Jews and the American Public Square

Jews and the American Public Square

Debating Religion and Republic

EDITED BY ALAN MITTLEMAN, ROBERT LICHT,
AND JONATHAN D. SARNA

ROWMAN & LITTLEFIELD PUBLISHERS, INC.
Lanham • Boulder • New York • Oxford

ROWMAN & LITTLEFIELD PUBLISHERS, INC.

Published in the United States of America
by Rowman & Littlefield Publishers, Inc.
A Member of the Rowman & Littlefield Publishing Group
4720 Boston Way, Lanham, Maryland 20706
www.rowmanlittlefield.com

12 Hid's Copse Road
Cumnor Hill, Oxford OX2 9JJ, England

British Library Cataloguing in Publication Information Available

Library of Congress Cataloging-in-Publication Data

Jews and the American public square : debating religion and republic /
  edited by Alan Mittleman, Robert Licht, and Jonathan D. Sarna.
    p. cm.
  Includes index.
    ISBN 0-7425-2123-0 (cloth: alk. paper) — ISBN 0-7425-2124-9 (pbk. : alk. paper)
  1. Jews—United States—History. 2. Jews—United States—Politics and
  government. 3. Jews—Legal status, laws, etc.—United States. 4.
  Judaism and politics. 5. Religion and state. 6. Constitutional
  history—United States. 7. United States—Ethnic relations. I.
  Mittleman, Alan. II. Licht, Robert. III. Sarna, Jonathan D.

  E184.36.P64 J48 2002
  322'.1'089924073—dc21   2002007468

Printed in the United States of America

♾™ The paper used in this publication meets the minimum requirements of American
National Standard for Information Sciences—Permanence of Paper for Printed Library
Materials, ANSI/NISO Z39.48-1992.
Managing Editor: Mark Ami-El
Typesetting: Ami-El Applications

*This volume is dedicated to the memory of
Professor Daniel J. Elazar,
founding President of the
Center for Jewish Community Studies
and the Jerusalem Center for Public Affairs,
scholar, and friend.
This project began under his inspiration and guidance.
May his memory be a blessing.*

Jews and the American Public Square is a three-year project of communal dialogue, research, and publication devoted to exploring the relationship between the faith and culture of American Jews and their civic engagement. Initiated by a major grant from the Pew Charitable Trusts, the project seeks to foster greater understanding among both Jews and non-Jews of the role of religion in American public life.

Also available:

Jewish Polity and American Civil Society: Communal Agencies and Religious Movements in the American Public Sphere, edited by Alan Mittleman, Jonathan D. Sarna, and Robert Licht (2002).

Contents

x   Contents

Introduction

Alan Mittleman

Concern for the proper ordering of religion and public life, including both the governmental and nongovernmental dimensions of the public sphere, goes back to the founding of the American republic. The distinctively American approach to these matters is encoded in the First Amendment. What the code meant in the eighteenth century, let alone what it ought to mean today, is endlessly controversial. At the time of the ratification of the U.S. Constitution, six states had established churches and eleven out of thirteen had religious qualifications for office-holding.[1] Far from being dismantled by the ratification of the First Amendment (which prohibited a *federal* establishment of religion), Massachusetts and Connecticut preserved their religious establishments into the nineteenth century. Their desire to do so probably influenced the amendment's compromising language. Prohibiting Congress from making any law "respecting an establishment of religion" does, after all, cut both ways. It prohibits Congress from establishing a would-be national religion and it prohibits Congress from infringing on the state establishments. Far from building a "wall of separation" between church and state (Jefferson's 1802 gloss on the amendment), the founders' constitution built a complex federal system where linkages between religion and government at various levels were acceptable. Nonetheless, these linkages were controversial even at the beginning. Founders like Thomas Jefferson and James Madison advocated a quite different approach to the problem of ordering religion and government from founders such as George Washington or Patrick Henry.[2]

1

Nor have the controversies been resolved. Americans have been arguing over the meanings ensconced in the Constitution's language
for over 200 years. One thing is indisputable, however. Whether the
founders were anxious about too close a relationship between government and religion, or whether they ardently desired to encourage
such intimacy, the American tradition of non-establishment has
brought blessings to both church and state. America remains exceptional among the advanced democracies for the pervasiveness and
vibrancy of its religious life.

This dynamic religious life informs the public culture of America. It fills the space of civil society. It shapes the cultural environment in which the judges who tell us what the Constitution means
do their work. Our collective religious life continues to inform our
public and private moral choices. It partially defines how we vote
for our politicians and how our politicians vote their consciences. It
contributes to how we Americans, at our most reflective, see our
nation and ourselves. As important, therefore, as the constitutional
dimension of church-state law is for any serious consideration of the
place of religion in American public life, we must also attend to the
larger historical, cultural, social, and philosophical settings that undergird and accompany the law. We must look not only to "church
and state" but to "religion and republic," to the great theme of how
religion in a free society relates to that society's highest ends.
Books on this topic abound. But specifically Jewish books on it are
few.

Why is this? For much of their recent history, American Jews
have been content to adopt the discourse of American liberalism as
their framework for considering the ordering of religion and the
public sphere. According to that framework, government—at all
levels—prescinds both from aiding religion and from interfering
with it. The ideal is for government and religious communities to be
hermetically sealed off from one another. Were government to be
supportive of religion, it would imply that government favors one
worldview, one encompassing scheme of values, over another. This
would infringe upon citizens' privacy and freedom. A free society,
on this account, is distinguished precisely by the refusal of its political institutions to prescribe to citizens what they should think or,
more minimally, to recommend to them what they should think. A
liberal society should be neutral toward all comprehensive visions
of the good life; it should provide a safe space where citizens can
work out their own vision of the good life rather than direct them
toward a favored, state-supported system. Freedom in general, in-

cluding freedom of religion, means primarily "freedom from" governmental coercion or endorsement.

This version of liberalism has been especially congenial to American Jews. If government is not allowed to provide support for religious beliefs or practices, then the historic edifice of vestigial Christian customs—prayer and Bible reading in public schools, the Ten Commandments posted in courthouses and other public buildings, symbolic images in governmental public spaces on holidays, and so on—can be dismantled. From 1947, when modern establishment clause jurisprudence begins, until the present, this dismantling of our once generic and pan-Protestant public culture has proceeded apace. Surging in the 1960s and faltering today, the unmaking of an unofficial Christian cultural establishment has been embraced by the courts and by most American Jews. What served to replace the older culture of diffuse public Protestantism (often called "civil religion") were a liberal confidence in social progress, good government, scientific and progressive education, and the steady expansion of social inclusion. American Jews may be counted among the architects as well as the beneficiaries of this project.

By the end of the millennium, however, confidence in the liberal project has faltered. The faith of the nineteenth and early twentieth centuries that scientific and technological progress was necessarily good, that they somehow brought moral progress in their train, was rendered incredible, if not obscene, by Auschwitz. The belief that social problems such as poverty had rational and technical solutions, that they could be solved on the federal level through grand initiatives, has largely been abandoned. Liberal philosophers themselves no longer speak with one voice about the secular character of "public reason." Many have come to believe that religious beliefs and values—comprehensive schemes of meaning—do have a valid and necessary place in public discourse. Rather than seeing religiously informed moral understandings as intruders in the democratic debate, liberal thinkers are now more concerned with clarifying when the public expression of religious perspectives is helpful and when it is hurtful. When candidate John Kennedy was running for president, he had to convince the Protestant establishment that he did not take his Catholicism too seriously. When candidate Joseph Lieberman was running for vice-president, he did not miss an opportunity to tell the public that he took his Orthodox Judaism very seriously indeed. This is a measure of the transformation of the liberal project.

The decline of the taken-for-granted milieu of secular liberalism is a matter of some perplexity for American Jews. Their investment in a constitutional interpretation of strict church-state separationism is threatened. The Supreme Court itself has edged away from the jurisprudence of "no aid" to religion and moved piecemeal toward a framework of "equal treatment." Rather than ruling out state support for religious entities *tout court*, the new approach considers disregard of religious groups a form of discrimination against them. For the state to favor secular entities alone constitutes, in this view, an establishment of secularism-as-religion. The growing case law that embodies the "equal treatment" approach provided the basis for the provision in the 1996 welfare reform legislation known as "charitable choice." That law allows for religious groups that offer social services to compete with purely secular service providers for government funds. It has been the case for decades that religious groups, which have set up nonprofit corporations at arm's length from their purely religious mission, have received government funds. Under the new scheme, religious groups need not entirely disentangle their social welfare activities from their confessional ones. Jewish groups have, for the most part, come out against charitable choice and its embodiment in the White House Office of Faith-Based and Community Initiatives. Jews continue to believe that strict separationism and "no aid" to religion are the gold standard of First Amendment interpretation.

The decline of taken-for-granted secular liberalism has also left American Jews without a sure-footed way of thinking about the larger cultural questions of "religion and republic." Unmaking the unofficial Protestant establishment and banishing its public culture to the history books allowed Jews in the postwar period to become full-fledged Americans rather than presumptive second-class citizens. Jewish inclusion in the society and the polity came at the price of a reduced Jewish particularism. Jews adapted the historic Jewish tradition to the inoffensive religiosity of the suburbs. They embraced liberalism, with a Hebraic accent, as the vibrant heart of their faith. This writer recalls his father telling him that the essence of Judaism is to believe in the Ten Commandments, a version of the faith calculated to ease one's acceptance into the middle-class world of postwar suburbia. But the big story of American Jewish history in the past decade has been the perceived need to return to a more intense, particularly Jewishly-specific form of life. If the Jews are to survive as a distinct group in America, so the argument goes, they need to cultivate their distinctiveness. They need to implement some boundaries vis-à-vis the larger society. To be sure, these boundaries should be elected by the Jews rather than imposed upon them, as was the case in a more anti-Semitic age. The emergence of Jewish day schools, even among that Jewish group most adapted to liberalism, Reform Jewry, is surely a sign of the times. How does the new emphasis on particularism, on a more rich and textured religious identity, impact on the earlier assumption that the public sphere is a neutral and secular sphere?

American Jews do not face this question alone. As the various modern surrogates for religious faith lose their intellectual prestige, return to religion or, more precisely, to the religious possibility presents itself to the postmodern imagination. For masses of Americans, of course, it never left. America was, famously, the nation with the soul of a church. But whatever faith characterized America's soul, its landscape came to be dotted not only with churches but with synagogues and mosques as well as Buddhist and Hindu temples. Religious pluralism on a scale unimaginable one or two centuries ago came to be a fact of life. American society is becoming in some ways post-Christian. It is not, however, becoming post-religious. Religious demographics have changed dramatically in the past three or four decades. The historic mainline churches lost both members and cultural visibility. Conservative Protestantism became a significant demographic and cultural force. Catholicism rose from acceptance to prominence. Orthodox Judaism, fated by sociologists in the 1950s to go the way of the dodo bird, succeeded in building strong institutions and now wields increasing clout. The liberalization of immigration laws brought Muslims and practitioners of Asian religions here to undergo those complex processes of Americanization experienced generations ago by Jews. The sheer profusion of religions brings cause for both celebration and perplexity. How should "religion" (always an abstraction in the singular) relate to public life, to our self-understanding as a people, in an era of innumerable religions? There is no civil religious template against which particular religions reshape themselves any longer. There seems to be nothing but open-ended particularity; nothing but morally perplexed people looking for norms that reach beyond their private lives. What fills the public space where we encounter one another as citizens in an age where confidence in purely secular values has eroded?

Increasingly, Americans have come to think of their particular religious communities as "seedbeds of virtue."[3] The principal philosophical contender against secular liberalism over the past decade, communitarianism, urges us to take religious communities seriously as incubators of distinctive moral outlooks. Communitarians prize freedom no less than liberals. No one advocates a stifling single code of virtue for a society as diverse as ours. Yet precisely because the liberal state must content itself with a minimal, rules-of-the-game sort of public morality, we must rely on the communal institutions of civil society to provide moral texture and depth in our lives. Exhortations to articulate and follow a common core of values are well meaning but inadequate. Character is shaped by the master stories and way of life of particular communities. In this argument, religious communities serve an important public good. They provide much-needed content for the moral life. They compensate for the relative vacuousness of public morality and public meaning in the liberal society. Inner-city Catholic schools, for example, not only provide poor children, most of whom are not Catholic, with an education superior to that of public schools but they also provide them with a moral orientation. This is not a purely private affair. Should the service that such schools perform for the public good be acknowledged and furthered by support from the public purse?

Citizens are divided over these questions. Does the establishment clause require government to take no account of and give no aid to religious groups insofar as they serve public purposes? Or does the Constitution allow for religious groups that serve the public good to be treated in a manner equal to secular groups that do so? Should the state and the particular religious/moral communities of civil society operate on parallel tracks that never touch, or can the state work with such entities, ceding some of its power to subsidiary groups? These are complex legal questions that will undoubtedly produce controversy for a long time to come. What seems uncontroversial, however, is the new awareness of how important religious communities are to American civil society. We do not yet know what will replace our once more uniform, civil religious culture. We have not yet decided what the limits of pluralism are—how much absorption in identity-shaping particularity is compatible with a common life in a mass society. But it does seem clear that we are on to the right questions. Policymakers, social scientists, and public philosophers must take the endurance and vitality of religious communities in America seriously, as must American Jews.

American Jews are well positioned to enter into a new discourse about religion and public life. The "hyper-organized" communal experience of American Jews can provide a trove of materials for reflection on how a particular religious-ethnic community serves the public good. Innumerable social welfare agencies, educational and cultural services, overseas relief activities, human relations organizations, and religious institutions generate tremendous "social capital" for Jews and non-Jews alike. The Jewish penchant for communal organization and involvement both bonds Jews to one another and bridges distances between Jews and others. It sustains in-group solidarity and generates activity outside of the community by orienting Jews to work for civic purposes. American Jews, while manifestly committed to their own communal life, have not yet made the leap to appreciate how other communities' networks of institutions also contribute to the common good. Although an awareness of this connection exists, American Jews remain skeptical that religion can serve as a profound source of civic health and, therefore, of democratic renewal. In a poll conducted for "Jews and the American Public Square" in 2000, for example, researchers discovered that only 11 percent of the Jewish public (compared to 42 percent of the non-Jewish public) thought that "democracy works better in the U.S. if Americans are religious." While 65 percent of the non-Jewish public thought that the influence of religion in American life should increase, only 30 percent of Jews agreed.[4] Jews remain concerned that religion will undermine the secular liberal order.

The purpose of this book is to provide American Jews and others with some basic tools as they begin the necessary process of rethinking the ties between "religion and republic." Assembled here are analyses of historic Jewish activity in the public square, approaches to constitutional law, studies of modern Jewish political culture and action, explorations of issues in Jewish organizational life, and constructive models for how to think about Judaism and public affairs. Once we move out of the narrow framework of "church and state" the issues appear in all of their cultural and intellectual complexity. Accordingly, the chapters in this book represent a diversity of viewpoints as well as intellectual styles. Neutral historical treatments are paired with engaged, polemic ones. The material is inherently controversial. Our intention has been to mirror the controversies both inherent in the material and in the Jewish community's encounter with it.

The volume begins with two historical treatments. Naomi Cohen reaches back into the first years of Jewish settlement in North America and focuses on the tradition of Jewish communal self-defense, the oldest manifestation of Jewish engagement with the public sphere. Cohen describes the classic, ongoing tension of Jewish modernity, the tension between participation in the larger civil culture and the survival of a distinctive Jewish subgroup. How have Jews remained both "a part and apart?" All subsequent Jewish engagement in the public sphere was—and is—marked by this tension. Jonathan Sarna focuses on a recurrent tension in how the American Jewish community, from early times to the present, has understood the constitutional framework within which it has articulated and fought for its interests. Are those interests best secured in a republic that accepts and promotes all faiths or in one that distances itself from religion altogether?

In Part II, Ralph Lerner considers different approaches to the place of religion in civil society at the time of the framing of the American Constitution. The Founders' generation was of several minds about the relationship of religious bodies to both state and society. He shows that the ongoing arguments about the public role of religion in the republic have deep and ancient roots. Martin Plax analyzes the cultural and intellectual setting in which modern church-state jurisprudence arose and argues that some of the assumptions and consequences of this jurisprudence actually undermine the rule of law. Both of these chapters cast doubt on the prudence of continued Jewish fidelity to the principle of strict separation of church and state. Finally, Marc Stern argues on behalf of that traditional fidelity that religion does have an important if sometimes disruptive role to play in a liberal society, but that the state must take little account of it. Together the three chapters engage constitutional issues from a distinctively Jewish angle of vision.

Jewish engagement with the public square involves, to be sure, much hands-on political activity. In Part III, Marshall Breger provides a road map to Jewish political activity in Washington, D.C. He describes the successes and failures of contemporary Jewish activism and seeks to define what is—or should be—Jewish about Jewish politics. Harvey Sicherman studies the problem of Jewish coalition-building with other groups. How are Jewish interests defined and articulated? Who are appropriate partners for the promotion of those interests? When do the differences so outweigh the commonalities that coalitions cannot be sustained? Finally, Jack Wertheimer explores an issue of considerable contemporary importance to Jews, namely, the increasing prevalence of day schools and the interface between "parochial" schooling and public funding.

In Part IV, two sociologists consider trends in contemporary Jewish public culture and their impact on Jewish civic engagement. Sherry Israel looks at the increasing privatization of Jewish life (the "bowling alone" phenomenon) and the corresponding decline of involvement in and support for Jewish civic organizations. Sylvia Barack Fishman visits the topic of feminism in the Jewish community and explores its impact on Jewish involvement in family policy issues. What, in turn, are the consequences of the liberal Jewish approach to family matters in public policy for the Jewish family? Insofar as families are the principal institutions of civil society, the "little platoons we belong to in society" as Edmund Burke called them, this is a key issue for both American Jews and civil society alike.

In Part V, the issues of "religion and republic" are plumbed to their philosophical depth. David Dalin contributes an intellectual history of Jewish dissent from the prevalent norm of strict separation of church and state. He essays the minority report of intellectual mavericks who believed that privatizing religion and secularizing society would be, in the long term, injurious to American Jews. Setting the same problem in a longer historical context, Hillel Fradkin considers how modern Jewish views of public religion contrast with the political philosophy of some of the American founders. He argues for the superiority of those founders' philosophy and urges a Jewish reappraisal. Finally, David Novak breaks new ground in proposing the parameters of a Jewish public philosophy, that is, a method for bringing Jewish religious tradition to bear on contemporary public policy. In an age of apparent religious renewal, Jews and others need disciplined models for relating the teachings of their faith to the lives that they hope to lead as citizens. If, in fact, our society is coming to rely more on the "seedbeds of virtue," the institutions of civil society, and less on the state for the solutions to social problems, the religious voice will only grow in importance. Judaism, with its rich heritage of practical reason and applied ethics, is well suited to add to the democratic conversation.

This volume does not promise to dispel the current perplexities that beset Jews in the face of resurgent and pluralist American religion and a conservative political climate that encourages a large public role for it. It will, we hope, provide stimulation and provocation. It is, after all, not the responsibility of any of us to finish the work. But neither are we free to desist from beginning it.

The editors wish to thank Paul Gottfried, editor of *This World*, for permission to reprint the chapter by Ralph Lerner. An earlier version of Professor Lerner's essay appeared in *This World* in summer 1989. The editors also wish to thank Mark Silk, director of the Greenberg Center for the Study of Religion in Public Life at Trinity College, for permission to reprint Marc Stern's chapter. An earlier version of the chapter was delivered at Trinity and distributed by the Greenberg Center. Mark Ami-El, publications coordinator of the Jerusalem Center for Public Affairs, assisted in preparing the manuscript for publication. His help is gratefully acknowledged. No list of acknowledgments would be complete without thanking the Pew Charitable Trusts and Dr. Luis Lugo, the religion program director of the Trusts, for their generous support of this project. The opinions expressed in this volume are those of the authors and do not necessarily reflect the views of the Pew Charitable Trusts.

Notes

1. Akhil Reed Amar, *The Bill of Rights* (New Haven, Conn.: Yale University Press, 1998), 32.

2. John Wilson, "Locating Religion in American Politics," in Mark Silk, ed., *Religion and American Politics* (Hartford, Conn.: Center for the Study of Religion in Public Life, 2000), 11.

3. Gertrude Himmelfarb, *One Nation, Two Cultures* (New York: Vintage Books, 2001), 35.

4. Steven M. Cohen, *Religion and the Public Square: Attitudes of American Jews in Comparative Perspective* (Philadelphia, Pa.: Center for Jewish Community Studies, 2000), 23.

Part I

Historical Dimensions

1

An Overview of American
Jewish Defense

Naomi W. Cohen

Jewish defense, American style, is as old as the settlement of Jews in North America. It began in 1655 when Asser Levy and Jacob Barsimon of New Amsterdam petitioned for the right to stand guard. From that time on, Jews have challenged disabilities and defended themselves against attacks and attackers. Their goal has been the attainment of Jewish equality, or the recognition by the government and Americans generally of the fundamental right of Jews, qua Jews, to live on an equal footing with their fellow citizens. That goal, as Rabbi Arthur Hertzberg once explained, has been their "deepest and most messianic need."[1] Realistic or not, it has motivated American Jewry for over three hundred years.

The early defense posture was usually reactive, as Jews sought to remove existing obstacles to full equality. During the second half of the twentieth century, however, Jewish agencies developed the active dimension of defense alongside the reactive, exploring new ways and devising new programs for their collective protection even *before* obstacles to equality arose. Jewish interests were thus subsumed within a universalist approach of defending the rights of all minorities and by improving society in general. More recently another shift took place in consonance with the ethnocentric tide of the

1970s and 1980s. The universalist approach was not discarded, but a greater emphasis was put on Jewish ethnic needs and on improving relations with other groups in a multiethnic America.

How to win American acceptance as equal citizens and as bearers of a distinct religio-ethnic tradition has been an ongoing task whose enormity is well nigh immeasurable. How could Jews and Judaism, targeted for many centuries as the enemies of Christians and Christendom, be absorbed unconditionally by Christian America? Indeed, until today true Americanism, at least in popular thought, had a Christian component, and in contemporary America the so-called secular society retained a Christian flavor. Milton Himmelfarb put it this way: "The secular society in the lands that used to be Christendom . . . is more neutral against Judaism than against Christianity."[2] It followed that Judaism was outside the pale for all time and that Jews, the "quintessential" minority according to Marshall Sklare,[3] were at best only qualified Americans.

Whatever the cause of discrimination—and nineteenth-century Jews openly blamed Christian contempt for Judaism—American Jews as individuals have been denigrated alongside their faith. Any preference for Christianity on the part of the government increased the possibility of converts and drop-outs from Judaism. More important, if Jews desired full equality, they had to combat long-standing laws, established institutions, and deeply rooted customs.

One struggle often led to another; it was not enough, for example, that most early state constitutions promised freedom of religion when in some of those same states Jews were denied the right to hold office or serve as jurors. At the same time, if they wanted acceptance of Judaism as a respectable *American* religion, most agreed that it behooved them to alter their public face by Americanizing their religious beliefs and practices. Complicating both tasks was the rampant divisiveness within Jewish ranks. Never a monolithic entity, American Jews were a group riven by the larger forces of voluntarism and sectionalism as well as by different social and religious customs within their own world. Rarely if ever did all agree on one definition of legitimate Jewish interests. The wonder is that, despite the obstacles, Jewish defenders operated creatively in order to register specific Jewish demands in the public square.

This chapter examines major aspects of American Jewish defense against the backdrop of the group's evolving interests. The first section focuses on the underlying principles and the basic methods of defense, and the second part treats the major issues of concern to Jewish defenders. Although the approach of this chapter is historical, the essay discusses implications that are still relevant today. It also suggests that the study of defense can serve as an index to Jewish feelings of security at any specific time.

I

Integration and Identity

The search for total acceptance as equal American citizens, *integration*, and fulfillment as Jews, *identity*, necessitated some sort of compromise or balance. Logically, as long as "American" signified "Christian," the two goals were contradictory. Furthermore, integration automatically put a constraint on identity; how could Jews bent on proving themselves worthy of acceptance admit to group interests different from most Americans? On occasion American law addressed the contradiction by granting exemptions to Jews, as in the case of Sunday laws. (Ohio, for example, once allowed Jews to work on Sunday provided they conscientiously observed their own Sabbath!) But exemptions, some Jews rightly maintained, still set them apart from the majority.

The inherent contradiction between integration and identity was played out most clearly in its extremist forms. Countless Jews, anxious for acceptance, were driven to sever all ties with Judaism, while a very few on the opposite end of the spectrum sequestered themselves from mainstream America in order to retain their identity intact. Most Jews—and here the reference is to those who, however tenuous their connection to Judaism, did not read themselves out of the community—have been somewhere in the middle. Some may have smarted under the Christian usages in the public schools, but they attended nonetheless. Tailoring their behavior to satisfy the demands of integration, they also tailored their own institutions. If they affiliated with a synagogue, be it any one of the major Jewish denominations, they expected American features originally copied from the churches—at least some English in religious services, a weekly sermon, and Protestant decorum.

Time and again Jews have faced the underlying question: How much Jewishness were they prepared to exchange for equality? The federal government never exacted a price for Emancipation, but public opinion was often more demanding. In 1819, John Quincy Adams explained what became a time-honored attitude: "They [the immigrants] must cast off the European skin, never to resume it. They must look forward to their posterity rather than backward to their ancestors."[4] In contemporary America, which prides itself on being a pluralistic society, American Jews have grown more secure, but the need to balance the bipolar pulls on a non-Christian minority still obtains.

The adoption by defense organizations of social welfare programs in the middle of the twentieth century qualified the concepts of both integration and identity. Defenders now stood for integration within mainstream America not as Jews but as Jewish *liberals*. The causes they championed as their own, resting on a broader interpretation of freedom, grew out of the liberal reformist consensus forged by Franklin Roosevelt and Harry Truman. Jews no longer were merely a distinct religious body; they became a group very much involved in matters of freedom and equal opportunity for all religious, racial, social, and economic minorities. Preoccupation with such matters subordinated particularist Jewish goals to universalist goals. It also justified defense activity for non-Jewish causes that admittedly had no connection with Jewish interests. (The Commission on Law and Social Action of the American Jewish Congress declared in 1945 that it was committed to work "for a better world . . . whether or not the individual issues touch directly upon so-called Jewish interests.")[5] As a result, the defense agencies have often appeared more liberal than Jewish.

True defenders could and did argue that *Jewish* concerns propelled them to social reform. Acting on the premise that liberty was indivisible, they maintained that curtailment of the rights of any minority made the Jewish minority more vulnerable. Moreover, Jewish tradition abounded with injunctions on the care of the needy. But how likely was it to find dicta in normative Judaism that plainly justified concern about gun control, neutral prayer in the classrooms, or rights of homosexuals? At times the defense agencies themselves considered how far they had strayed from strictly *Jewish* interests and, as some said, had become essentially Jewish branches of the American Civil Liberties Union. The process illustrated a fundamental rule—the more successful integration has been, the less the interest in Jewish identity.

To be sure, contemporary defense has not neglected strictly Jewish religious interests, like the right to construct an *eruv* (a divider or marker usually encircling a city or neighborhood) or the right to wear a *kippah* in the armed services. Most important, Jewish communal agencies have recently become very much involved in a new aspect of Jewish defense—encouragement and aid to Jewish education. But even as they shifted gears to accord with a multiethnic America, the public face of Jewish identity became more secularized than religious. Overall, contemporary Jewish interests on the domestic front conform to those of the mainline churches, and in the political arena Jews (except for pockets of the Orthodox) appear little different from liberal Protestants and Catholics in major urban centers.

Defense and Democracy

Jews based their defense on the principles of American democracy. The nation was forged in the crucible of religious freedom and political equality, and hence, the reasoning went, disabilities of a religious or political nature were false to the Founding Fathers and to the spirit of America. Jews who labored to remove obstacles to their equality, and not their opponents, were the true believers in the tenets of Americanism and the natural rights from which Americanism drew. Assuming the role of guardians and explicators of American precepts and the Constitution, Jewish defenders ventured over time to reinterpret and expand fundamental ideas of equality and freedom. In that manner they validated to both Jews and non-Jews the rectitude of a broad spectrum of Jewish interests. In the nineteenth century, the best example of a looser interpretation comes from the area of church/state relations, where Jews explained *freedom* of religion to mean *equality* of religion. After World War II, the Jewish commitment to social welfare programs for the have-nots and for all minorities was interpreted as inherent in the very meaning of equality. But irrespective of how radical such interpretations seemed, Jews always couched their interests within an American framework.

To be sure, it behooved a small minority dependent on the government and popular goodwill for the success of its endeavors to appeal to American principles, but more than pragmatic reasons accounted for the Jewish approach. In their case a commitment to democracy was matched by passion for the Constitution. Reverence for the fundamental law, the embodiment of democratic principles, was, as Jerold Auerbach has persuasively written, symmetrical to traditional devotion to Jewish law.[6] American Jews did not merely replace one law for another, but they argued that the two converged. The country's allegiance to constitutionalism and individual rights derived, like the Jewish heritage, from biblical teachings. Thus, in the words of Reform theologian Kaufmann Kohler, "We recognize

in the Fourth of July the offspring of the Sixth of Sivan" (the traditional date marking God's granting of the Torah to Israel.)[7] The
children of the Bible became, as it were, the children of the Constitution. By that reasoning Jews were worshipers of the fundamental
secular law before Americans made a virtual cult of the Constitution. So pervasive were those sentiments that even Jews born in
continental Europe "adopted" the *English* antecedents of American
basic rights as their own. Banker Jacob Schiff, of German extrac-
tion, once wrote to the Jewish Historical Society of England: "We
. . . cannot fail to appreciate that it was the dearly cherished 'British
Constitution' and the beloved 'English Common Law,' *which we
still share with you*, and their spirit, that made possible . . . Jewish
development on our respective countries" (emphasis added).[8]

Early American Jews also posited a contract they had with America. Not too different from a religious covenant, Jews pledged to
give their means, render service, and when necessary lay down their
lives on behalf of the country. In return America (and they often
meant the states as well as the federal government) was obliged to
protect the freedoms Jews earned by their loyalty. In a setting where
Jews were bound by contract to the nation, one could well ask if
Jewish defense was at all necessary. Wasn't defense by definition a
posture that belied Jewish faith in the all-protective shield of
American democracy? Rabbi Isaac Mayer Wise, the master architect
of Reform Judaism in the United States, made that point in 1860 to
explain his opposition to a national defense organization. He said
that the Constitution and the "spirit of liberty" were adequate
guardians.[9] Few concerned Jews, however, repudiated the need for
organized defense, and they would have probably explained that on
certain matters American public opinion required enlightenment.

Since America's Jews had never before lived in a democratic
society where Jewish identification was voluntary, their defense had
few precedents to follow. In pre-Emancipation communities that
were the home of Jewish immigrants to the United States, firm
boundaries set off the Jews from their Christian countrymen, and
Jewish rights that were granted arbitrarily were severely limited and
frequently temporary. Changed circumstances made American Jews
the pioneers who created new communal patterns of behavior that
were refined by succeeding generations. Rapid maturation of the
Jewish group contributed to greater sophistication in arguments and
methods of defense even as the overall approach—rationalistic, legalistic, and hyperaccommodationist—remained fixed.

Defenders and Defense Tactics

Over the years the leaders and tactics of Jewish defense have changed. At first, self-appointed prominent individuals or small ad hoc committees presented grievances of Jews in particular cities or states. They drew up petitions and resolutions that were presented to their community, to public officials, and at times to the larger society. National defense was not a concern until the Damascus affair of 1840. At the time, various communities held protest meetings and passed resolutions condemning the blood libel, and some recognized the need for an overall agency to coordinate the separate activities. From the 1840s until 1860 the interests of Jews locally and nationally were aired by major Anglo-Jewish periodicals like the *Occident*, the *Asmonean*, and the *Israelite*. Attracting a national readership, and more able than their predecessors to sustain Jewish interest and involvement over longer periods of time, the journals gave full coverage to Jewish grievances. The responses they suggested usually included tactics used earlier, but now they often counseled communal agitation and political action. They themselves set out to "enlighten" public opinion; steeped in the optimistic aura generated by the Enlightenment, they believed in the ultimate success of arguments based on reason. Since the periodicals also printed letters from readers as well as opinions which they solicited from non-Jews, they allowed for a measure of popular discussion. By adding new methods to the old, they proved the value of national, open-ended defense.

In 1859 a national organization was founded, the Board of Delegates of American Israelites, and one of its tasks was the defense of Jewish rights in the United States and abroad. Under that mandate it prepared appropriate responses to the curtailment of Jewish rights during the Civil War and Reconstruction era; it spoke too for the rights of Jews in Switzerland and Romania. While the Board did not mobilize the community at large for its campaigns, and while it never eclipsed the newspapers, it expanded the role of prominent individuals in the planning and execution of strategy. It also added another dimension to defensive tactics—cooperation with European defense organizations. The Board's successes were limited, however, and in 1878 it was taken over by Reform's Union of American Hebrew Congregations (UAHC).

Organizational activity increased during the Gilded Age. In addition to the Board of Delegates on Civil and Religious Rights of the UAHC, the far-flung fraternal order B'nai B'rith expanded its origi-

nal functions to include defense projects, and so did Reform's rabbinical organization, the Central Conference of American Rabbis
(CCAR). Ironically, from its very beginnings the CCAR, an organization of clerics, made the secular issue of church/state relations a
primary concern. Organizations did not limit individual leadership;
rather, they added strength to those who had already carved out positions of influence—men like Simon Wolf and Max Kohler of the
UAHC, Adolf Kraus of B'nai B'rith, and Isaac Wise of the CCAR.
Although such leaders, without the help of a professional or clerical
staff, still planned all strategic details, and privately approached
non-Jewish officials and opinion-molders, they could now argue
that their case commanded the support of significant numbers. The
idea of letting those they represented debate policy as well as leadership rarely constrained them.

The era of voluntary leadership by a few men peaked in the decade before World War I, but after the death of the "giants"—the cir-
cle of Jacob Schiff and Louis Marshall—impersonal defense
organizations run largely by paid and secular professionals assumed
control. Professionalization became more pronounced two decades
later when social welfare was incorporated into defense. Although
defenders increasingly resorted to newer methods like litigation and
the cultivation of non-Jewish allies, earlier tactics of petitions,
enlisting Christian supporters, public enlightenment, and the use of
the Jewish vote were never totally repudiated. (We may note parenthetically, however, that modernization has not always been an un-
mixed blessing. When the activism of volunteers is supplanted by
professionals who devise strategy, often without a knowledge of or
sympathy with the mandates of Judaism, the Jewish community at
large is paying a significant price.)

At no time in the evolution of American defense did defenders
win the endorsement of a united community. In the first place, a
portion of the Jewish population—even among those affiliated with
synagogues—has always been apathetic or silent on issues of defense. Furthermore, Jews gave their support to a variety of causes
and a variety of organizations that, despite different styles, often
duplicated each other's efforts. (The establishment of the Conference of Presidents of Major American Jewish Organizations [1955]
was a serious effort to achieve greater unity.) More important, Jewish groups at times worked at cross-purposes. The rabidly anti-
Zionist American Council for Judaism, for example, broke the
American Jewish consensus and lobbied strenuously during and after World War II against Zionist efforts for a Jewish state. The major defense agencies have frequently cooperated, particularly on

litigation, but on matters of church/state separation—like the recent Kiryas Joel case—Orthodox organizations have often been at odds with the secular agencies.

The story of Maryland's "Jew Bill" of 1826 provides a convenient starting point for briefly comparing early defense tactics with more recent ones. It began in 1776 when Maryland adopted a constitution that required a Christian oath for holding office. The test oath, which applied as well to lawyers and to officers in the state militia, was first contested by a petition from several Jews in 1797. It took twenty years, however, before the passage of a constitutional amendment that finally granted Jews the right to hold office (provided they declared a "belief in a future state of rewards and punishments"). Since Jews could not afford to alienate members of the all-Christian legislature by threatening the use of their votes, their defense weapons were severely limited; they resorted solely to petitions and quiet pressure on individual legislators. Interestingly, their arguments on behalf of equality, which were taken up and supported by influential newspapers, matured over the twenty years. The first petition in 1797, for example, merely mentioned that Jews were deprived of equal rights, but succeeding ones added other considerations—the patriotic service rendered by Jews to the country, the contradiction between Maryland's constitution and the federal Constitution, and the moral tenets of Judaism that made Jews eminently worthy. Above all, as the Jewish memorial of 1824 remonstrated, the disability on Jews conflicted with America's "political wisdom" and the nation's profound commitment to democratic ideals.[10]

Over 150 years later, some tactics of early-nineteenth-century Jews may appear outdated, but basic similarities still exist. Today a state or local church/state issue would doubtless be handled by the professionals of one or more of the Big Three defense organizations (American Jewish Congress, American Jewish Committee, Anti-Defamation League). Where they judge the matter grave, they, like the Jews in Maryland, would probably make overtures to Christian leaders in the community or to non-Jewish organizations for their support. Again, as in the pre-Civil War era, they would want press coverage, but now they would plan it in advance. If lawmakers were needed for remedial action, the defense agencies would also impress the seriousness of the issue on Jewish and non-Jewish politicians and political candidates. Then, as now, Jews were expected to reward such supporters with their votes or, in the case of organizations, by their cooperation on non-Jewish issues. Arguments, too, have been modified. Today, as in early Maryland, the case rests on a constitutional base, but now clauses like "due process of law" and "establishment of religion" are far more loosely construed. Moreover, whereas modern defenders stress the universal rights of mankind that brook no discrimination against any minority, Maryland's Jews asked for Jewish rights exclusively. Overall we may conclude that new approaches have been grafted on to old roots.

Constraints on Defense

Defenders of Jewish interests were constrained from the outset by the dictates of American public opinion. Representatives of a very small minority, they always considered whether any suggestion of defense activity would generate anti-Jewish sentiment. Could Jews afford, for example, to demand General Grant's resignation after his notorious Order #11 at a time when Judeophobia ran high and when the Union desperately needed generals who could win battles? Or, how wise was it for Jews in the 1920s to publicly condemn Henry Ford's anti-Semitic *Dearborn Independent* and risk worse prejudice in years when the auto king was at the peak of his popularity and when anti-Semitism was propagated simultaneously by the Ku Klux Klan and immigration restrictionists? Yet again, should Jews have challenged Senator Joe McCarthy during the second Red Scare of the twentieth century, thereby raising the taunt of Jewish disloyalty? In large measure, Jewish defense activity has been the inverse of the ebb and flow of popular prejudice and American hypernationalism.

Jewish defenders also took pains not to waste favor with the government. How many times could they plead with President Theodore Roosevelt to intercede on behalf of pogrom-stricken Russian Jews? In fact, Roosevelt did tire of the frequent requests, and only the feisty Jacob Schiff dared to persist. (At the same time, however, the banker counseled European Jews not to bother TR lest they alienate him.) Since even Schiff acknowledged some limits, he preferred not to raise the matter of Moroccan Jewry with the Roosevelt administration because it could deflect executive attention from the Russian problem. Appeals to presidents and prominent non-Jews in Congress also risked official goodwill if any advice received was not followed. In some instances, as in the approaches of Felix Frankfurter and Rabbi Stephen Wise to Franklin Roosevelt, heavy flattery could well mask the gravity of the Jewish request.

Another constraint on defenders has been the matter of image. Indeed, the image of Jews in American society determined if, when, and how defense activity should proceed. During the 1930s when American isolationism held sway and anti-Semitic organizations mushroomed, many Jews opposed public agitation against the Nazis. Then, the image of the "international " Jew loyal only to his own people, with scant regard for his country's interests, was the primary deterrent. The American Jewish Committee, for example, thought of educating the public to recognize the menace of Hitler's Germany to the free world and the need for national preparedness. But to avoid charges of Jewish warmongering on behalf of the European Jews, it dared not use Jews to head that campaign. It chose rather to sponsor an unpublicized trip by a prominent non-Jew who headed the Defense of Peace and Freedom movement in England. The Committee recognized the need to stop Hitler, but considerations of image at that particular moment seemed, at least to them, to proscribe publicity and overt Jewish participation. To be sure, not all defenders reached the same conclusions, and there were noisy anti-Nazi rallies and demonstrations staged by Jews, but no responsible groups would venture beyond some limit imposed by American public opinion.

At the same time, the Committee upheld the right of notorious Jew-baiter Robert Edmondson to freedom of speech and the press. The image of the Jew as a civil libertarian who fought even for Jew-haters superseded the desire to curb anti-Semitic agitation.

Considerations of image in the 1930s also led leaders like the men of the American Jewish Committee to focus on Jewish behavior—an admission that Jews themselves were responsible for anti-Semitism or at least for exacerbating it. A memorandum prepared for the Committee by Professor Alvin Johnson stressed that Jews should maintain a low profile and avoid public action that accorded with fixed anti-Semitic stereotypes. Among other things, Johnson advised that Jews not preach Zionism or ally themselves with other oppressed minorities. The Committee attempted to spread this message among American Jews but it was denounced for its timidity. Even if all Jews were saints, some asked, would anti-Semitism disappear? Nevertheless, the idea that Jews could avoid the antagonism of non-Jews by not advertising their Jewishness in extrareligious affairs is still rooted within the community.

The constraints mentioned above derived from Jewish perceptions of the majority's demands. Other constraints that deserve mention involved limits imposed by Jews themselves without direct prompting by the outside. One question was that of alliances with non-Jews. We might logically reason that a small minority would

seek allies to enhance its influence in the public square, but Jews
purposely refused to sustain working relationships with other minorities or religious groups until the twentieth century. Even when
others, like Catholics or Seventh-Day Adventists, suffered similar
legal disabilities, Jews engaged in no more than sporadic coopera-
tive ventures. Hostility and fear bred of memories of persecution
and Christian missionizing accounted for their behavior.

Noninvolvement, however, also exacted a price. If Jewish cooperation were solicited by a non-Jewish body, refusal could well
arouse non-Jewish surprise, if not hostility. When Jews as a group
stayed aloof from the numerous social reform movements of the
1840-1860 period, largely because of the prominence of Protestant
clergymen in those movements, some reformers criticized the Jewish posture. The abolitionists, for example, noted that "The objects
of so much mean prejudice and unrighteous oppression as the Jews
have been for ages, surely they, it would seem, more that any other
denomination, ought to be the enemies of CASTE, and the friends of
UNIVERSAL FREEDOM."[11] Similarly, in the second quarter of the
nineteenth century, the Know-Nothing Party, which crusaded
against Catholics and foreigners, doubtless expected Jewish support.
Indeed, some Jews were enticed by Protestant opposition to Catholicism, a religion that conjured up memories of the Jewish badge,
slaughter at the hands of the Crusaders, and the Inquisition. But the
major Anglo-Jewish periodicals advised noninvolvement. They argued that Jews would fare badly under either Protestant or Catholic
domination and that the wiser course was to steer clear of Protes-
tant/Catholic strife.

Considerations of public opinion reinforced avoidance of alliances. For example, Jews were long loath to identify with atheists.
Early Americans barely tolerated the "godless" atheists and agnos-
tics; in some colonies and states they even lagged behind Jews in
the acquisition of equal rights. In an early court case a Jew did join
an atheist in pleading the unconstitutionality of a Sunday law in
South Carolina. There, Judge John O'Neale, who ruled for the court,
found among other things that Judaism was inferior to Christianity.
But unable to accuse Jews as religionless, he nevertheless commented that the alliance between "the infidel and the Israelite" was
"altogether unnatural."[12] Some Protestant Americans also saw a
linkage between two of their enemies, the Catholic and the Jew. A
speaker for a postbellum group that worked to engraft Christianity
onto the Constitution once observed that there was a "confederacy
of the Jesuit and Jew, infidel and atheist" to eliminate Bible-reading
from the schools.[13] Those prejudices lasted well into the twentieth

century, and Jews weighed their importance before they embarked on church/state cases dealing with released time and Bible-reading in the classroom. After World War II, defense agencies forged close ties to liberal non-Jewish groups, but, as discussed below, they learned in the 1980s that alliances at times require reevaluation.

A second self-imposed constraint was the Jewish "code" of political neutrality. Formulated before the Civil War, the rules of political behavior rested on the premise that politics concerned the individual Jew but not the community. If Jews were, as Reform Judaism and others said, no more than a religious group, they were not entitled to a collective voice in politics. Both the *Occident* and the *Israelite* (at times inconsistently) preached against defiling the sanctity of Judaism with corrupt politics. It followed, therefore, that Jewish political clubs, or advice from rabbis and congregational leaders on how to vote, or support of a candidate just because he was Jewish, or appeals to a "Jewish vote," were wrong. It even meant that rabbis were muzzled by their congregations from discussing politics in their sermons. At bottom, those strictures questioned the existence and legitimacy of separate Jewish interests as well as the right of Jews *as Jews* to political self-defense. The most Jews could hope for was a sensitivity to their concerns on the part of non-Jewish officials. The code of neutrality, which spawned inconsistent and ambivalent behavior even on the part of its supporters, was at odds with the American pattern of resolving issues at the polls. Disregarded by politicians who wooed Jews for their votes and by Jews themselves, neutrality in practice was unreal. The wonder is that its teachings lingered into the twentieth century. The American Jewish Committee, for example, publicly defended Jewish political neutrality, but it used the Jewish vote as a weapon in bargaining with political leaders. Although it denied the existence of a Jewish vote, the Committee compiled statistics on how Jews voted.

To the extent that Jews behaved neutrally in politics, their posture weakened Jewish defense. So, too, until recently, and perhaps to some degree a result of the neutralist code, was the fact that comparatively few Jews won elective office in the United States. A study done twenty-five years ago of members of Congress revealed that through all of American history until 1970 only ninety-two Jews had been chosen for the House of Representatives and only twelve for the Senate. The percentage of congressional posts held by Jews thus amounted to under one percent, a figure far less than the percentage of Jews in the population. To be sure, a Jewish official did not necessarily act on behalf of Jewish interests just because he or she happened to be Jewish. But Jewish reluctance to run for office, and the community's reluctance to vote for one of their own, blunted any political leverage that the minority enjoyed.

Ever since the days of Franklin Roosevelt and the New Deal, organized Jewry made its political home within the Democratic Party. Nevertheless, half a century after Roosevelt, long-standing Jewish liberalism found itself in conflict with the new liberalism of affirmative action and racial quotas as well as the anti-Semitic overtones in the 1984 presidential bid of would-be nominee Jesse Jackson. Some predicted a shift by Jews away from the Democrats, and others noted that disaffection with the Democrats had made the Jews politically "homeless."[14] But since the threat of the Christian Right's influence with the Republicans appeared greater than the threat of Jackson's influence with the Democrats, Jewish voters stayed largely with the Democrats. As an observer cynically commented, some liberal Jews were inclined "to overlook anti-Semitism on the Left even when it flourishes, and to detect it on the Right even in those cases where it does not exist."[15] Today, when politicians continue to scramble for the Jewish vote, a return to the nineteenth-century Jewish stand of political neutrality and independence hardly seems likely.

II

Jewish Interests

This brief essay cannot do justice to the myriad of issues that have concerned American Jewish defenders. For example, a constant item on the defense agenda, anti-Semitism, is far too complex to discuss here; it is mentioned merely insofar as it impinged on other defense activity. Nor does this essay attempt to treat the vast number of social welfare projects undertaken by Jewish defense agencies in the last fifty years. Rather, here we will examine aspects of a few important defense reactions on matters that have been and still are of communal concern.

In Defense of Judaism

American Jews have frequently felt called upon to argue for the respectability of their faith. Indeed, early Jews believed that they suffered legal disabilities because they bore the mantle of Judaism. The petition for equality from Philadelphia's Jews in 1784 asserted that the denial of equal rights stigmatized "their nation and their religion," and that Jewish teachings in no way were "inconsistent with the safety and happiness of the people of Pennsylvania."[16] Forty years later a petition in Maryland against the test oath for office-holding similarly wondered what in Judaism warranted the state's departure from American justice. In some church/state cases after World War II, Jews who challenged Christian practices in public schools defended themselves and their religion against charges of secularism.

In the early nineteenth century, the defense of Judaism emerged principally in response to Protestant missionaries. Jewish spokesmen knew of the wave of conversions that attended the struggle for Emancipation in Europe, and they saw a similar threat to American Judaism in missionary activity. Since missionaries stood in the vanguard of the Christian-state idea, or the effort to shape America legally and socially into a Christian commonwealth (which reached a peak before the Civil War), their successes could well undermine the equality of Jews. Moreover, missionaries who canvassed outlying territories kept alive anti-Jewish stereotypes that readily translated to this-worldly situations. In response, Jews fought the common conversionist charges that Judaism was a dead religion and its precepts immoral. Rabbi Isaac Leeser's *Occident*, the first long-lived American Jewish periodical, and two other antebellum papers repeatedly lashed out against the missionaries and their abominable tactics. In this matter, as in others, defense rested on American rather than Jewish principles. By charging that the conversionists flouted the principle of separation of church and state, and crusaded for the establishment of Christianity as the national religion, the defenders called them un-American and unconstitutional. It followed that the Jews who defended separation and resisted a religious establishment were the better Americans.

The long antimissionary struggle led Leeser to prescribe new communal institutions, e.g., Jewish schools and a Jewish publication society, as the best methods of defense. They would guard the ignorant and the weak against missionary blandishments while they built up Jewish knowledge and pride. He also said that for its very survival the Jewish community would do well to adopt missionary zeal—and Christian devices like the Sunday school—as their own. Those suggestions showed how Jewish defense that began as reactive could become active, in this instance insofar as it initiated changes within the Jewish community.

Unlike other defensive battles, the case against the missionaries was directed primarily *at the Jews,* including those likely to succumb to missionary influence. While Jewish periodicals belittled the missionary societies, only rarely did Jews dare to mock the doctrines of Christianity. Fear of anti-Semitic backlash from Christian America inhibited them, as did the awareness that their words had no impact on the Christian zealots.

The missionary problem persisted into the twentieth century, manifesting itself at times of heavy Jewish immigration, and again Jewish education appeared to be the corrective. When, for example, the missionaries preyed upon the young children of Russian immigrants, Jews established and maintained a string of Hebrew Free Schools.

More recently, Jews were challenged by an ecumenical campaign known as Key '73. Rooted in the Evangelical churches but joined by the Protestants as well as the Catholics, the movement announced its intent "To Call the Continent to Christ in 1973." It spread its message nationwide through the media, billboard ads and auto stickers, Bible study groups, distribution of the New Testament, and crusaders who proselytized on high school and college campuses. Orthodox, Conservative, or Reform—all Jews were fair prey. Jews took the movement seriously; those who knew their history were reminded of debates and disputations in premodern times that often resulted in anti-Semitic excesses. Jewish religious, defense, and community relations organizations mobilized their resources; resolutions and action kits were distributed to congregations and community relations councils. None questioned the right of religions to proselytize, but Key '73, which resorted to deception and harassment particularly in connection with Jewish students, sounded to some Jews like an updated threat to religious equality. Focusing on Jewish teenagers and young adults, defenders prepared crash courses on Judaism and circulated material on campuses refuting missionary arguments. Rabbis and scholars visited students, and some antimissionary groups were formed. Only the Jewish Defense League resorted to violence. As it had always been, overall Jewish defense was rational, law-abiding, and concerned about equality. Here, too, a greater emphasis was put on educating Jews instead of confronting the missionaries.

Key '73 failed to achieve its stated goal, but it left an impact on Jewish defense. The American Jewish Committee (AJC), for one, realized that Evangelicals had changed radically since the days of

Sinclair Lewis's *Elmer Gantry,* and it began to work seriously to bring them into the fold of Jewish/Christian dialogue.

Evangelicals determinedly entered the political arena immediately before the elections of 1980. The program and campaign of the Christian Right, which charged the electorate to return the nation to Christian values, included statements that denigrated Jews and their religion. At a well-attended briefing on national affairs in the summer of 1980, Dr. Bailey Smith, president of the Southern Baptist Convention, set off one explosion when he said in a speech, "God Almighty does not hear the prayer of a Jew, for how in the world can God hear the prayer of a man who says that Jesus Christ is not the true Messiah." Smith denied that he was anti-Semitic; Jews were lost without Jesus, he said, but they were still "God's special people."[17] Not too different from traditional Christian teaching that underlay missionizing of Jews, Smith's message aroused the anger of many Christians and liberals as well as Jews. Although they called his remarks hateful, morally offensive, and destructive of American pluralism, Smith could not be dismissed as just another missionizing crank. The fundamentalist churches were gaining in strength— Southern Baptists alone numbered over thirteen million—and Jewish defenders knew from their own analyses that the stronger the fundamentalist beliefs, the higher the anti-Semitic quotient. Even more alarming was the attempt represented by Smith to inject those beliefs into politics. Nevertheless, Jewish spokesmen were divided on how to react. Reform Rabbi Alexander Schindler, president of the UAHC, called Smith an anti-Semite, "Julius Streicher with an Oklahoma twang"[18]; the AJC and the Anti-Defamation League (ADL) criticized Smith but continued efforts to arrive at a Jewish/Evangelical understanding; and some Orthodox leaders, more critical of the secular Jewish agencies and their support of a secular state than the Baptist leader, defended Smith's religious beliefs. At bottom, the way in which American Jews interpreted their priorities determined their response. Public pressure forced Smith to backtrack and, via the ADL, to work out a modus vivendi with the Jews, but the affair brought Reverend Jerry Falwell's Moral Majority and other Christianizers, similarly bent on political action, into the picture. As one Jewish leader said, the struggle was on "for the character and soul of America."[19]

The forces of the Christian Right held firm and so did most Jews, who believed that anti-Semitism and missionizing were "constants" in the Evangelical equation. They also feared the implications of Christian Right demands—their disdain for pluralism, their injection of religion into politics and repudiation of church/state separation, and their resurrection of a Christian state that would erase all the advances made by Jews in the name of equality. Second, Christian Right views on specific issues like the rights of women and homosexuals, pornography, and abortion clashed head-on with the liberal and egalitarian agenda of the postwar defense agencies on which they predicated their security. If not for Christian Right support of a strong Israel (separate from the theological connection between the ingathering of the Jews and their conversion), Jews of all stripes would have been less inhibited about condemning Bailey Smith and his ilk.

Some Jewish organizations resorted to public education of both Jews and non-Jews in their fight against the Christian Right. This time, however, the aim was not to teach the rudiments of Judaism but to teach about the far Right and how Jews should respond. Study groups and workshops abounded. The UAHC, for example, printed two handbooks for teachers, *Assault on the Bill of Rights* and *The Challenge of the Religious Right*, that presented historical examples, opinions of famous Americans, and court decisions in opposition to the platform of the Christianizers. One booklet discussed missionaries in a short section, and here the object was not to defend Jewish doctrines but to prove the illegality of the proselytizing methods. Jewish teachings were cited in the second booklet in a chapter on abortion, and only those that condoned abortion were mentioned. Clearly, at least to the UAHC, a pluralistic America was a priority demanding education that transcended the need to defend the tenets of Judaism against Christian missionizing.

The Christian Right did not score as well as it had hoped in the national elections of 1980 and 1984, but efforts at proselytizing, mandated by the Christian tenet of witness to the Jews, continued. (As recently as 1999, the Southern Baptist International Mission Board issued a pamphlet that counseled its members on how to pray for Jewish conversion.) The aims of missionaries prove that religious pluralism in its broadest sense, that is, the acknowledgement of the truth of all faiths, has bypassed a significant sector of "churched" Americans. In addition, missionizing still feeds Jewish suspicions of Christian good will and constitutes a major stumbling block to meaningful interfaith activities.

In Defense of Foreign Jews

Probably no issue has mustered greater unity among American Jews than concern for Jews abroad. Since the eighteenth century, when Palestinian messengers first canvassed the American colonies on behalf of scholars and yeshivot in Eretz Yisrael, Jews have responded sympathetically. (On at least two occasions in the nineteenth century, the Damascus affair of 1840 and the eruption of intense anti-Semitism in Bismarck's Germany, some worried lest the same hatred of Jews turn westward and reach the United States.) The number of cases in which Jews acted, and still act, is legion. Over the years, defense has encompassed far more than financial aid; it has meant protests against discrimination and persecution, resettlement of refugees, and, on rare occasions, direct diplomatic negotiations between American Jewish leaders and representatives of anti-Jewish governments. For the most part, the Americans never consulted with the objects of their assistance about their defense strategy.

An examination of the American Jewish response to the situation of Russian Jews between 1880 and 1914, a period when defense rested in the hands of a small group of prominent individuals, illustrates all the features mentioned above. No matter if they liked Eastern European Jews or not—and many of the German-born Jewish communal spokesmen did not—defenders called meetings and drew up resolutions and petitions protesting czarist anti-Semitism. They labored diligently to cultivate American public opinion *against* Russia and *for* the mass immigration of oppressed Russian Jews. The most prominent leader of the community, Jacob Schiff, who worked to cut off Russian access to international money markets, bargained repeatedly with high Russian officials; he was willing to trade financial support for Jewish emancipation.

One publicized meeting of leading American Jews with a Russian official occurred in the summer of 1905. At the initiative of the president of B'nai B'rith, a conference was arranged between Sergey Witte, who led a Russian delegation to Portsmouth, New Hampshire, to negotiate a settlement of the Russo-Japanese war, and five Jewish spokesmen. Officially, loans to the czarist government were not on the agenda, but all understood that Witte was anxious to cultivate Jewish goodwill. Bankers Schiff and Isaac Seligman were at the meeting, and remembering how Schiff had bankrolled Japan in the Russo-Japanese war, both sides knew that "goodwill" translated into loans. The Jews openly stated their case—Russia risked the loss

of American sympathy and financial support so long as Russian
Jews were not emancipated. Witte agreed in principle to equal rights
and, although tension ran high at the three-hour meeting, he remained conciliatory and promised to seek amelioration of the Russian Jewish condition.

The meeting attracted widespread comment. While the Jewish
press at first commended the stewards, Secretary of State Elihu Root
sneered at those Jewish leaders who merely sought notoriety, and
some secular papers talked of Jewish ultimatums. In the end, the
meeting proved to have been futile. Witte could neither deliver on
his promise of amelioration nor could he stop a new wave of po-
groms that erupted in 1905 and 1906. The one long-lasting result of
the episode was increased resentment from the rank-and-file of
American Jews against undemocratic leadership. Personal diplomacy has remained a method of defense, but lessons were learned
for the future. Now, negotiations are usually begun with the government's blessing, thereby avoiding snide comments from the State
Department; confidentiality is more carefully guarded; and the independence of organizational leaders is kept in check by their followers.

Most important of all in the defense of Russian and other Jews
have been the efforts of American Jews to secure government intervention on behalf of their beleaguered brethren. Defenders themselves were motivated by deeply rooted feelings of kinship and responsibility (did Jewish law not enjoin the ransoming of captives?),
but they cited American principles to justify official intercession.
Referring back to sentiments held by the Founding Fathers, who
viewed the new nation as the exemplar of liberty and a haven for the
persecuted, nineteenth-century Jews defended their interest as being
eminently compatible with the American spirit. They acted, they
said, according to America's tradition of humanitarian diplomacy, a
factor that legitimated American intervention.

Oscar S. Straus, the first Jew appointed to the cabinet (1906) and
one very much involved in Jewish affairs, defined humanitarian diplomacy in an address to the American Society of International Law
in 1912. He said: "There is [a] class of cases for which intervention
. . . is justified by a high act of policy above and beyond the domain
of law, especially if such intervention is free from the suspicion of
self-interest and is not used as a cloak for national ambition, but undertaken solely and singly in the interest of humanity for the purpose of ending revolting barbarities, inhuman oppressions or religious persecutions." Citing authorities on international law, he
acknowledged that a humanitarian posture in international affairs

could be justified on strictly legalistic grounds, but that "a large element of popular conscience at times enters into those relations and shapes the actions of states." His examples included American support of the revolutionaries in Greece and Hungary, and remonstrances on behalf of Jews and against oppression in Damascus, Romania, and Russia. Even Theodore Roosevelt had said in connection with the Kishinev pogrom that a nation like America "should desire eagerly to give expression to its horror." Straus himself looked forward to the time when enlightened public opinion and the development of democratic institutions would replace the doctrine of expediency with that of international morality and humanity.[20]

Christians, too, invoked humanitarian reasons to uphold the rectitude of American intercession for the sake of oppressed Jews. With respect to the Damascus blood libel that had resulted in the persecution of Syrian Jews, a group of non-Jewish citizens in Charleston offered their sympathy. "It becomes a solemn duty of all nations blessed with the enjoyment of Civil and Religious liberty," they said, "to raise their voices against such cruelties, to remonstrate against their repetition, and to invoke the aid of public opinion everywhere for their suppression."[21] Clearly, the fact that American Christians as well as enlightened opinion in Europe shared Jewish outrage made the American Jewish case more convincing.

The importance of humanitarianism in the formulation of foreign policy, particularly if it hinted at possible American involvement in Europe, faded rapidly in reaction to Wilsonian diplomacy, and it was quietly shelved by the State Department during the 1920s. In 1936, when American Jewry anxiously watched Hitler's anti-Semitic crusade and desperately sought expression of condemnation from the government, Secretary of the Interior Harold Ickes was advised by the State Department to delete references to humanitarian diplomacy in an address he prepared for a Jewish audience. At the same time, Zionists tried to resurrect humanitarian diplomacy, arguing for American intercession on the side of a Jewish state in Palestine that could save Jews from the hands of the Nazis. Here again the State Department was unmoved. Politicians continued to mouth platitudes on humanitarianism and morality when they talked of displaced persons or the Holocaust, but American Jews learned to couch requests in terms of America's pragmatic self-interest.

An appeal to Americanism, but with a different twist, was reflected in the Jewish campaign against Russia in 1911. Since Russia subjected foreign Jews to the same limitations it imposed on its own, American Jewish leaders successfully agitated for the abroga-

tion of a commercial treaty between the czarist government and the
United States. Their primary aim, however, was *not* the desire to
secure the rights of American citizens to enter and sojourn in Russia, but rather to force that country to emancipate its Jews. They
reasoned that if disabilities against foreign Jews were lifted, Russia
could do no less than lift the disabilities on its own Jews. In this
matter Jewish defenders masked their real goal and argued to the
public that America, so long as it took no action, was condoning
religious, and hence unconstitutional, discrimination against Americans. American Jews, the argument went on, were the zealous
guardians of the Constitution who rested their case on American
constitutional principles. Once again Jewish interests were equated
with true Americanism.

Defense of foreign Jews frequently included defense of free immigration into the United States. On this subject American Jews, or
at least some groups within the community, dared at times to contradict public opinion. The best example deals with the heavy pre-
World War I immigration from Eastern Europe. During the 1890s
American restrictionism, supported by organized labor, patrician
activists in the Immigration Restriction League, and racists capti-
vated by the pseudo-scientific theories of inferior and superior peoples, made rapid headway. Immigrants were blamed for the social
problems of the urban areas, and calls for restrictionist devices like
the literacy test grew louder. At the same time, concerned Jews,
who increasingly realized that oppression of Russian Jewry would
not end under czarist rule, determinedly took an opposite position.
Invoking the ideal of America as a haven for the oppressed, they
sought to preserve a safe haven for the persecuted. Their publicity
sought to defend the Russian Jews, both those who had recently
immigrated and those who desired to immigrate. Their lobbying ultimately succeeded in securing exemptions from the literacy test for
refugees fleeing religious persecution, and it helped delay the passage of a stringent restrictionist law until 1917. Unfortunately, the
Jewish position shifted after the war. During the 1930s, when their
own insecurities mounted because of the Depression and the bitter
isolationism of their fellow citizens, American Jews expended little
effort on behalf of German Jewish refugees.

In Defense of a Jewish State

Zionism posed a stickier problem. How could a movement positing
optimum security for Jews and Judaism only in a Jewish state be

squared with unqualified allegiance to the United States? How could it not taint its supporters with the charge of dual allegiance? In response, American Zionism fashioned a singular interpretation of the movement that applied strictly to the United States: America was different, and not exile in the conventional sense; Zionism did not call on American Jews to leave their country and settle in Palestine; a Jewish state was necessary for oppressed Jews abroad who were not fortunate enough to live in America. From its inception American Zionism became little more than a philanthropy (and Americans admired philanthropies). Justice Louis Brandeis went further in explaining the compatibility of Zionism with Americanism. Not only were the *halutzim* in Palestine akin to the "Pilgrim Fathers," but loyalty to one's heritage enriched the individual and the country: "Every American Jew who aids in advancing the Jewish settlement in Palestine, though he feels that neither he nor his descendants will ever live there, will . . . be a better man and a better American for doing so."[22] Since Zionism's appeal to deep ethnic interests could not be denied even in America, Zionists assumed the responsibilities of aiding settlement in Palestine and of representing the nationalist cause to the government and the public at large. As loyal Americans, they almost always ignored *aliyah*.

Toward the end of World War II, American Zionists campaigned for government support of a Jewish state. A congressional resolution of 1944 called for a haven for the homeless Jews of Europe—an echo of humanitarian diplomacy—but it was rejected in the Senate on the advice of the State Department. As they had since the 1920s, Zionists and their supporters had presented a variety of reasons at the committee hearings in support of the resolution: a Jewish state would be democratic and hence in America's interest; Arabs had supported the Axis; American Jews had made significant investments in the infrastructure of the Yishuv; the United States was bound legally by its official endorsement of both the Balfour Declaration and the Mandate to support the creation of an independent Jewish homeland; a homeland in Palestine would not involve the United States militarily. Similar arguments emphasizing American national interests were mustered immediately after the war when non-Zionists and Zionists lobbied feverishly for the creation of a Jewish state by the United Nations.

The establishment of the State of Israel did not end American Jewish concern. Israel's need for financial aid and military equipment, and its reliance on the United States in the unfriendly atmosphere of the United Nations, are as relevant today as they were in

1948. American Jewish defenders were the "honest brokers" who engineered and maintained the partnership between the United States and the Jewish state. To be sure, they have more often than not judged the behavior of the Jewish state according to American standards, and the obvious example is their condemnation of the preferred position enjoyed by the Orthodox in Israel, but defense of Israel's security remains uppermost for concerned Jews.

Like other American interest groups, defenders of Israel maintain a permanent lobby in Washington that is recognized as among the most effective. Although political action is now well organized, the older defense methods of individual pressure on officials and efforts to mold public opinion have not been totally abandoned. Nor have the reasons for requesting government aid been any less American. During the Cold War, Israel's defenders justified American involvement in terms of the nation's national interests, that is, for strategic reasons the United States needed a democratic ally in the Near East to counter Soviet expansionism. Whether other grounds for American support will prove as effective after the demise of the USSR has yet to be seen. Nevertheless, the friendship that developed during the first fifty years of Israel's existence is a firm and so far enduring one. Despite occasional grumbling by each side about the meddling of the other, the ties between American Jews and Israelis have remained equally firm. (When Israel protested the epidemic of swastika-daubings in the United States, or when David Ben-Gurion appealed to American Jews to encourage *aliyah*, Jacob Blaustein of the AJC felt impelled to reach an agreement with the prime minister that pledged noninterference in American Jewish internal affairs.) Although concern for Israel may have strengthened American Jewish identity, the impact of current trends within American Jewry to move the focus of communal attention from Israeli needs to those of the internal community may possibly alter the long-held priorities of American Jewish defense.

Defense of Israel has forced organized American Jews to give less weight at times to other interests. Conflicts over priorities could and did arise. How wise was it, for example, for Jews or Jewish organizations to litigate a specific church/state issue, or to agitate for civil rights legislation in the South, if the trade-off was congressional or executive support for Israel? Or, did a commitment to the security of Israel weaken alliances with Christian groups that supported the internationalization of Jerusalem or the return of Israel to its pre-1967 borders? In the same way that defenders worried about a rise in anti-Semitism if they diverged radically from their fellow Americans, so were they concerned about anti-Israel threats. An incident in 1966 appeared to substantiate such fears. According to a report in the *New York Times*, President Lyndon Johnson asked a representative of the Jewish War Veterans why Jews so loudly opposed involvement in Vietnam at the same time that they requested support for Israel. Johnson was a friend of the Jewish state, but he saw no difference between America's commitment to the independence of both of those small nations. His question underscored the constant need to balance the items on the communal agenda.

The balance of priorities raised a grave threat to Jewish defenders in the 1970s and 1980s when the mainline liberal Christian churches took an anti-Israel stand. The "silence in the churches"[23] during the Six-Day War of 1967 ushered in years of concern for the rights of Palestinian Arabs at the expense of Israeli security. Church groups, some with their own network of religious and social services in the Middle East, were seemingly captive to the liberationist ideology of the Third World. They blamed Israel for its aggressiveness (especially during the Begin era), for "Zionist racism," and for the failure to arrive at a lasting peace. Jesus may have been a Jew, the liberal *Christian Century* said, but he was not a militant Israeli. The Quakers added insult to injury; they attacked Israel and the pro-Israel American Jewish establishment at the same time they sought contributions from liberal Jews!

The situation threatened the interfaith activities in which the Jewish defense agencies had heavily invested. More important, it forced them to reconsider their choice of allies. Could they afford to abandon their long-time partners and even risk their identification as liberal Americans? But to protect their liberal domestic agenda should they abandon Israel, their high, if not highest, priority? When the Christian Right thrust itself into politics in the 1980s, another option surfaced—an alliance with the pro-Israel Christianizers.

On the surface at least, the Christian Right were not palatable allies. As discussed above, their crusade against secular humanism, the Antichrist that bred rampant social ills, alienated the vast majority of Jews, the most secularized of American religious groups. Moreover, Evangelical theology and missionizing were distasteful and their protestations of friendship for Jews highly suspect. Yet leaders of the Right, like Jerry Falwell, lobbied on the side of Israel against Arabs. Unlike the liberals, Falwell had no problem with Israel's bombing of an Iraqi nuclear reactor, Israel's rule over the territories, and Israel's war against its neighbors. Since Israel welcomed Evangelical support, leading Jewish defenders refrained from

denouncing the Right out of hand. Nor were some spokesmen deterred by missionizing or theological concerns. Nathan Perlmutter,
director of ADL, explained that the "real" anti-Semitism in America
was anti-Zionism,[24] and that the lineup of the churches on Israel dictated a fresh approach on the part of Jews to both the liberals and
the Evangelicals. Neoconservative Irving Kristol put it this way: "It
is their theology, but it is our Israel."[25] Jewish leaders and the rank-
and-file divided on whether to welcome the Right's interest in the
Jewish state. While some within the Orthodox camp sided with specific demands of the Right on domestic issues, those Jews most
committed to women's and gay rights, as well as Jewish critics of
Israeli hawkishness, rejected any thoughts of a Jewish/Evangelical
alliance.

In the end, the Christian Right was never totally embraced nor
were the liberal churches totally abandoned. The consensus of the
Jewish majority was to adopt a pragmatic approach—to work with
the Christian Right on issues of mutual concern and to part company
where there was disagreement. (Rabbi A. James Rudin of the AJC
illustrated the new phenomenon in a description of two congressional hearings in the spring of 1984. The first, which considered an
amendment mandating prayer in schools, found Jewish agencies allied with the liberal churches in opposition to the Christian Right.
The second, on the relocation of the American embassy from Tel
Aviv to Jerusalem, found Jews lined up with Falwell against the liberal National Council of Churches.) While the AJC and ADL broadened their outreach to Evangelical groups, the ADL stepped up activities on behalf of Israel. A balance had been found between
Jewish loyalties to both liberalism and Israel, but defenders were
forced to adjust to ad hoc instead of permanent alliances.

In Defense of Separationism

It has become commonplace for Americans to point to Jewish defense of church/state separation as a key characteristic of the minority's activity in the public square. The subject has also been discussed and studied by Jews and non-Jews in popular and scholarly
books as well as in recent symposia on the limits of separation.
They all show that whenever early American Jews fought against
test oaths or Sunday laws, or practices like prayer and Bible-reading
that kept Christianity in the public schools, their case rested primarily on the doctrine of separation as defined by Jefferson and Madi-

son. It must be remembered, however, that Jews in the early republic understood separationism differently from their descendants today. To the earlier Jews this meant a government neutral to all religions, while today's Jews supported a government divorced from all religions. As nineteenth-century Jews made clear in their petitions for equal rights, they did not contemplate a secular state but merely one that recognized and accepted the respectability of Judaism as it did Christianity. They, like their fellow Americans, rejected the concept of a religionless state and, as discussed above, they, too, wasted little sympathy on the much maligned atheists. Not until the last three decades of the nineteenth century were Jews, then engaged in a battle for religion-free schools, among the serious supporters of a secularist state.

"Secularist" and "secularism" remained pejorative terms to most Americans well into the twentieth century. Since they were used interchangeably with "separationist" and "separationism," they tainted the image projected by Jews. Moreover, secularism raised its own problems. For example, most agreed that a task of the public schools was to inculcate morality, but could morality be taught without a religious base? Was a secular school preferable to the need to acquaint children with the Bible? Was there not something incongruous about those who identified themselves as a religious group, and who were quick to defend Judaism, simultaneously defending secularism? Could a secular state guarantee equality to non-Christians when American culture was grounded in Christianity? In the 1870s, Reform Rabbi Max Lilienthal of Cincinnati came up with an alternate way for squaring religion and secularism. He thought that Americanism, acceptable to all denominations, could serve as a surrogate religion, and, as others have repeated after him, there is in fact an American civil religion.

Jewish defense of separation reached a new high after World War II. Since then, defenders acted primarily through state and federal courts, the final arbiters on the issues of Sunday laws, religion in the schools, and religious symbols in the public square. Here, too, traditional reverence for Jewish law and the way in which it was expounded contributed to their reliance on the judiciary. Alert to situations that touched matters on their agenda, defense agencies gave their support to litigants, non-Jews as well as Jews, who represented their point of view. (In some cases an agency purposely sought out individuals to file appropriate suits.) Before the court ruled on the case, the Jewish defenders often filed amicus curiae (friends of the court) briefs that buttressed the litigant's case. The

American Jewish Congress, following the lead of Counsel Leo Pfeffer, was the most important of the Big Three in matters of litigation. A survey done in 1958 disclosed that the Congress ranked among the most active filers of amicus briefs in the country.

With antecedents dating back to Roman and common law, the amicus curiae was originally a neutral individual who advised the court on the relevant legal issues. In time, the friend became an advocate of one side in the dispute and organizations took the place of individuals. The brief, a form of judicial lobbying, held out several advantages for the Jewish agencies. Free of personality and political implications, it permitted the faceless organization to take the initiative in arguing points of law. Since the same legal issue could be introduced repeatedly, it also freed the agency from the fear of wasting favor with government officials or other power brokers. Pfeffer, who often wrote the joint brief when Jewish agencies joined forces or when the Congress cooperated with organizations like the ACLU or the National Council of Churches, produced arguments that combined legal interpretations and precedents with evidence from history and the social sciences. Aside from its value in a specific case, the amicus brief contributed to public awareness of Jews as separationists.

Like other areas of Jewish interest, defense of church/state separation was subject to the constraints imposed by public opinion and considerations of image. Again, as in other matters of defense, concerned Jews reacted strongly to the results of their endeavors. At times, a rejection of their position by the court caused considerable anger or dismay within the Jewish community. Perhaps one of the best examples was the famous case of *Lynch v. Donnelly* in 1984 in which the Supreme Court upheld the legality of a municipal crèche in Rhode Island. Not all Jews agreed that litigation should have been undertaken; why risk anti-Jewish sentiment or jeopardize Christian support of Israel? they asked. When the ruling was handed down, many feared that *Lynch* might signal an oncoming erosion of gains made under separation or, worse still, even a reversion to the Christian-state idea. A Jewish student at New York University's law school told his dean, "I feel as if we have been betrayed." The implication of *Lynch*, the president of the American Jewish Congress stated, was that the Jewish community "is now a religious stranger in its own home."[26] Other suits were brought to resolve the issue, and, meantime, a rash of Hanukkah menorahs erupted in the public square. That, in turn, led to a parting of the ways between the Orthodox and the secular agencies on the legality of religious displays on public property. To the Orthodox, at least, separationism had limits.

A decision that occasioned an inordinate amount of criticism was that of *Engel v. Vitale,* the 1962 case that tested the constitutionality of a twenty-two word *nonsectarian* prayer in the classroom. The background of the Jewish reaction is important: Braving Christian animosity and anti-Semitic taunts of "godless" and "Communist," the organized Jewish community had closed ranks in opposition to the prayer instituted by the New York Board of Regents. Many defenders did not expect a favorable ruling by the Supreme Court, but to their surprise and delight the Court invalidated the prayer. The victory, however, was short-lived, as a torrent of popular abuse, from both Christians and Jews, fell on the Warren Court and on the Jewish separationists. In Congress several proposals for an amendment to the Constitution permitting prayer were introduced within hours after the decision was handed down. One congressman captured the Southern mood when he said, "They put the Negroes in the schools, and now they've driven God out."[27] The Catholic hierarchy was particularly enraged, and a leading (liberal) journal, *America,* responded with a vicious anti-Semitic editorial. It said in part: "What will have been accomplished if our Jewish friends win all the legal immunities they seek, but thereby paint themselves into a corner of social and cultural alienation? The time has come for these fellow-citizens of ours to decide . . . what they conceive to be the final objective of the Jewish community in the United States . . . what bargain they are willing to strike as one of the minorities in a pluralistic society."[28]

Prominent Protestant intellectuals, like theologian Reinhold Niebuhr and Dean Erwin Griswold of the Harvard Law School, also voiced their opposition. By no means anti-Semites, they supported the right of the Christian majority to retain their religious practices. Griswold maintained: "This . . . has been and is a Christian country, in origin, history, tradition and culture. It was out of Christian doctrine and ethics . . . that it developed its notion of toleration . . . but does the fact that we have officially adopted toleration as our standard mean that we must give up our history and our tradition?"[29] He and the others sent a clear message: Christian Americans had made ample room for non-Christian minorities, and for the minorities to expect the majority to obliterate all vestiges of a public Christian-flavored religion was both unnatural and wrong. Reminders to American Jews that they were at best a tolerated minority would have devastated nineteenth-century Jewry. The activist supporters of

Engel, however, were not deterred, and from then on they have rallied in opposition to prayer amendments.

Christian opinion, which at one time would have made Jews recoil and keep a low profile, did not squelch public criticism of *Engel* from within the Jewish camp. Aside from the need to rally public support for the ruling and to prepare for the congressional hearings on a prayer amendment, *Engel* gave rise to a serious debate among Jews on the desirability of limits to separation. Far different from the aftermath of *Lynch*, the community divided loudly over the decision. Ironically, in this instance the criticism was triggered by a case the Jews had won! Indeed, it was the victory in *Engel*, which supporters claimed enhanced Jewish security, that allowed a critical appraisal of the rectitude of that very same decision and the implications of extreme separationism.

Jewish critics of *Engel* were concerned less about the unfavorable public opinion than about the intrinsic value of a public square devoid of all religious trappings. (The internal debate over that issue was started in the 1950s by Will Herberg, who had argued against secularism and for public religious values in American Jewish life.) In 1962, Orthodox Jews, who were staunch opponents of communal leadership by the secularist defense agencies, were shifting to a more accommodationist stance on public religion. To be sure, school prayer had no effect on their own schools, but many believed that even the inoffensive Regents' prayer could arouse a wholesome sensitivity to religion in secular schools. Spokesmen of Reform and Conservative Judaism were similarly disturbed. They argued that a totally secular state was alien both to Americanism and Judaism; Judaism needed a state sympathetic to religion in order to flourish. Rabbi Seymour Siegel, a Conservative theologian, warned: "If we completely desacralize our culture, we will be in danger of creating a kind of bland, common Americanism which in the end will progressively wear away Jewish consciousness and commitment." Furthermore, the idea that public religion widened the gulf between Jews and Christians was erroneous. Even America was *galut*, and in *galut*, Jewish separation from Christians was the normative situation. Attempts to obliterate the dividing lines, practically or theologically, only bred a "false messianism."[30] As one Reform rabbi wrote, "A Jew . . . who thinks that he is not surrounded by a majority that considers itself Christian, and involved in a culture and history that is saturated with Christianity, and with Christian judgments about Jews—is surely fooling himself."[31] Far better, therefore, for Jews to accept limitations, like religious usages in the schools, which were the fate of a non-Christian minority. The message of those two rabbis sounded very similar to that of the Nie-buhrs and the Griswolds.

The debate over *Engel*, and the criticism of extremist separation-ism from both Christian and Jewish intellectuals, hinted at a signifi-cant shift in the Jewish posture on church/state affairs. Rarely after World War II had American Jewish defenders been so berated for their stand on separation, and rarely had they been so harshly re-minded even by "friends" that the Jewish goal of complete equality *as Jews* was unrealistic and unattainable. If the logic of the critics were followed, a reversion to the neutralist position of early-nineteenth-century Jews was possible. Nevertheless, despite an in-crease in the number of dissidents, the rank-and-file of American Jews remained committed to separation in its purist sense. Perhaps, as some speculated, the commitment reflected the persuasive Jewish belief that anti-Semitism was more than a relic of the past. If so, Jews could not abandon separationism, a tried weapon that so long aided them in the struggle for equality.

Conclusion

The story of American Jewish defenders can be read as a study in acculturation or Americanization. Like the Jewish community at large, defense was accommodationist. Nonetheless, within the pa-rameters of accommodation, defenders redefined American princi-ples, and, like the premodern rabbis, they built fences around the law. Since accommodation worked in tandem with integration, de-fense spurred on Americanization. It followed that the more Jews integrated into American society, the better able they were to ex-plain their interests in the public square.

Overall, defense has been more American than Jewish. Although the interests at stake were Jewish, defenders defined those interests in American terms. Whatever their approach—conservative or lib-eral, legalist or populist—they argued within the conventional legal framework, and the points they raised derived from interpretations of American principles as well as their readings of the national in-terest. In most instances they also took care to plot their activities in accordance with American views of proper Jewish behavior.

Jewish defense has left an impact on American policy. Lobbying efforts on behalf of foreign Jews, most notably on behalf of Israel, have sensitized the government to an awareness of the minority's priorities. Even if officeholders and would-be officeholders were not convinced of the intrinsic merits of the Jewish case, defenders taught them the importance of the Jewish vote. On the matter of church/state separation, the results were more substantive. Together with other religious minorities, Jews helped to expand the liberties of all Americans and to transform the United States from a Protestant nation into one that acknowledges the needs of different religions. Thanks to such labors, Jewish defenders contributed to a change in America's definition of itself.

The costs of defense have been high. The greater the attention to outside issues, the less the focus on the internal community and the needs of a vibrant Judaism. Indeed, as explained above, the emphasis on integration lessened concern for Jewish identity. For example, Reform's CCAR was more involved before World War I with affairs of church/state than it was with issues like Jewish education or attracting Jewish youth to the synagogue. Only in recent decades, when confronted by the twin challenges of intermarriage and population loss, has organized Jewry reread its priorities and turned its attention to the theme of American Jewish continuity.

Jewish defenders scored numerous victories as well as failures. None can deny, however, that over the years they have contributed significantly to the security and well-being of American Jews. Nonetheless, the "messianic need" of full equality as Jews is still elusive. As long as Jews pursue that goal in a country steeped in Christianity, Jewish defense, in whatever form it takes, will continue.

Notes

* Having studied and written about American Jewish defense for several decades, I find that the references for each subject mentioned are far too numerous to cite in notes. Most appear in the books and articles I have published. Therefore, only direct quotations are footnoted.

1. Arthur Hertzberg, "Church, State and the Jews," *Commentary* 35 (April 1963): 277-88.

2. Milton Himmelfarb, "Secular Society? A Jewish Perspective," *Daedalus* 96 (1967): 220-30.

3. Marshall Sklare, *America's Jews* (New York: Random House, 1971), 4.

4. Moses Rischin, ed., *Immigration and the American Tradition* (Indianapolis, Ind.: Bobbs-Merrill, 1976), 47.

5. Arthur A. Goren, *The Politics and Public Culture of American Jews* (Bloomington: Indiana University Press, 1999), 191.

6. Jerold S. Auerbach, *Rabbis and Lawyers: The Journey from Torah to Constitution* (Bloomington: Indiana University Press, 1990), chaps. 1-3.

7. Naomi W. Cohen, *Encounter with Emancipation: The German Jews in the United States 1830-1914* (Philadelphia: Jewish Publication Society, 1984), 169.

8. Jewish Historical Society of England, *Transactions* V, Sessions 1902-1905, 301.

9. Naomi W. Cohen, *Jews in Christian America: The Pursuit of Religious Equality* (New York: Oxford University Press, 1992), 53.

10. Morris U. Schappes, ed., *A Documentary History of Jews in the United States,* 3rd ed. (New York: Schocken Books, 1971), 170.

11. Schappes, *Documentary History,* 333, 607.

12. *Occident,* 5 (March 1847): 597.

13. Cohen, *Jews in Christian America,* 70.

14. Irving Kristol, "The Political Dilemma of American Jews," *Commentary* 78 (July 1984): 23-29.

15. Werner Dannhauser, "Election '84," *Congress Monthly* 51 (December 1984): 5.

16. Schappes, *Documentary History,* 63.

17. Naomi W. Cohen, *Natural Adversaries or Possible Allies?* (New York: American Jewish Committee pamphlet, 1993), 8.

18. *Report of the President of the Union of American Hebrew Congregations,* November 21, 1980, 3-6.

19. Annette Daum, ed., *Assault on the Bill of Rights* (New York: UAHC booklet, 1984), 4.

20. Oscar S. Straus, *The American Spirit* (New York: Century Co., 1913), 19-38.

21. Joseph L. Blau and Salo W. Baron, eds., *The Jews of the United States, 1790-1840,* 3 vols. (New York: Columbia University Press, 1963), 3:940-42.

22. Arthur Hertzberg, ed., *The Zionist Idea* (Philadelphia: Jewish Publication Society, 1960), 519-20.

23. A. Roy and Alice L. Eckardt, "Silence in the Churches," *Midstream* 13 (October 1967): 27-32.

24. Nathan Perlmutter and Ruth A. Perlmutter, *The Real Anti-Semitism in America* (New York: Arbor House, 1982).

25. Noah Pickus, "'Before I Built a Wall'—Jews, Religion and American Public Life," *This World,* no. 15 (fall 1986): 31.

26. Cohen, *Jews in Christian America,* 243.

27. Cohen, *Jews in Christian America,* 172.

28. *America,* September 1, 1962, 665-66.

29. Erwin N. Griswold, "Absolute Is in the Dark," *Utah Law Review* 8 (1963): 167-82.

30. Seymour Siegel, "Church and State," *Conservative Judaism* 17 (spring-summer 1963): 13-38.

31. Herbert Weiner, "The Case for the Timorous Jew," *Midstream* 8 (December 1962): 3-14.

2

Church-State Dilemmas of American Jews

Jonathan D. Sarna

"The government of the United States of America is not in any sense founded on the Christian religion." This statement, found in Article 11 of a 1797 treaty between the United States and the Bey and subjects of Tripoli, encapsulates what may safely be seen as a near-unanimous Jewish view on the relationship of church and state in America. It is a manifestly negative view, a statement of what America is not. It also turns out to be somewhat misleading, for although the English-language version of the treaty was ratified by Congress, the Arabic original omits the controversial statement concerning "the Christian religion"—a fact discovered only some 133 years later. It is, however, a classic text, "cited hundreds of times in numerous court cases and in political debates whenever the issue of church-state relations arose"[1] to reassure the faithful that *no* religion obtains special treatment in America. However much Christianity might be the law of the land in other countries, in America, Jews have insisted, religious liberty is guaranteed by the Constitution itself.

But what does religious liberty mean? How are those who adhere to the religion of the majority, those who adhere to the religion of the minority, and those who adhere to no religion at all supposed to

interrelate? If America is not a Christian society, what kind of society is it and what is the relationship of that society to the state?
Elsewhere, David Dalin and I have shown that American Jews "have
never been of one mind" concerning these questions. Indeed, "over
the long span of American Jewish history there has been far less
communal consensus on the subject than generally assumed."[2] Here,
I will extend this conclusion by focusing on two major themes:
First, in response to claims that America should be a "Christian nation," Jews have put forth two alternative and in many respects contradictory models of religion-state relations in the United States, one
that points to the equality of all faiths under the Constitution, and
the other that stresses church-state separation. Second, in so doing,
Jews have confronted three central dilemmas, posed here as questions, that remain both difficult and nettlesome: (1) Are Jewish interests better served under a system that guarantees equality to *all*
religions or one that mandates complete state separation from any
religion? (2) Should Jews, in defense of their minority religious interests, ally themselves only with other minority faiths, or also with
atheists? (3) Should Jewish organizational policies on questions of
religion and state privilege broad national goals, like church-state
separation, or be directed instead toward the promotion of Jewish
group interests, as determined by constituents?

I

The great fear of the American Jewish community—well reflected
in their frequent invocations of the treaty with Tripoli—was that
America would someday officially define itself in Christian terms,
thereby reducing Jews to the level of a tolerated minority and second-class citizenship. True, George Washington had promised the
Jewish community of Newport in his famous letter of 1790 that "it
is now no more that toleration is spoken of as if it was by the indulgence of one class of people, that another enjoyed the exercise of
their inherent natural rights."[3] Nevertheless, Jews knew that the
conception of America as a Christian country—a tolerant one—lay
deeply rooted in both American history and culture. The earliest
charter of an English settlement in America, the First Charter of
Virginia (1606), granted by King James I, associated the settlement
with missionary work, the "propagating of Christian religion." Connecticut's Fundamental Orders (1639), the first to be drawn up by
the colonists themselves, pledged to "maintain and preserve the lib-

erty and purity of the gospell of our Lord Jesus which we now profess." Maryland, in a special act concerning religion that actually became known as the Toleration Act (1649) owing to its pathbreaking effort to guarantee tolerance for minority Catholics, forbade blasphemy, religious epithets, and profaning of the Sabbath, and explicitly promised freedom of religion without fear of molestation or disrespect—but, again, only to those "professing to believe in Jesus Christ."[4]

Nor was Christian triumphalism confined to the colonial period. "For more than three centuries," Robert Handy has shown, "Protestants drew direction and inspiration from the vision of a Christian America. It provided a common orientation that cut across denominational differences, and furnished goals toward which all could work, each in his own style and manner."[5] The Constitution and the Bill of Rights (which, of course, applied only at the federal level, and did not become binding upon the states until the twentieth century) did not dampen the ardor of those who embraced this Christian America ideal, for they interpreted these documents narrowly. Their reading—and whether it was correct or not is less important than the fact that they believed it to be so—was summed up by Justice Joseph Story in his famous *Commentaries on the Constitution* (1833): "The real object of the amendment was, not to countenance, much less to advance Mahometanism, or Judaism, or infidelity, by prostrating Christianity; but to exclude all rivalry among Christian sects, and to prevent any ecclesiastical establishment, which should give to an hierarchy the exclusive patronage of the national government."[6]

Story's view was buttressed by a long string of court decisions which, in accordance with British precedent, assumed that "the Christian religion is recognized as constituting a part of the common law."[7] Chancellor James Kent, chief justice of New York's highest court, held in 1811 that religious freedom and church-state separation did not stand in the way of a common law indictment for malicious blasphemy, for "We are a christian people and the morality of the country is deeply ingrafted upon christianity." Justice David Brewer, writing for a unanimous Supreme Court in 1892 (*Church of the Holy Trinity v. United States*), ruled that "we find everywhere a clear recognition of the same truth: . . . this is a Christian nation." In 1931, the Supreme Court (*U.S. v. Macintosh*) described Americans just as Chancellor Kent had, as "a Christian people." Eight years later, the Georgia Supreme Court, upholding a Sunday closing law, reiterated the same point—that America is "a Christian nation."[8]

Individual Americans have been even more outspoken in associating the state with the religion of the majority. Daniel Webster, for example, argued eloquently before the Supreme Court in the case of *Vidal v. Girard's Executors* (1844) that "the preservation of Christianity is one of the main ends of government." He claimed that a school "derogatory to the Christian religion," or even a school "for the teaching of the Jewish religion" should "not be regarded as a charity," and that "All, all, proclaim that Christianity . . . is the law of the land." He lost his case, but won cheers from members of the Whig Party. Furthermore, his views with regard to the illegitimacy of schools "for the propagation of Judaism" won support from the Court, even as it rejected his claims on other grounds.[9] Webster may well have changed his mind later on.[10] Still, the views he expressed in this case clearly reflected the sentiments of a significant minority of Americans in his day. At the end of the nineteenth century, a similar view was put forth by the Presbyterian minister Isaac A. Cornelison, who described America as "a state without a church but not without a religion." Even as he endorsed church-state separation, he argued that "Christianity in a proper sense is the established religion of this nation; established, not by statute law, it is true, but by a law equally valid, the law in the nature of things, the law of necessity, which law will remain in force so long as the great mass of the people are Christian."[11]

II

American Jews have, broadly speaking, offered two meaningful alternatives to these kinds of "Christian America" claims. Both are historically well grounded, both appeal to American constitutional ideals, and both claim to promote American and Jewish interests. Yet they are very different. One stresses the broadly religious (as opposed to narrowly Christian) character of the American people, the other stresses church-state separation and the attendant secular nature of the American government. Each reflects a different reading of history, involves Jews with different kinds of friends and allies, and translates into radically different policy positions.

The first alternative conjures up an image of Americans as a religious people, committed to no religion in particular but certain that some kind of religion is necessary for the well-being of all citizens. This idea finds its most important early legislative expression in the Northwest Ordinance of 1787, in which "religion, morality and knowledge"—not further defined—are termed "necessary to good government and the happiness of mankind." Leading Americans from Benjamin Franklin (who proposed that nondenominational prayers be recited at the Constitutional Convention) to Dwight D. Eisenhower ("Our form of government has no sense unless it is founded in a deeply felt religious faith, and I don't care what it is") have championed similar views, as have some proponents of what is now known as civil religion.[12] The concept is somewhat nebulous, and means different things to different people. What is important here, however, is the existence of an ongoing tradition, dating back to the early days of the republic, that links Americans to religion without entering into any particulars. It is a tradition that counts Judaism in among all other American faiths, Christian and non-Christian alike.

This tradition, although rarely appealed to by American Jews today, forms the basis for almost every important American Jewish call for religious freedom in the early decades following independence. A 1783 Jewish petition to the Council of Censors in Pennsylvania, for example, attacked a test oath demanding belief in the divinity "of the old and new Testament," on the grounds that it conflicted with the state's own declaration of rights—"that no man *who acknowledges the being of a God* can be justly deprived or abridged of any civil rights as a citizen, on account of his religious sentiments." That this declaration of rights, while inclusive of Jews, allied the state with theism did not trouble Jews at all. Similarly, the German-Jewish merchant Jonas Phillips, in the only petition on the subject of religious liberty sent to the Constitutional Convention meeting in Philadelphia in 1787, declared that "the Israelites will think themself [sic] happy to live under a government where all Religious societies are on an Equal footing." He too offered no brief for those outside the pale of religion. Indeed, when Pennsylvania adopted a new constitution in 1790 that qualified for office all who acknowledged "the being of a God, and a future state of rewards and punishments," the Jewish community raised no objections and was satisfied. As a rule, early American Jews sought religious equality, not a state divorced from religion altogether. Jacob Henry of North Carolina, when efforts were made in 1809 to deny him his seat in the state legislature for refusing to subscribe to a Christian test oath, underscored this point: "If a man fulfills the duties of that religion which his education or his conscience has pointed to him as the true one; no person, I hold, in this our land of liberty has a right to arraign him at the bar of any inquisition."[13]

Nowhere in any of these statements do Jews suggest that their rights should stand on an equal basis with those of nonbelievers. Nor did Jews protest when Maryland, in its famous "Jew Bill" of 1826, specifically accorded them rights that nonbelievers were denied.[14] Instead, most early American Jews accepted religious freedom as a right rooted within a religious context. They defined it, in the words of Mordecai Noah, perhaps the leading Jewish figure of the day, as "a mere abolition of all religious disabilities." Jews, as a rule, did not mind that America firmly committed itself to religion. Their concern was mainly to ensure that this commitment carried with it a guarantee to them that, as Noah put it, "You are free to worship God in any manner you please; and this liberty of conscience cannot be violated."[15]

Jewish support for this essentially pro-religion position remained strong throughout the first two-thirds of the nineteenth century. One well-versed student of the subject, Shlomith Yahalom, concludes that American Jews during this period were concerned with "freedom *of* religion and not freedom *from* religion." Rather than siding with the demands of antireligious organizations, she writes, many Jews supported "impartial aid to *all* religions."[16] A prime example of this may be seen in the Civil War when, in connection with the mustering of troops, Congress provided for the appointment of chaplains to the armed forces. Previously, only Protestants had served as military chaplains, but Congress, under the sway of "Christian America" proponents and Catholics, broadened the qualifications somewhat to embrace any "regularly ordained minister of some Christian denomination." Voting down a proposal to widen the qualifications more broadly, Congress consciously ignored the interests of the "large body of men in this country . . . of the Hebrew faith." When, as a result of this law, the soldiers in a heavily Jewish regiment were denied the right to hire a member of their own faith as their chaplain, the outraged Jewish community responded with vigorous protests and an extensive campaign of lobbying. What most Jewish leaders of the day sought, however, was not total abolition of the military chaplaincy, which a secularist interpretation of America's religious tradition might have demanded, but only religious equality. Once Congress amended the chaplaincy law so that the word "Christian" was construed to mean "religious," allowing chaplains of the Jewish faith to be appointed, the Jewish community pronounced itself satisfied.[17] Nor was this a unique case. As Professor Naomi Cohen explains in her study of German Jews in the United States:

The Jewish pioneers for religious equality generally asked for government neutrality on matters of religion . . . a neutral-to-all-religions rather than a divorced-from-religion state. Indeed, the latter concept, which in the climate of the nineteenth century was tantamount to an anti-religion stance, was as abhorrent to Jews as it was to most Americans. Rabbis, long the most influential leaders of the community, taught that religion was a vital component of the good life and, like Christian clergymen, inveighed against the inroads of secularization.[18]

While this response to the challenge of "Christian America" never completely lost its appeal, Jews in the last third of the nineteenth century found to their dismay that calls for religious equality fell more and more on deaf ears. The spiritual crisis and internal divisions that plagued Protestant America during this period—a period that confronted all American religious groups with the staggering implications of Darwinism, biblical criticism, and burgeoning agnosticism—drove evangelicals and liberals alike to renew their particularistic calls for a "Christian America." Evangelical leaders championed antimodernist legislation to protect the "Christian Sabbath," to institute "Christian temperance," to reintroduce Christianity into the schoolroom, and to write Christian morality into American law codes.[19] The National Reform Association, founded by Conservative Evangelicals in 1863, for example, defined its objectives in 1888 as follows:

The object of this Society shall be to maintain existing Christian features in the American Government; to promote needed reforms in the action of government touching the Sabbath, the institution of the Family, the religious element in Education, the Oath, and Public morality as affected by the liquor-traffic and other kindred evils; and to secure such an amendment to the Constitution of the United States as will declare the nation's allegiance to Jesus Christ and its acceptance of the moral laws of the Christian religion, and so indicate that this is a Christian nation.[20]

Liberal Christians may have been somewhat more circumspect in their public pronouncements, but as Robert Handy indicates, their goal too was "in many respects a spiritualized and idealized restatement of the search for a specifically Christian society in an age of freedom and progress." The liberal Congregationalist minister Washington Gladden, for example, looked forward to the day when "every department of human life—the families, the schools, amusements, art, business, politics, industry, national politics, international relations—will be governed by the Christian law and controlled by Christian influences."[21]

For Jews, the frightening implications of this renewed Protestant hope for a "Christian America" were candidly spelled out as early as 1867 by a writer in the *American Presbyterian and Theological Review*. Instead of placing all religious Americans on an "equal footing," as Jews had hoped, the article insisted that non-Protestants in America could never win full acceptance as equals:

> This is a Christian Republic, our Christianity being of the Protestant type. People who are not Christians, and people called Christians, but who are not Protestants dwell among us, but they did not build this house. We have never shut our doors against them, but if they come, they must take up such accommodations as we have. . . . If any one, coming among us finds that this arrangement is uncomfortable, perhaps he will do well to try some other country. The world is wide; there is more land to be possessed; let him go and make a beginning for himself as our fathers did for us; as for this land, we have taken possession of it in the name of the Lord Jesus Christ; and if he will give us grace to do it, we mean to hold it for him till he comes.[22]

The National Reform Association's proposed "Christian Amendment," designed to write "the Lord Jesus Christ" and the "Christian" basis of national life into the text of the U.S. Constitution, attempted to ensure that these aims would be speedily and unambiguously satisfied.[23]

Jews, new to America and all too familiar with the anti-Jewish rhetoric of Christian romantics in Europe, were understandably alarmed by these efforts. As in the Old World so in the New, they thought, proponents of religion were allying themselves with the forces of reaction. "The Protestants come now and say defiantly that this is a Protestant country," Rabbi Max Lilienthal warned in a celebrated public address in 1870. "When I left Europe I came to this country because I believed it to be free."[24] In search of a safe haven, many Jews now settled down firmly in the freethinking liberal camp; it seemed far more hospitable to Jewish interests. Jews also turned increasingly toward a more radical alternative to "Christian America"—the doctrine of strict separation.

III

Church-state separation is, of course, an old idea in America; its roots lie deeply imbedded in colonial and European thought. The idea was warmly embraced by Thomas Jefferson and James Madison who believed that the state should be utterly secular, religion being purely a matter of personal preference. "The legitimate powers of government," Jefferson wrote in his *Notes on Virginia*, extend to such acts only as are injurious to others. But it does me no injury for my neighbor to say there are twenty gods or no God."[25] While certainly not hostile to religion, Jefferson and Madison believed that religious divisions were salutary and that religious truth would be most likely to flourish in a completely non-coercive atmosphere. "While we assert for ourselves a freedom to embrace, to profess, and to observe the religion which we believe to be of divine origin," Madison wrote in his *Memorial and Remonstrance* (1785), "we cannot deny an equal freedom to those whose minds have not yet yielded to the evidence which has convinced us." Jefferson refused to proclaim so much as a Thanksgiving Day, lest he "indirectly assume to the United States an authority over religious exercises." We owe to him the famous interpretation of the First Amendment as "a wall of separation between church and state."[26] Jefferson and Madison's view was, to be sure, a decidedly minority opinion that fell into disfavor with the revival of national religious fervor early in the nineteenth century. But later, in the post-Civil War era and as a response to "Christian America" agitation, its message of "strict separation" attracted a whole new school of adherents, Jews prominently among them.

It is by no means clear when Jews first began to express support for this model of "secular government." In the election of 1800, a majority of the few thousand Jews in the country supported Jefferson, but his religious views were not the reason why. Indeed, Benjamin Nones, a Philadelphia Jewish merchant and broker, pointed out in his public endorsement of Jefferson that the future president "in his very introduction to the Declaration of Independence, declared all men equal, and implores a Divine Providence"—a clear indication of where Nones's own priorities lay.[27] Isaac Leeser, the most important Jewish religious leader of the pre-Civil War period, stood much closer to the radical Jeffersonian view. He repeatedly invoked the principle of church-state separation in defense of Jewish rights, took an active role in the battle for Jewish equality on the state level, and was vigilant in his opposition to such alleged Christian intrusions into American public life as Sunday closing laws, Christian pronouncements in Thanksgiving proclamations, official references to Christianity in state and federal laws, and Christian prayers and Bible readings in the public schools. Even Leeser, however, was primarily motivated by a desire to assure Jews equal rights and to prevent their assimilation into the mainstream. While he was more wary of religious intrusions into public life than were some of his Jewish contemporaries, he by no means advocated a secular government. "The laws of the country know nothing of any religious profession, and leave every man to pursue whatever religion he pleases," he insisted. "Nevertheless it is not an atheistical country."[28]

It was, then, only in the post-Civil War era, with the revival of efforts to create a "Christian America" and the resulting ties between Jews and advocates of religious radicalism and free thought (themselves on the rise during this period), that American Jews began unequivocally to speak out for a government free of any religious influence. Leading Jews participated in such groups as the Free Religious Association and the National Liberal League, both dedicated to complete church-state separation, and many Jews, among them such notable Reform Jewish leaders as Rabbis Isaac Mayer Wise, Bernhard Felsenthal, and Max Schlesinger, as well as the Jewish leader Moritz Ellinger, embraced the separationist agenda spelled out in *The Index*, edited by Francis Abbot. As Professor Benny Kraut has pointed out, during this period "the issue of church-state relations precipitated a natural, pragmatic alliance uniting Jews, liberal Christians, religious free thinkers, and secularists in common bond, their religious and theological differences notwithstanding."[29] The result, particularly in terms of Reform Jewish thought, was a clear shift away from emphasis on Americans as a religious people, and toward greater stress on government as a secular institution. Thus, in 1868, Rabbi Max Lilienthal elevated total church-state separation to one of the central tenets of American Judaism:

> [W]e are going to lay our cornerstone with the sublime motto, "Eternal separation of state and church!" For this reason we shall never favor or ask any support for our various benevolent institutions by the state; and if offered, we should not only refuse, but reject it with scorn and indignation, for those measures are the first sophistical, well-premeditated steps for a future union of church and state. Sectarian institutions must be supported by their sectarian followers; the public purse and treasure dares not be filled, taxed and emptied for sectarian purposes.[30]

Lilienthal's Cincinnati colleague, Rabbi Isaac Mayer Wise, proclaimed a year later that "the State has no religion. . . . Having no religion, it can not impose any religious instruction on the citizen, adult or child."[31] Rabbi Bernhard Felsenthal of Chicago, in an 1875 polemic written to prove that "ours is not a Christian civilization," went even further:

> God be praised that church and state are separated in our country! God be praised that the constitution of the United States and of the single states are now all freed from this danger-breeding idea! God be praised that they are "atheistical," as they have been accused of being by some over-zealous, dark warriors who desire to overcome the nineteenth century and to restore again the fourteenth century. God be praised that this has been accomplished in our Union and may our constitutions and state institutions remain "atheistical" just as our manufactories, our banks, and our commerce are.[32]

This soon became the predominant American Jewish position on church-state questions. During the latter decades of the nineteenth century, the organized Jewish community consistently opposed "religious legislation" in any form, and, in one case, applauded liberal efforts "to secularize the State completely."[33] Although, as we shall see, the early decades of the twentieth century witnessed some significant debates over the wisdom of this policy, Jewish organizations later in the century, especially following World War II, generally lined up behind what came to be known as the "separationist agenda," taking their lead from Leo Pfeffer, general counsel of the American Jewish Congress, and "America's foremost author, scholar, and jurist of church-state relations," who famously argued that "complete separation of church and state is best for the church and best for the state, and secures freedom for both."[34] Pfeffer won significant Supreme Court victories on behalf of the position that he espoused, and he assembled a powerful coalition of secular and liberal Protestant organizations that associated themselves with him. By the 1950s, separationism became for many Jews a critical plank of the liberal agenda that they took up in the postwar era. Just as they opposed all forms of discrimination, and allied themselves with supporters of civil rights and civil liberties, so they advocated an end to prayers and Bible readings in the public schools and to other religious practices that, they felt, placed members of minority faiths (like themselves), as well as nonbelievers, in the position of second class citizens.[35] A "high wall of separation" between church and state, they believed, would help to bring about "liberty and justice for all." Indeed, into the 1960s, one study indicates, "American Jews under the leadership of their defense organizations went on record time after time in significant court cases on behalf of separation. . . . For the most part they eschewed completely the idea of equal government recognition of all religions or of nondenominational religious practices, and they called for nonrecognition of any form of religion."[36]

In the waning decades of the twentieth century, the separationist consensus within the American Jewish community came under increasing pressure. A few critics, notably the Jewish thinker Will Herberg, spoke out as early as the 1950s against the community's "secularist presupposition" on questions of religion and state. In March 1961, according to the *American Jewish Year Book*, "unexpectedly strong support" for federal aid to religious schools "appeared within the Jewish community, especially among the Orthodox." Several Orthodox Jewish organizations publicly supported congressional proposals favoring state aid to parochial schools, and a leading Conservative Jewish leader, Charles H. Silver, declared that any plan of "federal aid that excludes nonpublic schools" would "tend to . . . do a disservice to our country." In the hope of obtaining funds for Jewish day schools, these Jews argued (as Catholics had before them) that education in a religious setting benefited not only members of their own faith but also the nation as a whole, and that funds used to support secular studies at these schools should not be denied just because the schools happened to teach religious subjects on the side. They also cast doubt on the whole Jewish separationist approach to the problem of church and state, terming it "robot-like" and "unthinking." By 1965, according to the *Year Book*, "these groups began to challenge the non-Orthodox hegemony in Jewish communal life and to lobby independently for their interests." They also established the National Jewish Commission on Law and Public Affairs (COLPA) to promote the rights and interests of the "observant Jewish community" concerning church-state questions. In the 1970s, the Habad (Lubavitch) organization joined the fray, arguing for the controversial right to construct privately funded Hanukkah menorahs (candelabra) on public property, a right that Rabbi Menachem Schneerson privately linked with state aid to parochial schools. At the close of the twentieth century, the "separationist" and "accommodationist" camps within the American Jewish community were again crossing swords, this time over the highly controversial church-state issue of vouchers, a proposal aimed at providing parents with tuition vouchers redeemable at the public, private, or parochial school of their choice.[37]

IV

The breakdown of the twentieth-century American Jewish consensus on the subject of church and state should come as no surprise. If anything, the fact that the consensus lasted as long as it did is a surprise, for it effectively masked the three agonizing dilemmas on the question of religion and state with which we began. Having summarized the two alternative models of church-state interaction that Jews put forth in response to Christian America claims, we can now return to these dilemmas to see how they played out over time.

Taking them up in reverse order, we begin with the question of group interests, specifically: *Should Jewish organizational policies on questions of religion and state privilege broad national goals, like church-state separation, or be directed instead toward the promotion of Jewish group interests, as determined by constituents?* In a sense, this question is a subspecies of one that lies at the heart of all minority group politics, pitting "universalists" against "particularists." Under universalism, Murray Friedman has observed, Jews "helped shape the 'good society,' in which they saw the fulfillment of Judaism's prophetic ideals. Those drawn to particularism, on the other hand, have argued that as a small and historically detested minority, Jews must frame their public policy positions on the basis of self-interest."[38] For some time, American Jews insisted that there was no dichotomy here at all: promoting universalistic ideals, they believed, was the very essence of Jewish self-interest. Thorny church-state issues (among other things), however, called this comforting assumption into question.[39]

Where secular advocates of the doctrine of church-state separation, for example, advocated taxation of church property, elimination of chaplains from the public payroll, abolition of court and inaugural oaths, and removal of the phrase "In God We Trust" from the currency, not one of these causes found significant support within the Jewish community. All these causes clashed with Jewish group interests that were, in the final analysis, not totally secular at all.[40] Indeed, in the late 1960s, the leadership of the American Jewish Congress specifically *refused* to challenge the principle of tax exemption for religious institutions (including synagogues), over the objections of Leo Pfeffer (who ultimately ghost-wrote an amicus brief on the subject for the American Civil Liberties Union).[41] In an earlier case involving Pfeffer, in 1956, the American Jewish Congress heeded the concerns expressed by local Jewish communal leaders and withdrew from a challenge to the constitutionality of a

Tennessee law mandating Bible reading in the public schools.[42] In both cases, internal Jewish interests, however parochial, overrode the more universalistic "separationist" goal to which so many within the Jewish community supposedly subscribed.

On the other hand, one can also point to cases where the goal of separationism overrode Jewish group interests. In Indianapolis, for example, the Jewish Community Relations Council and the Indiana Civil Liberties Union came out, in 1976, in opposition to a Christmas manger scene erected at public expense by the city government. A firestorm of anti-Semitism resulted, and some within the Jewish community felt that the issue should not have been made a priority, especially given the damage done to local Jewish interests. Others, however, including the community's leading rabbi, insisted that the constitutional principle involved—the goal of maintaining a high wall of separation between church and state—overrode these parochial interests, and they ultimately won the day.[43]

Disputes surrounding the display of Hanukkah menorahs on publicly owned land resulted in similar clashes between those who put "national interests" first, and those who made Jewish group interests their highest priority. In every city where the issue arose, the Jewish community divided internally between those who opposed the menorah on broad constitutional grounds, citing church-state separation (an argument that the Supreme Court in *County of Allegheny v. American Civil Liberties Union Greater Pittsburgh Chapter* [1989] did not ultimately vindicate), and those who supported the menorah on Jewish grounds, as a symbol of ethnic pride and as an appropriate counterpart to publicly funded Christmas displays. Admittedly, supporters of the menorah advanced constitutional arguments on behalf of its public display, and opponents insisted that Jewish interests, ultimately, were better served by "strict separation" than by "accommodation." Underlying the dispute, however, was a basic dilemma that we have seen played out repeatedly in American Jewish life: a clash between those who ranked church-state separation at the top of their list of priorities and those who insisted that the Jewish community's primary goal should be to advance its own group interests—first and foremost.[44]

A second dilemma that American Jews have faced in their long history of involvement in church-state questions is *whether, in defense of their minority religious interests, they should ally themselves only with other minority faiths, or also with atheists?* Historically, as far back as the Middle Ages, persecuted Jews allied themselves from time to time with a variety of "heretics." Eighteenth-century Jews made similar unofficial alliances with deists.[45]

In America, as early as 1820, the Jewish community seems tacitly to have sponsored a pamphlet by a radical freethinker named George Houston entitled *Israel Vindicated,* aimed at refuting "calumnies propagated respecting the Jewish nation," and specifically the "objects and views" of a missionary society designed to convert Jews to Christianity (the author's name was hidden behind the moniker "An Israelite"). Probably American Jews were motivated in their support of this radical freethinker by the same impulse that motivated Jews in previous eras: self-interest. Adversity, they understood, sometimes makes for strange bedfellows.[46]

Publicly, however, Jews rarely supported atheists at that time. Indeed, as we have seen, Jews in several states, including Pennsylvania and Maryland, won rights that nonbelievers were denied. Rather than allying themselves with the small freethinking minority that was without faith, nineteenth-century Jews, at least until late in the century, generally preferred to claim equality ("equal footing") with the Christian majority that took its faith seriously.[47]

In the early twentieth century, the question of whether or not to ally with the forces of irreligion arose anew in conjunction with the Jewish debate over the "Gary Plan," a scheme initiated in Gary, Indiana, in 1913 that permitted released time during the public school day for moral and religious instruction outside of school property. In the debate over the plan before the Central Conference of American Rabbis, one rabbi strongly urged his colleagues to line up with the "Free Thinking Society" in total opposition to the "released time" plan. But Rabbi Samuel Schulman, a leading Reform rabbi in New York, explained publicly, and then even more clearly in a private letter, why he felt that such a course of action would be a mistake:

> In America, we have a unique and, therefore, very delicate problem. We, of course, want to keep religion, Bible reading, hymn singing out of the public schools. At the same time we know that there is not enough efficient moral and religious education in the country. . . . Jews make a mistake in thinking only of themselves and assuming always a negative and critical attitude. They must supplement that negative attitude with a constructive policy. Otherwise, they will soon be classed in the minds of the Christian men and women in this country with the free-thinkers and with those who have no interest in the religious education of the youth. That, of course, is undesirable.[48]

In the end, the Central Conference of American Rabbis compromised, agreeing to a plan that shortened the school day in order to make religious instruction outside of school possible. The dilemma over whether or not Jews should lend their support to freethinking atheists, however, remained unresolved. It surfaced anew just after World War II in the well-known case of *McCollum v. Board of Education*. Vashti McCollum, the appellant in the case, challenged an Illinois "released time" law that permitted religious groups to use public school classrooms during school hours to teach religion. An avowed atheist, she depicted religion as an opiate of the masses and as a virus injected into the minds of public school children. She called for the prohibition of all religious education within the public schools of her district. Faced with this antireligious rhetoric, the question for Jewish leaders was whether to support McCollum as a means of ending a series of well-documented abuses that had turned many "released time" programs into forums for promoting state-sponsored Christianity, or whether to sit out the case for fear of being associated with a "Communist attempt to do away with religious instruction." As Gregg Ivers has shown, Jewish organizations are divided on the question: The American Jewish Congress was eager to support McCollum's case, while the American Jewish Committee and the Anti-Defamation League of B'nai B'rith felt that it was not in the best interests of American Jews "to be perceived as rushing to support a professed atheist's attack on the well-established practices of the Protestant and Catholic majorities in the public schools." In the end, all of the Jewish organizations agreed to support the amicus (friend of the court) brief written by the American Jewish Congress's Leo Pfeffer, and he specifically disassociated Jews from McCollum's antireligious sentiments, insisting that the church-state principle involved in the case was so significant that Jews had to overcome their "natural reluctance" to participate in it. "The importance of the issues to Jews," he explained, "requires intercession regardless of the risk of defamation."[49]

The court's verdict in the McCollum case, which declared released-time programs unconstitutional, by no means resolved the Jewish community's dilemma over whether or not to ally itself with atheists. Indeed, in 1959 both the Anti-Defamation League and the American Jewish Committee refused to become involved in the case of a nonbeliever who, under Maryland law (which required a religious test oath), was denied the right to become a notary public. "An interference in the case might be misconstrued as an ungodly attitude and, therefore, be inadvisable," a Washington-area ADL executive committee member explained.[50] The central question— with whom American Jews should ally themselves on church-state issues and what the implications of such alliances were—remained a significant bone of contention into the 1960s, and it has not been fully resolved to this day.

As important as that question has been, however, it pales in comparison with the most important church-state dilemma facing American Jews: the central policy question of *whether, in fact, Jewish interests are better served under a system that guarantees equality to all religions or one that mandates complete state separation from any religion?* As we have seen, over the long span of American Jewish history the American Jewish community has been of two views concerning this question: some have emphasized "equal footing," others "church-state separation." The majority of American Jews today support the separationist approach, but the dilemma has by no means been conclusively resolved—and for good reason. Persuasive historical arguments buttress both sides in the debate.

On the one hand, history teaches Jews to favor strict church-state separation as the only defense against a Christian-dominated state. Those who emphasize this reading of history think that sooner or later "so-called non-denominational religious exercises" inevitably acquire "sectarian additions and deviations," and that "non-denominational" then becomes the majority's term for what the minority views as decidedly partisan. They fear that calls for religion in American life, given the record of the past, will likely turn into calls for a "Christian America." To prevent this, they argue for "a fence around the law so as to avoid approaches to transgression as well as actual transgression." They understandably worry that once religion gains entry into the public square, majority rule will come trampling down over minority rights, Christianizing everything in its path.[51]

On the other hand, history also teaches Jews to oppose secularization as a force leading to assimilation, social decay, and sometimes to persecution of all religions, Judaism included. Those who emphasize this reading of history welcome appropriate manifestations of religion in American life, and they propose a less absolutist approach to church-state separation—freedom *for* religion rather than from it. They insist that "support for religion is basic to the American system," and they fear that completely divorcing religion from national life will result in "a jungle where brute force, cunning, and unbridled passion rule supreme." Only the idea "that wrongdoing is an offense against the divine authority and order," they argue, can protect society against delinquency and crime. They also point out that Jews, as a small and often persecuted minority, should be wary of setting themselves too far apart from the majority lest anti-Semitism result.[52]

What then of Jews in the American public square? They are caught, repeatedly, on the horns of agonizing dilemmas, faced with multiple arguments that are, at once, historically legitimate, ideologically convincing, and fraught with dangers. Experience has taught Jews conflicting lessons, for, historically, those who have focused on "principles" and those who have focused on "group interests" have at different times both been right. So have those who have made common cause with nonbelievers and those who have sought alliances only among the faithful. As for those who have held aloft the banner of religion and those who have trampled down upon it, both groups, we know, have over the course of time proven friendly to Jews, but only sometimes, and sometimes they have not proven friendly at all. In their dreams, most Jews long for an America where they and their neighbors can live as equals, safe from the fire and brimstone of the Christian state and the desolate barrenness of the secular one. How best to achieve such a society, however, remains an unsolved riddle.

Notes

* This is an expanded and revised version of an article that appeared originally in *Jews in Unsecular America*, Richard, J. Neuhaus, ed. (Grand Rapids, Mich.: Eerdmans, 1987); see also my introduction to Jonathan D. Sarna and David G. Dalin, *Religion and State in the American Jewish Experience* (Notre Dame, Ind.: University of Notre Dame Press, 1997).

1. Morton Borden, *Jews, Turks, and Infidels* (Chapel Hill: University of North Carolina Press, 1984), 76-79.

2. Sarna and Dalin, *Religion and State in the American Jewish Experience*, 29-30. The standard chronological history is Naomi W. Cohen, *Jews in Christian America: The Pursuit of Religious Equality* (New York: Oxford University Press, 1992).

3. A facsimile of Washington's letter is reproduced in Morris A. Gutstein, *To Bigotry No Sanction: A Jewish Shrine in America* (New York: Bloch Publishing, 1958), 91-92.

4. Sarna and Dalin, *Religion and State*, 45-50.

5. Robert Handy, *A Christian America* (New York: Oxford University Press, 1971), viii.

6. Reprinted in Sarna and Dalin, *Religion and State*, 101.

7. *Shover v. The State*, 5 Eng. 259, as quoted in Bernard J. Meislin, "Jewish Law in America," in Bernard S. Jackson, ed., *Jewish Law in Legal History and the Modern World* (Leiden: Brill, 1980), 159; cf. Borden, *Jews, Turks, and Infidels*, 97-129.

8. *People v. Ruggles*, 8 Johns Re (N.Y.) 294 (1811); *Church of the Holy Trinity v. United States*, 143 U.S. 457 (1892); *U.S. v. Macintosh*, 283 U.S. 605 (1931); *Rogers v. State*, 60 Ga. A722; cf. John Webb Pratt, *Religion, Politics and Diversity* (Ithaca, N.Y.: Cornell University Press, 1967), 138, 142; Leonard W. Levy, *Treason against God* (New York: Schocken, 1981), 34; Meislin, "Jewish Law in America," 159.

9. *The Works of Daniel Webster* (Boston: Little, Brown, 1851), 6, 166, 175-76; cf. Anson Stokes and Leo Pfeffer, *Church and State in the United States*, rev. ed. (New York: Harper & Row, 1964), 105; and Borden, *Jews, Turks and Infidels*, 102-3.

10. See Ferenc M. Szasz, "Daniel Webster—Architect of America's 'Civil Religion,'" *Historical New Hampshire* 34 (1979): 223-43; and Max J. Kohler, "Daniel Webster and the Jews," *Publications of the American Jewish Historical Society* 11 (1903): 186-87.

11. Isaac A. Cornelison, *The Relation of Religion to Civil Religion in the United States of America: A State without a Church but Not without a Religion* (1895; reprint, New York: Da Capo Press, 1970), 362, as quoted in Robert T. Handy, *Undermined Establishment: Church-State Relations in America 1880-1920* (Princeton, N.J.: Princeton University Press, 1991), 11.

12. Sarna and Dalin, *Religion and State*, 3, 85, 254; Benjamin Franklin "Motion for Prayers in the Philadelphia Convention," in N. G. Goodman, ed., *A Benjamin Franklin Reader* (New York: Thomas Y. Crowell, 1945), 242; Patrick Henry, "'And I Don't Care What It Is': The Tradition-History of a Civil Religion Proof-Text," *Journal of the American Academy of Religion* 49 (1981): 41; cf. Russell E. Richey and Donald G. Jones, eds., *American Civil Religion* (New York: Harper & Row, 1974); John F. Wilson, *Public Religion in American Culture* (Philadelphia: Temple University Press, 1979); Martin Marty, "A Sort of Republican Banquet," *Journal of Religion* 59 (October 1979): 383-405.

13. All of these documents are reprinted in Sarna and Dalin, *Religion and State*, 69-74, 82-85 (italics added); see also Edwin Wolf 2nd and Maxwell Whiteman, *The History of the Jews of Philadelphia from Colonial Times to the Age of Jackson* (Philadelphia: Jewish Publication Society, 1975), 146-52.

14. Edward Eitches, "Maryland's 'Jew Bill,'" *American Jewish Historical Quarterly* 60 (March 1971): esp. 267, 277, 279. The distinction between Jews and unbelievers lasted in Maryland until 1961 when the Supreme Court overturned it in *Torcaso v. Watkins*. Jewish organizations were initially divided over their support for the atheist appellant in this case; see below at n. 50.

15. Morris U. Schappes, *A Documentary History of the Jews in the United States, 1654-1875* (New York: Schocken, 1971), 281; Jonathan D. Sarna, *Jacksonian Jew: The Two Worlds of Mordecai Noah* (New York: Holmes & Meier, 1981), 132-35.

16. Shlomith Yahalom, "American Judaism and the Question of Separation between Church and State," Ph.D. dissertation, Hebrew University, 1981, English section, 14; Hebrew section, 260.

17. Sarna and Dalin, *Religion and State*, 129-31; Bertram W. Korn, *American Jewry and the Civil War* (New York: Atheneum, 1970), 56-97.

18. Naomi W. Cohen, *Encounter with Emancipation: The German Jews in the United States, 1830-1914* (Philadelphia: Jewish Publication Society, 1984), 77.

19. James Turner, *Without God, without Creed: The Origins of Unbelief in America* (Baltimore: Johns Hopkins University Press, 1985); Ferenc M. Szasz, "Protestantism and the Search for Stability: Liberal and Conservative Quests for a Christian America, 1875-1925," in *Building the Organizational Society*, ed. Jerry Israel (New York: Free Press, 1972), 88-102; Paul A. Carter, *The Spiritual Crisis of the Gilded Age* (DeKalb, Ill.: University of Illinois Press, 1971); Jackson Lears, *No Place of Grace: Antimodernism and the Transformation of American Culture, 1880-1920* (New York: Pantheon, 1981).

20. Quoted in Handy, *Undermined Establishment*, 25-56; see also Cohen, *Jews in Christian America*, 69-72.

21. Handy, *A Christian America*, 101, 161-62.

22. *American Presbyterian and Theological Review* 5 (July 1867): 390-91.

23. Borden, *Jews, Turks and Infidels*, 62-74; Cohen, *Encounter with Emancipation*, 254-56.

24. David Philipson, *Max Lilienthal* (New York: Bloch Publishing, 1915), 121.

25. Quoted in Anson Phelps Stokes and Leo Pfeffer, *Church and State in the United States* (New York: Harper & Row, 1964), 53.

26. James Madison, "A Memorial and Remonstrance to the Honorable the General Assembly of the Commonwealth of Virginia" (1785), and "Thomas Jefferson to the Rev. Mr. Millar" (1808), both reprinted in John F. Wilson and Donald L. Drakeman, *Church and State in American History* (Boston: Beacon Press, 1987), 69, 79; see Robert M. Healey, "Jefferson on Judaism and the Jews: 'Divided We Stand, United We Fall!'" *American Jewish History* 73 (June 1984): 359-74; and more broadly, William Lee Miller, *The First Liberty: Religion and the American Republic* (New York: Knopf, 1986), 5-150.

27. Wolf and Whiteman, *History of the Jews of Philadelphia*, 213. On Jewish support for Jefferson in 1800, see Jonathan D. Sarna, "American Jewish Political Conservatism in Historical Perspective," *American Jewish History* 87 (1999): 118-19.

28. Sarna and Dalin, *Religion and State*, 103; Lance J. Sussman, *Isaac Leeser and the Making of American Judaism* (Detroit: Wayne State University Press, 1995), 147-49; 225-27; Cohen, *Jews in Christian America*, 50; Maxine S. Seller, "Isaac Leeser, Architect of the American Jewish Community," Ph.D. dissertation, University of Pennsylvania, 1965, 136-

75; Borden, *Jews, Turks and Infidels*; see Isaac Leeser, *The Claims of the Jews to an Equality of Rights* (Philadelphia: C. Sherman, 1841).

29. Benny Kraut, "Frances E. Abbot: Perceptions of a Nineteenth Century Religious Radical on Jews and Judaism," in *Studies in the American Jewish Experience*, ed. J. R. Marcus and A. J. Peck (Cincinnati: American Jewish Archives, 1981), 99-101.

30. Reprinted in Philipson, *Max Lilienthal*, 456-57, cf. 109-25.

31. Reprinted in Sarna and Dalin, *Religion and State*, 188.

32. Reprinted in Emma Felsenthal, *Bernhard Felsenthal: Teacher in Israel* (New York: Oxford University Press, 1924), 267-68.

33. Sarna and Dalin, *Religion and State*, 173.

34. James E. Wood, Jr., "Preface," *Religion and the State: Essays in Honor of Leo Pfeffer*, ed. J. E. Wood, Jr. (Waco, Tex.: Baylor University Press, 1985), ix-x; the quotation is from the concluding words of Pfeffer's *Church, State and Freedom* (Boston: Beacon Press, 1967).

35. Arthur A. Goren, "A 'Golden Decade' for American Jews: 1945-1955," *Studies in Contemporary Jewry* 8 (1992): 3-20, esp. 7-10; Stuart Svonkin, *Jews against Prejudice: American Jews and the Fight for Civil Liberties* (New York: Columbia University, 1997), esp. 79-112.

36. Naomi W. Cohen, "Schools, Religion and Government—Recent American Jewish Opinions," *Michael* 3 (1975): 343-44.

37. Sarna and Dalin, *Religion and State*, 25-29, 245-69, 292-94; *American Jewish Year Book* 63 (Philadelphia: Jewish Publication Society, 1962), 176-77; 67 (1966), 128-29; Marshall J. Breger and David M. Gordis, eds., *Vouchers for School Choice: Challenge or Opportunity? An American Jewish Reappraisal* (Boston: Wilstein Institute, 1998).

38. Friedman, *Utopian Dilemma*, 97-98.

39. Of course, other issues challenged this assumption as well. The 1976 "Centennial Perspective" of American Reform Judaism makes this point explicitly: "Until the recent past our obligations to the Jewish people and to all humanity seemed congruent. At times now these two imperatives appear to conflict." See the text and Eugene Borowitz's commentary in his *Reform Judaism Today* (New York: Behrman House, 1977), xxiv; and part III, 128-36. More broadly, see Jonathan D. Sarna, "The Cult of Synthesis in American Jewish Culture," *Jewish Social Studies*, new series, 5 (1998-99): 52-79.

40. Cf. Yahalom, "American Judaism and the Question of Separation between Church and State," esp. 257-64; Anson Phelps Stokes, *Church and State in the United States*, 3 vols. (New York: Harper's, 1950), 3:592-95.

41. Gregg Ivers, *To Build A Wall: American Jews and the Separation of Church and State* (Charlottesville: University of Virginia, 1995), 165-68.

42. Ivers, *To Build a Wall*, 127-28.

43. Gerald Houseman, "Antisemitism in City Politics: The Separation Clause and the Indianapolis Nativity Scene Controversy," *Jewish Social Studies* 42 (winter 1980): 21-36, esp. 32-33.

44. Sarna and Dalin, *Religion and State*, 288-300.

45. David Berger, "Christian Heresy and Jewish Polemic in the Twelfth and Thirteenth Centuries," *Harvard Theological Review* 68 (1975): 287-303; Daniel J. Lasker, *Jewish Philosophical Polemics against Christianity in the Middle Ages* (New York: Ktav, 1978): 164-65; Isaac Bazilay, "The Treatment of the Jewish Religion in the Literature of the Berlin Haskalah," *Proceedings of the American Academy for Jewish Research* 24 (1955): 39-68, esp. 49-50; Moshe Pelli, "The Impact of Deism on the Hebrew Literature of the Enlightenment in Germany," *Journal of Jewish Studies* 24 (1973): 127-46; Shmuel Ettinger, "Jews and Judaism in the Eyes of British Deists in the Eighteenth Century," *Zion* 29 (1964): 182-207.

46. Jonathan D. Sarna, "The Freethinker, the Jews, and the Missionaries: George Houston and the Mystery of Israel Vindicated," *AJS Review* 5 (1980): 101-4.

47. See, for example, Mordecai Noah's comments on the death of the self-professed atheist Charles C. C. Cohen, reprinted in Morris Schappes, *A Documentary History of the Jews in the United States 1654-1875* (New York: Schocken, 1971), 192-94.

48. Sarna and Dalin, *Religion and State*, 19-20, 203-8.

49. Quotations are all from Ivers, *To Build a Wall*, 75-80.

50. The American Jewish Congress did intervene in the case, and in 1961, in the case of *Torcaso v. Watkins*, the Supreme Court unanimously overturned the Maryland requirement. By then, both AJC and ADL had altered their positions and filed amicus briefs with the court. See Ivers, *To Build a Wall*, 107-12, esp. 109.

51. Quoted material is drawn from Cohen, "Schools, Religion and Government," 354, 345.

52. Quoted material is drawn from Alvin I. Schiff, *The Jewish Day School in America* (New York: Jewish Education Committee Press, 1966), 177; and Cohen, "Schools, Religion and Government," 364.

Part II

Constitutional Dimensions

3

Believers and the Founders' Constitution

Ralph Lerner

When thoughtful men and women turn to wonder about a possible divine presence in human affairs, they join in an activity as old and widespread as our species itself. Often enough that private silent speculation becomes public and soon displays the heat and discord common to political life—even while trying to transcend it. An age's puzzlement over the meaning of its existence may also express itself in an emblematic yearning for some decisive instant resolution, as in recovery of the holy grail or conquest of the holy land.

But in this American world of ours, yearning takes another form—public discourse about God seems to implicate domestic institutional arrangements to a point that even constitutional interpretation is affected. Perhaps it is not altogether strange that a universal search for an immutable Presence should manifest itself in our time and place as a search for an authoritative eighteenth-century prooftext, as an uncovering of the Founders' original intent.

Where avid interest fuels the search, zealous claims of success will not be wanting. Equally predictable is the regularity with which such simple solutions fail to compose political differences, let alone resolve the deeper human puzzlement they reflect. Rather than add to that heap of misleading answers, this author questions their common premise. When viewing the Founders coolly and from afar, can it be said that they shared some coherent understanding of the proper relation of religion and politics? After viewing that distant scene, a closer look will be taken at the handiwork of the Founders from within, indeed, from an emphatically parochial perspective.

I

Leaving self-serving legal polemics behind, we are confronted at once with the question, whom does one count as being Founders? There is good reason to look beyond those attending the Constitutional Convention in Philadelphia in the summer of 1787, even beyond those attending the state ratifying conventions in the following months. For if that great era of constitution-building is viewed as being, among other things, a deliberate and serious-minded effort to gain some clarity about the terms of collective life, then some who were present at none of those conventions but nonetheless were participants in the broader public debate need to be included among the Founders. Among such would be Richard Henry Lee, Thomas Jefferson, and John Adams. The Founders, so defined, would be a very diverse lot indeed, and especially in matters having to do with religion and politics.

Broadly speaking, they were the sons of Protestants, but not exclusively so. They included believers, deists, and some unspecifiable others, all holding positions with various degrees of intensity. On the whole, though, they tended toward muted rather than enthusiastic expression. Indeed, when viewed against the backdrop of the beliefs and concerns of their contemporaries in the several states or of the people of America at large, the Founders appear as a class apart. They strike one as more worldly, as more open to the issues stirred in the great political and philosophical debates of the preceding century. They also appear more measured and cautious; these were public men speaking to a public record.

All that has been said so far, however, presumes that the Founding ought to be viewed from the standpoint of the federal Constitution. But in fact the federal Constitution's prescriptions and silences need to be considered against the background of the state constitutions—and this for several obvious, even simpleminded, reasons.

First, it is well to remember that by 1787 the several states—and before them the several colonies—had had a long history of experience with varying degrees of self-governance. The length of time that elapsed between the founding of Jamestown and the Philadelphia Convention corresponds to the number of years separating the Philadelphia Convention from the administration of Lyndon Baines Johnson.

Second, the states were the main arenas in which religious principles were given political expression. It was there that the religious sects fought out their sometimes bitter battles.

Third, it is not surprising, therefore, that the efforts and experiences of the states in settling on constitutional forms appropriate to their several situations were very much present to the minds of those deliberating over the federal Constitution.

In this sense, then, individuals prominent in even only a restricted sphere might nonetheless be thought of as participants in the larger debate about religion and politics. If some of those individuals were not founders in the strict bicentennial sense, they were participants in a debate to which the celebrated authors of the federal Constitution were by no means the only contributors.

To complicate matters further, let us remember that even that debate at the state and local levels took on a variety of forms and concerns. Congregationalist Connecticut and Massachusetts had their distinctive coloration, Quaker Pennsylvania its own, Catholic Maryland another, and a riven, yet formally Anglican, Virginia still another. In all or most of the states, religion was a subject of legislation, regulation, and controversy. Charters, constitutions, and statute books bear witness to an established church or multiple establishments, to the use of general tax revenues to support the ministers of a particular denomination, to ordinances aimed at keeping the Sabbath holy and fostering church attendance, to the regulation of marriages and the registration of births by religious, not civil, authorities, and to the use of test oaths as a condition for holding public office.

As though all this variety and range were not enough, there was a further complication that forbids giving simple answers to simple questions. Even those who, so to speak, held a common position on the larger issue spoke in changing accents. To illustrate this one can observe four Massachusetts writers in the period 1776 to 1786, each of whom favored governmental support for religion. Just as one swallow does not make a spring, so, too, do four Congregationalists not make an historical movement. The thesis of this author is that religion, as viewed by believers themselves, came to be presented to the public at large in increasingly political terms. Confronted by the undeniable social facts of religious diversity and this-worldly preoccupations, defenders of old establishments had to trim both their claims and their supporting reasons.

None of this is to assert that the cool latitudinarianism that might be found in parts of Pennsylvania was already visible in Massachusetts. Rather it is to suggest that social conditions might already have been moving in that direction. Further, the old kind of arguments for monolithic establishments, now no longer seen as comfortable or credible, gave way to a new kind—less assertive, high-toned, and righteous. If these new arguments were still a long way from that system of principled indifference to be embodied in the Constitution of the United States, they were nonetheless prefigurations, or at least preparations, for that system. The terms of debate were changing.

The first author, writing in the *Massachusetts Spy* in September 1776 under the name of "Worcestriensis," was no canting, persecuting zealot.[1] He rejected outright any coerced conformity in matters of conscience, and yet he was for a religious establishment. In his view, the legislature was well within its proper authority to promote the general principles of religion and "good and rational sentiments." It was right to take "mild and parental measures" to bring that about. He had no qualms about bringing the state's penal jurisdiction to bear upon notorious violations of the "laws of natural religion" and upon the openly profane—in that they were disturbers of the public peace.

Nor is that all. This particular author's commitment to toleration of conscientious diversity in no way dissuaded him from urging the "positive interposition of civil magistracy in behalf of religion." Thus the legislature was perfectly within its right to promote *its* religion over that of others, as an exercise of its members' right to private judgment. Nor had other sectarians cause for complaint when general tax revenues were used to support the religion of the prevailing majority. They had, he said, as little reason to protest as in the analogous case when general funds were used to support a war that a minority held to be unnecessary or imprudent. Were it otherwise, greed would entice many to discover in themselves new money-saving scruples.

The second text is taken from the 1778 Massachusetts election sermon by Samuel Phillips Payson of Chelsea.[2] The occasion called for a political treatment, and the Reverend Mr. Payson rose to it. He plainly spelled out the social utility of religion in that it gives force to an oath, keeps alive the sense of moral obligation, and invokes the "most powerful restraints upon the minds of men." Here, he thought, were patent reasons indeed for the "civil fathers" of the community to guard against any innovations in the public worship of God—even when "urged from the most foaming zeal." At bottom, it was a question of law and order, and that great concern clearly could not be left to "the humors of the multitude."

The third example is from another election-day sermon, delivered in 1782 by an Adams of Lunenberg.[3] This divine, Zabdiel, was cousin to John and Samuel. Once again religion and general morality were joined as a proper object of the civil magistrate's attention. The Reverend Mr. Adams had no thought of molesting the modes, forms, or doctrines of other folks' religion. In accents strikingly reminiscent of Adam Smith's rejoinder to David Hume in Book V of the *Wealth of Nations*, this divine held forth on the advantages to state and religion that attend a multiplicity of sects.

> If coercion would bring mankind to a uniformity of sentiment, no advantage would result therefrom. It is on the contrary best to have different sects and denominations live in the same societies. They are a mutual *check* and *spy* upon each other, and become more attentive to their principles and practice. Hence it has been observed that where *Papists* and *Protestants* live intermingled together, it serves to meliorate them both. The same may be observed of any other sects. It is however greatly to be lamented that there is not a more catholick and comprehensive spirit among different denominations of Christians. Bigotry and censoriousness sour the temper and interrupt the happiness of society. The diffusion of light lessens this unhappy temper; and among people of knowledge, though of different communions, a harmonious intercourse commonly takes place. With madmen and enthusiasts there can be no agreement, except among people as distracted as themselves. But even such, where they put on a religious guise, and do not interrupt the peace of society, are not to be disturbed by the civil arm.[4]

This display of near impartiality ought not to be mistaken for indifference. A general encouragement to religion was the end in view, just as the mutual checking and spying were supported as means leading to a purer religion. Yet religion, even for the Reverend Mr. Adams, might be said to be too important to leave to the divines. In its worldly or social respects, religion is fit matter for legislative regulation. Hence, he would require that the young in the schools be instructed in the principles of morality. Further, he would compel adults to attend religious services *somewhere*, viewing this "most benevolent exercise of power" as a way of countering barbarism and profaneness. Most striking of all is this—even while reminding us that "righteousness exalteth a nation" (Proverbs

14:34)—Adams found his most pertinent examples of the political benefits of public morality and religion in Sparta and ancient Rome.

The fourth example is from an essay written in 1786 by a Congregationalist minister from West Springfield, Joseph Lathrop.[5] Boldly addressing the question, "Why should government have anything to do with religion?" this divine gave what he thought was an "obvious" answer: "Because religion has much to do with government." Even viewed politically, as an instrument of social control, the promotion of religion by the state makes more sense than its alternative. It is more consistent with human dignity and liberty to promote society's existence and happiness through public worship "than to do everything by whips, prisons, and cords."

The Reverend Mr. Lathrop was thus led to justify governmental compulsion in these matters, not for the sake of a great end—the salvation of individual souls—but because public worship served the present peace and happiness of society. As long as Christians were left free to determine their own manner of worship, they had no cause for complaint. Their rights of conscience were no more invaded by compulsory sabbatarianism and church attendance than by the compulsory maintenance of the poor and by public support for schools.

The arguments can be reviewed as they developed. In 1776 the case was made for some favored establishment, but without coerced conformity by others. In 1778 religious innovations were opposed— on law and order grounds. By 1782 a case was being urged for the multiplicity of sects, but under a general legislative regulation and promotion of religion out of regard for its social effects. Finally, in 1786 the problem was treated as one of social control, religious instruction and molding being held vastly preferable to corrective whips and prisons.

It is striking and curious that these divines so stressed the political utility of state intervention and support at a time when some opponents of governmental intervention were making their case from the standpoint of religion.

This chapter will look briefly at two such cases. The first and most famous of all was James Madison's 1785 Memorial and Remonstrance against a bill supporting teachers of the Christian religion.[6] The subscribers to this petition to the General Assembly of Virginia presented themselves first of all as "faithful members of a free state," and one is inclined to view them as loyal sons of Virginia, or as believers bound by some higher duty, or indeed as both. This artful melding is furthered by the premise of the Memorial and by the use Madison made of it. The first reason given by the subscribers for their remonstrance was their holding for "a fundamental and undeniable truth" that the duty owed the Creator and the discharge of their duty are matters of conviction, of individual conscience, not coercion. The source of this truth is not left to conjecture or vague recollection. Instead Madison put its precise formulation in quotation marks and, by appending a reference to Article 16 of the Virginia Declaration of Rights, reminded Virginians of 1785 that this was the authentic voice of 1776. Madison apparently thought that Virginians of 1785 also stood in need of a gloss on that hallowed language, and this too he was ready to supply.

The "unalienable right" of 1776 was a right only as against other men; that is to say, it was an assertion against their presumption. But more fundamentally it was unalienable because it was "a duty towards the Creator," a duty "precedent, both in order of time and in degree of obligation, to the claims of Civil Society." From such beginnings Madison was able to move with great address to the necessary conclusion that religion is "wholly exempt" from the cognizance of civil society. Every man remains unencumbered to do his duty, "to render to the Creator such homage and such only as he believes to be acceptable to him." From this standpoint, a magistrate's use of "Religion as an engine of Civil policy" is nothing less than "an unhallowed perversion of the means of salvation." Madison's argument thus moved smartly along to its main appeal to the legislators of Virginia: disestablishment *for the sake of religion.*

Yet it was not only a religious case that the subscribers made against state religious establishments in all their forms. There was a political case as well. But in making that case Madison called upon a sense of duty, nobility, and more:

> Because it is proper to take alarm at the first experiment on our liberties. We hold this prudent jealousy to be the first duty of Citizens, and one of the noblest characteristics of the late Revolution. The free men of America did not wait till usurped power has strengthened itself by exercise, and entangled the question in precedents. They saw all the consequences in the principle, and they avoided the consequences by denying the principle. We revere this lesson too much soon to forget it. Who does not see that the same authority which can establish Christianity, in exclusion of all other Religions, may establish with the same ease any particular sect of Christians, in exclusion of all other Sects? That the same authority which can force a citizen to contribute three pence only of his property for the support of any one establishment, may force him to conform to any other establishment in all cases whatsoever?[7]

In short, Americans had not fought a bloody revolution only for the privilege of substituting a home-grown Declaratory Act for that of Whitehall. In remembering their political principles they also would be revering their hard-won lessons. The sacred and the profane both pointed in the same direction.

A final example is from a little theologico-political catechism entitled *The Yankee Spy*, issued in Boston in 1794 under the alias of Jack Nips.[8] Its author is the famous Baptist preacher and lobbyist John Leland, who by this time had switched his attentions from Virginia to the Bay State. Much of the pamphlet is a critique of several provisions of the Massachusetts Constitution of 1780, most particularly those proclaiming a duty of public worship, requiring suitable provision for the support of public Protestant teachers, and authorizing compulsory church attendance on the Christian Sabbath. For none of these exercises of public power did the Reverend Mr. Leland have a good word. Rather he saw them all as products of a confusion of mind, one that confounded sins and crimes together, with a result that public authority could no longer distinguish moral evil from state rebellion. It was no surprise, then, that civil rulers so befuddled should "often run to grand extremes."

Overall, the Reverend Mr. Leland's approach was both political and religious. He sought in vain for some "principle of natural right" upon which the people of Massachusetts could rightly invest their legislature with these kinds of religious powers. What he found instead was the "havoc rulers make of good sense" when they fail to leave religion to the care of those who care most about it. Just as religion was purest and strongest when resting on the support of its voluntary adherents, so too was the state on firmest footing when considering its subjects without regard to religion. Neither motive nor object matters, however exalted the claim. "Should a man refuse to pay his tribute for the support of government, or anywise disturb the peace and good order of the civil police, he should be punished according to his crime, let his religion be what it will." All others, keepers of the peace, deserve full liberty of private conscience.

In sum, these opponents of state intervention in matters of conscience argued that such intervention is bad for religion and bad for the state. Religion is of too great a dignity and importance to be left to the uncertain supervision and control of those who may abuse powers not rightly theirs. "May" is almost certainly too cautious a term, for the experience of mankind showed that compulsion in matters of conscience was productive of corruption, hypocrisy, and persecution. This was no path for Americans to follow.

The point in mentioning these diverse opinions is to suggest how fatuous it is to speak of a monolithic original intent in these matters. For here we are touching on the very core of our private beings, and on these things, then as now, individual men and women divide deeply. Today it may be enough to note that this highly charged and divisive background, not to speak of all those people's long remembrances of religious struggles in the old country, had to be vivid in the thoughts of those Founders who met at Philadelphia in the summer of 1787. The political expression of those thoughts—that is to say, the text of the proposed Constitution—was an amalgam of hopes and fears, of existing political constraints and new anticipations. By saying little and requiring even less in matters of conscience, the new Constitution skirted the impossible task of assimilating highly diverse actual arrangements. At the same time, it opened a broad field for ever more liberal accommodations. As in its treatment of suffrage, the Constitution posed no additional restrictions and left it to the several states to take the hint, or not, as the case may be.

It is to that new vista that this essay now turns with remarks that might be called not "The Constitution and 'The Jewish Question,'" but rather "Jewish Believers and the Problem of the Constitution."

II

The point of departure, less a text than a puzzle, is Genesis 49:20. Jacob's blessings of his sons bristle with ironies, so much so that at times we are hard pressed to refrain from calling some of them curses. In any event, the prosperity promised Asher—"Asher's bread shall be rich, and he shall yield royal dainties"—has indeed fallen to his American descendants. Yet if these are dainties fit for a king, they are being savored at an emphatically republican table, a table set by others.

In the beginning, it is fair to say, Jews were not among those who sought a Zion in America. For some it might have been such: for Puritans setting up their city on a hill by the shores of Massachusetts Bay, for Moravians founding a city of refuge in Salem in the Carolina piedmont, for Mormons ending their decades-long trek through the wilderness at Deseret, complete with its own Dead Sea. Jews, however, were different. For them salvation was less a matter of heavenly bliss awarded those who conformed to a creed than the joyous daily fulfillment of the Law's commands in a commonwealth

of one's own. That political restoration, in turn, awaited the coming
of the Messiah. For Jews, then, the promised land still lay elsewhere, and Zion was where it had always been. At best—and this
was surely no small thing—America could be a new Ararat, a resting place after great tribulations.

Yet Jews, like those other peoples, separated themselves from
ancestral homes and sorrows to find a new place and make a new
beginning here. In leaving Europe or Latin America, they sought to
preserve themselves, and like those other migrants, Jews may further have separated themselves once they were here, the better to be
free to serve God in their own ways. For, as in the case of those Puritans and Moravians and Mormons mentioned above, but even more
than most, the daily round of Jewish practice requires a density, a
concentration of like-minded people in a compact territory so that
the most ordinary business of life and of the Lord can go forward.
All this points to psychic separation as well as physical concentration.

In these respects early America was indeed a promising land.
That vast and empty territory, ever so thinly settled along a narrow
littoral, insulated and protected such separatist and self-protecting
tendencies. One might join with one's fellows and, huddled together
in an untroubled corner of the wild, follow some particular road to
salvation. To be a free people in one's own land, to be secure
against the prying authority of hostile others, this was a dream the
New World's isolation made possible. Those early impulses and
tendencies may account in large measure for the peculiar motley
appearance of the theological and political landscape in the colonies
and then in the states. The expression of those impulses only rarely
took the form of a nearly homogeneous Connecticut, but it was by
no means uncommon for there to be enclaves, even extensive ones,
where shared religious preferences and restrictions were supported
by custom and by law. The legal establishments of many of the
colonies and some of the states, extending down to the age of Jackson, bear witness to this. They testify, no less, to a widespread assumption that state government and local community might well
have a visible religious aspect.

But with growing numbers and a relative concentration of the
population, another side of human nature, well known from Europe,
asserted itself in America. The claims of any one sect soon came to
be seen as immodest, indeed as impinging uncomfortably on the legitimate claims of others. Holiness is much impressed by the scandal of difference—especially when it is under its nose. It was certain
that our species' capacity for ingenuity and perversity would supply

much matter for scandal. Not surprisingly, the colonies' assemblies and other institutions were arenas where contending claims of right were voiced and voted on and contested yet again.

How striking, then, must have been the original Constitution of 1787 as it came from the hands of the Philadelphia Convention. We refer here not only to its forthright and unequivocal prohibition of test oaths as a condition for holding national office or public trust but even more to its pregnant silences as compared to a number of the state constitutions of the day. Add to this the language of the First Amendment as composed by the First Congress, and it is not hard to read the intended conclusion. From then on, at least as far as federal constitutional law was concerned, the focus of attention was to be shifted from groups to individuals, from sects to consciences. The new enlightened regime—one of the nobler products of an age that had more than its share of absurdities and travesties—made a new world safe, not for church or chapel or synagogue, but for each and every believer, indeed for each and every person's private conscience.

The implications of all this have been momentous, and not least for Jews. In emphasizing those implications the author does not mean to suggest that they made themselves felt at once in the tone and behavior of society at large or in the actions of state and local governments (a level at which they had no legal force until recent decades). American Jews, Catholics, and other religious minorities have long remained subject to scorn, abuse, and worse—sometimes even with the sanction of public authority. Thus, when Thomas Jefferson (in 1818) remarked to a Jewish correspondent on the Americans' response to the universal spirit of religious intolerance, he also took note of its insufficiency. "Our laws have applied the only antidote to this vice, protecting our religious, as they do our civil rights by putting all on an equal footing. But more remains to be done."[9] Yet looking back over the intervening years, one cannot deny that the national Constitution's principles and premises did indeed open new prospects.

Here was a world safe for Jews, not by grace of the man who happened at that moment to be seated on the throne, not by virtue of the intercession of a favored *Hofjude*, but on the same general juridical ground as left Anglican and Congregationalist and Quaker and a totally unspecifiable multitude secure in the privacy of their several thoughts and in the notoriety of their public worship or nonworship. As George Washington reassured the Jews of Newport in 1790, the governing principle under the new Constitution was no longer toleration or indulgence but natural rights.[10] What was required of them was that they comport themselves as good citizens, that they give effectual support to the new regime, and that they "continue to merit and enjoy the good will of the other inhabitants" of the land. In return, the American descendents of Abraham might at long last savor the tranquillity and safety promised by Micah's vision of every man sitting under his own vine and fig tree with none to make him afraid.

Nor was that all. The new constitutional regime promised a world safe for Jews, however they might choose to define themselves. Should they choose publicly and loudly to join in singing a joyous song—fine. Should a Jew choose rather to commune with his own heart upon his bed and be still—also fine. Should they even cease being Jews or believers at all, public authority neither knew nor noticed. For the first time (or at least to a degree unprecedented) all of these outcomes were equally available to individual Jews and, as far as the formal constitutional system was concerned, equally eligible. Here, then, was the ultimate word in indifference.

It was a new kind of promised land, at once more seductive and subversive perhaps than anything seen since the days of Alexandria. Here were possibilities and challenges barely dreamt of outside Spinoza's study. For an oppressed and hounded people to have stumbled upon such a land was as disconcerting and delightful as for someone to sail for China but to come instead upon an even vaster and unknown El Dorado. In its ideal American form, democratic society presented an "easy, tolerant, and contented" face. But, if like the Pennsylvania of Henry Adams's depiction,[11] this was a society gentle toward differences, it was also, ultimately, uncomprehending of deep differences. The very gentleness that it bore toward parochialisms of every sort was in itself a fierce corrosive upon those particularistic ways. Nor, of course, did those affecting such gentle toleration or acceptance perceive the parochial ground on which they themselves stood.

For all practical purposes it was enough to know that American society under the Constitution was open to all kinds of voluntary associations and that religionists who meant to enjoy the benefits of that regime had to quietly accept their place as one kind of association among many. Those unable to bear this muting of their clarion call would soon discover that society was equally uncomfortable with them. Like John Bunyan's Christian, they might shake off the dust from their feet as they left the city. For such, Jerusalem still lay ahead.

For the vast majority of believers, however, Jews as well as others, the new constitutional regime made an offer too great to be

withstood. Eschewing any pretensions to holiness or divine direction, this system of secular, enlightened indifference is large enough
and generous enough to shield almost any kind of holiness so long
as it minds its civil manners. Within these sprawling confines, and
along with many, wildly differing others, the Jew may find his or
her niche; if need be, even an enclave of kindred souls. But again,
the very openness of society cuts both ways. That which permits and
eases entry into any particular enclave at least as readily invites ex-
iting from it. That corrosive gentleness, which was referred to, is at
work here too. If this is so, then it is futile to look for or think of a
static equilibrium in the retort of democratic society. The possibility
of even a stable dynamic equilibrium may be equally remote. The
persistence or survival of a recognizably distinctive Jewry is profoundly in question.

This leaves us with the ultimate irony. A God, the plenitude of
whose powers and the mysteriousness of whose ways defy predic-
tion or analysis, has left the Jewish remnant today with not one but
two promised lands. In the Jewish state one finds the long-awaited
Jewish majority being pulled and tossed by competing promoters of
a new Zion. These heated enthusiasts seek a little world dedicated in
its entirety to either the austerities of Me'ah She'arim or the flesh-
pots of Dizengoff Street, as though the Chosen People's vocation
lay in replicating either Carpathia or Manhattan. Meanwhile, in the
goldene medinah, in the attenuated Christian environment of commercial, polyglot America, a minuscule Jewish minority is free to
flourish in such manner as each member sees fit to attempt. It is altogether a setting that neither invites nor rewards Jewishness, however defined. While government avoids direct assault or insult,
while society by and large even averts its eyes, American Jews are
left without the usual stimuli to taking collective self-preserving
measures. Instead, the staying power of Jewish belief and thought,
of Jewish loyalty and concern, is left to the impulses and deliberations of freely willing individuals. What they choose and how they
choose is, so to speak, only their private affair.

This is the continuing and lasting legacy of the Constitution of
the United States to believers of almost every sort. It fits awk-
wardly, if at all, with the daily prayer that praises God for establishing the singularity of the Jewish people. "It behooveth us to praise
the Lord of all, to ascribe greatness to him who formed the world in
the beginning; that he hath not made us like the nations of other
lands, and hath not placed us like other families of the earth, that he
hath not given unto us a portion as unto them, nor a lot as unto all
their multitude." The bended knee with which Jews traditionally

have acknowledged and celebrated their idiosyncrasy—and striven to preserve it—is yet another expression of human wonder and insufficiency and awe. Knowing, or at least sensing, before whom they stood, Jews and other believers living in America among their own, long tended to their divine concerns. Their parochial behavior may have been quaint and colorful within their little enclaves but could not help grating upon the sensibilities of the larger world without, a complacent society that increasingly sought to camouflage or airbrush away hues of a distinctly different kind. Nor could the children of those believers be shielded from that sense of awkwardness.

One might wonder, how could a proud assertion of distinctiveness, maintained for countless generations at a fearful cost, succumb so quietly to nothing grander than a sense of social embarrassment? Though this was and is a problem for Jews, it is not a Jewish problem. Austere orthodoxies of every kind posit a God who is not to be trifled with. The very harshness of His created world underlines that point. But America has presented a different prospect. Its geographic and social and political landscape suggested conclusions deeply at odds with earlier modes, leading believers of all kinds to relax their thoughts in certain directions. This has been described memorably by Henry Adams in the concluding pages of his monumental *History of the United States*.[12] "Only when men found their actual world almost a heaven, could they lose overpowering anxiety about the world to come. Life had taken a softer aspect, and as a consequence God was no longer terrible."

Most Jews, like most other democratic believers, have been drawn down new roads by new vistas and by promises of individual self-fulfillment. They have fully accepted the world that the Constitution has made possible. If some few, a saving remnant, still keep to ancestral ways that lead back toward the terebinths of Mamre, they too have fully accepted the peaceful opportunities that the Constitution has made possible. Like some Jews in America, so have some other believers also found themselves at the parting of the ways. At that junction of conflicting hopes and memories they may be jolted into discovering a few important truths about their deeper yearnings. They are certain, however, to discover this truth about their country: that America's blessings, like Jacob's blessings, have their concealed edge.

Notes

1. "Worcestriensis," no. 4, *Massachusetts Spy,* Boston, September 4, 1776, reprinted in Charles S. Hyneman and Donald S. Lutz, eds., *American Political Writing during the Founding Era, 1760-1805,* 2 vols. (Indianapolis: Liberty Press, 1983), 1:449-54.

2. Samuel Phillips Payson, *A Sermon,* Boston, 1778, reprinted in Hyneman and Lutz, 1:523-38.

3. Zabdiel Adams, *An Election Sermon,* Boston, 1782, reprinted in Hyneman and Lutz, 1:539-64.

4. Adams, "An Election Sermon," 1:556.

5. Joseph Lathrop, "The Reformer," no. 3, Springfield, 1786, reprinted in Hyneman and Lutz, 1:668-70.

6. James Madison, "Memorial and Remonstrance against Religious Assessments," Virginia, 1785, reprinted in Hyneman and Lutz, 1:632-7.

7. Madison, "Memorial and Remonstrance," 1:633.

8. [John Leland], Jack Nips, *The Yankee Spy,* Boston, 1794, reprinted in Hyneman and Lutz, 2:971-89.

9. Thomas Jefferson to Mordechai M. Noah, May 28, 1818, Thomas Jefferson Papers, Series 9, Collected Manuscripts, 1783-1822, Images 76-78, Library of Congress.

10. George Washington to the Hebrew Congregation, Newport, R.I., 1790, reprinted in Jacob Rader Marcus, ed., *The Jew in the American World: A Source Book* (Detroit: Wayne State University Press, 1996), 109-10.

11. Henry Adams, *History of the United States of America during the Administrations of Thomas Jefferson* (New York: The Library of America, 1986), 80.

12. Henry Adams, *History of the United States of America during the Administrations of James Madison* (New York: The Library of America, 1986), 1344.

4

The Rule of Law and the Establishment Clause

Martin J. Plax

The Problem and the Argument

The fascination with origins is often a signal that something revolutionary is taking place. This was certainly the case when the Establishment Clause of the First Amendment was defined by the Supreme Court in 1947, in *Everson v. Board of Education of the Township of Ewing, et al.* Although the justices divided over whether to uphold public funding of the transportation of students to and from public and private (secular and parochial) schools, they all agreed that the Establishment Clause meant that there should be a "wall of separation between Church and State." In asserting this, the justices claimed that the Establishment Clause gave equal protection to both religious believers *and* nonbelievers. The justices also agreed that, in interpreting the Constitution in that manner, they were following the principles articulated by Thomas Jefferson and James Madison.

From the start, the justices' interpretation of the Establishment Clause, and their claim to historical continuity, touched off a polemical debate. That debate continues to this day, largely because the Supreme Court has continuously settled cases on the basis of the *Everson* reading of the Establishment Clause. But in spite of the dif-

ferences between and among the conflicting parties, all share certain
premises that make both sides of the historical continuity question
self-contradictory. These contradictions, in turn, make a new analysis of the problem necessary in order to understand the true nature
of the problem posed by the *Everson* interpretation of the Establishment Clause.

In a 1995 article, "What to Do about the First Amendment,"[1]
Robert Bork argued that the Supreme Court has perverted the com-
mon-sense interpretation of the First Amendment by interpreting the
Establishment Clause to mean strict separation of church and state
instead of prohibiting an established religion in America. In doing
so, he argued, the justices had, in effect, denied the rights of religious liberty to many citizens. The Supreme Court, having "developed a severe aversion to connections between government and religion, had placed the First Amendment ahead of all other sections
of the Constitution, as though it were attached to the Preamble."[2]

Because, he argued, "the vast majority of Americans are believers, these holdings [on behalf of a strict separation] are fiercely resented by most of them."[3] It was this resentment, Bork argued, that
led to the call by then representative Newt Gingrich for a constitutional amendment permitting prayer in schools. But Bork was not
sanguine that such an amendment would ameliorate the problem.
Prayer in school would only be a Band-Aid for a more serious hem-
orrhaging.

The problem for Bork was that the Court had been contributing
to a growing support for secularism at the expense of religion and
that this was at odds with the original intent of the Founders. The
antireligious preference of the court was made even more evident in
the decision rendered by the justices in *Lemon v. Kurtzman* (1971).
There, the majority opinion stated that a law must satisfy three criteria: it must have a *secular legislative purpose;* its effect must be one
that neither advances nor inhibits religion; and it must not foster an
excessive governmental entanglement with religion. Bork argued
that the first criterion prohibited *any* government concern with religion. Therefore, by itself, it inhibited religion. From this, one could
infer that Bork saw the word "excessive" in the third criterion as not
just extraneous but deceptive.

Were the justices to review the legislative intent of the authors
and ratifiers of the religious clauses of the First Amendment, Bork
argued, they would discover that the First Amendment was intended
to assure that government was neutral as between religions, but not
as between religion and irreligion. But Bork had to contend with the
fact, however, that Jefferson and Madison had written of the desir-

ability of a wall of separation between church and state. He resolved this contradiction by asserting that both Jefferson and Madison held *radical and unrepresentative positions* on what constitutes the establishment of religion. But, were Jefferson and Madison unrepresentative of those who wrote and ratified the First Amendment, then Bork had, in effect, admitted that there is a radical disjuncture between the theory and practice of the Founders from the start. By making this concession, Bork, in effect, admitted that his insistence on returning to the "original intent" of the Founders did not necessarily lead to a clear and distinct conclusion.

That same admission was implicit in the argument made by Professor Leonard Levy, who wrote a response to Bork's article.[4] He based his argument on a 1962 *Commentary* article "School Prayers & the Founding Fathers," in which he provided an account of the drafting history of the Establishment Clause and concluded that the Founders *did* intend the language of the First Amendment to mean a strict separation of church and state. In responding to Bork in 1995, Levy argued that Bork's understanding of Establishment was drawn from the European notion, which was "the union of a government and a single or preferred church or religion."[5] This condition did not exist in America, *even in colonial times*. Among the states that ratified the First Amendment, seven authorized establishments of religion, but none of them fit this old understanding. Rather, "each had a general or multiple establishments of religion, benefiting all churches."[6] In other words, even prior to the First Amendment, in those states with established churches, there was no absolute exclusion of the free exercise of other religions. Religious civil wars did not occur in America, even prior to the ratification of the First Amendment.

Unlike Bork, who was willing to dismiss contrary information as irrelevant, Levy argued statistically. He asserted that "the preponderance of evidence" supported the thesis that the justices' opinions in the *Everson* case are consistent with the intentions of the Founders.[7] But this argument, like Bork's, logically leads to the conclusion that because the Founders were seemingly inconsistent, *any* conclusion about "original intent" would be equivocal.

This chapter will argue that the issue of original intent is not equivocal but has been misinterpreted by both sides in the debate, as well as by the justices who wrote opinions in *Everson*. That misinterpretation is traceable to the fact that the justices, and proponents for both sides in the debate over the meaning of the Establishment Clause, have framed their arguments by emphasizing *church* and not *state*. The proper understanding of the original intent of the Foun-

ders, including Jefferson and Madison, begins only when one considers the problem from the perspective of the state, and the good of
all, taken collectively. At the foundation of all the controversies
about the Establishment Clause is an issue that is coexistent with the
major problem of modern constitutionalism, namely, the grounds of
the authority of the rule of law. The issue can be framed in the form
of two questions: does the rule of law require religion as a necessary
condition for its authority and, hence, its stability? If not, can the
rule of law be sustained by the conscience of humans guided solely
by human wisdom?

These questions were answered in both Thomas Hobbes's *Leviathan* and John Locke's *Second Treatise*. These two founders of
modern constitutionalism began their inquiries by postulating humans in a "state of nature." Humans, by nature, are vain and rapaciously acquisitive. They grounded their construction of the rule of
law on that specific understanding of human nature. When one looks
to the foundations of modern constitutionalism, one discovers that
government by consent of the governed is predicated on that unflat-
tering portrait of human nature. One also discovers that the stability
of the rule of law founded on that understanding of human nature
requires ongoing prudential judgments about ways of harmonizing
the state *with* religion. Because the Founders of the American constitutional system shared those notions, they shared the same position with respect to the relationship of the state and religion.

On the basis of this analysis, this chapter will argue that the justices who decided the *Everson* case initiated a radical experiment in
American statesmanship.[8] They chose to rest the authority of the
rule of law in America on the basis of human wisdom alone and on
the conscience of the autonomous individual. The justices interpreted the Establishment Clause as they did because they were
forced, with the rise of totalitarianism and especially Nazism, to
consider the meaning of democracy and how it differed from totalitarianism. This historical factor accounts for the reason that the issue of Establishment was raised and settled only after World War II.

The reason the justices in their *Everson* opinions thought they
were following Jefferson and Madison was that they were, unknow-
ingly, the products of another twentieth-century revolution—the absorption of the language of sociology and psychology into the language and practice of law. The vocabulary of social science gave
new meanings to traditional words like "conscience," "religion,"
and "democracy." The adoption of the language of social science
also led the justices to believe that by defining the Establishment
Clause in clear and distinct terms, they would be able to unequivo-

cally differentiate American democracy from totalitarianism on the basis of the relationship between the state and religion.

Having identified the revolutionary nature of the 1947 experiment, this chapter will conclude by considering the effect of the *Everson* interpretation of the Establishment Clause on the problem of the rule of law in America in the year 2000. It will argue that, by defining the Establishment Clause in clear and distinct terms, the justices freed members of minority religions from religious impositions by members of majority religions. At the same time, however, having defined the Establishment Clause in absolute terms, they abandoned any semblance of prudential balancing that the Founders had argued was necessary for the maintenance of the Constitution and the rule of law in America. As a result, religion has, today, become radicalized politically and threatens to challenge the sanctity of the very institutions the Court exists to uphold.

Modern Constitutionalism and Religion

Jefferson and Madison, as Founders, of necessity had to be concerned with the problems inherent to the founding of a stable constitutional order. Both men were familiar with, and profoundly affected by, the philosophers who were the founders of modern constitutionalism. Considering the concerns of *these* philosophers provides some clue as to what the Founders of the American Constitution understood was *their* challenge.

Modern constitutionalism was grounded on ambivalence toward religion. On the one hand, the Founders were hostile to religion and created the distinction between state and society on the basis of that hostility. On the other hand, they were protective of religion. Nowhere is this more evident than in the fact that the three major founders of modern constitutionalism wrote works devoted to this relationship. Two of the four parts of Hobbes's *Leviathan* (1651) were devoted to examining how Christian theology could be made compatible with his notion of sovereignty. Spinoza's *Theological-Political Treatise* (1670) was devoted almost entirely to a critique of the Bible so that religion could be made compatible with his vision of modern democracy. Locke's *First Treatise on Government* is devoted to refuting the claim that the Bible supported only patriarchal polities, namely, those grounded on the divine right of kings. For the founders of modern constitutionalism, the problem of the legitimacy of the rule of law is the relationship of government and religion.

At stake was the question of whether or not humans and the state were created and therefore ruled by God, or whether government could be created and sustained by humans themselves. Divine right as a political concept meant the subordination of the state to theology. Rulers were, to speak metaphorically, the chosen, by God and not men. By extension, Establishment was an affirmation of the religion of those who were the chosen.[9]

In theocracies, religion and the state are one. By contrast, modern constitutionalism presupposes the distinction between state and society. But on what grounds could the idea of society be said to exist separately from the state? The answer to this question goes to the heart of the revolution that was modern constitutionalism. The division of the one into two, that is, state and society, meant the separation of religion from the state. Society became an entity of its own and the relationship with the state became a matter of philosophic inquiry.

Thomas Hobbes was the first philosopher to distinguish between state and society. Motivated by the desire to moderate religious partisanship, he turned the story of the Garden of Eden on its head with his own story, which he called the state of nature. Humans, no longer understood to have been created in the image of God, were also no longer described as living in peace. Life in the state of nature was a life of war of all against all. This was the case because Hobbes inferred, from history and from his own experience, that humans are, by nature, vain and rapaciously acquisitive. Civil society, or the condition of peace among and between residents of the state of nature, was motivated by fear of violent death. The contract creating civil society is grounded on consent, but because humans cannot be trusted to continue to believe that they are obligated to what they agreed on in the past, the state became a necessity. The state existed for society and was authorized by the social contract, but only to create peace or balance and to maintain it. The ruler, or sovereign, was the chosen, not by God but by those choosing to join civil society.

At its origins, modern constitutionalism placed the rule of law as its primary end. In Hobbes's state, the just became equivalent to the legal, and virtue came to be understood solely as obedience to the law. This meant that there were no legitimate claims to justice outside of what the law said was just. By inventing the idea of civil society from which the state was created, Hobbes not only separated religion from the state, but also weakened the claims of religion. This is the ground of the modern doctrine of the rule of law.

What is law for Hobbes? Law is a command that is obligatory under the following conditions. Commands are "authored" by an agent, called the sovereign. This sovereign, by virtue of the social contract, is authorized (has the right) to issue such commands. Those who receive the commands must know that the sovereign is the author of those commands (laws). If questions arise about the meaning of those commands (laws), an authentic interpretation of those commands has to have been given by the sovereign. Finally, the commands (laws) must be communicated so that those upon whom they impose a duty will know the commands and know that they are commands.

But this understanding of law creates a difficulty for the rule of law. Since the obligatory nature of law is linked with the author of the law, this means that it is not the law itself that obligates the citizen. The obligation is to the author of the law. The sovereign may have been authorized to make laws by those who have agreed to limit their liberties by agreeing to the social contract, but what is to insure that the citizen will continue to honor the contract by continually performing the duties imposed on him by the law? What if he no longer acknowledges the authority of the lawmaker? Is he then obligated to obey the laws made by the lawmaker? Is there any law, other than the civil law, which binds him? "There is little in Hobbes . . . to suggest that he held the making of the Covenant [besides being a prudent act] to be also a moral obligation, and that "keeping the covenant" and "obeying the law" were not inseparable activities. . . . But . . . if it is conceded that for there to be a duty to "keep the covenant" there must be a law imposing this duty and it cannot be the civil law itself, then . . . for Hobbes there was no specific duty to keep the covenant."[10]

There is one law that exists prior to the concluding of the contract. That is the law of nature that obligates everyone to seek peace. But who was the author of that law? Did the law of Nature have an author? If not, why would it be obligatory?

If the state was to remain limited and in the service of society, then individuals must be capable of self-rule. "Individuals must be able to rule themselves, at least to some extent, and to do this, religion—which reminds us of the importance of our souls—might seem indispensable."[11] Traditionally, that is to say, theologically, the soul was understood to be the human source of self-rule or self-control.

The distinction between state and society created by Hobbes was predicated on the theological distinction between body and soul. The state was no longer to be concerned with the salvation of souls.

This meant that concern for souls was left to private individuals in society. Since men were expected to obey the law, however, they were, in effect, abdicating any obligation to accept personal responsibility. "If individuals are not to be responsible for others' souls, why should they be responsible for their own? To enjoin citizens from tyrannizing over their fellows, constitutional government runs the risk of leaving them unconcerned, both for their fellows and themselves."[12] In effect, the doctrine of the rule of law opened the door to a decline of responsibility of citizens to rule themselves.

The final two sections of the *Leviathan* treat the issue of God. If the law of nature is known naturally, it could not be a human who established such a law. By inference, one would be led to conclude that it is known because God was the author of that law. With respect to God, however, Hobbes said two opposite things. On the one hand, by reasoning humans *can* know God to be the author of moral law. On the other hand, by reasoning we *can know nothing* of God as the author of the moral law.

What might account for these two opposite determinations? Michael Oakeshott suggested that Hobbes intended the second explanation for "those whose heads were strong enough to withstand the giddiness provoked by skepticism" and the first one "for ordinary men who must be spoken to in an idiom and a vocabulary he is accustomed to."[13] In other words, Hobbes presupposed that, by nature, there exist two kinds of individuals—extraordinary and ordinary. Despite his effort to understand humans as not created by God, he was compelled by the need to strengthen the obligations of ordinary humans to conform to the rule of the sovereign to import the language of religion. In effect, the state had a compelling interest in religion. But if religion is required to maintain responsibility and autonomy in society, how does the state keep religion within constitutional bounds?

Spinoza recognized the difficulty and made his own critique of revealed religion even more extreme. He treated the Bible as though it were any book written by a human being and subjected it to a critique according to philosophic reasoning. In doing so, he revealed the Bible's logical flaws. But Spinoza's politics did not support Hobbes's claim that the contractual creation of the sovereign established the rule of law. On the contrary, the sovereign was as "natural" as the state of nature. The rule of law, for Spinoza, was the rule of the strongest. People obey the law only because they are fearful of failing to do so.

Spinoza, unlike Hobbes, favored democracy. He understood that democracy can be stable, however, only if it rests on "republican virtue," which, he had learned from Machiavelli, was martial virtue moderated by the love of one's neighbors, or what Spinoza referred to as "charity." Such love, however, cannot be supported by reason alone, since reason teaches men to take and keep what they can. Charity had to depend on faith. "The main work of charity being to counteract religious fanaticism, it is the one delusion set against another, worse delusion. After beginning from the standpoint that religion is *the* enemy of human reason and freedom, Spinoza conclude[d] that religion, suitably redefined so that it amounts to charity and nothing more, is a necessary foundation of democracy."[14]

Even though both Hobbes and Spinoza conceded that the state (the rule of law) needed religion, both were reviled because they supported religion on purely utilitarian grounds and not because of its claim to be the truth.

John Locke was more prudent in his treatment of religion. As a result, his work was met with less hostility. Locke offered a constitutional politics that did not force anyone to oppose religion with constitutionalism. He did so, however, by claiming initially that he was not questioning the Bible, but defending it against false interpretations. In his *First Treatise on Government,* he challenged Filmer's claim that, because the Bible taught that God created Adam, neither freedom nor equality was natural. In doing this, he prepared the way for indirectly supporting Hobbes's doctrine of natural freedom.

The *Second Treatise* began, like Hobbes, with man in a state of nature. Unlike Hobbes, however, his language was tempered, and couched in words that were familiar and traditional. If the Bible must be interpreted according to reason, it was not the kind of reason that made it subservient to revelation. His goal was not simply to undermine the foundation of the theory of the divine right of kings (which rested on the principle of patriarchy that was derived from the account of the creation of man by God). He also aimed to create God in the image of the philosopher, or to create a "reasonable concept of *nature's* God."[15]

Locke's challenge to traditional political teachings arose in his understanding of property and the grounds of its acquisition. He rejected any notion that the appropriation of property was based on consent. On the contrary, property rights preceded government. Man in the state of nature was not merely possessive, but acquisitive and productive. It was man's labor that created property. Furthermore, there were no natural restrictions on the acquisition of property, including enclosed land. Because of this, man in the state of nature could ignore the obligation to be charitable with his property. It was the inconvenience that the conflict over property engendered that provided the motive for the social contract and the establishment of a government that would mediate those conflicts.

Locke, again following Hobbes, proposed that there existed a law of nature. One of the laws of nature is that "men should keep their compacts." But, as with Hobbes, one was again left with the question of why the natural law would be obligatory. Locke knew from experience of the many violations of the law carried out in private and in secret. He was, therefore, also forced to say publicly that "the true ground of Morality" can "Only be the Will and Law of God, who sees Men in the dark, [and] had in his Hand Rewards and Punishments."[16]

But in *An Essay Concerning Human Understanding*, Locke argued that experience also demonstrated that while "self-interest and the Conveniences of this Life make many Men own an outward Profession and Approbation of religion, [their] Actions sufficiently prove that they very little consider the Law-giver that prescribed these Rules."[17] In other words, success tended to breed a forgetfulness of the fears of eternal damnation and the obligations taught by religion. This is why religious faith could not be a strong enough foundation for keeping contracts and, by extension, for insuring the obligation of citizens to obey the law.

From the writings of Thomas Aquinas, who had synthesized revelation with the reason of ancient philosophy, Locke recognized that Christianity was hospitable to reason. Locke endeavored to regulate it in such a way as to make it compatible with modern constitutionalism. He encouraged religious education in the state. Locke's religious education was to be limited, however, to "imprinting" on the child's mind "a true Notion of God, as of the independent Supreme Being, Author and Maker of all Things" and to telling biblical stories. In particular, children were to be told the stories of Joseph and his brothers, of David and Goliath, of David and Jonathan, those stories that taught children that "what you would have others do unto you, do you the same unto them."[18] This negative statement of the Golden Rule followed Hobbes rather than Jesus. It was the teaching of self-defense or self-preservation first. But since humans wish others to be charitable to them in their judgment and actions, charity was also to be the lesson of religious education. Locke's doctrine then, led to an emphasis on toleration as the highest social virtue.

Religion, therefore, was not to be denied entirely. Instead, it had to become an aid to the promotion of a universal sense of obligation to obey the law by means of the "law of opinion or reputation." Locke knew, from experience, that humans have a desire for honor and a fear of being shamed, and that this could be used to support the rule of law. But given the variety of opinions regarding what may be honorable and shameful, one was left with only one basis of obligation, the multiplicity of "community standards." This meant that were people to conform to the religious standards of the community in which they live, it would be more for the sake of their reputations than out of concern for the salvation of their souls.[19]

Locke's transformation of religion was matched by a transformation of the idea of the state and of the rule of law. The rule of law was made by "representatives," and not by the wise and the virtuous. But since laws needed also to be administered and enforced, they had to be shaped to fit specific circumstances and had to be promoted in terms of the public good. Given that Locke also provided for a rationale for the popular right of resistance, the rule of law was also dependent on a healthy fear and respect of the people. In effect, the rule of law meant a balance of mutual fear and respect between state and society. "Because the nature and condition of man, even man in civil society, is so recalcitrant to law or reason, law . . . sometimes [had to] be suspended or even violated in order to promote the public good. In other words . . . there is no possibility of purely lawful rule."[20]

To summarize—the founders of modern constitutionalism were compelled, by their concern with the stability of the social contract and of the state, and therefore, of the rule of law, to balance the requirements of the state *with* religion. This was possible because they were able to redefine biblical religion in such a way as to mod-erate the universal claims made by its adherents. But the balancing that was necessary meant that they could not speak directly to everyone equally, nor could they articulate, in clear and distinct terms, what should be the relationship between state and religion that would hold absolutely in each and every instance.

Jefferson and Madison as Modern Constitutionalists

Thomas Jefferson is known to have been familiar with the writings of John Locke and to have been influenced by him. The Declaration of Independence was predicated on principles articulated in Locke's *Second Treatise*. Locke, as Hobbes before him, had established the equality of humans in the state of nature. It is a necessary assumption for the claim that government depends on the principle of consent. This is the same assumption that Jefferson made when, in the Declaration of Independence, he asserted the right of the American people to independence. In the Declaration of Independence, Jefferson asserted that it is self-evident that all men are created equal. In what are humans self-evidently equal? In their need for government, that is, for a state that will be authorized to make rules, in the form of laws, for society. Humans are also equal in authorizing a state that will be based on consent rather than on the claims of natural or divinely sanctioned superiority.

In writing the Declaration, Jefferson did not make his assumptions about human nature, or about the state of nature, explicit. He was not writing as a philosopher but as a statesman. Yet the Declaration's recitation of the "long train of abuses and usurpations" by the king of England was offered as proof—to the king and to the rest of the world—that the American people were withdrawing their consent to be governed by the king. The document declared that they were choosing to return to the state of nature, in preparation for the creation of a new social contract.

The new contract, first in the form of the Articles of Confederation and later the Constitution, created a new people. The new American people (which found expression in the Preamble of the Constitution, "We the People") was to be formed, not on the basis of a common culture or language or religion. It was to be grounded on the basis of the natural right of each to form a government on the basis of consent. A people, Jefferson implied, consists of humans who are aware of their natural rights and who are prepared to exercise those rights.

In the only book that Jefferson published, *Notes on the State of Virginia*, he demonstrated that Americans were capable of self-government by proving that Americans were capable of reform. The proof is in the form of a discussion of how Virginia's initial constitution, which was created when the people of the state were inexperienced, was corrected. The reformed constitution established and protected the self-evident truth of human equality.

Since the constitution of government protects the very possibility of reform, Jefferson understood that it has, or should have, a special status and should not be, in his words, "alterable by the ordinary legislature."[21] For Jefferson, the rule of law presupposes a distinction between constitution and the laws. This distinction, understood by Americans today, however, reflects the problem posed to every Founder, that is, affirming the doctrine of the rule of law. That doctrine is embodied not in the obedience to particular laws, which are changeable, but to what gives lawmakers authority to make laws, namely, the Constitution.

Jefferson, like Locke and Hobbes, faced the question of the special sanctity of the Constitution. If laws are changeable, what truly distinguishes a claim for the sanctity of a constitution that differs from any other law? Since humans, on the basis of consent, also create constitutions, one is entitled to ask, on what grounds is the citizen obligated to treat the constitution differently from ordinary laws? With this question, one is returned to the problem posed by the construction of the distinction of state and society by Hobbes and followed by Locke.

Hobbes and Locke, in order to protect the sanctity of the rule of law, were compelled, on grounds of prudence, to protect religious freedom and at the same time to favor religion over nonreligion. Jefferson was compelled to make a similar compromise. It is true that in *Notes on the State of Virginia* he claimed that "it does me no injury for my neighbor to say there are twenty gods, or no god. It neither picks my pocket nor breaks my leg." But Jefferson's neighbor's religious opinion, and his tolerance of it, was an insufficient ground for providing the security of the rule of law. Jefferson supported the idea that the testimony of an atheist be rejected in a court of law. "Can the liberties of a nation be thought secure when we have removed their only firm basis, a conviction in the minds of the people that their liberties are a gift of God. That they are not to be violated but with his wrath?" Only on the grounds of such a belief will it be likely that the rule of law, and thereby the constitution, will be treated as sacred. But it is important to notice that neither the rejection of an atheist's testimony in court nor Jefferson's toleration of any and all religious and irreligious convictions speak to the truth or falsity of religion. They do speak to religion's political utility.

Jefferson did write of the wall of separation of church and state. But did he mean by that phrase the same as the justices in *Everson*? Given Jefferson's concern with the sanctity of the Constitution, the proper meaning of the doctrine of separation could not readily be determined by abstract argument alone. It would be dependent on the success of its end, namely, to make religion harmless to the constitution. If, in the application of a separation doctrine that required neutrality between the religious and irreligious, government failed to make religion harmless, one would properly infer that Jefferson would argue that such a doctrine ought to be seriously moderated. If, by upholding such a doctrine, government was forcing religious advocates to challenge the sanctity of the Constitution itself, then one would properly infer that Jefferson would argue that such a doctrine was dangerous. The statesman's need for prudential balancing made it impossible for Jefferson to absolutely reconcile the tension between the rule of law and the principle of government by consent.

Was he as confident that the advancement in science would be matched by advancements in politics? Reminiscent of Rousseau's *Discourse on the Arts and Sciences*, which had demonstrated that the expansion of science was perfectly compatible with tyranny and not with freedom, Jefferson wrote to John Adams in 1812: "If science produces no better fruits than tyranny, murder, rapine and destitution of national morality, I would rather wish our country to be ignorant, honest and estimable as our neighboring savages are."[22] In *Notes on the State of Virginia* he stated that the "only firm basis [for] the liberties of a nation [was the] conviction in the minds of the people that these liberties are the gift of God [and] . . . that they are not to be violated without his wrath." Religion was at the least "a vast additional incitement" to virtue (Letter of August 10, 1787).

James Madison held a similar view, out of similar concerns. Even more than Jefferson, he wrote as a statesman and not as a philosopher. Therefore, his concern about a possible return to a state of nature was implied rather than explicitly stated. But his Hobbesian/Lockean assumptions about human nature were expressed in *Federalist* No. 10, where he asserted that the spirit of faction is sown into the souls of men. It was on the basis of this assertion that Madison argued that the Constitution's provisions for the separation of powers contained the harmful effects of that spirit. It was the spirit of faction that threatened any and all government and the rule of law.

In his *Memorial and Remonstrance*, Madison contrasted the religious history of European nations with that of America. He did not find America's experiences cataclysmic. Americans had largely experienced "equal and complete" religious liberty. While religious conflict was never totally eradicated, in his view Americans never experienced the same "malignant influence" of religion on the "health and prosperity of the State" that Europeans had experienced. However, he argued that man's moral duties, which are derived from religion, have prior claim to his loyalties over his political duties. Although he objected to government involvement in religion, he did not deny that religion is the *guardian* of morals.

Madison grounded the right to inalienable political liberty on man's nature and on man's relation to God, "which is that of a subject bound by a duty to his Creator."[23] As he stated in the *Remonstrance,* "what is here a right towards men (toleration) is a duty towards the Creator. It is the duty of every man to render the Creator such homage and such only, as he believes to be acceptable to him. . . . Before any man can be considered as a member of Civil Society, he must be considered as a subject of the Governor of the Universe."

Religious liberty is based on man being both free *and* being created. It required attention to the obligations of religion, not its blessings. Madison acknowledged that there had been an increase in moral laxness and lawlessness following the repeal of the original establishment laws in Virginia, but he asserted that the restoration of religious establishments would *not* solve the problem. He argued that the negative effects of the decline of religious involvement in public life, and in the schools, could be deferred by "the promulgation of laws that promote virtue [and] actions by religious organizations that would provide personal examples of morality. Government should not be indifferent to the promotion of values that would elevate the populace, such as those taught by religion. Therefore, he gave no consideration to political claims on behalf of irreligion, secularism, or "humanism."

Dissatisfied that there was no greater protection for religion in the Constitution than Article VI, prohibiting a religious test for national office, some members of state ratifying conventions urged the national government to amend the Constitution soon after the document was ratified. It was at this urging that the Bill of Rights was developed. Madison reworked many of the proposals and submitted them to a specially created select committee. After a series of delays a debate was scheduled. The language of the Establishment Clause was the focus of some serious debate. Benjamin Huntington expressed concern that the language should not harm religion and should secure the rights of conscience and the free exercise of religion. But he urged the Congress to refrain from including language that would "patronize those who professed no religion at all." Madison, while he "privately questioned the efficacy of governmental assistance to religion, accepted [this] view throughout the First Congress debates."[24]

The Senate drafted its own language, which was unsatisfactory to the House. A conference committee, which included Madison, was established. The final language was agreed upon there and in both Houses of Congress.

The final wording of the amendment embodied key compromises on both the national/state and the aid/no aid issues. . . . [T]he phrase "an establishment" seems to ensure the legality of nondiscriminatory religious aid. Had the framers prohibited "*the* establishment of religion," which would have emphasized the generic word "religion," there might have been some reason for thinking they wanted to prohibit all official religion over irreligion. But by choosing "an establishment" over "the establishment," they were showing that they wanted to prohibit only those official activities that tended to promote the interests of one or another particular sect.[25]

The one piece of evidence that supports this contention is that in 1789 the First Congress reenacted the Northwest Ordinance of 1787. In that second ordinance, Congress set aside federal land and offered federal dollars for schools in which "religion, morality and knowledge" were to be taught.

Both the actions taken by the First Congress and the words uttered by Jefferson and Madison raise serious doubts as to whether they were consistent with the justices' opinions in the *Everson* case. Jefferson and Madison, like Locke, were more inclined than the justices to consider the negative political implications for the rule of law of putting religion and nonreligion on the same plane. In holding this opinion they, again like Locke, recognized the political problems created by trying clearly and distinctly to reconcile practice with principle or, in the language of political philosophy, of absolutely reconciling theory and practice.

Sociology and the Rise of Judicial Realism

How was it possible that the justices were able to believe that they and the Founders were merely two ends of an unbroken chain of history? They, and Jefferson and Madison, used the same words. The justices, however, used those same words in ways that had been radically altered in meaning. The transformation had been prepared by the development of a new science of society, based on the findings and methods of the physical sciences.

Sociology arose after contradictions were exposed in classical political economy and utopian socialism. The founders sought to develop a science of society that would be able to account for economic relations without economics.[26] Sociology developed in the aftermath of the Kantian critique of reason. Kant had made the distinction between the noumenal, or what cannot be known empirically, and the phenomenal, what can be known through sense data. Since God was the noumenal,[27] any empirical science that depended on Kant's distinction had to be agnostic.

The introduction of science into the study of society also implied an emphasis on scientific integrity. What developed from this was what is called the scientific conscience, or probity. Probity denies that it is necessary to live with, and by, contradiction. In fact, it requires that all contradictions, especially that between thought and action, be resolved by reason. It therefore rejects any activity that "attempts to mediate between the Enlightenment and (any) orthodoxy."[28] Conscience predicated on probity is conscience that is ruled by reason, not the heart. There can be no "bad conscience" or "good conscience," as there is in the idea of religious conscience, which implies that there are divine commands and duties that are either followed or not. Conscience grounded on probity cannot be either bad or good. Conscience, in this sense, is simply a euphemism for autonomous choice. It may also be a reflection of will.

The scientific study of politics contributed to a serious reevaluation of American life, including American political life. "In empirically examining human behavior and the actual process of American politics, scientific political scientists came to question and often reject three cardinal principles of democratic government: the possibility of a government of laws not men, the rationality of human behavior, and the practical possibility of popular government itself."[29]

The scientific study of society also contributed to the development of new meanings of "democracy" and "religion." When understood scientifically, the traditional system of values were exposed as ideals, which meant they were treated as though they were myths or, even more negatively, as dogmas. This treatment of values in political life was the basis of Thurmond Arnold's The Symbols of Government (1935). Arnold transformed what had traditionally been understood as fundamental principles of right into functional symbols for the society. He was able to legitimate the translation by arguing that "almost all human conduct is symbolic" and symbols are the expression of the human desire for social control. If students of American politics had earlier "revealed many of the inconsistencies and weaknesses in traditional democratic theory," Arnold "made those contradictions the very bone and marrow of the political structure. Democratic theory was not simply inconsistent and therefore false, but it was necessarily inconsistent and false."[30]

The rise of communism and fascism forced liberal democrats not only to define for themselves what democracy was but also to prove why and in what way liberal democracy was superior to these new forms of government, which they named "Totalitarianism." The new "realists" may have been firm believers in democracy, but their scientific studies raised serious questions about the nature of democratic government. Realists proved that there were practical injustices in American society and sought to determine how human relations could be made more just, in practice. "The most important practical point of their argument was the questioning and in many cases rejecting the idea of a government of laws rather than men"[31]

Both communism and fascism claimed to be grounded on scientific thinking and both claimed to be superior to Western democracy. In defense of democracy, advocates of scientific theory argued that it was necessary to test the traditional democratic system of values by scientific methods with the aim of producing a realistic democratic theory that could justify democracy on rational and ethical grounds.

Unable to account for the rise of illiberal governments in the midst of what appeared to be progress, social scientists, influenced by the idea of symbols, found an explanation in the idea of "culture," or the product of some unconscious human process. They coined the term "totalitarian" to describe it. It referred to what appeared to be the total collapse of the distinction between state and society and the incorporation of the society by the state. They also determined that the cause of this collapse and incorporation was in the rise of what they judged to be an absolutist culture. Politics no longer was understood to be the element that shaped citizens and held people together. What held them together were common cultural traditions, which were largely unconscious.

As Americans sought ways to defend democracy and democratic ideals against this new phenomenon, social scientists began to argue that political democracy depended on a democratic social structure and a democratic culture. With the exception of the defenders of natural law, most Americans came to believe that values like political freedom and personal dignity were essential to democracy and could *only* be defended within a framework of relativism.

A political scientist, Pendelton Herring, asserted that "the unvarying truth or falsity of the democratic dogma is not of determinant importance. . . . The significant thing is that the ideology of democracy permits the peaceful resolution of interest conflicts through accepted institutions."[32] Democracy was reduced to a method for making compromises between diverse interests. This method depended less on the form of government and more on the character of American society. Jacques Barzun declared that democracy is "an atmosphere and an attitude,"[33] by which he meant a culture. The concept of culture evolved as the comprehensive concept. Culture was the totality of ways that influenced the behavior of humans, both individually and collectively. The study of anthropology confirmed the belief that there were no absolutes of any kind.

Throughout the period of the 1930s and 1940s, a serious debate developed about the nature of the law. Catholic legal scholars and non-Catholic educators like Robert Maynard Hutchins and Mortimer Adler attacked social scientists for conspiring to suffocate religion and the theological foundations of law and to replace it with moral relativism. They argued that democracy could only be preserved if there were a rational ethical system, which could be discovered by reason, supported by religious faith, and applied to the making of legal and political decisions.[34]

This proposal moved the philosopher John Dewey to accuse Hutchins and Adler not only of supporting philosophical absolutism but of desiring political absolutism as well! Dewey claimed they were calling for an elite group that would identify those absolute principles and then impose them on everyone else. "Only an intellectual conviction that all ideas were tentative and subject to constant criticism could prize a free and flexible order."[35] Democracy and freedom depended on a total negation of the idea of absolutes. Americans, he argued, had two options, either authoritarianism or democracy; either absolutism or experimentalism.

What Pendelton Herring did to democracy, theologians such as Reinhold Niebuhr did to religion. He redefined it, thereby making it compatible with the new idea of a democratic society. Writing in the 1930s, he argued that whatever could be said about God's transcendence, when put in the hands of humans, revelation became relative to the person who accepted it. Truth, therefore, even religious truth, was necessarily personal and subjective. On the basis of this interpretation of man's relationship to God, he concluded that men's relations with each other must be grounded on the principle of toleration. Biblical faith, having been transformed, could now stand side by side with relativism.[36]

It was in this context of change that the justices of the Supreme Court faced questions of religious toleration and, subsequently, the question of the meaning of the separation of state and religion.

The introduction of science changed the meaning of law itself. It was no longer to be understood as an abstract problem of logic but a practical problem of social management.[37] Louis D. Brandeis, as a practicing attorney, introduced what came to be called the "Brandeis brief," which contained not merely legal arguments but sociological statistics and analyses outlining possible social consequences of the courts' decisions.[38] Later, Clarence Darrow, as counsel in the Scopes trial, defended science against the absolutist claims of religion.

When he served as counsel for Leopold and Loeb, he introduced psychological evidence in an attempt to persuade the judge not to impose the death penalty. In doing so, he changed legal procedure from judging an action to explaining it. His strategy was predicated on the assumption that science could make the law more progressive, that is, more humane.[39]

These changes took place in the context of another change in American political and legal life, the incorporation of the Bill of Rights by the Fourteenth Amendment. Initially meant to overturn the *Dredd Scott* decision, which denied citizenship to blacks, the Fourteenth Amendment was used for its first fifty or so years almost entirely in the area of property rights and the relationship between government and business. It was used to insure that government would not "unduly impede" American industrial growth.

In the early 1920s, the Court began to use the Fourteenth Amendment to focus on the personal rights of citizens. By extending the Equal Protection Clause to cover not just Congress but the governments of the states, the justices authorized the national government to protect the citizens of any state against the state itself. The Equal Protection Clause became an active principle by which the Court could do what the legislatures could not or would not, namely, induce equality between rich and poor, between urban and rural, and between black and white.

In the late nineteenth and early twentieth centuries, the justices adjudicated religious questions on the basis of constitutional principles other than the First Amendment. There was good reason for that. In 1833, in *Barron v. Baltimore*, the Court decided that the religion clauses were not enforceable against the states. Sixty-six years later, when the Court decided a challenge to the use of federal money for the improvement of a Catholic hospital (*Bradfied v. Roberts*), it treated the case as a matter of contract law. The issue, said the Court, was whether the hospital fulfilled its contract to treat ill patients, not whether it was operated by a religious order. Similarly, in 1908, in *Quick Bear v. Leupp*, the Court decided that federal money could be used to pay for the education of Native American children in Catholic schools because it was their money and not the government's money that was being spent.

In 1925 the Court decided a case involving an Oregon state law requiring all "able-bodied" children to attend public schools, *Pierce v. Society of Sisters*. The effect of such a law was to deny the right of parochial schools to exist. The Society of Sisters, representing Catholic schools, sued on the grounds that the Oregon law violated "the corporation's rights guaranteed by the 14th Amendment." It was on the basis of this amendment that the Court found the law unconstitutional.

Justice Reynolds, who wrote the majority opinion, sought to resolve the question of law without distorting the understanding of faith by the religiously faithful. In his judgment, "parochial" Catholic education meant providing "systematic religious instruction and moral training" according to the tenets of Roman Catholicism. Morality was the purview of religion, even though religions differed. Whatever those differences, the special claims of all religion were acknowledged. "Religion" was distinguished from the "temporal," so that morals were to be understood as derived from what was eternal in contrast to what was simply changing. "Religious training" was also distinguished from "mental" training. Religion and morals were matters of values rather than facts, or in the most abstract, matters of metaphysics rather than science. This contrast left unresolved the questions of whether religion was limited to matters of conscience and whether values were manifestations of the "heart" as opposed to "reason."

In the course of describing the religious education provided by the school, Justice Reynolds observed that "[s]ystematic *religious* instruction and *moral* training according to the tenets of the Roman Catholic Church are also regularly provided. All courses of study, both *temporal and religious*, contemplate continuity of training. . . . After setting out the above facts, the Society's bill alleges that the enactment [of the Oregon law] conflicts with the right of parents to choose schools where their children will receive appropriate *mental and religious* training" (author's italics).

In support of the Society of Sisters's claim, Reynolds noted that the Founders, in promulgating rights to be guaranteed by the Constitution, offered "appropriate prayers" to insure their fulfillment. Such an action would be consistent with the Declaration of Independence's reference to the self-evidence of man's being a created being. The prayer said by the Founders, and noted by Reynolds, presumed that the protection of constitutional rights was not entirely separable from some faith in a providential God.

But from that time on, the Court took a turn away from prudence and toward an attempt to harmonize theory and practice, to the detriment of practical wisdom and attention to the mixed views of the populations being affected. This new harmonization substituted a consistent application of clear and distinct principle for prudence.

Totalitarianism and the Justices' Struggle with the Meaning of Democracy

During World War II, the Court sought to resolve several issues that arose over the religious liberty of Jehovah's Witnesses: what are the limits of religious proselytizing? Should a religious group be required to salute and pledge allegiance to the American flag? Could a state require a religious group to acquire a vendor's license to sell religious books and records? In resolving the question of saluting and pledging allegiance to the flag, the justices, albeit in a peripatetic fashion, began using an entirely secular definition of religion. When combined with the concern to more clearly and distinctly distinguish democracy from totalitarianism, they were compelled to consider for the first time the meaning of the Establishment Clause.

Totalitarianism in Europe could hardly have been far from the justices' minds when they heard cases involving Jehovah's Witnesses, starting in 1939. At stake were two issues. First was the claim to the right to exercise their religion freely, even though the religious exercise included verbal assaults on other religions, especially Roman Catholicism. Second was the claim, on grounds of religious conscience, for exemption from a requirement, imposed on the children of all Americans during World War II, to publicly pledge allegiance to the American flag. The first issue was a matter of religious practice, the second a matter of religious conviction as it affected political practice. Both tested the meaning of American democracy as it dealt with a dissenting religion.

The language of the law, having incorporated the vocabulary of sociology, used words like "religion" and "conscience" in radically altered ways. While in the past, justices used these words as they might have been used and understood by believers, now justices used them as they would be used by sociologists. The consequence of this shift in meaning was that the justices were able to treat religion and irreligion as though they were two examples of a more general notion of "belief systems."

In 1940 the Court, in *Cantwell v. Connecticut*, reversed a state court's conviction of three Jehovah's Witnesses on charges of disturbing the peace. At stake was whether or not Connecticut could enjoin Jehovah's Witnesses from going house-to-house to spread their faith, especially in a neighborhood highly populated by Roman Catholics. While in the process of spreading their faith, the Jehovah's Witnesses had played a phonograph record, to those who agreed to listen to it, that made a general attack on all organized religious systems as "instruments of Satan." The recording also singled out the Roman Catholic Church for special attack.

The rise of Nazism in Europe was not far from the Court's mind when it faced the question of protecting those dissenters in America. Justice Roberts acknowledged that the Witnesses at times resorted to "exaggeration, to vilification . . . and even to false statement." Although he admitted that there were ways to test the truth-value of the evangelizers, neither he nor the other justices applied such tests. It was necessary to avoid doing so, he said, because the danger, "in these times, from the coercive activities of those who in the delusion of racial or religious conceit would incite violence and breaches of the peace in order to deprive others of their equal right to the exercise of their liberties is emphasized by events familiar to all." It did not matter "how misguided" others may have thought them to be, the evangelizers acted on behalf of what they "conceived to be true religion."

The Cantwells sued on the basis of the free exercise provision of the First Amendment. The justices, however, supported their claim on the grounds of the First Amendment's protection of free speech. The Court found that, by being arrested, the Cantwells had been deprived of their liberty without due process of law "in contravention of the Fourteenth Amendment, . . . [which] embraces the liberties guaranteed by the First Amendment." Justice Roberts, writing for the majority, asserted that, "in the realm of religious faith *and in that of political belief*" (author's emphasis) the effort to persuade could be expected to include exaggeration, vilification, and even false statement.

Justice Roberts also considered whether the "clear and present danger" rule was applicable in this case. In doing so, he moved toward equating evangelizing with political speech and thus treating Jehovah's Witnesses as though they were comparable to political dissidents. He found that "the profane, indecent, or abusive remarks" were not "directed to the person of the hearer," and did not lead to violence. The Jehovah's Witnesses were only making an effort "to persuade a willing listener. . . . In the realm of religious faith, *and* (author's emphasis) in that of political belief, sharp differences arise." The conjunction implied equivalence.

In the course of his opinion, Justice Roberts spoke of religion in terms of "creed or the practice of any form of worship." This meant "the freedom to believe and the freedom to act" on the basis of that belief. These two were encompassed by a broader principle, "freedom of conscience." In this context, conscience had a thoroughly secular, that is, irreligious, meaning. As it was used, it obscured the distinction between religion and irreligion.

It was possible for Justice Roberts to do this because he assumed that all groups, whether based on natural differences or conventional ones, were to be understood as the products of "systems of belief." He asserted that the "perpetuation of religious views or *systems*" (author's emphasis) was necessary to protect the democratic nature of American society. His silence about ritual, morals, or matters of eternal versus temporal, such as "salvation," revealed that religion had been emptied of dogma and has come to be treated as merely another belief *system*.

Jehovah's Witnesses made other claims based on their religious beliefs. In *Minersville School District v. Gobitis* (1940), the Court was faced with deciding whether a school system could compel students to salute the flag and pledge allegiance to it. The Jehovah's Witnesses claimed that their children should be exempted from such exercises because their religion taught that pledging allegiance to the American flag was equivalent to bowing down to an idol and that such action was prohibited by the Second Commandment. To compel the children of Jehovah's Witnesses to do so was to compel them to engage in a sin against God and a violation of their right to the free exercise of their religion.

Justice Frankfurter, the author of the majority opinion, indicated that this case involved "conflicting claims of liberty and authority." When such a conflict arises, *"judicial conscience* is put to its *severest* test"* (author's emphasis). At stake was the question of which source of authority would take precedence, the legislative authority of the state or the authority of God. The justices had to decide whether forcing a child, who refused "upon *sincere* (author's emphasis) religious grounds" to salute and pledge allegiance to the flag, "infringes without due process of law the liberty guaranteed by the Fourteenth Amendment."

Justice Frankfurter added the word "sincere" when referring to a child's religious beliefs. Of what necessity was this adjective to his case? The issue arose and was decided prior to Pearl Harbor, the one event that galvanized American sentiment about entering the war. There was still some resistance among Americans to the country's entrance into the war in Europe. Draft boards were faced with judging the sincerity of religious convictions with respect to conscientious objectors to the draft.

As Justice Roberts did in *Cantwell*, Justice Frankfurter spoke of religion in terms of "liberty of conscience." The question of the legislative authority of the state involved the authority of government "to safeguard the nation's fellowship." By that, Frankfurter meant the promotion of "national cohesion" or "national unity" in support of the war effort. "The ultimate foundation of a free society is the binding tie of cohesive sentiment." The flag, which Frankfurter acknowledged was a symbol, was the symbol of national unity that "transcended all internal differences." While there are many influences promoting "common feeling," Frankfurter expressed no doubt that the development of "common feeling" was legitimate. It was this consideration that the majority determined was paramount and concluded that the children could be required to salute and pledge allegiance to the flag.

Frankfurter made explicit the nature of the problem for the justices and their judicial consciences. "The effective means for its attainment are still so uncertain and so *unauthenticated by science*" (author's emphasis). This reference to science made explicit that the justices were looking for scientific grounds for determining their decision. But their decision could not be supported by scientific evidence, so they came to a conclusion on political grounds instead. Frankfurter, in effect, admitted that political grounds were far less secure than scientific ones.

He further noted that the history of religious conflict reflects a battle over "the erection of particular dogmas or all-comprehending faiths" and it was these conflicts that led to the guarantee of religious freedom. The First Amendment prohibited "the establishment of a state religion" which insured the free exercise of "every sect." Were this to be taken to its logical extreme, the government might never be able to deny to a religious sect any claim, even when it may disrupt the rest of society, which is being mobilized by flag ceremonies for building morale during war.

Frankfurter's vocabulary in speaking about religion proved even more revealing of his dependence on scientific thinking. He spoke of "the affirmative pursuit of one's convictions about the ultimate mystery of the universe and man's relation to it" and asserted that this was "beyond the reach of law." This understanding of religion reflects the language of the agnostic or the atheist.

He went on to argue that "government may not interfere with organized or individual expression of belief or disbelief. Propagation of belief—*or even disbelief in the supernatural* (author's emphasis)—is protected." Frankfurter's insertion of the phrase "even disbelief in the supernatural" added a dimension to the argument that was beyond the issues raised by the case. Frankfurter's very choice of the word "supernatural" contrasted faith with rational skepticism and hinted at the superiority of the latter. Not only were the special claims of religion rejected, but also the cornerstone of the Declaration of Independence was implicitly denied validity. Jefferson's phrase that "we hold these truths to be self-evident, that all men are *created* equal and are endowed by their Creator with certain inalienable rights" meant that it is self-evident that we are *created* beings and that our rights are inalienable precisely because they are not man-made either.

Justice Frankfurter's inclusion of disbelief also blended the Free Exercise Clause of the First Amendment with the Free Speech Clause. In effect, if not intent, his decision also linked religious and political dissidence.

That linkage was made even more explicit by Justice Jackson three years later in a dissenting opinion in *Douglas v. Jeannette.*[40] There he asserted that the First Amendment as a whole "assures the broadest tolerable exercise of free speech, free press, and free assembly, not merely for religious purposes, but for political, economic, *scientific, news* (author's emphasis), or informational ends as well." The First Amendment's aim was to limit religion in an effort to equalize it with any and all secular speech. That included scientific information. Furthermore, sensitive to the use of propaganda and censorship during war, Justice Jackson held that religious evangelizing is protected in the same way that the simple publication and broadcast of news are protected. In effect, for him morning prayer became equivalent to the morning news, and even less.

The Court had faced a serious question. Does religious liberty exempt a citizen from "doing what society thinks necessary for the promotion of some great common end?" In attempting to resolve the claims of two absolutes, Justice Frankfurter explicitly stated that in the realm of political action there could not be just one absolute governing all cases. In asserting this, he, in effect, stated the case for relativism. "The right to freedom of religious belief, no matter how dissident and however obnoxious . . . is itself the denial of an absolute."

The justices, faced with this dilemma, concluded that as with freedom of speech, there were limits to freedom of conscience. It cannot be given the liberty to destroy the government by undermining loyalty. In effect, legislative authority to compel citizens to publicly announced obedience to the regime was of a higher priority than the particular claims of religious duty.

Justice Stone dissented. He defended the view that the Jehovah's Witnesses should not be compelled to salute and pledge allegiance to the flag. He argued that to compel Jehovah's Witnesses to make public affirmation would not only violate their religious *conscience*, it would compel the Witnesses to bear false witness. This, he argued, was of graver importance to a democracy than any claim on behalf of "righteousness and the public good." Such claims had been used historically to infringe on any number of personal liberties. Without the benefit of science, Justice Stone argued on behalf of justice and moderation by government and on behalf of free government.

But he also made a claim about what he believed was the premise underlying the decision of the majority. Democracy was not just process, it was defined also by its ends or goals. The Constitution rested on more than a foundation of "democratic processes (that) must be preserved at all costs." It was "also an expression of faith and a command that freedom of mind and spirit must be preserved, which government must obey, if it is to adhere to that justice and moderation without which no free government can exist." Using what appeared to be biblical language, Justice Stone asserted that democracy meant a faith that "freedom of mind and spirit" was the prime value and that this end or goal absolutely required government to refrain from any interference with that freedom.

The *Gobitis* decision was overturned in 1943 in *West Virginia State Board of Education v. Barnette*. Justice Robert Jackson wrote the majority opinion. While affirming the opinion about the freedom of religious conscience articulated by Justice Stone in *Gobitis*, in fact his reasoning was closer to that of Justice Frankfurter.

Justice Jackson argued that the *Gobitis* decision rested on the assumption that the state has the authority to impose the obligation on all citizens to salute the flag. He recalled that Justice Frankfurter had found precedent for the use of the authority to do so in President Lincoln's suspension of the writ of habeas corpus during the Civil War. Lincoln had justified his action by claiming that there was a national emergency and the government might fall for being too weak if he failed to do so.

Jackson argued that Frankfurter's use of Lincoln's action was not analogous to the matter of children saluting and pledging allegiance to the flag. Coercing people into unity by threatening to expel a handful of children from school for not saluting the flag was not a sign of strength of government. Whatever unity might be produced would be artificial and certainly not sincere. In this instance the government could "limit its authority and not become weak."

Jackson's opinion reflected a different concern, namely, trying to define the proper meaning of American democracy. He argued that this case provided the Court with an opportunity to restore American democracy to its founding principles. In his judgment, the New

Deal had moved American government away from them. This issue
was the relation of liberty and coercion. In his judgment, the New
Deal was a revolution against the intentions of the Founders "who
produced a *philosophy* that the individual was the center of society
and his liberty was entrusted through mere absence of government."
This laissez-faire concept had been "withered away" by the New
Deal's control over economic matters. The suspension of freedom in
economic matters that had occurred with the New Deal, in Jackson's
judgment, had been the true ground of Frankfurter's opinion, in *Gobitis*, about the legitimacy of the legislature to compel the children
of Jehovah's Witnesses to salute and pledge allegiance to the flag.

Jackson had no question as to whether national unity or a uni-
formity of sentiment about the nation was a legitimate end of government and the laws. The question, for him, was whether the Constitution permitted compulsion as a permissible means to achieve
that end. Jackson argued that, on the basis of historical record, if the
government used coercion in this case, it would be inclined to use it
with less moderation in the future. "Probably no deeper division of
our people could proceed from any provocation than from finding it
necessary to choose what doctrine and whose program public education officials shall compel youths to unite in embracing." In other
words, if compulsion is used in the area of education, the schools
will prove to be *the* battleground for dividing people rather than
building unity.

Jackson's emphasis on educational programs led him to the question of the end or goal of education in general. In his judgment, the
goal was to free the mind of the individual. The reason that he
judged this as the goal of education was that, for him, it was the defining characteristic of American democracy and the one element
that differentiated Americans and American democracy from "our
present totalitarian enemies." By the "free mind," Jackson meant the
freedom to be "*intellectually* and spiritually diverse or even contrary." This formulation reflected the influence of the new social
science on him. In his judgment, culture, not the regime, defines
democracy. A democratic culture, that is, a diverse one, will make
intellectual individualism possible. For Justice Jackson, that is the
end or goal of education.

Intellectual individualism was understood by him to be the kind
of individualism that results from freedom from any compulsion,
not only from government but also from any orthodoxy, no matter
what its source. Jackson's own intellectual individualism was revealed in the way he disagreed with the religious teaching of the
Jehovah's Witnesses, all the while protecting their legal claims for

exemption from the provisions of the law requiring saluting and pledging allegiance to the flag. He argued that they sincerely believed that the children fear "spiritual condemnation" for having to salute and pledge allegiance to the flag. Jackson asserted that he believed that such fears were groundless.

Justice Murphy, unlike Justice Jackson, used language that was respectful of those with religious faith. He was silent about intellectual freedom but spoke directly of spiritual freedom, which he characterized as the "freedom to worship one's own Maker according to the dictates of one's conscience." This was the only time any of the justices ever entertained the idea of a creator, a term used by Jefferson; however, not once did any of the justices use the word "God."

Justice Jackson's majority opinion was more powerfully met in Justice Frankfurter's dissent. It began with an odd confession about his own tradition followed by a denial of its relevance to his judgment in this case. After admitting he was a Jew and associated with "general libertarian views," Justice Frankfurter argued that, as judges, "we are neither Jew nor Gentile, neither Catholic nor agnostic." Frankfurter's language revealed the nature of the author. To contrast Jew with Gentile was to contrast himself as a Jew with all non-Jews. That is what the word Gentile necessarily implies. But contrasting Catholic with agnostic both silently denied the salience of Protestantism and set belief in God in contrast with skepticism. Frankfurter, the Jew, thereby gave equal weight to religion and non-religion.

What might explain Frankfurter's decision to set these particular characteristics in the opinion? They were the products of *his* claim about the true nature of American democracy. He began his characterization of democracy by asserting that the duty of the justices is different from the duties of ordinary citizens. The responsibility of the justices was to ascertain whether or not any law that was enacted could be judged to have been *reasonable*. This was the beginning of his argument against what he considered to be excessive judicial authority. Excessive judicial authority exists when justices act as though their primary purpose is to protect any particular liberty. When the justices take this position, they are fundamentally usurping the legislative power that had already been given by the Constitution to the legislature.

The law requiring all children to pledge allegiance to the flag, he argued, was not discriminatory in intent. Therefore, accommodations to the specific claim for exemption by Jehovah's Witnesses should not be made by the judiciary but by the legislature. *For Frankfurter, democracy meant legislative sovereignty and judicial oversight, not the reverse.* It was undermined when one branch usurped the power of another branch. He characterized "judicial activism" as an abuse of power and the major contributing factor in undermining the citizens' faith in the rule of law.

The Constitution gave religious equality, he argued, but it did not provide religious groups with civil immunity from the law. The only freedom assured by the First Amendment was freedom from conformity to religious dogma, "not freedom from conformity to law *because* of religious dogma." Frankfurter's argument boiled down to the following: the rule of law depends on *equal application of conformity with law, without exception.* This is especially necessary when the exception is grounded on religious dogma.

The majority, he asserted, in deciding to overturn their decision in *Gobitis,* and to give an exemption to the Jehovah's Witnesses from the law, had given religion power *over* the state. As a result, there would be no secular limit on state power but a religious limit to state power. *In effect, by granting the exemption on the basis of religious conscience, the majority had created an establishment of a religion.*

The *Everson* Decision

It was in this dispute between the opinions of Justices Jackson and Frankfurter that the justices of the Supreme Court faced the question of the meaning of the separation of state and religion in the *Everson* case.

This case involved a suit by a taxpayer objecting to a New Jersey law that authorized reimbursement to parents of bus fares they paid to send their children to nonpublic schools. The law specified reimbursements would be paid to parents of children sent to public schools and to private schools not operated for a profit. The Board of Education of Ewing Township specified the private schools in its district to be the Catholic schools.

Justice Black, writing for the majority, noted that the suit was not brought on the ground that the state law or the school board's resolution was a violation of the Equal Protection Clause of the Fourteenth Amendment. The issue at stake was whether the First Amendment had been violated, specifically, the prohibition against the establishment of religion. On the facts of the case, the Court upheld the law.

Justice Black's opinion also spelled out the Court's reading of the history and intent of the First Amendment. Citing both the Free Exercise and Establishment Clauses of the Amendment, he argued that both "reflected in the minds of the early Americans a vivid mental picture of conditions and practices which they fervently wished to stamp out." He recounted the religious history of America, revealing a history of religious establishments in various colonies and in some states and the harassment and even the jailing of some members of sects who "steadfastly persisted in worshipping God only as their own conscience dictated." Referring to both Jefferson and Madison, Black concluded that "the 'establishment of religion' . . . means at least this: Neither a state nor the Federal government can set up a church. Neither can pass laws which aid one religion, aid all religions, or prefer one religion over another."

Justice Rutledge, in dissenting to the majority's decision to uphold public funding of the transportation of students to and from public and private (secular and parochial) schools, supported Justice Black's definition of the Establishment Clause as meaning a "wall of separation between church and state." He quoted from the Preamble to the 1786 bill "Establishing Religious Freedom" in Virginia, written by Jefferson, which stated that compelling a man to contribute money "for the propagation of opinions, which he disbelieves, is sinful and tyrannical." To that, he added a quote from Madison's *Memorial and Remonstrance*, in which Madison opposed a bill that would have used public taxes to support Christian religious teachers. On the basis of his reading of American history, Rutledge concluded that the Court's definition of establishment was entirely consistent with the intent of both of these Founders.

Rutledge was not unsympathetic to the parents of children in Catholic schools. "No one conscious of *religious values* can be unsympathetic toward the burden which our constitutional separation puts on parents who desire religious instruction mixed with secular for their children. . . . Hardship in fact there is which none can blink." However, this was not sufficient reason for aiding those parents with public funds. "Like St. Paul's freedom, religious liberty with a great price must be bought."

One might think that this represented a religiously sensitive view of the problem, but it was not. For Rutledge, the issue was more than a matter concerning those who were faithful to one creed paying for the propagation of another. "The person of no creed also would be forced to pay for teaching what he does not believe." In this, he affirmed Black's position that the First Amendment "requires a state to be a neutral in its relations with groups of religious believers and non-believers."

What this neutrality meant was more forcefully articulated in Justice Jackson's opinion, in which he directed his attention to the relation of religion in education. Justice Jackson described the public school system in America as, "if not the product of Protestantism, at least . . . more consistent with it than with the Catholic *culture and scheme of values*" (author's emphasis). On this ground, he affirmed an earlier Court decision that found the existence of Catholic parochial schools constitutional.

But the influence of Protestantism had to be neutralized in the public schools as well. Tax-raised funds may not be used "to induce or reward piety, to secure religion against skepticism, or to compensate people for the adherence to a creed." The goal of education, therefore, was the rationalization of everyday life, which, in effect, meant isolating "temporal knowledge" from religion. The effect of this was to make moral judgment a matter of personal choice rather than a product of religious or family heritage.

When Justice Black, writing for the majority, defined establishment in strict separationist terms, he interpreted religion as the expression of the feelings of the individual toward *"ultimate issues of existence* (author's emphasis) in any creedal form." What he meant by "creed" was merely "opinion." Such language was not neutral, but a reflection of the sociological understanding of religion that had already been articulated by Justice Frankfurter in *Gobitis*. Religion was a matter of conscience rather than dogma, and conscience was a matter of personal opinion absent any duty to anything collective, such as a religious institution.

Justice Black's interpretation of the Establishment Clause had been articulated with the goal of setting the individual entirely free. What that freedom meant, however, was more fully articulated by Justice Jackson in his dissent in *Everson*. While dissenting on the disposition of the case, based on the facts presented, Jackson's opinion regarding the meaning of the Establishment Clause was congruent with that of Justice Black. It articulated, without fanfare, what was truly revolutionary about the *Everson* decision. *"After the individual has been instructed in worldly wisdom he will be better fitted to choose his religion."* This would include, as he suggested later, even the choice of no religion. Each and every child in the public school was to be treated as a potential *autonomous individual*. Such an individual's education was to be aimed at making every culture and scheme of values a matter of personal choice rather than a heritage passed on by his or her family, or his or her religion.

The justices insured that this process would occur when, in *Illinois ex rel. McCollum v. Board of Education* (1948), they supported the claim of an avowed atheist that "released time" (that is, children being allowed to leave public school early for religious instruction) constituted an establishment of religion. Justice Black, writing again for the majority, asserted that the definition of establishment that was used by the Court was not hostile to religion but was neutral. The problem was that, as Justice Jackson's opinion in *Everson* revealed, the use of the word "neutral" was not free of a polemical meaning or intent. By having treated religion as a manifestation of culture, he gave conscience an agnostic meaning. His was an agnosticism that sided with those who were hostile to religion. Thus, his claim to the contrary, Justice Black's assertion of neutrality was an expression of a creed, not a statement of fact.

In *Barnette*, Justice Jackson had expressed utmost confidence that the bonds of American society were strong enough to allow for "occasional" idiosyncrasies. "We apply the limitations of the Constitution with no fear that freedom to be intellectually and spiritually diverse or even contrary will disintegrate the social organization. . . . We can have intellectual individualism and the rich cultural diversities that we owe to exceptional minds only at the price of occasional eccentricity and abnormal attitudes."

Justice Jackson's confidence that the bonds of society were strong enough to tolerate eccentric religious views rested on the assumption that it was impossible for the idiosyncratic to become the norm. Yet when it finally became sensitive to the matter of establishment and defined it explicitly, the Court turned the law on the path of the normalization of the unconventional, the idiosyncratic, and the eccentric.

This process began when the agnostic conscience of the justices deemed it necessary to legally protect anyone who feels different. This doctrine was articulated by Justice Frankfurter, in *Barnette*. Although he claimed that his being a Jew was of no legal relevance, it is not at all evident that it was *not* relevant when he articulated the doctrine of compassion.

> The fact that this power (of the school system) has not been used to discriminate (on behalf of one religion) is beside the point. . . . That a child is offered an alternative may reduce the constraint; it does not eliminate the operation of influence by the school in matters sacred to conscience and outside the schools' domain. *The law of imitation* (author's emphasis) operates, and non-conformity is not an outstanding characteristic of children. The result is an obvious pres-

sure upon children to attend. . . . The children belonging to these non-participating sects will thus have inculcated in them *a feeling of separatism* (author's emphasis) when the school should be a training ground for habits of community.

The autonomous individual, whom Justice Jackson idealized as what public education was supposed to produce, was judged in *McCollum* not to be in existence yet and needed help in being created. The justices understood children to be "other-directed," that is, they are "feeling I's" rather than "thinking I's." The ethics of compassion, however, may inadvertently produce something other than the autonomous individual. The autonomous individual is what David Reisman (in the *Lonely Crowd*) termed "inner-directed."

Frankfurter's doctrine expressed sensitivity toward "feeling I's" by articulating a doctrine that amounted to the institutionalization of compassion toward anyone who felt separated from others due to belonging to different religious groups. In reality, whatever the intent, its effect was to contribute to the weakening of the autonomy of the individual and the weakening of the autonomous will, which is grounded in certitude and confidence in one's own uniqueness or difference. It contributed to making the "exceptional" individual more, rather than less, fearful of being different. Instead of building internal strength, such compassion leaves a child ashamed of being different and too emotionally weak to tolerate any difficulties that might arise from being different. It also encourages hypersensitivity at any and all disturbances to one's comfort and fosters perpetual irritability and unhappiness with the world as it is—populated with other people with passionate concerns and a willingness to compete on behalf of those concerns.

This sensitivity and weakness was evidenced in *Lee v. Weisman* (1992). The justices supported Deborah Weisman's claim that her rights had been violated when her high school principal asked a rabbi to offer a nonsectarian prayer at graduation. They found that this act constituted government coercion because she would feel pressure to stand and maintain a respectful silence during that prayer. In the name of religious liberty, the Court affirmed the claim that any prayer would be an infringement, even though it was only a nuisance. Any compromise, such as a moment of respectful silence, was too much to ask of anyone.

The detection of establishment in such innocuous situations may have been an unintended consequence of Justice Jackson's vision of the proper goal of secular education, but it is a palpable consequence nonetheless. The effect of *Everson* is that the *idiosyncratic has become the norm.*

Evaluating the Experiment

Everson set in motion a new experiment in American political life. By granting irreligion equality with religion, the justices, with a strong faith in the impact of science on politics, determined that the United States would be a laboratory for a radical principle—that the rule of law in a modern constitutional democracy could be sustained without the aid of religion. Is the experiment working or failing? From simple observation, one might feel compelled to give an equivocal "yes" to both. For members of minority religions, the separation doctrine has been successful in freeing their children from having a foreign religious teaching imposed on them in school. Indirectly, it has contributed to opening doors for adults in areas ranging from housing to executive suite positions to membership on previously closed boards of trustees. On the other hand, one also observes a growing number of lawless incidents in the society. Is it possible that the separation doctrine has contributed to the production of a more insolent American democracy? Is there any evidence that the battle over religion and irreligion is affecting the rule of law in America or, worse, the sanctity of the Constitution?

Just as the roots of the Establishment Clause are grounded in the philosophic development of modern constitutionalism, so does the evaluation of the effects of the experiment require a philosophic framework. The success of the experiment initiated by *Everson* appears to rest on the idea of the extraordinary individual, which had been articulated by Justice Jackson. Such an individual was the model of the autonomous individual. In several opinions, Justice Jackson referred to Socrates as just such a person.

There is a Platonic dialogue, the *Crito*, which is devoted to the issue of the rule of law and Socrates' relationship to that issue. This dialogue contains a conversation between Socrates, in prison and about to be subject to the death penalty, and his friend and financial benefactor, Crito, who has bribed the prison guard and made it possible for Socrates to escape. Not only does Socrates resist the idea but also he attempts to convince Crito that it is unjust to escape from prison.

To counter Crito's enthusiasm for personal justice, Socrates narrated an imaginary conversation between himself and the Laws of

Athens. In effect, the Laws argued that they are like parents and citizens are like children. There is a religious quality about the speech of the Laws of Athens. They assert that humans are the creation of the Laws. The Laws also provide education and security. Therefore, humans ought to be grateful to the Laws for what they have received. The rule of law, in effect, depends on the gratitude of children for the many "services" that the parents provide. If gratitude is not present in the recipient, the respect for the city will disappear.

Crito is willing to undermine the rule of law for his friend Socrates by bribing the guard and stealing Socrates out of prison in darkness. He is fearful of death. The law, especially the criminal law that prescribes the death penalty, is harsh. Socrates' imaginary dialogue with those Laws was a way of deterring Crito from believing that he could, and therefore should, exempt himself from the harshness of the law. If the idea of "exemption" should become a categorical imperative, then everyone could claim individual exemption from the law. The rule of law itself would therefore be jeopardized.

Plato's answer to the question of providing stability to the rule of law was predicated on serious thought about the difference between ordinary and extraordinary individuals. Only the extraordinary individual, in this case Socrates, who is free of the fear of death, free from envy and from the desire for vengeance, will be capable of being autonomous *and* supportive of the rule of law. Accepting the death penalty, in the face of a choice not to do so, required courage. Socrates' action implies that this also is the key to the stability of the rule of law.

The founders of modern constitutionalism understood that the stability of the rule of law required some sense of obligation to obey the law, including laws that would be harsh. Were it possible to create humans who could be autonomous and at the same time obligated to the law, there would be nothing to be concerned about. Hobbes and Locke, and Jefferson and Madison, did not believe that most citizens of the state were extraordinary individuals. That was why they were compelled to make a practical compromise with religion.

By contrast, Justice Jackson, in his *Everson* opinion, believed that a secular education could produce autonomous individuals who would also feel obligated to obey the law, including harsh laws. But American education since *Everson* has been negatively affected by a democratic dogma that insists that all people are equal. Educational standards have been lowered rather than elevated. The effect has been to produce individuals who are neither extraordinary nor autonomous. Nor do they appear to be free from envy or the desire for revenge. This tendency has been exacerbated by the doctrine of compassion articulated by Justice Frankfurter in *McCollum*. The effect of the doctrine of compassion has been that the demand for exemption from the law has become the norm.

Seven years after the *Everson* decision, the Supreme Court issued its decision in *Brown v. Board of Education*. President Eisenhower used force to integrate Central High School in Little Rock, Arkansas. At the same time, there were billboard signs in the South saying "Impeach Earl Warren." Those who objected to the Court's decision still indicated their respect for the Constitution. Their protest amounted to a rectification of their discontent by means of the rule of law. But is that same faith still evident today?

The direction that *Everson* took did not solve the problem of tempering religion. Instead, by excluding religion from the public sphere, the experiment did two things at once. First, it educated Americans to be free from the influences of tradition. Simultaneously, it intensified the desire of those who found living as an autonomous individual troubling (either for themselves or because of what they judged were the negative effects on society) to want to sack the experiment entirely and try a new, although really old, one.

Religion has become a major source of ideological conflict today, not simply within the schools, but over other issues, abortion being the most visible and audible. There appears to be *more* rather than *less* intolerance today being expressed not only by the religious but also by the irreligious; not merely by the Christian faiths that represents the majority, but by dissenting Christians, and by non-Christians who still resent Christianity of any kind. However much the justices hoped to resolve the problem posed by Justice Frankfurter in his *Barnette* dissent, from the opinions that followed *Everson*, the separation doctrine may have exacerbated the problem rather than resolved it.

First Things is a journal created and edited by Father Richard John Neuhaus, the author of *The Naked Public Square*. The November 1996 issue of the journal gave expression to hostility to the government. Articles with titles such as "The Tyrant State," "A Crisis of Legitimacy," "A Culture Corrupted," "The End of Democracy?" and "Our Judicial Oligarchy" appeared, each of which, either explicitly or implicitly, called for resistance to the government. When reprimanded for their political excessiveness, the editors of the journal recanted. But whether the authors who expressed those views merely bowed to coercion, in an act of political correctness, or were genuinely convinced of their error, was unclear. For that moment, however, those authors encouraged civil disobedience and called for a change of government.

On the other hand, the *Weisman* case was a good indication that the fear of an absolutism from religion has spawned, and sustained, an equal and opposite absolutism. It ought to make one wonder if the result of secular education, among secularists, has been to breed more tolerance or intolerance of religion, including one's own. However humane it may appear in providing a judicial remedy for everyone who feels they are vulnerable, the numbers of actions by others that make people feel vulnerable has widened.[41] If Socrates was Justice Jackson's model for the autonomous individual, Socrates' courage is evidently missing.

Some American scholars are sensing that political problems being raised today by conflicts within society, including religion, are surfacing as an attack on the Constitution itself. *The New Federalist Papers,*[42] a collection of essays written by a political scientist, an historian, and a professor of law, expresses such a view. Concerned with the revival of populism in American politics, all three authors have argued that the new populists' activities aimed at making the government more accessible to citizens is, in reality, potentially dismantling the Constitution. The history of western expansion shows there has always been an anarchic streak among some Americans, so it is reasonable to argue that it is an exaggeration to say that there is a danger to the Constitution only from "armed militia, nativist bigots and mad bombers."[43] The disregard for law is far more widespread and expressed daily by nearly everyone who drives a car, van, or truck. The number of people driving motor vehicles without licenses appears to be growing. Worse, both licensed and unlicensed drivers summarily ignore legally posted speed limits and those who abide by those limits are sometimes subjected to what has come to be called "road rage." Growing numbers of Americans seem to consider themselves to be exempt from these laws. The exemption is proving to be the rule.

The more serious concern is the growing tendency to propose constitutional amendments to solve political conflicts.

> More constitutional amendment proposals have been taken seriously now than at any other recent time. Some have come close to passing. An amendment calling for a balanced budget passed the House twice and came within one and then two votes of passing the Senate. An amendment allowing punishing of flag burners easily passed the House and fell just three votes short in the Senate. These and other proposed amendments continue to circulate—including

amendments that would impose term limits on members of Congress, permit subsidies for religious speech with public funds, confer procedural rights upon crime victims, denaturalize children of illegal immigrants, or require a three-fifths vote to raise taxes, to name a few.[44]

In effect, the Constitution itself has become increasingly politicized. Lurking behind the concerns and fears of the authors of *The New Federalist Papers* is the possibility of a Constitutional Convention!

While such a radical alternative seems improbable, if not impossible, it may be closer to the horizon than anyone wishes. David Broder, in *Derailing Democracy: Initiative Campaigns and the Power of Money*,[45] has revealed the growing tendency in America to use the initiative and referendum as a mode of political expression. This book documents the growth of an "initiative industry" comprised of professional signature gatherers, initiative drafters, and marketing specialists for initiative campaigns, especially through television. In documenting this new group of political advocates, Broder voiced his concern that direct democracy is increasingly replacing legislative institutions as the lawmakers of this country. This concern was best expressed in the title of his last chapter, "Law without Government."

With the growth of daily polling of public opinion by the electronic and print media, on one policy question after another, citizens are being asked to adopt opinions about issues that have no direct, or in some cases, even indirect, effect on their daily lives. Is it any wonder that citizens have become increasingly morally indignant?[46] Perpetual indignation should be of concern when it is being expressed toward changing the Constitution. Nowhere is this more evident than in the fact that presidential candidates are being questioned far more today than even a decade ago about whom they plan to appoint to the U.S. Supreme Court.

Although the courts remain able to judge the constitutionality of laws made even by initiatives and referenda, can we remain confident that the politicizing of the Constitution will remain within bounds? Is it not possible that the American public, already skeptical of elected officials, and inclined to use ballot initiatives to take decision-making power away from those officials, may become increasingly disrespectful of the justices of the Supreme Court?

Can this challenge be addressed? Resistance to any change has been based on an ill-defined notion called "the slippery slope." In effect, it argues that any deviation from the current wall will provide the opening for a complete reversal and a return to the pre-*Everson* relationship of church and state. This notion, borrowed from physics, in particular the Newtonian notion of an inertia-free incline, is only an expression of fear based on a very limited, if not totally absent, understanding of the art of statesmanship that the Supreme Court is capable of.

The problem that the separation doctrine has created is with the rule of law, not with the free exercise of religion or irreligion. The rule of law cannot simply be asserted. It is predicated on the consent of those who are the subjects of law. Jefferson and Madison, the sons of Hobbes and Locke, were aware that the alternative to the rule of law based on the principle of consent was the state of nature. If we, today, forget that possibility, then we may discover, to our horror, that "not for nothing is history associated with the figure of Nemesis, which defeats man by fulfilling his wishes in a different form or by answering his prayers too completely."[47]

Decisions made by the justices are not limited to simply judging between disputing parties. They have political implications.

> It is not customary to regard judges as statesmen, but the unique powers of the Supreme Court of the United States make it easier for an American judge to gain this distinction. In a very real sense the task of expounding the Constitution converts the Supreme Court into a lawgiver, because to expound the meaning of the powers granted, the limits imposed, and the relations established by this document is to give the nation the law by which it lives. Nor is this merely law in the narrow sense of the term. On the contrary, in the course of its regular work the Court has the opportunity to give the nation the principles by which it governs itself.[48]

The justices in *Everson* articulated a *clear and distinct* interpretation of the Establishment Clause. The response was equally unequivocal, and the conflict today apparently remains so. The question one must pose is whether it is always best for lawgivers and statesmen to give *clear and distinct* interpretations of the principles by which citizens are to live or whether it is wiser to allow those principles to remain equivocal. Perhaps absolute clarity is not the highest form of statesmanship. As the philosopher Stanley Rosen has forcefully pointed out, there may be a kind of "Goedel's Theorem in human affairs: Every attempt to systematize life or to govern by a set of axioms rich enough to encompass the totality of experience leads to a contradiction."[49]

The problem that the absolute application of the separation doctrine has created is with the rule of law, not with the free exercise of religion or irreligion. Humaneness and the rule of law may, in the end, be contradictory. This possibility opens the door to a consideration of a possible defect, or at least weakness, in modern constitutionalism itself. The problem has to do with relating theory and practice. Prudential considerations are always grounded either on some notion of utility or on what is noble. The outcomes of any decision based on utility are always difficult to determine ahead of time, since there are unintended consequences of every action. What of the grounds of nobility? Perhaps it is no better. Nobility, as Rosen, reminded us, "is a perception, not a concept . . . [it] is a value, an estimation, a ranking, and therefore an ambiguous mixture of aesthetic and moral qualities."[50] Furthermore, "the relation between theory and practice . . . is such that we cannot apply the classical doctrine of virtue as a standard for improving modern moral and political life except by transforming that life beyond recognition, and indeed, in the extreme case, by destroying it."[51]

Statesmen know that crises must be negotiated. That is why a judicial retreat from an absolutism that ranks vouchers and funding for educational items in parochial schools as the same as prayer in schools may, in the name of prudence, be a first step.[52]

Notes

1. Robert Bork, "What to Do about the First Amendment," *Commentary* (February 1995): 23-29.
2. To demonstrate his charge, Bork noted that

orthodox standing doctrine withholds the power to sue from persons alleging an interest in an issue only in their capacities as citizens or taxpayers. An individualized personal interest, some direct impact upon the plaintiff, such as loss of money or liberty, is required. But in 1968, in *Flast v. Cohen*, the Supreme Court created the rule that taxpayers could sue under the establishment clause to enjoin federal expenditures to aid religious schools. . . . Every single provision of the Constitution from Article I, Section I to the 37th Amendment is immune from taxpayer or citizen enforcement—except one. *Only under the establishment clause is an ideological interest in expunging religion sufficient to confer standing* (author's emphasis).

3. Bork, "What to Do about the First Amendment," 23.
4. "Letters to the Editor," *Commentary* (September 1995): 13.

5. "Letters to the Editor," 13.

6 "Letters to the Editor," 12.

7. Levy tried to strengthen his claim by turning the tables on his religious critics. He argued that strict separationism had its roots in religion. "The driving force in Virginia for separation of church and state came from evangelical Christians who believe that Christ's kingdom is not of this world," and that religion is best served when left alone by government. Government aid would actually injure religion by compelling believers to give "ceremonial obedience to the state." While this argument certainly supports the Free Exercise Clause of the First Amendment, it could as well support Bork's thesis that establishment means neutrality only as between religions. It is not likely that evangelical Christians would ever have supported neutrality as between religion and irreligion.

8. The source of the justices' decision appears to be Henri Bergson's *Two Sources of Morality and Religion*, which distinguished between an "open society" and a "closed society." An open society is one in which science frees the individual from being a slave to traditions, especially traditional religions, and substitutes a rational morality defined by science and technology. Each individual's morality will then be grounded in the openness of scientific inquiry and experimentation. Bergson presumed that human nature is historical or perpetually unfinished and that the source of moral judgment was the individual conscience educated in modern science and history. Bergson's argument was the source of Karl Popper's *The Open Society and Its Enemies*. See Dante Germino, "Preliminary Reflections on the Open Society: Bergson, Popper and Voegelin," in Dante Germino and Klaus Von Beyme, *The Open Society in Theory and Practice* (Amsterdam: M. Nijhoff, 1974), 1-25. See also, Dante Germino, "Henri Bergson: Activist Mysticism and the Open Society," *Political Science Reviewer* 9 (fall 1979): 1-37.

9. The Protestant challenge to Catholic political rule meant a challenge to Catholicism as the chosen religion. Calvin energized his followers by utilizing the same principle, via predestination.

10. Michael Oakeshott, "Moral Life in the Writings of Thomas Hobbes," in his *Rationalism in Politics* (New York: Basic Books, 1962), 270-71.

11. Harvey C. Mansfield, Jr., "The Religious Issue and the Origin of Modern Constitutionalism," in Robert A. Goldwin and Art Kaufman, eds., *How Does the Constitution Protect Religious Freedom?* (Washington, D.C.: American Enterprise Institute, 1987), 4.

12. Mansfield, "The Religious Issue."

13. Oakeshott, "Moral Life," 287.

14. Mansfield, "The Religious Issue," 10-11.

15. Thomas L. Pangle, *The Spirit of Modern Republicanism* (Chicago: University of Chicago Press, 1988), 135.

16. Cited in Pangle, *The Spirit of Modern Republicanism,* 191.

17. Cited in Robert H. Horwitz, "John Locke and the Preservation of Liberty: A Perennial Problem of Civic Education," in Robert H. Horwitz, ed., *The Moral Foundations of the American Republic* (Charlottesville: University Press of Virginia, 1979), 137.

18. Horwitz, "John Locke and the Preservation of Liberty: A Perennial Problem of Civic Education," 137.

19. In effect, Locke created the grounds for what, in the 1950s, David Riesman, Nathan Glazer, and Ruel Denny called "the other-directed individual." *The Lonely Crowd* (New Haven, Conn.: Yale University Press, 1961), 17-24. Locke's doctrine was challenged by Rousseau, who sought to liberate men from dependence on the opinion of others. As will be shown below, Rousseau's doctrine was the basis of at least one justice's opinion in *Everson.*

20. Riesman, Glazer, and Denny, *The Lonely* Crowd, 255.

21. Cited in Harvey C. Mansfield, Jr., "Thomas Jefferson," in Morton J. Frisch and Richard G. Stevens, *American Political Thought: The Philosophic Dimensions of American Statesmanship* (New York: Charles Scribner's Sons, 1971), 34.

22. Cited in Mansfield, "Thomas Jefferson," 41.

23. Eva T. H. Brann, "Madison's 'Memorial and Remonstrance,' A Model of American Eloquence," *The St. John's Review* (summer 1981): 55-73.

24. Michael Malbin, *Religion and Politics: The Intentions of the Authors of the First Amendment* (Washington, D.C.: American Enterprise Institute, 1978), 9.

25. Malbin, *Religion and Politics,* 14.

26. Georg Lukacs, *The Destruction of Reason* (Atlantic Highlands, N.J.: Humanities Press, 1981), 585.

27. The term was used by Rudolf Otto, *The Idea of the Holy* (London: Oxford University Press, 1950).

28. Leo Strauss, *Philosophy and Law* (Albany: State University of New York Press, 1995), 37.

29. Edward A. Purcell, Jr., *The Crisis of Democratic Theory* (Lexington: University Press of Kentucky, 1973), 11.

30. Purcell, *The Crisis of Democratic Theory,* 113.

31. Purcell, *The Crisis of Democratic Theory,* 88.

32. Purcell, *The Crisis of Democratic Theory,* 215.

33. Purcell, *The Crisis of Democratic Theory,* 213.

34. Purcell, *The Crisis of Democratic Theory,* 139-58.

35. Cited in Purcell, *The Crisis of Democratic Theory,* 205.

36. Purcell, *The Crisis of Democratic Theory,* 154-55.

37. Cited in Purcell, *The Crisis of Democratic Theory,* 76.

38. Alpheus Thomas Mason and William M. Beaney, *The Supreme Court in a Free Society* (New York: W. W. Norton, 1968) 238-41.

39. I found the best treatment of this in a dramatization of Darrow's defense. See John Logan's *Never the Sinner,* Act II, Scene 16.

40. This case was one of three that overturned a previous case, *Jones v. Opelika*, that allowed licensing fees to be charged for selling religious books and records by Jehovah's Witnesses.

41. Support for this claim was provided in two "Letters to the Editor" in response to Robert Bork's 1995 article. Borrowing from John Stuart Mill, Samuel Rabinove asserted that "the right to engage in voluntary prayer does not include the right to *coerce* other students to participate." But he extended the notion of coercion to include any situation in which someone who disagrees with prayer or a prayer is upset but not necessarily threatened with coercion. The right to engage in voluntary prayer also does not include "the right to have a captive audience *listen*." *Commentary* (May 1995): 7-10. Adam Simms expressed the feelings of such a person, all the while admitting that he was not being coerced. He recalled being at Mt. Rushmore and hearing a choir singing "a number of revivalist songs, all of the Christian faith." As a Jew he objected that tax money was being used to support one religion over another, even though the direct impact of those songs was *"perhaps ephemeral"* (author's emphasis). Simms's response to Bork is a plea for pity or compassion for those Americans who feel themselves to be "outsiders." He was expressing explicitly a sentiment implicitly expressed by Bork, on behalf of those he designated as "believers" and who resented what they judged to be discrimination against their views. *Commentary* (May 1995): 11.

42. Alan Brinkley, Nelson W. Polsby, and Kathleen M. Sullivan, *The New Federalist Papers: In Defense of the Constitution* (New York: W. W. Norton, 1997).

43. Richard C. Leone, president of the Twentieth Century Fund, wrote this in the preface, not the authors of the essays.

44. Kathleen Sullivan, "What's Wrong with Constitutional Amendments?" in Brinkley, et al., *New Federalist Papers,* 61-62.

45. David Broder, *Democracy Derailed: Initiative Campaigns and the Power of Money* (New York: Harcourt, 2000).

46. An interesting study of this subject was Sven Ranulf, *Moral Indignation and Middle Class Psychology* (New York: Schocken, 1964).

47. Henry E. Kissinger, *A World Restored* (Boston: Houghton Mifflin, 1957), 1. The separation of church and state, as a political doctrine, has hardened into an antireligious ideology—separationism. People who are addicted to ideological thinking refuse to view or accept anything "as it is" and insist on interpreting everything as being only a stage for some further development. This is the root of the mentality that sees, in any deviation from what is, the immediate potential for the start of a "slippery slope," that is, a precipitous decline. The fear of a slippery slope, however, is not always a conclusion based on empirical fact, but it is an ideological expression of the ordinary autonomous I, who feels rather than reasons.

48. Walter Berns, "Oliver Wendell Holmes, Jr.," in Frisch and Stevens, *American Political Thought,* 167.

49. Stanley Rosen, *The Ancients and Moderns: Rethinking Modernity* (New Haven, Conn.: Yale University Press, 1989), 17.

50. Rosen, *The Ancients and Moderns*, 12.

51. Rosen, *The Ancients and Moderns*, 11.

52. As this chapter was being completed, at the end of the Court's 2000 term, the justices, by a 6-3 margin, determined that federal financing of computer equipment for parochial schools did not violate the Establishment Clause. See *Mitchell v. Helms*.

5

Religion and Liberal Democracy

Marc D. Stern

I

Democracy itself means only that the people rule. Other than, perhaps, freedom of speech and equal access to the ballot, the notion of democracy itself sets no limits on what the people may do when acting in their sovereign capacity.

The American constitutional tradition is not one of pure democracy. As the Supreme Court has repeatedly reminded us, in recent years, federalism is one important restraint on democracy. The Constitution imposes other limits—most important, that which is embodied in the Bill of Rights—on what democratic government may do. More generally, the American political tradition imposes informal, non-constitutional limits on what is appropriate for government.

The United States is not unique in this. All liberal constitutional democracies impose restrictions on what government may do and how it may act, including, in particular, religion, and what values it may assimilate, including, again, religious ones.

In liberal democracies, citizenship is not dependent on adherence to an official state religion, or even to a state-approved religion. Religion is not a necessary constitutive element of citizenship. Equally well accepted is the notion that in a liberal democracy government may not penalize citizens (i.e., persons within its jurisdiction) because they choose to adhere to a faith not shared by their fellow citizens. Similarly, it is a postulate of liberal democracy that citizens enjoy freedom to express and practice their religious views publicly without fear of punishment or civic disability.

It is equally settled that liberal democracies cannot compel the doing of religious acts, or attendance at worship services, although the exact extent of this principle as it applies to children in state-run schools is disputed.

Liberal democratic theory assumes as well the importance of a sharp demarcation between the state and the private sector. This demarcation distinguishes liberal democracy from fascist or totalitarian states. This demarcation—in American constitutional law the problem of state action—means that it is a given that citizens may order their own values and act in ways government may not. This principle suggests, among other things, that citizens acting in a nongovernmental capacity may create communities in which religion is the constitutive element, and which are in every way permeated with religious values.

There is, however, an important limitation on the scope of this private right. Liberal democracies generally mandate equal treatment of citizens in private economic and social activities. Enforceable prohibitions on racial, religious, and sexual discrimination by private actors who serve as gatekeepers to social and economic benefits are universal features of liberal democracy.

It is assumed, quite soundly, that substantial inequalities of social and economic opportunity are fundamentally inconsistent with a society in which individuals are regarded as being of equal worth. Not only the reality of equal worth, but a citizen's self-perception of equal worth, is essential to the well-being of the liberal democratic society.

This is why the struggle for gay rights looms so large today in American politics, not because discrimination against gays in employment is such a pressing problem, but because it is assumed in a liberal democracy that personal characteristics such as sexual orientation are not relevant to a person's economic and social possibilities. The failure to include sexual orientation in the now standard list of prohibited forms of discrimination is seen as relegating homosexuals to second-class citizenship. For opponents of gay rights laws, it is precisely the symbolic message of these laws—their affirmation of the equality of homosexual and heterosexual sexual activity—which makes them so objectionable.

Liberal democracies also assume that citizens should not be prevented from practicing their faith and that the government ought not to interfere with the religious decisions of citizens or their institutions. This last principle is not always observed. In the United States today it means only that the government may not single out religious practices for regulation. In the name of equal treatment of religious and nonreligious citizens (an important value in a liberal democracy) the courts refuse to recognize a right to exemption from ostensibly neutral government regulation for religious practice, even though the constitutional text reads as if one was intended. ("Congress shall make no law respecting . . . the Free Exercise of religion.")

Curiously, many civil libertarians who usually support the broadest reading of the Bill of Rights insist on a narrow reading of the Free Exercise Clause, asserting a fear that religion will be above the law. Part of what is at work here is a notion of equal treatment trumping individual liberty, that is, the claim that religious citizens should not have access to exemptions denied nonreligious citizens. But also at work is a dislike of traditional religion and the notion that government should take no notice of religion, religion being a private affair with no public implications. The latter is not a religiously neutral position.

The insistence on religious equality both in governmental activities—in the age of the regulatory and welfare state, government occupies a far larger sphere than it did when the Constitution was written—and in the larger society suggests real limitations on religious liberty. On the one hand, liberal democracy assumes freedom of religion; on the other, it assumes restrictions on that freedom, not because a particular religious practice is too dangerous to tolerate (all agree that religiously motivated child sacrifice can be banned), but because powerful religious groups with counter-majoritarian and antiegalitarian views are antithetical to liberal democracy.

The more or less universal acceptance of the liberal democratic attitude toward religion in the Western world has, from a historical perspective, come in an astoundingly short time. Two hundred years ago, the twin ideas of freedom of religious belief and separation of church from state were accepted principally in some parts of the United States and Holland—and some of the United States did not accept all of these principles until well into the nineteenth century.

In Europe, these developments came still later and not without substantial resistance. Even today the newly formed democracies of Eastern Europe are struggling with the question of the extent to which the national church should have a preferred role in public life. In other words, they are deciding whether the national church should have a defining and constitutive role in defining the nation.

The breadth of the achievement is quite stunning. On the whole it has contributed to the well-being of both religious and nonreligious individuals and churches.[1] It is important to bear in mind how new the consensus about the role of religion in a liberal democracy is, because it should serve as a caution not to insist with puritanical rigidity on an ideal model of liberal democracy, one which risks alienating the many citizens who are deeply religious and who would be inclined to abandon the project altogether if it stood in irreconcilable conflict with their religious commitments. But we must be equally certain not to overestimate the resilience of liberal democracy, and to think that departures from principle will do no harm to the larger public weal.

II

Many have concluded that in a liberal democracy religion is a purely private affair. Persons are free to believe and practice what they please, but at the price of that liberty, they may not make religion a public affair, whether public encompasses the government or large social institutions. Surely, in this view, public means that the government must not involve itself in religion, or alter its own practices and policies to advance religious interests. Some, for example, go still further and insist that religion may play no role in the formation of policy in a liberal democracy; religious views are refracted through the individual citizen's own view of appropriate policy. Others insist that the idea that religion should be privatized often means direct restrictions on religion.

The emphasis on individual, not social, religion fits well with the general individualistic theme of contemporary democratic theory[2] and American life. It is also compatible with a long-standing trend in American religious life, which is to emphasize individual over institutional religion. Some would go further and insist that even in nongovernmental activities, public activities must be free of religious influence. The Supreme Court has rejected the last position, recognizing a right to associate—and to refuse to associate—along religious or other ideological lines, but when push comes to shove the right is rarely vindicated, certainly not in the commercial sphere.

The Supreme Court has also made it clear that as a legal matter, religious leaders and institutions have the right to participate fully in political activities, in part because it judges that in the American experience such participation is not likely to undermine the constitutionally required separation of church and state, but also because a ban on such speech would be difficult to square with the secular value of freedom of speech.

This theoretical liberty is, however, limited by a practical reality. Congress has denied tax exemption to religious institutions which endorse or oppose candidates for election to office, a restriction which has minimized open religious involvement in political campaigns. Without tax-exempt status, most religious groups could not survive. Most are forced to either abandon or at least disguise political involvement.

The United States has no tradition of political parties organized along religious lines, although surely religion has played a key role in several great struggles including slavery, equal rights for women, temperance, labor, civil rights, nuclear disarmament, and abortion. Alexander Hamilton once suggested a religious party, and the Know-Nothing party of the mid-nineteenth century came close, but we certainly have had nothing resembling European Christian Democratic parties or the religious (and antireligious) parties in Israel. This nontradition, too, has minimized the extent of religious involvement in politics, and it has helped create a tradition of secular liberal democracy.

The debate over whether religion has any "public" role in a liberal democracy is not limited to the question of electoral and legislative involvements by religious groups. Consider the following examples, most from the United States, but some from elsewhere.

1. A town in Missouri refuses to lease school buildings for privately sponsored social dancing, in recognition of religiously generated community sentiment which regards dancing as immoral.
2. States refuse to fund abortion because many citizens object to being taxed to fund a procedure that they regard, as a matter of religious teaching, as murder.
3. The Boy Scouts insist that every scout believe in God. The Scouts also reject homosexual scoutmasters because their acceptance would be inconsistent with traditional morality. Both policies are challenged as violations of civil rights laws. The Scouts insist they are free as a private group to impose these discriminatory restrictions. The New Jersey Supreme Court sided with a dismissed gay assistant scoutmaster; a closely divided U.S. Supreme Court sided with

the Scouts. With the exception of Orthodox Jewish groups, the Jewish community sided with the scoutmaster. Since the decision, many Jewish groups have severed their own ties with the Scouts, not wishing to be associated with discrimination.

4. Yale Law School refuses to allow the Christian Legal Society to recruit on campus because it discriminates in hiring—hiring only believing Christians. Yale also refuses to accommodate Orthodox Jewish students who seek an exemption from a requirement that they live in a coed dorm, which they claim violates their faith. Yale readily accommodates the dietary and Sabbath observance requirements of such students.

5. In order to preserve a secular society, France and Turkey refuse to allow Muslim girls to attend public schools wearing religiously mandated head scarves.

6. In Israel, daylight savings time was ended earlier than usual in order to facilitate the practice of Sephardic Jews reciting early morning penitential prayers forty days before the Jewish New Year. The change brought sharp criticism from secular Israeli Jews, who complained of religious coercion. One complained to the *New York Times* that the change made it more difficult for her to swim at the beach after work.

7. In a similar vein, religious and secular Jews fight over street closings which made it more difficult for those wishing to drive on the Jewish Sabbath to reach their destinations, but which promote a "Sabbath atmosphere" in neighborhoods in which the overwhelming number of residents are Sabbath observers and do not drive. In commenting on these disputes, a retired Israeli judge insisted that religion is purely a private matter which has no public place.

8. Private landlords in various states refuse to rent to unmarried cohabiting couples, insisting that they should not be required to facilitate sin. Civil rights and civil liberty organizations insist that when one enters the commercial marketplace, he or she can no longer insist on observing religious precepts which disadvantage anyone else. The courts have been receptive to these arguments, which have created a furious reaction among more traditionally religious communities that object to being told they must leave religion at the door to the economic marketplace.

9. Georgetown University was the scene of a battle between students who support the hanging of crucifixes in each classroom and administrators (many of them priests) who oppose such displays because they discourage recruitment of non-Catholic faculty and students.

Some of these cases involve governmental decisionmaking based on religion—the refusal to fund abortion and the refusal to permit social dancing. None of the cases involves coercing anyone to abandon his or her own faith and none involves coercion by government or anyone else to perform a religious act. Some, indeed, involve coercing religious people to violate their religious beliefs.

Take the housing discrimination cases. The cohabiting couple remains free to cohabit. Almost always, alternative housing will be available in the same housing market. The Boy Scout oath requirement, in fact, denies a conscientious atheist access to the Scouts, but, as disappointing as that may be, it hardly denies access to an opportunity without which one cannot succeed in life.

Yale is quite willing to accommodate private religious observance. What it is not willing to accommodate is communal expression of religion which departs from the principle of nondiscrimination and which allows the creation of separate religious communities. Allowing the Christian Legal Society to recruit only Christians would be an acknowledgment that essential differences between believers and nonbelievers justifies discrimination in access to economic benefits.

Allowing students to refuse to live in coed dorms on grounds that they are a breeding ground for immoral behavior would implicitly concede that egalitarian principles are not acceptable to all, that there are some religious groups that cannot or will not meet on common ground with fellow students, and that students who hold such beliefs must be permitted to create their own communities. This, too, is thought to threaten the principles of religious egalitarianism which undergirds liberal education and democracy. Yale insists that it cannot tolerate separatist religious enclaves. It seems beyond Yale's grasp that for the students involved its existing dormitories were not neutral but openly hostile to their religious beliefs, and that liberal democracy also countenances the formation of private religious enclaves.

It is hard to credit the fear that the personal act of a woman covering her head from a sense of sexual modesty threatens to call a theocracy into being, even given the anticlerical grounding of French church-state relations. It does, however, threaten the notion (read broadly) of religion as a purely private matter. (It also may threaten some understandings of gender equality.) In the case of France, anti-Muslim prejudice cannot be excluded.

Furthermore, what are we to make of the Israeli daylight savings case? Is it really true that religious forms of human activity cannot be given any consideration by liberal democratic government?

Something revealing is at work in these cases. It is the notion that religion is purely a private affair that has no place in the larger public arena, even where its appearance does not threaten any of the principles essential to a liberal democracy.

The people who advocate a private role for religion are not necessarily bigoted. Few sanction, and most would and do protest, efforts to punish believers because of their beliefs. They may even be quite religious themselves. Still, the forced confinement of religion to purely private and intimate settings is inconsistent with liberal democracy, at least that much of it which depends on the existence of a private sector, where citizens are free to put into place their own vision of the good life.

Let us expand on a controversy over religion and politics which was mentioned above in passing. The dispute is largely confined to academics, though it does surface from time to time in public debate. Are citizens or legislators permitted to cast votes based on religious beliefs? As to citizens at least, this is not a legal question, since citizens are legally free to cast their votes for any reason they choose.

The question is whether there is a moral duty of citizenship in a liberal democracy to act in one's capacity as a citizen without regard to one's religious beliefs. Professor Bruce Ackerman thinks that such a duty exists. John Rawls thinks it exists as to crucial constitutive decisions. Others are not so sure. After much hesitation, Professor Michael Perry of the University of Michigan has now concluded that no such duty exists. Professor Robert Audi has suggested that such a rule applies only to coercive legislation, but not otherwise. What constitutes noncoercive legislation is not altogether clear. Professor Kent Greenawalt of Columbia Law School believes citizens should make political decisions based on rational secular reasons, but that in those cases in which decisions involve ethical values not given to rational resolution—such as abortion or animal rights—religious reasons are as acceptable as irrational secular ones.

There is much to be said for a rule which requires citizens to at least try to carve out a secular space, not too closely tied to particular religious views. On the other hand, this author is skeptical of rules which are wholly unenforceable, even by individuals sitting in judgment on their own consciences. It is impossible for the deeply religious person to ever be sure that his or her views on some civic issue are unaffected by religious teachings. It is nevertheless revealing that so many prominent thinkers are prepared to exclude religion from impacting on political debate.

Consider abortion. The Catholic Church insists that its opposition to abortion is not religious but based on natural reason, the conviction that the fetus is human. Ronald Dworkin once wrote a book claiming that no rational person could believe the fetus was human and that therefore restrictive abortion laws were necessarily religious and unconstitutional. With regard to the proposed duty to use secular reasons only, who decides who is right?

The question is not so easily dodged elsewhere. One can easily argue that the debate in Israel over recognition of marriages not sanctioned by Jewish law can have no secular justification. But that would be wrong. The secular justification is that civil marriage would lead to the birth of children who many citizens would regard as illegitimate and refuse to marry. Can one not argue in secular terms that a nation has an interest in discouraging the birth of such children?

This may or may not be a sufficient argument to justify the restriction—and one could challenge the morality of a rule of religious law which visits the sins of the parents on the children—but it is assuredly a secular argument. In short, we do not think the arguments for a rule of secular citizenship would accomplish much, and it would come at the price of punishing citizens with particular views, itself of questionable validity in a democracy where decisions flow from the people.

Matters are more complicated with regard to legislators. They act not as private citizens but as holders of political power. May they allow religious motivations to dictate how those powers are used? Here the question is one not only of what should be but also of law. If it can be shown that a legislator (or a majority of legislators) acted out of a religious motive, should the result be invalidated?

It seems that most legislators make an attempt to act only for secular reasons, although the legislators of Alabama frequently test this thesis. Senator Lieberman struggled through the last presidential campaign to explain precisely where he drew the line. Some legislators, however, make no effort to disguise their religious motivations.

The Supreme Court has been of two minds on the subject. On the one hand, it is reluctant, for reasons not peculiar to religion, to question legislative motivation. On the other, it has said that where there is clear proof of a religious motivation, it will invalidate the resulting legislation. Justices Rehnquist and Scalia have written scathing criticisms of this rule, but it remains the law. Justice O'Connor has defended it, pointing to the importance in a secular democracy of government legislating for secular reasons only.

Although there are good reasons for rejecting the secular citizenship rule, there are also good reasons for imposing one. We would err greatly in not accounting for these reasons in ordering communal behavior.

Advocates of only a private role for religion rightly insist that for a liberal democracy to function effectively there must be the possibility of shared political and social language. Discussions of public policies must be equally accessible to all. An argument contesting which of two flatly contradictory things God said cannot be resolved in a secular democratic state. What God said cannot be debated in a meaningful way in a legislative body representing a religiously pluralistic community. Unless a community is prepared to allow itself to dissolve into separate faith communities, held together by only God knows what, we must forge a common identity, of necessity a secular identity.

The people who advocate a private role for religion are not necessarily bigoted. Few sanction, and most would and do protest, efforts to punish believers because of their beliefs. They may even be quite religious themselves. Still, the forced confinement of religion to purely private and intimate settings is inconsistent with liberal democracy, at least that much of it which depends on the existence of a private sector, in which citizens are free to put into place their own vision of the good life.

More important, religious views cannot easily be compromised, for religious arguments, reflecting absolute truths revealed (in Western religious thought) by God himself, do not lend themselves to resolution, debate, or compromise. Again, consider the intractable abortion debate. In over twenty-five years since *Roe v. Wade* we are about where we were the day after the decision was handed down. Relief is not on the horizon. The Republic can withstand one or two debates like those over abortion, but it could not survive many.

Abortion raises fundamental issues of morality, of the role and place of women, and the permissible role and scope of government. In a democracy, liberal or otherwise, there is no way to exclude such issues from public debate. As Professor Greenawalt of Columbia has persuasively argued, the arguments for choice are no more subject to scientific verification than those in opposition. But even with regard to abortion, it would be best if the arguments were, to the extent possible, cast in secular terms accessible to all. It is worth remembering—as pro-life advocates often do not—that protecting choice leaves women (and doctors) free to reject abortion, while a mandatory no-abortion rule enforces one moral vision on all. On the other hand, pro-choice advocates are equally prone to dismiss moral objections to abortion, and they run roughshod over those who regard abortion as some form of illicit killing.

Second, and here we refer to those issues which do not necessarily implicate direct government action (i.e., the discrimination in the rental of private housing, or discrimination by the Boy Scouts), we should not underestimate the impact on the equality norm which is essential, perhaps indispensable, for a liberal democracy. It has been only a generation, or at most two, since the elimination of the gross social inequalities that relegated certain religious groups—Catholics, Jews, and everyone not a Protestant—to de facto second-class status. The problem was not formal legal restrictions but private social and economic ones.

The Constitution prohibits religious tests for public office, and that proscription plainly applied to protect the candidacies of both Al Smith and John Kennedy. But success was by no means a sure thing for John Kennedy until he persuaded Protestants that the Republic would not collapse if the president were Catholic. It was denied to Al Smith at least in part because he did not make that case. The problem was social, not legal.

Jews and, to a lesser extent, Catholics at the end of World War II faced any number of social and economic restrictions—in employment, housing, education, and access to various social amenities. The demise of those restrictions, both by act of law and, more important, and earlier, by changes in social thought, have greatly empowered the Jewish and Catholic communities. That occurred not only because government is more active in protecting civil rights but also because religion is less salient in important social and economic institutions.

The restrictions the Boy Scouts impose do not look terribly threatening. But would we feel the same way if those restrictions were race-based? What if it were not just the Boy Scouts which imposed religion-based restrictions? Does it matter if the restriction is limited to a belief in God? What if the Boy Scouts insisted on an acceptance of Christian, Muslim, or Jewish beliefs?

On the other hand, it must be acknowledged that some "secular" decisionmakers regard religiously constituted communities as particularly dangerous. Thus, at least one court has allowed racial boycotts of merchants but not religious ones. It is hard to explain the decision on any ground but an unreasoned fear of organized expression of religious power.

A third objection to a public role for religion is that in a diverse society there is no religion which predominates to the point where it is acceptable to impose any religious view on everyone. Although this is a matter of principle, it is also a question of prudence. Religious leaders and religious believers often generally tend to greatly undervalue the resentment felt by other believers or nonbelievers when they are compelled—or believed they are compelled—to observe the religious views of others. Although this is most plainly true when government compels "observance," it is not much mitigated when the compulsion comes from other important social institutions.

A fourth objection to religious intervention in public affairs, particularly political affairs, is that religious folk are thought to defer to religious leaders, to the point at which they are not exercising independent judgment, and that those religious leaders get far more than "one" vote.

This argument is singularly unpersuasive. There are relatively small numbers of believers in the United States who blindly follow their religious leaders' dictates. When Rush Limbaugh, Jerry Springer, Oprah Winfrey, and Matt Drudge command a high level of loyalty from mass audiences, and politicians actively solicit endorsements from Hollywood or athletic celebrities, one is hard pressed to defend a rule against listening to religious leaders.

Finally, in a democracy it is difficult to accept the legitimacy of any a priori restriction on what or whom a citizen may base his or her vote. Still, both because they often do not have the expertise, and because ex cathedra religious endorsements smack of imposed religion, it is wisest if religious leaders refrain from them.

This author does not feel the need for a permanent, overarching, theoretically complete answer to these questions. By and large, the situation in the United States is healthy. The following principles could be laid down for the United States:

1. Government may not use religion (including atheism) as a constitutive device for holding society together. Religion, or its absence, cannot be used as a prerequisite for citizenship, exercise of the franchise, or government benefits.
2. Private groups may use religion as a constitutive device, even beyond the confines of the house of worship, so long as such discrimination does not, in either the individual

case or in gross, threaten the creation of religious castes. In judging whether a particular private discrimination is acceptable, we must assume neither that any discrimination threatens secular democracy nor that religious liberty cannot ever be bounded by civic needs. We must keep firmly in mind that the creation of unregulated private space is an affirmative value in a liberal democracy.

3. Government may not coerce the doing of religious acts, nor should it restrain—barring some compelling reason—private performance of religious acts.

4. There should be a strong prejudice against making religion the organizing principle of political or governmental life. It is for this reason that the Hassidic school district in Kiryas Joel, New York, was so objectionable. As a practical matter, it makes religion the central organizing principle of political life, albeit on a small scale, and in a good cause.

5. Religious groups should, as a matter of prudence, refrain from advancing purely religious arguments for governmental action, but they are legally free to do so.

6. The frequently expressed view that religion is a matter of individual belief must be understood as having either a basis in a desire to limit the role of religion, often itself rooted in a denial of the possibility of ascertaining religious truth, and/or in a somewhat distorted form of Protestant piety, emphasizing belief, not action. To the extent that it stems from the latter, it is surely not consonant with much of the Jewish tradition and assuredly not with the Catholic tradition, both of which accept the use of compulsion to enforce religious norms and emphasize the importance of group adherence to religious norms. Neither of the latter groups (and Islam appears to fit here as well) accept the prevailing (Protestant) individualistic view of the role of faith.

There are two distinct but overlapping points here; one, the creation of religious communities, and the other, the question of state enforcement of moral norms. We have no social consensus on whether the state has any role to play in enforcing purely moral norms. Plainly, this is part of the debate over abortion, adultery, and gay rights.

But what of the intrusion of religious communities in the public sphere? This seems to be the hardest question we face. It encompasses the Missouri school district that would not facilitate social dances, the wearing of head scarves in public schools, and the closing of streets in religious neighborhoods.

Considering again abortion, one of the current disputes involves the right of those who object to the practice to refrain from performing, assisting, advising, or subsidizing abortion. Pro-choice groups concede that no individual can be compelled to participate in an abortion. Grudgingly, if at all, they concede that religious hospitals cannot be forced to provide abortions—how they ask, can an institution have a conscience?

But they are completely unwilling to concede that a Catholic employer should have the right to refuse to pay for health insurance coverage. This, they say, is forcing the employer's belief on the employee. It eludes them that forcing the coverage of abortion forces the employee's religious faith on the employer. (Note that the employers are not claiming the right to fire an employee who has an abortion.)

It may be that compelling employers to provide insurance covering abortion or contraception is a just result, or the most just possible result, but it is not because the employer has no claim at all. The fact that pro-choice groups simply miss the point is reflective of an individualistic understanding of religion, one which grants no legitimate social or corporate role to public, nongovernmental religion.

On the other hand, it is not clear that we would allow religious groups with substantial economic power to use that power to impose religious views on others. Too much of that, and the autonomy and equality which are essential for a liberal democracy are destroyed.

7. Those who favor a greater role for public religion sometimes do so because they conceive of the world in monochromatic fashion—there is religion and there is anti-religion. Their world outlook leaves no room for secular society, which neither favors nor limits religion. This view is inconsistent with liberal democracy, for it leaves no room for a secular—not secularist, but secular—government.

Our society could not withstand too many efforts to insist on communal religious observance, at least where these observances impact on others. As difficult as it is, and at a substantial price for religious believers, religious groups in a modern democracy should be chary of insisting on creating religious communities which will impact on the broader community.

As a theoretical matter, whether such communities are, as a matter of principle, wholly incompatible with liberal democracy is far more doubtful. One cannot conceive of a truly liberal democracy which does not tolerate such communities, but that does not mean that if too many such communities exist, and touch on too many areas of life, the common ground essential to a well-functioning liberal democracy will cease to exist.

The content of liberal democracy was not handed down to Moses at Sinai. Those who challenge the toleration of private, but not public, religious communities at the level of principle should remember that the people can alter the principles of democracy at any time. If "liberals" push too hard, the terms of the social compact can be rewritten. The result may violate every theoretical description of liberal democracy, but it would be politically and legally unassailable.

III

Different elements of the American Jewish community can be found supporting either the privatization of religion or protesting any limitation on religious involvement in the public square. Historically, the community has tended to favor confining religion to purely private activity. In part, this is a reaction to the oppression that Jews associated with Old World partnerships of government and religion. It is more a visceral reaction than a philosophically grounded one. History can be a powerful and wise teacher, so this position should not be dismissed merely because it lacks theoretical grounding. The fear American Jews have of a Christianizing America, a fear out of all proportion to its possibility, reflects this historically grounded reaction.

Several recent studies indicate that Jews are formally religious in far lower numbers than almost any other major faith group. They are thus proportionately more likely than most to be suspicious of the intensive religions which seek actively to impose themselves on the world, either through active involvement in politics or through domination of public institutions. Thus, many Jewish organizations have paid only scant attention to free exercise claims, and they have devoted even less in the way of resources to these problems compared to the considerable efforts deployed on nonestablishment issues. When free exercise of rights comes into conflict with cherished secular egalitarian values (abortion, civil rights), these people inevitably denigrate free exercise concerns.

Some of the debate over these issues in the United States reflects a spillover from the debates in Israel over the roles of religion and state. In recent years non-Orthodox groups in the United States have tended to be even more separationist than previously, an apparent reaction to the refusal of the Orthodox establishment to recognize non-Orthodox movements.

On the other side are interesting combinations of neo-conservatives and Orthodox Jews. Both urge the desirability of greater religious involvement with political and public life, albeit not always for the same reason. The neo-conservatives seem motivated by the idea that increased religious involvement in public affairs will lead to less social deviance, an empirical proposition not sustained by proof. The Orthodox community is reacting to what it perceives as an increasing secularization of society, one which makes it and its religious framework—a framework which is largely communal and not individualistic—for approaching many of life's questions socially marginal, or even impossible.

In analyzing these differences, one may not ignore their theological dimension. Those who emphasize the importance of individual religious experience and judgment, and the mutability of religious teaching, are more likely to challenge the state's efforts to ensconce a theological vision into law. Those who believe in a revealed "immutable" Torah, with demands directed to the community as well as to the individual, will not share that opposition; indeed, they are likely to view it as rejecting their worldview.

Finally, one should also not overexaggerate the practical extent of these differences. The Reform movement is associated in the public mind with limiting the role of religion in public life. Yet both at the national level (in the form of its Religious Action Center), and at the congregational level, it takes an active role in advancing religious positions on a wide range of public issues. The Orthodox community, which is theoretically wed to a more activist stance, is often passive and silent on public issues not of direct interest to it.

Notes

1. Less universally accepted are other aspects of the American church-state arrangement, notably our notion that the state cannot evenhandedly subsidize religious activity. This idea has not been accepted outside the United States. In the United States, it is today under attack. The univer-

sally accepted principle of evenhandedness requires that subsidies be generally available, a provision that has caused some difficulty in Canada and Western Europe. Still, it cannot be said that the availability of subsidies has led to religious persecution. Whether subsidized churches are and will remain as free as unsubsidized ones remains to be seen.

2. Legal theorists, both right and left, have attempted recently to forge a "communitarian" vision of liberal democracy. On the right, the motivation is greater social control of "deviancy" (i.e., premarital sex, drugs, etc.) and on the left, largely to provide a more solid grounding for affirmative action and antipoverty programs.

Part III

Political Dimensions

6

Jewish Activism in the Washington "Square": An Analysis and Prognosis

Marshall J. Breger

Jewish history is replete with recourse to the *shtadlan* or "intercessor"—a high-level intermediary, often a businessman, who in the period prior to "emancipation" ran interference with kings and potentates on behalf of the Jewish community.[1] The *shtadlan*'s influence with European rulers was personal and his focus (and it was inevitably a he) was on individual cases, and rarely on general rules of law.[2]

Jewish groups in Washington today continue to do a great deal of the *shtadlan*'s work, both in terms of individual case-handling and facilitating individual grants and contracts. The case servicing of grant and regulatory problems of yeshivas and Orthodox community organizations by Agudath Israel is a good modern-day example of *shtadlanut*.

These groups also focus on a form of postemancipation Jewish politics "informed by the liberal politics of individual rights."[3] This approach concerns itself with the protection of the civil and political rights of individual Jews. Thus, Jewish organizations in both Washington and New York have long supported the claims of individual Jews who sought to be free of discrimination in housing, employment, and in the provision of government services. The 1960s saw

the disintegration of this approach "due to the impact of ethnic pluralism, whose two main features were the legitimation of claims
upon American society in group terms and the use of public and
militant ethnic assertiveness."[4]

Not surprisingly, then, recent years have seen the growth of a
different kind of Jewish representation in the Washington public
square. Such an approach is less personal and less focused on individual requests and more attuned to public policy issues, both those
obviously of concern to the Jewish community and those less so.

This chapter will consider the internal dynamics of Jewish public
policy organizations in Washington, describing the various players
in the Jewish community who purport to represent Jewish leadership
in the national political arena. It will consider a number of issues
including the Jewish groups in the Washington political arena, the
reality of Jewish liberalism, the question of Jewish unity, the prolif-
eration of Jewish issues, the problem of coalitions, and the problem
of priorities. It will close with some ruminations about the future of
Jewish political power in the nation's capital.

Who Are the Jewish Groups Who Play in the Washington Political Area?

Historically, the nexus of Jewish political life in America was New
York City because, after all, that is where the Jews are most concentrated. Thus, the Conference of Presidents of Major American Jewish Organizations, created to be the main address for Jewish groups
in their representations before the U.S. government, is based in New
York. So are the three so-called defense agencies: the American
Jewish Congress, the American Jewish Committee, and the Anti-
Defamation League. So is the central address for Jewish community
fund-raising, the United Jewish Communities (the Federation
movement), and the lead office of the local community relations'
agencies, the Jewish Council on Public Affairs (JCPA, formerly
known as NJCRAC). There are also the Zionist groups, from the
Zionist Organization of America (ZOA) to the American Zionist
Movement (AZM), all arguing American public policy with their
eyes eastward, all firmly attached to New York.

For many years the only membership organization centered in
Washington, D.C., was B'nai B'rith, because "its membership
strength lay in the Midwest and South," not the urban northeast.[5]
The Jewish groups with Washington headquarters, as opposed to

Washington offices, were those whose very purpose was focused on the federal public square. Their focus, in one way or another, is the federal government. Indeed, they are viewed as inside the beltway habitués. Prominent among these is AIPAC—the American Israel Public Affairs Committee, which has been called by *Fortune* magazine the second most powerful lobby in Washington.[6] Others with headquarters in Washington include the National Conference on Soviet Jewry (NCSJ) and smaller groups like the Jewish Institute for National Security Affairs (JINSA).

Numerous other organizations play in the Washington public square by opening government affairs offices to stake their places. Groups with Washington offices include the three defense agencies—the Anti-Defamation League, the American Jewish Committee, and the American Jewish Congress—JCPA, and the United Jewish Communities. While these are branch offices only, to a growing extent the Washington perspective often impacts on headquarters' decisionmaking. This reflects the increasing impact of the federal government on Jewish communal affairs. It reflects as well the extent to which Jewish communal organizations have become lobbyists in the Washington arena.

A more recent development has been the growth of religious organizations in the public policy arena. The Reform movement's Religious Action Center (RAC) first opened a Washington office over twenty-five years ago. Led by the charismatic Rabbi David Saperstein, RAC covers the waterfront with a wide social justice agenda. It maintains key organizational links with women's and civil rights organizations, Saperstein being one of the two Jewish leaders serving on the board of the umbrella Leadership Conference for Civil Rights. More recently, the *haredi* Agudath Israel opened a Washington office led by Abba Cohen. As noted earlier, Cohen's focus has been servicing the needs of yeshivas and other Orthodox institutions in their interfacing with government regulators. He may be found as often negotiating with mid-level Department of Education officials regarding the interpretation of regulations as writing op-eds or traversing the halls of Congress.[7]

Other religious groups have heeded the capital's siren song. The Orthodox Union's Institute of Public Affairs recently opened a Washington office. Their agenda is more focused on issues of concern to the Orthodox community. The Conservative movement has talked about opening an office and is, at this moment, in the process of doing so. Until that is finalized, most of their Washington work will still come out of their government affairs office in New York.

Further, a number of Jewish women's groups also maintain an outpost in the nation's capital. Hadassah keeps a presence as does the National Council of Jewish Women (NCJW). While these groups man the barricades for the general run of Jewish issues, they take leadership positions on women's issues, particularly those surrounding a woman's freedom of choice.

Finally, Jewish groups in Washington have specifically organized around the political process. The National Jewish Coalition was founded in 1985 as a home for politically conservative Jews close to the Republican Party. It specifically abjured the Republican label, however, fearing that institutional identification with the GOP would scare off otherwise ideologically compatible adherents. The distinction proved artificial and, by 1999, the organization changed its name to the Republican Jewish Coalition (RJC) and became an autonomous yet interconnected part of the party's outreach efforts. Indeed, much of its attractiveness to new members comes from its connection with the organized Republican Party institutions.[8]

For its part, the Democrats only created an analogous organization in 1990. The National Jewish Democratic Coalition (NJDC), as it was styled, contains as members most of the major contributors to the Democratic National Committee. As such, its relevance and impact on the Washington public square is problematic. After all, the Democratic Party itself is so heavily engaged with matters Jewish, one more internal pressure group will likely make little impact.

Undergirding Jewish legislative advocacy efforts is the notion of Jewish power, which is usually understood as Jewish money. There are at least seventy-five political action committees (PACs) organized to contribute money to elect officials who support Israel. This does not include individual contributors ($1,000 per person per primary and general election), whose donations can often be bundled and delivered by an identifiably Jewish source.[9] The combined contributions of Jewish money donated through Jewish PACs and individuals in the 2000 election totaled just shy of $5 million.[10]

One ritual device of the Washington scene—used by both Jewish PACs and communal organizations—is the ubiquitous Washington mission. These missions bring large dollar contributors to Washington and set up briefings with executive branch officials as well as with members of Congress. The missions allow the Jewish organizations to wave the flag and display their clout to their members and contributors. At the same time these meetings allow major contributors to press the flesh of members of Congress. One perennial highlight of the Washington mission is the congressional lunch, held in a Senate or House hearing room, where large numbers of congressmen and senators line up to thank the organization for their support or contributions and swear fealty to Jewish causes, especially Israel. Organizations compete for the number of members they can muster for these "grip and grope" sessions. The missions serve as a way of attracting high-roller contributors by displaying the PAC's political clout.

Jewish money is clearly a bipartisan affair. Commentators suggest that the four pillars of financial support for the Democrats are trial lawyers, Hollywood, labor unions, and Jews (and these often overlap). J. J. Goldberg, author of *Jewish Power*, has noted that Jewish money is believed to account for roughly half the funding of the Democratic National Committee and about half of the funding for the Democratic presidential campaign.[11] Republican Jews have suggested that they provide up to a third of the party's financial contributions. While this claim is likely exaggerated, the dollar figures are no doubt substantial. Indeed, much of the fund-raising leadership of the party is Jewish. In the 2000 election cycle, Republican Jewish Coalition lenders served as party finance chairs in nine states. The three most important Republican Jewish fund-raisers during this period were RJC members—Mel Sembler, finance chair of the Republican National Committee (RNC) (who raised over $484 million during his tenure), Stu Bernstein, cochair of Team 100, and Eric Javits, co-chair of the Republican Eagles. In fact, Jews constituted 15 percent of the Republican Eagles.

Tensions often exist between the Washington-based groups and their New York confreres. The New York groups tend to be membership-based organizations and believe that, as a result, they have more legitimacy and should have the right to, in some sense, set communal policy. At the same time, the New York groups fear that the Washington advocacy groups, most of which lack a membership base, nonetheless, as single-interest groups, wield an inordinate amount of power. Historically, AIPAC and NCSJ were created, in part, to service the New York groups. When AIPAC sought to set up regional offices in cities like San Francisco, Tucson, and New York, the New York groups strenuously (albeit unsuccessfully) opposed this move, fearing that this might justify the Washington groups following their own policy inclinations. Indeed, many Jewish professionals fear that is what has happened to AIPAC. But this concern has been vitiated by its startling success.

Similarly, when the predecessor organization of the JCPA, the National Jewish Community Relations Advisory Council (NJCRAC), announced the establishment of a Washington office in 1997, the plan met with resistance from Jewish defense agencies suggesting that at a time when the Jewish community "should be trying to concentrate resources, this seems to be moving in the opposite direction."[12] After much debate, the NJCRAC Washington office "pledged not to engage in activities on Capitol Hill without prior agreement with the defense agencies."[13]

Those Jewish groups without Washington offices do not ignore the axiom, "render to Caesar the things that are Caesar's and to God the things that are God's." Numerous rabbinical delegations from all four Jewish denominations travel to Washington regularly. The United Jewish Communities has an active Washington mission program that at one time was the single largest group visitor to the White House for briefings. It is hard, however, to be a player if you are coming down once a week on the Delta shuttle and have no one on hand to do "set ups" for you.

The activities of a Washington office are varied and in many ways not much different from traditional trade associations. There is a significant amount of reporting (usually by junior staff) of what went on at congressional hearings. This monitoring function provides data to be disseminated both to New York and to the grassroots. There is the servicing or case handling function alluded to earlier by which Washington reps run interference with government agencies on behalf of Jewish community clients. There is the servicing of volunteer leaders, often a high maintenance activity.

Finally, there is the time-consuming lobbying function in which community representatives work an issue. This can include bill comment and, in some cases, bill drafting as well as coalition-building, both public and private.

The most important aspect of the Washington reps working an issue is, in an ironic sense, just being there. As Nathan Diament, head of the OU's Institute for Policy Analysis, has said, "What is most important is exposure to the Congressman or Senator. Through me, he learns about the OU and hopefully gets a comfort level about the organization."[14] Thus, Diament touches base with those senators key to the OU's domestic agenda at least every other week, not only providing the OU message but also looking to see "what I can do for you." The other Washington reps do the same, for propinquity is often the source of power inside the beltway.

We must remember that the Washington office tends to be legislatively driven, its work program is infused by legislative priorities. It operates in fast, perhaps more fruitful, fashion. Indeed, one Jewish Washington rep suggested that her office operates in campaign mode. As such, it is often pragmatic (some would say realistic) in its approach. The New York (or central) office tends to be policy-driven, it looks toward the big picture; indeed, it tries to place the Jewish interest within the framework of general public policy.

To What Extent Do the Jewish Groups Cooperate?

How do these myriad entities work together, or do they? One historic meeting ground was a "First Tuesday" meeting of Jewish representatives to discuss common issues. When these sessions were called by lobbyist giants like Hyman Bookbinder in the 1970s and 1980s, "First Tuesday" was a meeting ground of some significance. This was particularly the case in the 1970s when AIPAC, lacking its own internal lobbying capacity, relied in large measure on the Jewish organizations for its lobbying clout. By the 1980s, however, AIPAC had bulked up its internal lobbying capacity and their participation became more desultory. Over time the meetings diminished in importance, and when they occur, they are attended in the main by juniors, if not interns. Rabbi David Saperstein of the Religious Action Center tries to bring all the principals into one room at least once a year but time does not always allow for it. More recently, Riva Price of the JCPA has called such meetings to order but on a sporadic basis only.

The Joint Policy Plan of the JCPA is an annual statement of the broad common denominator of Jewish communal concerns. It reflects a substantive agenda, however, and there is no one annual program or publication which sets the tactical agenda or shells out lobby tasks. Rather, there are overlapping reference points that allow Jewish professionals to know what is going on. Sometimes one gets a "heads up" from a colleague. Information often flows informally. The winter *mincha minyan* at the Agudath Israel offices, for example, allows Orthodox professionals to trade the latest Hill information without a formal meeting. As a result, the Jewish groups often receive tactical information from local sources rather than from their headquarter offices. This is but one additional piece of evidence for the shift of Jewish communal decisionmaking ever so slightly to D.C.

Jewish groups tend to belong to specific coalitions in which they are interested, such as the immigration coalition or the Leadership Conference on Civil Rights. Often these are ad hoc groups that assemble based on specific bills such as the charitable choice coalition. These coalitions often call weekly, if not daily, meetings when in the middle of a legislative struggle.

On the conservative side, the Republican Jewish Coalition convenes two semiregular meetings, one on domestic policy and one on foreign policy. The meetings are held in conjunction with the Senate Republican Conference whose chair in 2001, Rick Santorum (R-Pa.) was charged with ethnic outreach. The domestic group includes the OU, Agudath Israel, RJC, United Jewish Communities, and the American Jewish Committee. The foreign policy group is more inclusive, including Agudath Israel, Americans for a Safe Israel, AJC, B'nai B'rith, AIPAC, ZOA, JCPA, JINSA, NCSJ, and the National Unity Coalition for Israel.[15]

The Goal of Communal Unity

One feature of Jews in politics that stands in sharp contrast to Jewish communal life generally is the high premium placed on communal unity in the political sphere. This communal obsession with unity has been very successful in the past. But this unity has not come about because of Jewish skill in political tactics or strategy. It has come about because of the existence of a real singleness of purpose.

The politics of power requires internal discipline in agenda-setting. In large measure, Jewish strength comes from Jewish unity. The member of Congress who believes that Jews everywhere will hate him forever if he votes against foreign aid exemplifies this. Rightly or wrongly, most non-Jewish congressmen expect that there exists a Jewish point of view.[16]

Historians will differ on the actual extent of unity within the Jewish community. With the hindsight of nostalgia, stippled realities have turned into softer hues. Just as all Jews remember their ancestors in "the old country" as rabbis, so all immigrants inhabited Irving Howe's "World of Our Fathers."[17] The recalibration of memory aside, the rite of passage for the Jewish immigrant generation was remarkably similar. As American Jews learned English, entered trades, and moved from the working to the middle class, their group interests were largely similar, and their politics were as well. By the New Deal, American Jews were a basic part of the Roosevelt coalition. That a common experience should lead to a homogeneous political perspective ought not to surprise us.

This is not the place to discourse on the relationship between American Jews and political liberalism. Suffice it to say that the wellsprings run both wide and deep.[18] While the numbers today are not so commanding as in the past, it is clear that the bulk of American Jews still resonate (and self-identify) with the appellation: "liberal."[19] Thus, it should be no surprise that the Jewish public square in Washington is largely a liberal square. Indeed, it would be odd if it were not. Any analysis of Jewish political activity in Washington must start from this reality. The Jewish community's closest ties are with the liberal Democrats, the congressmen who keep a spare yarmulke in their pocket just in case. The community's nascent relationship with the Republican right, whether based on support for Israel or other reasons, is still too young for the fruit it may bear to be appropriately graded.

On most domestic issues, the Jewish communal representatives in Washington speak as one. OU and RAC have worked together on gun control issues such as the gun show loophole, and on cloning issues. Recent years, however, have seen a falling away in homogeneity in the American Jewish community. In some measure this reflects the level of acceptance of Jews within American society. The need for unity as a protective device is simply less. Two areas where this falling off has been most marked have been in social issues, especially the issue of aid to parochial schools, and approaches toward Israel.

Aid to Parochial Schools and the Orthodox Community

It is no surprise that the Orthodox community has found itself in a kind of structural dissent in the Jewish community regarding aid to parochial schools. The Orthodox are committed to day school education and self-tax themselves considerably for this purpose. Thus, this is far more than an abstract issue of principle for the Orthodox but rather a pocketbook issue of great significance.

Since the 1960s, when the issue of aid to "parochial schools" first surfaced as a debate over tax credits or parochaid, it was accepted that the Orthodox would provide a minority report on Jewish community proposals regarding aid to parochial schools. They would do so "religiously" at every NJCRAC meeting, but traditionally that dissent was sotto voce and had little effect on Jewish communal positions regarding aid to parochial schools.

More recently, however, with the increased political strength of the Orthodox community, the divisions have pierced the myths of communal unity on church-state matters. The OU and Agudath Israel regularly testify on legislation promoting aid to parochial schools and charitable choice, while the "big three" defense agencies testify on the opposite side. When it comes to the social issues broadly defined, conservatives have their Jews and liberals theirs.[20] There is little pretense of Jewish unity on issues like school vouchers, abortion rights, or charitable choice.

Israel Issues

Before World War II the Jewish community was of two minds on Zionism. The established Jewish groups, including the Reform movement and the American Jewish Committee, were clearly anti-Zionist, as were many Orthodox. Only with the end of World War II and the recognition of the catastrophe that had befallen the Jewish people did the community's support for a Jewish state coalesce. Even here support was modest until the Six-Day War. After 1967, the Jewish community was fully unified in its support for Israel, right or wrong (and it could do no wrong).

Today, however (writing from the vantage point of spring 2001), unity in the American Jewish community on the issue of the peace process just does not exist. A poll by the American Jewish Committee taken before the Rabin assassination showed that 68 percent of American Jews supported the peace process—a drop from 84 percent at the time of the mythic Arafat-Rabin handshake. Far more important, however, 64 percent of the Orthodox in America opposed the direction of the peace talks. Indeed, the February 2001 poll (four months into the "Al-Aksa intifada") found that 53 percent of American Jews strongly support the peace process,[21] and 33 percent were prepared to divide Jerusalem for peace.[22] Given these numbers, it is hard for any side in the Israel political system to claim that there is unity among American Jewry.

True, the Conference of Presidents of Major American Jewish Organizations and other Jewish groups have long sought to mandate a single political line in the Jewish community (given the plethora of Jewish organizations, one could never envision a single political voice). But in the past, except for short periods of time, there had been a broad consensus of support among American Jews for policies of the government of Israel, whether those of Golda Meir or Menachem Begin.

As the American Jewish consensus on Israel has broken down, umbrella organizations sought frantically to shore up the facade of unity. But the differences were deep and often moved from the political to the personal. In 1997 Mort Klein, the feisty head of the Zionist Organization of America (ZOA), attacked the ADL for inviting *New York Times* columnist Thomas Friedman to speak at their 1997 West Coast dinner.[23] ADL president Abe Foxman rose to Friedman's defense, calling Klein an "attack dog of the thought police."[24] Foxman, in turn, was admonished by the President's Conference for his use of intemperate language.

Klein himself had been censured by the Presidents Conference a year earlier for what many viewed as a call to boycott a 1996 pro-Israel rally after Prime Minister Rabin's assassination.[25]

A little over a year later the Presidents Conference drafted regulations that "imposed limitations" on members' dissent from conference policy (a sure sign of organizational disarray), noting that "no Member of the Conference may, expressly or by nuance, demean or denigrate consensus statements of the conference."[26] As one might expect, this effort at preserving "symbolic" unity did little to resolve the deep divisions within the Conference.

Given this history, resuscitating a united Jewish consensus over Israel will prove a daunting and perhaps impossible task.[27] The current violence in the Middle East has covered up many of these differences, however, as the Jewish groups in Washington and elsewhere seek once again to create a united front of support for Israel.

Israeli Actors in Washington

The challenge of seeking unity regarding Israel is made even more complex by the increasing tendency of the minority parties in the Israeli government to send emissaries of their own directly to Congress. It means that Israelis are criticizing the Israeli government to American officials. This, of course, undercuts the unity message from the source.

The phenomenon first surfaced in 1991 when American Friends of Peace Now brought a delegation of Labor and left-wing members of Knesset to Washington for the express purpose of meeting with American officials to "lobby" for continued use of pressure on Prime Minister Shamir in favor of "land for peace"[28] and to urge the

George H. W. Bush administration to withhold U.S. aid money to
Israel that might be used for settlement activity.[29] This, of course,
was at a time when Prime Minister Shamir was expanding West
Bank and Gaza settlements. It grew more explicit during the Rabin
years when the Likud "gang of three" offered up a "Team B" analysis of the Arab-Israeli conflict on a regular basis to American lawmakers. They opposed the possibility of an American presence as a
buffer force in the Golan Heights after a hoped for Syrian peace
deal, and they criticized the Palestinian Authority for a failed fight
against terrorism.[30]

Today, any hope that Israelis will keep their disputes at home is a
notion from a bygone era. Often in tandem with ZOA and other
right-wing Jewish groups, dissident MKs are paraded before Congress on a regular basis. At the same time, peace process support
groups like the Israel Policy Forum (IPF) bring pro-peace process
intellectuals and former government officials into the Washington
policy world.

The introduction of the Israeli element creates real problems for
Jews in the Washington public square. The premise of much American Jewish support for Israel is that such support is in America's
best interests. For Israelis to second-guess Americans about American interests places that premise under a cloud.

A relatively new institutional form has begun to be used to advance various conceptions of Jewish interests. This is the Washington policy think tank, an enterprise that attempts to wed academic
scholarship to public policy. Their goal is not basic research or objective analysis but to advance public policy positions associated
with the think tank's weltanschauung. As has been well discussed,
groups such as the Brookings Foundation, the American Enterprise
Institute, and the Heritage Foundation have become centers of influence in Washington. Specifically, foreign policy groups like the
Center for Strategic and Institutional Studies have also proliferated
and had similar impact. It should be no surprise that the Jewish
community joined the fray.

One Israel-oriented group that has had particular success in the
Washington policy world is the Washington Institute for Near-East
Policy (WINEP) founded in 1985 as a pro-Israel but not specifically
Jewish think tank. Its founders were largely AIPAC board members
led by Lawrence Weinberg of Los Angeles. Unlike AIPAC, the
Washington Institute is a nonprofit research center (rather than an
advocacy organization), but it has generally been viewed as a source
of quality scholarship with a pro-Israel flavor.

WINEP joined the Washington scene at an unusual moment. In the late 1980s and early 1990s there was a need for a place where moderate Arabs (including diplomats) could meet and talk with Jewish and Israeli officials informally. WINEP filled that function. Then, in the post-Oslo euphoria, it became a place where third track conversations could take place. The fact that Dennis Ross, President Clinton's special representative to the Middle East, and Martin Indyk, Clinton's assistant secretary of state for Near East Affairs, were former WINEP staff members helped undergird the notion that it spoke with quasi-official authority. WINEP's success has led other advocacy groups to develop policy centers in Washington. It is instructive that when the Israel Policy Forum, a center-left group of Jewish leaders formed to support the "peace process," set up a Washington office, it was styled the Washington Policy Center. While none would explicitly say so, one purpose of this center was to provide a counterweight to WINEP's increasingly "right-wing" analysis of the Arab-Israeli conflict. Among the Jewish think tanks in Washington is the Jewish Policy Center, a conservative think tank spawned and largely controlled by the Republican Jewish Coalition.

It is interesting that few Jewish domestic think tanks have been created in Washington. Perhaps this is because there is less consensus on the Jewish interest in domestic policy. More likely, however, this think tank function is undertaken in New York where, as already noted, the agencies take a longer view. For example, the American Jewish Committee includes institutes like the William Petschek National Jewish Family Center, and the American Jewish Congress has a National Commission for Women's Equality and its Commission on Law and Social Action (CLSA). The ADL conducts symposia and studies on hate crimes and church-state relations.

Does the Jewish Lobby Pursue Too Many Issues?

Some have criticized Jewish organizations for taking on too much when they extend their reach to non-Jewish issues. This problem surfaced in a rash of letters during spring 2000 between the New York and Chicago Jewish Community Relations Councils and the JCPA (the former NJCRAC). The New York letter charged JCPA with focusing on too many issues, many of which were not Jewish. The suggestion of issue promiscuity, as it were, reflected more than a debate over tactics. Those who supped at the larger table did so

because their view of the Jewish prophetic tradition required them
to enter the fray across the board. But this often meant taking up
cudgels for a wide variety of liberal causes including those with
only a seemingly tangential relationship to Jewish communal needs.

From a strictly *halakhic* perspective, the charge of issue promiscuity is difficult to sustain. It is hard to argue *halakhically* that in
the world of public policy there are non-Jewish issues. After all,
Jewish law has a view on the warp and woof of life's details ranging
from how you wash to the timing of sexual relationships. Furthermore, the doctrine of *da'at Torah*, which attributes expertise and
authority on all public issues to the rabbinic sages and is embraced
by some fervently traditional Jews, underscores this approach. If
there is a Jewish way to live privately, there is perhaps a Jewish
way to live in the public sphere. In that respect one cannot, as a
matter of principle, accept the view of the large Federations. Prudence, however, may suggest a different path.

Some might take umbrage that we label Jewish communal interests a "lobby," but on the American political scene that is what it
essentially is. A lobby has a finite amount of resources and, thus,
can promote only a finite number of agenda items. Taking, for example, something other than the Jewish agenda, some commentators
have pointed out that the current AFL-CIO agenda includes too
many political goals: striker replacement, unemployment insurance,
free trade, and more. Returning to the subject at hand, one cannot
move from loan guarantees to Cardinal Glemp without dissipating
one's strength, input, and impact. While politically, Jews should
have input on the exact contours of loan guarantees or hate crime
legislation, we would emphasize that they need not and should not
assume a similar role on a wide range of political issues, which are
often incorrectly classified as Jewish *moral* issues but do not directly affect the Jewish community.

This author can provide anecdotal but absolutely compelling
proof that the Jewish political agenda has been too broadly diversi-
fied, having once shepherded a group of Jewish leaders to their first
meeting with Don Regan, then president Reagan's chief-of-staff.
The meeting, planned for twenty minutes, was stretched to forty-
five. One subject dominated the discussion, a matter on which a
Senate or House vote was scheduled for the next day. As we left,
Don Regan turned to me and said, "I never knew that aid to dependent children was a Jewish issue." On whether it was or was not we
will not opine, but Regan walked away with the view that it was.
While somewhat dated, this example emphasizes that the Jewish
political agenda, as defined by NJCRAC and the various defense

committees, includes a laundry list of issues only marginally related to Jewish survival.

A review of the Agenda for Public Affairs (formerly the Joint Program Plan[31]) of the Jewish Council for Public Affairs (JCPA) for 2000-2001 suggests an exceedingly wide variety of issues to be addressed by the Jewish community. The Agenda (and its predecessor plans) include issues which all Jewish groups recognize as involving and/or protecting Jewish identity, such as Israel, Soviet Jewry, and domestic issues such as intergroup relations, anti-Semitism, and separation of church and state. However, there are items on the JCPA political agenda that are not so obviously related to Jewish communal interests, such as urban sprawl, the WTO, and global warming. We would even venture to say that the issue of abortion falls into this nonidentity category (although many Jewish groups classify it as an issue of religious freedom). It should be noted that the New York Federation in June 1999 chastised the JCPA as "out of touch," pointing to its opposition to school vouchers and support for affirmative action. The Federation further wondered "whether it is even appropriate for an organization to speak on behalf of the Jewish community on some of these issues."[32] Two months later the Chicago Federation sent a similar letter.[33] Although the local Jewish Community Relations Councils spiritedly defended their wide-ranging perspectives, the most recent JCPA meetings have focused on more traditional Jewish concerns.[34]

This author once believed that there was a surplus of Jewish organizations and that the chaotic situation in which each fell over the other to gain the attention of government officials and megadonors served to injure Jewish communal interests. Thus, he supported historical efforts to merge the three defense agencies as well as more recent (failed) discussions regarding the merger of the AJCommittee and AJCongress. This author still believes that there is a surplus of organizations, but he now considers that the inefficiency and cacophony may be positive. The more noise, the more result, notwithstanding the lack of institutional tidiness.

What Is a Jewish Issue?

The effort to ascertain what Jewish interests are requires a review of the changing ways Jews have understood themselves over the last century. The rise of ethnicity and cultural pluralism has added group interests to the panoply of so-called Jewish interests.[35] Furthermore,

different issues are often rediscovered—a cynic might say manufac-
tured—as Jewish issues. One such example is the environment, once
rarely considered a Jewish problem. In the 1990s, however, the
JCPA spun off a Jewish environmental coalition, the Coalition on
the Environment and Jewish Life (COEJL), that has done much to
foster a "greening" of the American Jewish Community.[36] Eco-
Shabbat seminars have been developed for synagogues, Jewish day
schools have added environmental modules, and Tu b'Shvat has become a resuscitated Jewish holiday. Rabbis and scholars have begun
to publish on the theme, often from a new age perspective.[37] With
this heightened Jewish sensitivity, it is understandable that Michael
Newmark, president of the JCPA in 1997, explained its support for a
strengthened Endangered Species Act in Jewish terms. It is our "ark
of choice" he stated, arguing, "Jewish tradition teaches that the protection of species is a moral act."[38]

The following four definitions may be useful to test public policy
positions from a specifically Jewish perspective.

Jewish Interests Are Matters That Affect Jews as a Group

In the nineteenth century, defining the Jewish agenda was rarely a
problem for Jewish political activists. The central Jewish political
issue was civil emancipation—the effort to eliminate political disabilities of Jews as a class. Issues included the right to vote, the
right to hold public office, and the right to own land. These status
disabilities were more easily susceptible to collective remedies.

In the twentieth century, the impetus shifted to assistance to dis-
tressed communities abroad and the removal of social and economic
discrimination at home. After World War II and the Nazi destruction of European Jewry, all of the major Jewish organizations saw
support for Israel as vital to Jewish communal survival. Efforts to
win freedom for Jews in the Soviet Union, Syria, and Ethiopia were
seen in similar terms. The recent use of racial quotas by U.S. government agencies in distributing government grants and contracts
has been seen as detrimental to Jews as a group, even by those organizations that support the ultimate goal of compensating for past
discrimination.

The defense of religious freedom has been a continuing concern
of Jewish defense organizations. In America the increased interpen-
etration of the public and private sectors in our century has made

this problem especially acute. In protecting religious freedom, government must at times promote specific practices or institutions that make religious expression possible. In the United States, government intervention has been used to require places of employment to protect the rights of Sabbath observers, to require nursing homes to make kosher food available, and to protect the rights of students at every level of education to worship or not to worship.

At times this presents difficult choices. In *Wilder vs. Sugarman*,[39] black children represented by the New York Civil Liberties Union attacked New York State's policy of permitting Jewish, Catholic, and Protestant children to be placed in foster families of the same religion through denominational family services. Since Jewish agencies provided high-quality services to primarily white Jewish children, the Civil Liberties Union claimed racial discrimination. Yet without the opportunity for a denominational focal point, the very raison d'etre of sectarian social services is undermined.

Jewish Interests Heed Jewish Law and Tradition

From the perspective of traditional Judaism, the only area in which rabbinic statements carry religious authority is when they are interpretations of *halakhah* (Jewish law). As noted above, it is very difficult to say that Jewish law should be limited to religious matters because it is not. Its scope includes guidance and even legal decisions on commercial matters as well as social and political issues. It is, therefore, difficult to say that Jewish law is not relevant to political decisionmaking.

From the perspective of Reform Judaism, the pursuit of social justice is a religious imperative that must be implemented by public policy. From this vantage point, Jews must take a Jewish position on the full range of social and economic policy issues.

Jewish Interests Promote the Self-Interest of Many Individual Jews

The fact that significant numbers of individual Jews may be affected by particular government policies may create a Jewish interest. Thus in the 1980s, the JCRC of New York lobbied in Washington to preserve the deductibility of state and local taxes from federal income taxation. Their justification was that since many Jews live in high tax areas, there was a Jewish interest in maintaining the current system of deductions, which gave an advantage to large urban states with a significant state income tax (where Jews just happen disproportionately to live). Similarly, Jewish organizations would lobby to maintain current levels of student aid since a high percentage of Jews go to college, and would support an increase in federal urban grants since many Jews are city-dwellers. They would make these representations not as members of the public, nor as city-dwellers, but as guardians of the Jewish interest. Though these matters affect large numbers of Jews, they are not uniquely Jewish issues. They affect the economic well-being of individual Jews and thus have an indirect impact on the financial strength of communal institutions.

Jewish Interests Are What Jewish Leaders Say They Are

From a religious perspective this classification is self-evident. Jews seek, or at least ought to seek, the guidance of Torah in determining their public affairs. Even from a secular perspective, reliance on the insights of the *shtadlan* makes eminent sense—the *shtadlan* is the expert in what is possible for Jews in the public sphere.

This approach has been incisively criticized by J. J. Goldberg who complains that American Jewish decisionmaking is undemocratic, depending in the views of *machers* (influential people) or successful businessman rather than intense popular participation. Goldberg's palliative, however, a greater local involvement by *amcha*, the general Jewish population,[40] is not likely to come to pass.

E Pluribus Unum?

It is worth considering the approach by which Jewish groups relate to the political process in Washington. At one level they articulate arguments that their goals are in the public interest, for example, AIPAC's continual refrain that support for Israel is in America's interest. At the same time, many Jewish goals, particularly among the ultra-Orthodox, are really another species of, as it were, pork by which the Jewish groups, like corporate lobbyists, seek to sup at the public trough. The ill-fated effort of Senator Inouye (D-Hawaii) to use American funds to subsidize Sephardic religious schools in

France is but one prime example.[41] The continual efforts of New York State to create a special school district for Hasidic Jews in Kiryas Joel may be another.[42]

In the main, Jewish expression in the public square has tended to be an affirmation of political pluralism in its classic form, reflecting the views of political scientists like Arthur Bentley who suggest that "[t]he phenomena of government are from start to finish phenomena of [pressure]. . . . Pressure . . . is always a group phenomenon. It indicates the push and resistance between groups. The balance of the group pressures is the existing state of society."[43] On this view politics is little more than the process of interest groups "struggl[ing] for a shot at using the fulcrum of the state."[44] In turn, the interests of the state are nothing more than "a reflex of an adjustment of power groups."[45]

This is particularly true for single-issue defense organizations like AIPAC that specifically claim interest group pluralism as the American way and define democracy as the aggregation and reconciliation of the projected power of interest groups in the political arena. What these organizations do is identify the Jewish good with the public good. Whether this description of democratic pluralism is empirically correct or not, it undercuts normative efforts to apprehend our democratic institutions through the lens of civic republicanism[46] or other forms of public interest analysis. Given the Jewish community's strongly held position that its goals are in the American public interest there is no little irony in their largely successful effort to become one of the nation's premier "special" interest groups.

Speaking for Jewish Self-Interest

When individuals or groups claim to speak for the Jewish community, they may be making a number of different claims. They may be claiming to speak in the self-interest of the Jewish community, along the lines of what piece of the pie the Jewish community will or should have. For example, when the Anti-Defamation League supported the Reagan administration's decision to classify Hasidic Jews as "socially and economically disadvantaged," thus rendering them "automatically eligible for management aid and technical assistance from the Commerce Department's ever friendly Minority Business Development Agency (MBDA),[47] it was speaking not out of religious motives but out of Jewish self-interest. It is arguing that if other groups are going to get special privileges, why should not the Jewish poor?[48] Similarly, the Jewish position on quotas and affirmative action is, in some measure, one of self-interest. Because they have a long legacy of having suffered from quotas, it is natural for Jews to fear that the new breed of quotas—those carrying "benign intent"—will affect them adversely. This is especially true for Jews in civil service and public education, where the merit system, while often imperfect in implementation, has protected minorities from the ravages of discrimination and the arbitrary use of discretion.

They also may be claiming that the promotion of universal liberal concerns has been good for the Jews, that the fate of the Jews is indissolubly bound with the fate of liberalism. In this view, then, it is in the long-term self-interest of the Jews to have universal concerns rather than to focus on narrow, particularistic concerns. There is much historical support for this view. In the nineteenth century, those groups that wanted to grant full citizenship to the Jews and bring them into the wider community were generally from the liberal side of the political spectrum. Those who opposed emancipation for the Jews came mainly from the conservative parties. In the twentieth century, conservative parties (often blinded by their anti-Bolshevism) were generally the last to understand the threat of Hitler to Western values. Is it surprising to find that since the Enlightenment, Jews have been liberal, both in politics and in culture?[49]

Carl Perlstone, a former ADL board member, describes one allegation of such a conflation of categories. In the past, Perlstone tells us, "the ADL mission was defined on a banner frequently displayed at the front of our meetings . . . to stop the defamation of the Jewish people and serve justice and fair treatment to all citizens alike." Recently, he tells us he saw a supplemental banner at an ADL function proclaiming that ADL was "dedicated to translating democratic ideals into a way of life for all Americans in our time."[50] This shift in arguable mission reflects the growth of the universalist approach.

Speaking for Jewish Tradition

A second kind of claim that one speaks for the Jews is a claim that one speaks for Jewish tradition. For most Jews, this claim depends on the weight one gives to the institutional body or the rabbi making the pronouncement. In a hasidic community, for example, where the rabbi is revered as wise in all things, his pronouncements on morality would be attended to very carefully. In other religious contexts, while the rabbi may be listened to as an informed, if not revered, figure, his views will, perforce, lack the mandate of religious authority.

From the perspective of traditional Judaism, the only area in which the statements of the rabbi carry religious authority is when he speaks as an interpreter of Jewish law or *halakhah*. We can speak here only sketchily of the *halakhic* process, the method of decision-making in Jewish law. For our purposes, it is sufficient to recognize that the process is dyadic in character—an observant Jew asks a learned rabbinical authority what *Jewish* law requires in such and such a circumstance. While an actual case or controversy may not be required (as in the American judicial system), judicial decisions are generally made in the light of specific facts. Taking a strict-constructionist rather than judicial-activist approach, the rabbi looks at the individual case brought before him. He then tells an inquiring Jew what Jewish law requires in a particular situation. Only rarely are *takkanot,* or general regulations, laid down for the entire community. The emphasis on the factual context of legal decision-making limits a rabbi's capacity to speak of political issues in *halakhic* terms.

On the other hand, from the perspective of rabbinic Judaism—of normative Judaism—it is, as stated above, very difficult to say that Jewish law should be limited to religious matters because it is not. Jewish law is not limited to matters of ritual and prayer. Its scope allows it to give guidance and, indeed, to give decisions on commercial matters and on social and political issues. Therefore, it is difficult to say, in principle at least, that Jewish law is not relevant to political decisionmaking. How it should be relevant, the way in which it should relate to political matters, what particular laws should be used, is a different story.

This is both a theological and a methodological point. Recent Christian political activism notwithstanding, this distinguishes Judaism from many Protestant confessional denominations and underscores what many have called its "this worldly" aspect. If a religion is intimately involved in this world (in contrast to "the world to come"), it cannot avoid social, economic, and political matters, and, indeed, Judaism does not. The problem, of course, is how and when to speak.

The Problem of Coalitions

One argument in support of the maximalist approach claims that Jews need to form coalitions with other interest groups in order to maintain power and, therefore, take on non-Jewish issues in exchange for support on Jewish issues. Senator Carl Levin (D-Mich.) has stated: "If we do not fight the injustices that affect others, will they fight the injustices that affect us?" On the conservative side, Irving Kristol has noted that for Jews to expect conservative support for Jewish concerns, they "must have a large portfolio of issues with which to deal."

Historically, Jewish groups have been part of the grand coalition of blacks, liberals, and labor. In the 1970s this coalition grew to include women's groups. The ADL and the Reform Religious Action Center are part of the Leadership Conference on Civil Rights. The Religious Action Committee works closely as well with women's groups on issues such as a woman's right to choose. These coalitions were in difficult straits in the 1980s as Jewish groups found themselves on opposite sides with blacks on a number of issues, but the "grand coalition" returned in force during the Clinton years.

On the Republican side it would be incorrect to say that Jewish groups entered into coalitions with other conservative groups. Rather, for the first time, conservative groups felt it necessary, or at least useful, to include organized Jews on their list of supporters. Thus, groups like Toward Tradition and the Jewish Policy Center were added to the list of conservative causes. They have joined, however, as add-ons to allow conservative groups to show Jewish support for their side.

For Jews to be part of such coalitions, they have to make policy concessions and take on the causes of other groups. In short, participating in such coalitions requires a diversion of resources to non-Jewish issues. In addition, such coalitions often have little direct control over the policy-making process so that the advantages that accrue from this distortion of the Jewish agenda are either indirect or tangential.

Outreach efforts designed to forge or reinforce coalitions have not produced any measurable increase in support for Israel. The best attempts to increase conservative support for Israel barely altered the fact that most conservative congressmen supported the AWACS sale in 1981 and more recent Saudi arms sales. Similarly, the American Jewish Congress and the Union of American Hebrew Congregations (UAHC) joined the 1983 March on Washington commemorating the twentieth anniversary of Martin Luther King's march in order to preserve the black-Jewish alliance and, by extension, black support of Israel, despite the fact that the sponsors of the march included PLO supporters and leaders who condemned Israel and Zionism.[51]

Jewish support of an event tinged with anti-Semitism suggests another drawback to a coalition strategy. Many of the issues for which other groups seek support can divide the Jewish community. When issues on which Jews disagree such as school prayer, quotas, Central America, and women's rights are defined as Jewish and added to the Jewish agenda, it contributes to needless discord and diversion of resources.

It is not clear that coalitions are more essential to Jewish political effectiveness than the direct grassroots support reflected by the ability of the Jewish community, in Bookbinder's words, "to mobilize influence within their local constituencies." Nor are coalitions the best mechanisms for advancing particular Jewish interests. Indeed, when forced to choose between maintaining an alliance with Jewish groups and pursuing an area of specific concern, other interest groups have not hesitated to part company. Why should Jewish groups have behaved differently from organized labor, normally one of Israel's staunchest supporters, when it lobbied vigorously against the Free Trade Agreement with Israel? As an American Jewish Committee task force concluded, "in any coalition of interests, if one party pursues the 'general good' while the other parties advance their constituents' interests, the result must invariably be the victimization of the constituency whose representatives pursue the 'general good.'"[52]

The fact is that a minimalist notion of Jewish interests is the most effective way to get policymakers to pay attention. The important coalitions are those formed by PACs with key policymakers and political parties seeking Jewish backing precisely because Jewish support is targeted to potential allies who support Jewish issues in particular.

The Problem of Priorities

Perhaps the most difficult challenge to the organized Jewish community is the need to set priorities among the issues on its political agenda. The JCPA policy statement has the organized Jewish community taking an official Jewish stand on almost every issue before

Congress. This mélange of public policy interests does a disservice
to Jewish communal interests and blurs the message sent to policymakers. This extension of the Jewish imprimatur to issues outside
the core scope of Jewish concerns weakens community unity.
Nearly all Jews support Israel, but they differ on AFDC. The failure
to set priorities mutes the intensity of focus on the central concerns
of the Jewish community.

The Future of Jewish Political Power

Despite the trappings of influence Jews have accumulated, the un-
spoken secret is that Jewish political power in America is commenc-
ing a significant decline. Unless they identify why this is happening,
Jews will be unable to slow it down and will find its reversal all but
impossible.

Five factors contribute to this impending diminution of Jewish
influence.

The Balkanization of America

Twenty years ago, any discussion of ethnic-based political action on
foreign policy issues in the United States would focus on the Jewish
community. Today, with the increased balkanization of America,
more and more ethnic groups are organizing politically to protect
their interests here and abroad.

These groups are now emulating the Jewish model (indeed, when
the Cuban American Foundation was first formed in the 1980s, they
came to AIPAC to "learn the ropes"). These ethnic groups are increasingly pressing the United States to care about the country from
whence they (or their ancestors) came. Unlike in the 1980s, requests
for such care in the form of foreign aid have overwhelmed congressional interlocutors. The psychological energy of the American public is limited as well. As Albanian, Ukrainian, and African "AI-
PACs" (not to speak of Arab variants) grow and prosper, there is
less money and less concern for Israel. The more pieces that make
up the foreign aid pie, the smaller each piece becomes, and the pie,
if anything, is getting smaller.

The effects of this balkanization can be seen both in the details
and in grand policy approaches. Now all sorts of other groups are
organizing to create a domestic impact on foreign policy.[53] If Con-

gress has to worry about domestic pressure from supporters of India,[54] Greece, and Ireland, it simply has less time for supporters of
Israel.

One result of this balkanization is the increasing influence of
American Muslims who are organizing themselves in ways similar
to the Jewish community. There are at least five million Muslims in
the United States,[55] some say more than six million.[56] Already they
comprise substantial voting blocs in states like Michigan. They are
just beginning, however, to play the great game of politics in America. As they progress, pressure on American politicians to stay evenhanded between Israel and its Arab neighbors will increase. U.S.
Congressmen will hesitate before venturing into a fight among their
constituents. The important feature of wall-to-wall American support for Israel may well be shattered.

Campaign Finance Reform

Historically, the Jewish community has been able to exert a disproportionate political influence, in part because of Jewish campaign
contributions. Jewish money is vital to the Democratic Party, com-
prising close to half of its financial support. Jews are increasingly
important in Republican fund-raising as well, providing more than a
quarter of the high-dollar donors in the 1992 presidential elections.
There are over sixty active pro-Israel PACs steering over $4 million
each election cycle to pro-Israel congressional candidates.[57]

Whether a good idea or not, it is clear that there will be some
kind of significant campaign finance reform in the next ten years
and perhaps sooner. That reform is likely to reduce Jewish political
power in some way. The Senate variant of the proposed Campaign
Finance Bill, for example, prohibits candidates from accepting out-
of-state contributions except in the two years before an election. (It
is through such out-of-state contributions that Jewish political mus-
cle is flexed.)

Jews Dispersing Geographically

The Jewish population is large enough to make a difference in eight
states: New York (9.1 percent), New Jersey (5.5 percent), Florida
(4.6 percent), Massachusetts (4.6 percent), Maryland (4.4 percent),
California (3.1 percent), Pennsylvania (2.9 percent), and Illinois

(2.2 percent). Only in Florida is the percentage of the Jewish population significantly increasing. As Jews disperse geographically into the Southwest they lose much of their electoral (although not necessarily their financial) clout.

Further, the Jewish community itself is declining in numbers. At 5.8 million, Jews are still a little less than 3 percent of the population but barely. Through intermarriage and a low birth rate, the Jewish population is dropping even in absolute numbers. That even Federations and fund-raising agencies have been forced to become introspective and think about issues of Jewish continuity suggests the seriousness of the data.

The End of Jewish Cultural Homogeneity

The cultural homogeneity that defined American Jews—the Eastern European "World of Our Fathers"—is fast dissipating as Jews assimilate pell-mell into American culture. This diminution of a Jewish way of apprehending the world will naturally lead to splits in the long vaunted notion of Jewish political unity, which will in turn diminish Jewish political clout.

At the same time, those who knew the Holocaust firsthand grow older, and while Jews see today an effervescence of interest in the Holocaust, it is, in truth, a swan song. In the next decade, Jews are going to have to fight for the sympathy received by the generation following the Shoah.

Israel's Diminishing Centrality

For years, support for Israel has been the alpha and omega of politically active Jews. But the centrality of Israel in Jewish life is in contention. As Steven Rosenthal has suggested "Opinion polls, changes in synagogue programming, and tourist demographics all suggest the diminishing connection of American Jews to the Jewish State."[58] A 1989 survey by Steven M. Cohen asked Jews under the age of forty how they would react if the State of Israel was destroyed. Only 34 percent suggested it would have a profound effect on their lives.[59] In a recent study of the entire community by Cohen and Eisen, only 27 percent of Jews declared themselves emotionally "very attached" to Israel.[60] This distancing from Israel is significant, the more so because it reflects a generational shift. The explanations are many and varied, but they reflect at least three reasons: (1) the troubled state of the "peace process;" (2) the disputes over religious pluralism in Israel and the severe conflicts between Orthodox and non-Orthodox; and (3) the waning of the generation that knew the Holocaust and saw the creation of the State of Israel in some sense as a response to the travail of the Jewish people through the Shoah.[61] Given the secular diminution of support for Israel among the Jewish community, is it surprising that similar shifts may well take place in the non-Jewish world as well?

Concluding Observations

Jewish organizations in the Washington public square reflect the views of the Jewish community generally. As the community struggles with the challenge of tendencies pointing to a structural decline in Jewish political power, Washington Jewish groups have to navigate newfound rapids and unexpected shoals. Their job is to maximize Jewish interests in the Washington square while withstanding those broader social and political trends.

The community will have to learn to live without unity on major political issues. Rather than a single Jewish perspective, both conservatives and liberals will call on their predesignated Jewish support groups. Thus, politicians will be less interested in finding out where the weight of Jewish opinion might lie than in ensuring that they have enlisted their house Jews in their partisan lists. This same lack of unity will exist in foreign policy, specifically in policy regarding Israel. This lack of communal unity will make the job of the Washington rep that much more difficult.

Politicians understand the need to have Jewish support for their positions, particularly on issues that impact on Jewish concerns. But they now are well aware that they have a choice of Jewish perspectives. This will lead to less of a need to adapt their views to that of the Jewish community, in that they will have friendly Jewish groups "on point" with their views. The one exception will be in instances when they are so far off from the center of gravity in the Jewish community that even Jewish groups over which political organizations have considerable influence or control cannot go along. At that point, they will know they have gone too far. One such example occurred in the run-up to the Bitburg crisis when leaders like Max Fisher and groups like the Republican Jewish Coalition found they

could not support the president. Seeing Max Fisher in opposition
had a real impact on the White House of the day.

As a result, there is an urgent need for the Jewish community to
seek out new coalitions. The historical coalitions of Jews, labor, and
blacks live largely in retirement and memory. Coalitions for the future, whether with Asians, Latinos,[62] Christians, or others, are
needed particularly in regard to support for Israel.

There can be little doubt that Jewish organizations in Washington
make a substantial public policy impact. That impact mostly reflects
whatever clout the Jewish community at large may hold. However,
Washington efforts provide added value and increase Jewish clout.
In this regard, Jewish organizations have become more like trade
associations than religious clarions. While these Jewish lobbyists
provide added weight to Jewish involvement in the public square,
that involvement may well take somewhat different forms in the
decades to come.

Appendix

Jewish Organizations in Washington

Agudath Israel	
ADL	Anti-Defamation League of B'nai B'rith
AIPAC	American Israel Public Affairs Committee
AJC	American Jewish Committee
AJ Congress	American Jewish Congresses
B'nai B'rith	
Hadassah	
IPA	Institute for Public Affairs of the Orthodox Union (OU)
IPF	Israel Policy Forum
JCPA	Jewish Council for Public Affairs
JINSA	Jewish Institute for National Security Affairs
JPC	Jewish Policy Center
NCJW	National Council of Jewish Women
NCSJ	National Conference on Soviet Jewry
NJDC	National Jewish Democratic Coalition
RAC	Religious Action Committee
RJC	Republican Jewish Coalition
UJC	United Jewish Communities

Notes

1. Parts of this chapter are drawn from earlier forays on this general topic by the author including: "For Ourselves and for Others: Defining Jewish Interests" in Daniel Elazar, ed., *The New Jewish Politics* (Lanham, Md.: University Press of America and Jerusalem Center for Public Affairs, 1988), 57-64; "Political Interest vs. Moral Agenda," in Letty Cottin Pogrebin, Marshall J. Breger and Steven Windmueller, *Shaping the American Jewish Agenda* (Los Angeles: Wilstein Institute, 1992), 12-23; "Responses by Marshall Breger," in Seymour N. Siegel, ed., *Who Speaks for American Judaism? Competing Approaches to Public Issues* (Washington, D.C.: Ethics and Public Policy Center, 1983), 5-9, 18-22

2. See, generally, Selma Stern, *The Court Jew* (Philadelphia: Jewish Publication Society of America, 1950).

3. Peter Y. Medding, "The 'New Jewish Politics' in the United States: Historical Perspectives," in Zvi Gitelman, ed., *The Quest for Utopia: Jewish Political Ideas and Institutions through the Ages* (Armonk, N.Y.: M. E. Sharpe, 1992), 125.

4. Medding, "New Jewish Politics," 126.

5. Deborah Dash Moore, *B'nai B'rith and the Challenge of Ethnic Leadership* (Albany: State University of New York Press, 1981), 208. Prior to 1937, the seat of office was in the hometown of the incumbent president. The B'nai B'rith convention of 1935 voted to change this peripatetic approach and chose Washington, D.C., as a permanent base. See Maurice Bisgyer, *Challenge and Encounter: Behind the Scenes in the Struggle for Jewish Survival* (New York: Crown Publishers, 1967), 48-49.

6. *Fortune* magazine rated AIPAC the second largest lobby in both 1997 and 1998. See Jeffrey Birnbaum, "The Power 25," *Fortune,* December 8, 1997, 144. By 1999 AIPAC continued to maintain its top five position, ranking fourth in the top twenty-five. See Jeffrey Birnbaum, "The Power 25," *Fortune,* December 6, 1999, 206.

7. I am grateful to James David Besser for contributing this comparison.

8. The RJC has a small, nonprofit spin-off, the Jewish Policy Center, which has been active intermittently in the "culture wars" of the last decades of the twentieth century.

9. See Bradley A. Smith, *Unfree Speech: The Folly of Campaign Finance Reform* (Princeton, N.J.: Princeton University Press, 2001), 37.

10. $4,927,303 to be exact. The actual dollars involved are uncommonly difficult to total up, for the Jewish PACs rarely advertise themselves as such. The most assiduous efforts to collect numbers have been made by "pro-Arab" groups generally viewed as antagonistic. See Richard H. Curtiss, *Stealth PACs: Lobbying Congress for Control of U.S. Middle East Policy,* 4th ed. (Washington D.C.: American Educational Trust, 1997); Richard H. Curtiss, "Pro-Israel PAC Donations Soared in Final Months of 1996 Election Cycle," *Washington Report on Middle East Af-*

fairs, April/May 1997, 43-50; Richard H. Curtiss, "Pro-Israel PAC Donations Up in 1998 Election Cycle," *Washington Report on Middle Eastern Affairs,* 42 (October-November 1998).

11. See J. J. Goldberg, *Jewish Power* (Reading, Mass.: Addison-Wesley, 1996), 276.

12. Daniel Kurtzman, "More Jewish Groups to Join DC Arena," *Metrowest* (N.J.) *Jewish News,* January 9, 1997, 34.

13. Kurtzman, "More Jewish Groups, 34.

14. Interview with Nathan Diament, OU, May 2001.

15. Republican Jewish Coalition, *Hill Roundup,* June 14, 2001.

16. But it must be recognized that conflict exists. This conflict cannot be repressed or even ignored. It tells one something about one's body politic and no lobby can get too far away from its body politic. As a method of dealing with conflict, we should study other lobbies. Trade associations often issue a statement explaining that no position will be taken because the membership is split. Alternatively, where there is a lack of consensus, we see no reason why groups cannot put forward their own position in their own name. This would be efficacious in situations in which recognizing other views does not nullify the impact of the position taken. This practice has been implemented by the Leadership Conference on Civil Rights which places a premium on talking it out, but, if there is disagreement, will note in a footnote to their statements which groups do not go along. JCPA has adopted an even more open approach. Not only do they note who dissents from a particular policy position, but the JCPA policy document also provides an explanation of the rationale for that dissent. In contrast, the Presidents Conference believes in unity, even at the price of silence. This is because the Conference operates by consensus, and, in order to maintain consensus, it will either dilute a policy position to its lowest common denominator or will front load authority onto the president and executive director so as to avoid the debilitating aspects of open controversy.

Other agenda-creating, decision-making mechanisms are worth exploring. The National Federation of Independent Business (NFIB), an organization of over 600,000 small businesses, polls its members monthly to ascertain the five most important issues of concern. No doubt the NFIB staff have some input in the way the questions are asked, but the answers, democratically counted, then govern the work of the association's lobbyists. It is unknown if the Jewish community could stand such a radical infusion of democracy. Nonetheless, the goal is worthy and there may be mechanisms worth pursuing.

17. Irving Howe, *World of Our Fathers* (New York: Harcourt Brace Jovanovich, 1976).

18. Michael Walzer incisively points out that liberalism, as we know it today, is among the Jews a product of emancipation or, more precisely, "emancipation in exile." Michael Walzer, "Liberalism and the Jews: Historical Affinities, Contemporary Necessities," in Peter Y. Medding, ed.,

Values, Interests and Identity: Jews and Politics in a Changing World (New York: Oxford University Press, 1995) (Studies in Contemporary Jewry XI), 3.

19. A 2001 Zogby poll finds the number to be 48.5 percent. James J. Zogby, *What Ethnic Americans Really Think*, Zogby Culture Polls 52, Zogby International, 2001. In an earlier survey conducted by Steven Cohen, 32 percent of Jews classified themselves as liberal or very liberal, Steven M. Cohen, *The Dimensions of American Jewish Liberalism* (New York: American Jewish Committee, 1989), 39.

20. The conservative side includes the OU, Agudath Israel, the Republican Jewish Coalition, and a small social conservative group closely aligned with the Christian Right—Toward Tradition. The liberal team, while they would not style themselves as such, includes JCPA, the three defense agencies, the Religious Action Center of Reform Judaism, and the Democratic Party's Jewish spin-off, the National Jewish Democratic Coalition.

21. Conference of Presidents, American Jewish Committee, Anti-Defamation League, and United Jewish Communities, *American Attitudes towards the Crisis in the Middle East*, Table 10A (January 25-February 17, 2001).

22. *American Attitudes,* at Table 34A.

23. Neal Sher, "A Jewish 'Thought Policeman,'" *Jerusalem Post*, January 17, 1997, 6.

24. Morton Klein, "So Who Are the Real 'Thought Police'?" *Jerusalem Post*, January 17, 1997, 6.

25. Marilyn Henry, "Presidents Conference Censures ZOA over Ad," *Jerusalem Post*, January 10, 1997.

26. Rebecca Spencer, "Lauder, Conference Bigs Erupt in Public Feuding over Leaks and Dissent," *Forward*, September 9, 1999; see also, "Lauder Defends Conference's Policies: Sharon Warns Prexies to Avoid Erkat," *Forward,* September 24, 1999, 1.

27. See, generally, Steven T. Rosenthal, *Irreconcilable Differences? The Waning of the American Love Affair with Israel* (Hanover, N.H.: University Press of New England, 2001). It must be recognized, however, that the so-called Al-Aksa intifada which erupted in the fall of 2000 after the failure of Camp David II has increased levels of unity in diaspora. How permanent this development may be remains to be seen.

28. See Michal Yudelman, "Peace Camp's Visit to the U.S. Draws Wide Criticism," *Jerusalem Post,* May 6, 1991; Allison Kaplan, "Left-Wing MKs Defend Their Meeting in U.S.," *Jerusalem Post,* May 8, 1991.

29. David Singer, ed., *American Jewish Yearbook 1999*, vol. 99 (New York: American Jewish Committee, 1999).

30. The so-called "gang of three" included Yossi Ben Aharon, former director general of the Prime Minister's Office under Menachem Begin, Yoram Ettinger, former council-general in Houston, and Yigal Carmon, former special advisor on terrorism to Yitzhak Shamir. See Jim Besser,

"The Capital Column," *Jewish Week* (New York), March 29, 1996. See also Rosenthal, *Irreconcilable Differences?* 128.

31. Jewish Council for Public Affairs, *Agenda for Public Affairs, 2000-2001* (New York: JCPA, n.d.).

32. J. J. Goldberg, "Family Feud: Two Big Jewish Federations Seek to Rein in an Outspoken Jewish Advocacy Group," *Jewish Week,* November 5, 1999. See also Ami Eden, "Big Donors Seen in Move to Rein in a Policy Council, Curb 'Inappropriate' Debate," *Forward,* September 22, 2000.

33. Eden, *Forward,* September 22, 2000.

34. Eden, *Forward,* September 22, 2000.

35. See Arthur A. Goren, *The Politics and Public Culture of American Jews* (Bloomington: Indiana University Press, 1999), 205-23. "While we oppose the concept of group rights, we see no problem with the concept of group interests. Group interests are just as real and just as legitimate as transcendent common interests." Bertram Gold in Goren, *Politics and Public Culture,* 262, n. 37.

36. James D. Besser, "The Greening of Jewish America," *Jewish Week* (New York), December 21, 1999.

37. For a review of the field, see David Vogel, "How Green Is Judaism? Exploring Jewish Environmental Ethics," *Judaism,* vol. 59, no. 197 (winter 2001): 66-81; for a "new age" perspective, see Ellen Bernstein and Dan Find, *Let the Earth Teach You Torah* (Philadelphia: Shomrei Adamah, 1992).

38. Cited in Ira Stoll, "The Stoll Report of News from the Nation's Capital," *Forward,* August 1, 1997.

39. *Wilder v. Sugarman,* 385 F. Su 1013, (S.D.N.Y. 1974), re-filed sub.nom., *Wilder v. Bernstein,* 479 F. Su 980, (S.D. N.Y. 1980); later proceeding at *Wilder v. Bernstein,* 545 1292 (S.D.N.Y. 1986); aff'd 848 F. 2d 1338 (2d cir.1488); *Wilder v. Bernstein,* 725 F. Supp 1324 (S.D.N.Y. 1989); aff'd 965. F. 2d 116 (2d cir.), cert den. 588 U.S. 954 (1992).

40. See J. J. Goldberg, *Jewish Power,* 357-58.

41. Senator Inouye successfully secured an $8 million appropriation from Congress to support construction of Orthodox Sephardic Jewish day schools in France. The funds were to go to Otzar Hatorah ("Treasure House of the Torah"), a little known Jewish organization established in 1940 to aid Sephardic Jews from North Africa. After much controversy when the grant became public, Inouye undertook the unusual step of requesting that Congress rescind the appropriation. See Elaine Sciolino, "Religious Schools Get U.S. Aid Abroad," *New York Times,* January 24, 1988, A11. See also Martin Tolchin, "Washington Tales: Federal Aid: How $8 Million Was Won and Lost," *New York Times,* March 3, 1988, A28.

42. Kiryas Joel's first attempt came in 1989, when 15,000 residents, all members of the Satmar Hasidic sect, successfully petitioned the state legislature to create a public school district for their disabled children, allowing the children to receive government-financed services for their disabili-

ties. The 1989 law was declared unconstitutional as amounting to favoritism of a single religious group. Subsequent attempts by the state in 1994 and 1997 to pass laws that avoided the favoritism problem while creating a special district were also found to be unconstitutional. See Joseph Berger, "Hasidic Village Has Few Ways to Get Own School District," *New York Times*, May 28, 1999, B5.

43. Arthur F. Bentley, *The Process of Government; A Study of Social Pressures* (Chicago: University of Chicago Press, 1908), 258-59. Bentley's views were developed in David Truman, *The Governmental Process* (New York: Knopf, 1951). See also Robert Dahl, *Democracy in the United States; Promise and Performance,* 3rd ed. (Chicago: Rand McNally College Publications, 1970).

The theory of "public choice" advanced by many economists and legal scholars supports the view that governmental actions are designed to serve selfish private ends. The classic text is James M. Buchanan and Gordon Tullock, *The Calculus of Consent* (Ann Arbor: University of Michigan Press, 1962).

44. John Chamberlain, *The American Stakes* (New York: Carrick & Evans, 1940), 32.

45. Chamberlain, *The American Stakes,* 27.

46. By which we refer to models of democratic society that focus less on popular participation as justifying the democratic process and more on "deliberation in politics." See Cass R. Sunstein, "Beyond the Republican Revival," 97 *Yale Law Journal* 1539, 1541 (1988). See also Richard H. Fallon, Jr., "What Is Republicanism, and Is It Worth Reviving?" 102 *Harvard Law Review* 1695 (1989); Steven G. Gey, "The Unfortunate Revival of Civic Republicanism," 14 *University of Pennsylvania Law Review* 801 (1993).

47. Daniel Seligman, "Making It in Brooklyn," *Fortune*, August 6, 1984, 128.

48. See Richard Severo, "Reagan Grants Hassidim 'Disadvantaged' Status," *New York Times*, June 29, 1984, B5; see also "Hasidic Jews Fight Change in AIDS Project," *New York Times*, May 6, 1984, 45.

49. A vigorous argument that the greater danger to Jewish security today comes from "left" oriented parties is made in W. D. Rubinstein, *The Left, the Right and the Jews* (New York: Universe Books, 1982).

50. Carl Perlstone, "The ADL Pushes "Tolerance"? Why I'm Leaving after 25 Years," *Jewish World Review*, June 4, 2001.

51. See Marjorie Hyer, "Jewish Groups Plan Their Own Programs to Honor Dr. King," *Washington Post*, August 6, 1983, B6; Karlyn Berher, "March Upsets Some Jewish Groups," *Washington Post*, July 23, 1983.

52. See Breger, "For Ourselves and for Others," 57-64.

53. For one example, consider Armenian-Americans and their efforts to secure congressional "recognition" of the Armenian genocide. See Michael Doyle, "Armenian-Americans as Political Players," *California Journal*, April 2001.

54. Jeffrey Birnbaum, "Money, Money Everywhere: Sidebar: A Sacred Cash Cow," *Fortune,* July 19, 1999, 80 (discussing creation of the India caucus).

55. The Census Bureau cites 5,270,000 Muslims in the United States. See U.S. Census Bureau, *Statistical Abstract of the United States: 2000,* 61, no. 74 (2000).

56. See Richard N. Ostling, "Comprehensive Survey of US Muslims," *AP,* April 26, 2001 ("6 million to 7 million is a reasonable estimate for Americans who would consider themselves ethnic Muslims"). But see Gustav Niebuhr, "Studies Suggest Lower Count for Number of US Muslims," *New York Times,* October 25, 2001, A14, for a different view (citing a case study conducted by the Graduate Center of the City of New York released in October 2000, estimating the number of U.S. Muslims to be 1.1 million). In another survey, commissioned by the American Jewish Committee, estimates reach 2.8 million Muslims making up 1 percent of the total U.S. population. See Tom W. Smith, *Estimating the Muslim Population in the United States,* National Opinion Research Center, University of Chicago, prepared for the American Jewish Committee, October 2001.

57. See discussion on PACs at n. 10 above.

58. Rosenthal, *Irreconcilable Differences?* 170.

59. Steven M. Cohen, *Ties and Tension: The 1989 Survey of American Jewish Attitudes toward Israel and Israelis* (New York: American Jewish Committee, 1989).

60. Steven M. Cohen and Arnold M. Eisen, *The Jew Within: Self, Family and Community in America* (Bloomington: Indiana University Press, 2000), 143.

61. Parts one and two are well discussed in Cohen and Eisen, *The Jew Within,* 142-52.

62. For one effort in this regard, see Jewish Labor Committee, "Latino-Jewish Institute Forms in LA," *JLC Review* (summer 2001): 8.

7

Uncertain Steps: American Jews in the New Public Square

Harvey Sicherman

Senator Joseph Lieberman's run for vice-president of the United States on the Democratic Party ticket marked a new level of Jewish integration into American public life. Lieberman was not only Jewish, he was Orthodox. His campaign proved, beyond doubt, that America's highest elective office did not require a Jew to abandon a stringent religious life. Thus did religion enter into the very center of the public square.

This moment of triumph was followed by an unsettling sequel. It turned out that Senator Lieberman was very much an exception to the general Jewish rule. His religious practices were common to only 7 to 8 percent of American Jews. His views on such issues as affirmative action and school vouchers were out of step not only with the official position of most Jewish organizations but also with their allies in the Democratic Party: the African Americans, the feminists, and the teacher's unions. While he revised or reversed those views soon after nomination, he incurred the ire of prominent Jewish leaders when he offered a message of faith and the need for religion in the public square during his campaign.[1] Lieberman had called the discussion of religion in public affairs a "discomfort zone."[2] While certainly uncomfortable for Jews, it was not so for either Vice-President Al Gore or Governor George W. Bush. Both candidates were quick to cite their own religious experiences and to tout the virtues of faith-based organizations. Despite the decline of the Christian Coalition and other so-called religious Right groups, it appeared that religion has moved into the public square to stay.

What effect has this had on American Jews and their traditional approach to the public square? The answer appears to be: not much. Jewish relations with "others" in the political rough and tumble remain much the same. Although various observers have been detecting a shift in Jewish voting patterns since the 1980s, under the pressure of changing community and public mores, Jews remain second only to American blacks in their allegiance to the Democratic Party. The public positions of most American Jewish organizations and their preferred political allies seem firmly fixed on the liberal side of the spectrum. Yet, the pressure for change has increased. Foremost among these pressures is the growing alarm over the very survival of the community itself. This has led inevitably to a fresh discussion of the role of Judaism in preserving American Jewry. An articulate, if not very numerous, group of writers and thinkers has also been arguing for some time that Jewish survival and influence requires a more conservative political direction.[3] Last, though surely not least, historic coalitions, notably with African Americans, have been strained over issues such as Israel, affirmative action, and anti-Semitism.

This chapter seeks to assess the potential for change as American Jews work in a public square newly shaped by religion, including Judaism. Its argument proceeds in four parts:

The American Jewish Tradition: The traditional American Jewish approach emphasizes individual rights, the steady separation of religion from the public square, and coalition with the modern Democratic Party. This structure has enormous resilience because it fits in well with the social impulse and religious attitudes of the Jewish community.

"Identity" Politics: The Jewish community's attempts to deal with the danger of assimilation puts new emphasis on Judaism and challenges traditional approaches, especially separation of church and state with regard to school financing. It is not clear, however, just how influential Judaism will be on what for now is a diffuse form of identity politics.

The Coalition That Was: One of the proudest Jewish achievements in the old public square was the alliance with African Americans in the quest for social justice. Strains in this coalition, including black anti-Semitism, racial preference politics, and antagonism to Israel, have dealt a hard blow to the Jewish "civil religion" that identified Jews and blacks as minorities with common interests, and new trouble may be in store.

The Coalition That Wasn't: The sudden emergence of the Christian Coalition, Moral Majority, and other groups of the social-religious Right appeared to be a new American religious revival that threatened separation of church and state. These same groups, however, were very supportive of Israel. American Jews proved unwilling or unable to form a lasting coalition with the religious Right. Still, the new emphasis on "faith-based groups" and on religious values as a way of dealing with social pathologies seems firmly lodged in the public square.

As a result of these different developments, the major institutions of organized Jewish life, notably the Federations, the defense agencies, and the Jewish Council for Public Affairs, are facing the wrench of change, partly as a consequence of new ideas both within and without, and partly as a consequence of financial dilemmas. To make their maximum influence felt as a small but wealthy minority, especially in the context of an unsettled American cultural and political divide, Jews will have to find their place in more than the familiar liberal camp. Given the lack of Jewish consensus on this and other issues, however, the transition to a more balanced set of relationships with others in the public square will be neither neat nor clear. Yet, the first uncertain steps in this new public square are about to be taken.

The American Jewish Tradition

The American Jewish community, as Daniel Elazar wrote, is the "first fully emancipated Jewish community" in the history of the diaspora.[4] The community itself represents a sharp break from the traditional Jewish organizations of Central or Eastern European origin. The Jews who came to the United States did not do so with a "contract" that set out what the local authorities expected of them, as was the case throughout medieval Europe, nor were Jews singled out for a distinctive political or communal status. Unlike the Russian Empire, Jews were not restricted in place of residence or occupation; unlike the German or Austro-Hungarian Empires (or the French Republic), there were no government regulated and supported religious communities, even after emancipation recognized individual rights. While one can draw precedents from the German experience such as the development of self-defense agencies, these still came in the context of an historically separate, publicly recognized, and government-approved Jewish community.

"Full emancipation" thus meant the absence of an imposed structure, or even the history of one, for the first time in the diaspora. There would be no Exilarch or official "court Jews," no government-enforced communal taxation systems, no public sanction to Jewish courts of law. In this the Jews would share the same conditions as their fellow Americans, who, as de Tocqueville noted, were great voluntary organizers but were under no compulsion, except that of belief or self-interest, to do so. Another sharp break from the Old World was the nature of the immigration itself, largely motivated by economic reasons and therefore by definition composed of the poorer members of Jewish society. According to one estimate, in 1906 when 200,000 Jews entered the United States, only fifty listed themselves as professionals as compared to the 5 to 10 percent who fit that description in Eastern Europe.[5] The poor Jewish immigrants may have remained loyal to the relatives left behind, but they "were not predisposed to construct in North America a replica of their unhappy European past."[6] As Irving Howe and others have recounted, the world of our fathers contained a large share of frustrated revolutionaries and many who were intensely opposed, if not to Judaism itself, then to rabbinical authority. What they shared was a distinctive, if chaotic, ethnic heritage, often mixed up with religious practices, and a burning desire to "do better," whether as entrepreneurs or, in many of the big cities, as unionists or socialists advocating fundamental social change.[7]

Individual versus Community

The result was that the political and religious institutions the immigrants left behind made a tardy and sometimes unsuccessful appearance on the American Jewish scene. This was especially the case with the Orthodox. The most religious elements of European Jewry found the working conditions of the New World extremely hostile to such things as Sabbath observance, *kashruth*, and intensive Jewish education. For them, it was a *"treif"* (unkosher) land, not a "golden one." Rabbinical leaders were traumatized by the disastrous attempt to create a Kehilla in New York City and the personal tragedy for the eminent scholar and preacher recruited to head it, Rabbi Jacob Joseph.[8] The absence of European-style institutions and the immigrants' break with the past were important components of the new community-in-the-making. Another equally significant component was the discovery of America's emphasis on the individual. In the United States the individual's rights counted for more than membership in a religious community.

Thus, unlike Europe, the American public square was not restricted or off-limits for Jews in religious terms. The Establishment Clause and the Free Exercise Clause of the Bill of Rights did not allow Jews admission to all schools or hotels, or even to many professions, but equality was there to be invoked. Even before the Civil War, a pugnacious figure like Captain Uriah Philips Levy could sue and embarrass the U.S. Navy into an admission of anti-Semitism and gain promotion as a result.[9] The legal public square, the Jews discovered, made as much room in theory for Judaism as for Christianity, even though in practice, American laws (such as prohibition on Sunday sales) often reflected Christian practices. These broad brushes will suffice to sketch the portrait of an American Jewry that was organized under the fundamental impulses of survival and self-defense but that also created its own "tradition," a new one very different from its European origins. The Jews in the United States would not organize a Kehilla and would not respond to a central, nationwide organization with government-appointed leaders. They would have, as other Americans had, a plethora of groups, springing from the desire for individual advancement and acting in a public square that, unlike Europe, was not simply the forecourt of the cathedral.

A Minority in America

In establishing their own tradition, however, American Jews faced one condition that replicated exactly their situation in Europe. They were a small minority living in a society the majority of which professed a religion that had been occasionally tolerant but far more often hostile and physically threatening to Jewish survival. The public square in America may not have been the forecourt of the cathedral but the cross certainly cast its shadow. America was not a Christian state, but it was arguably a Christian nation dominated by Protestant sects.

Moreover, American political rhetoric was always "entangled" with religious references. American politicians invoked the deity often, used Christian metaphors, and engaged easily in such practices as public prayer. The Congress that composed the Constitution began with a prayer (at Benjamin Franklin's suggestion, to cool tempers) and continued to pray thereafter to this day. But the piety that still amazes foreigners—the apparent religiosity of American life—was combined with a pragmatism that generally confined the religious impulse to private mores and public customs rather than legal ordinances. To Jews acutely conscious of their minority status, this offered a unique opportunity. The more general the religious expression and the less Christian its specifics, the easier it would be for Jews to take a place in the public square out of the shadow of the cross, or better yet, to lift that shadow.

To sum up, then, the traditional American Jewish approach to the public square emphasized individual rights rather than communal rights, a "civil" rather than a doctrinal religion, and a strong emphasis on social justice, often defined by the working-class component of the original immigrants. A profound irony lurked beneath the surface of this approach. To enter fully into both the public square and American society, the People of the Book would work to diminish the role of the Book—the Christian Bible, but by inference the Hebrew Bible as well—in America's public life.

Coalitions and Organization

What remained to be found was a set of reliable coalition partners to advance Jewish interests, whether in separating religion from the public square, strengthening the case for individual merit as the key to advancement in society, or easing the task of Jewish integration. Early in the history of the republic, the Jews had already begun to master the art of coalition, whether on behalf of coreligionists in Syria or Russia, or at home in the case of General Grant's insulting prohibition of Jewish tradesmen in a southern military district.

The most lasting modern political relationship was formed with the Democratic Party created by Roosevelt during the course of the Great Depression. FDR proved a master of assembling groups whose distrust for each other was overcome by far greater overriding interests, the biggest one being change from the status quo. Liberalism in the New Deal sense offered Jews a political acceptance they had never known before by giving them charter membership in a powerful coalition. The minorities would become a majority and the economically weak would become strong, all parading under the banner of justice and America's promise of individual rights. As one historian wrote: "Jews used liberal politics to power their move from the margin to the mainstream of American life. They emerged as a model ethnic minority and credited the Democratic party for much of their political and social success."[10]

It is important, of course, not to exaggerate the Jewish community's affection for liberal causes; notable differences existed on such issues as anticommunism, support for Israel, and the extent of separation of church and state.[11] But liberalism had and retains a powerful appeal. Thus, the dominant patterns in American Jewish life were well set by the end of World War II: individual rights in a secular public square flanked by a broad objective of social progress secured by active government.

Also set during this time was the community organization, or more accurately, organizations. To the outside observer, Jews in America have been excessively creative in this field, multiplying groups and structures, many overlapping, all hard to coordinate. In fact, once the overall objectives are understood, these groups and their relations to others may be easily comprehended.[12] The historic national organizations—the American Jewish Committee, the American Jewish Congress, and the Anti-Defamation League—have as their primary mission the defense of Jewish rights: the Committee investigates, the Congress litigates, and the League activates.[13] The "defenders" continue to rely on American Jewish unease, a wariness that the apparent decline of anti-Semitism may conceal a dormant rather than defunct disease.[14]

Partly separate and much more local are the various agencies that serve (or served) Jewish social and employment needs, educational services, hospitals, and the like. The Federations, as central fundraisers, are the key local or regional instruments that rely upon and stimulate the "grass roots." Another function is fulfilled by the synagogues, the most numerous of the Jewish organizations, all of them offering religious services and most providing Jewish education for children and adults several hours each week.

Finally, the community relations councils have as their direct function the contacts with "others" in the public square. These are the repositories of much coalition activity because they serve local and regional constituencies and cover the state and local political arenas of the American federal system. By virtue of their self-selected, cumulative representation drawn from all local communities, the councils can claim to be the most democratic of all Jewish organizations. Inevitably, functions overlap and organizations change. Support for Israel is a good example. When AIPAC, as a consequence of the 1982 fight over the American sale of AWACS aircraft to Saudi Arabia, expanded from a small Washington, D.C., lobby into a national organization, it poached on the preserve of the defense agencies and the community relations councils. Another group, the Conference of Presidents of Major American Jewish Organizations, was actually created at the behest of the Eisenhower administration, specifically Secretary of State John Foster Dulles. He told the Jews they would be more effective (and take up less of his time) if the "community" spoke with one voice. The influence of the Presidents Conference has waxed and waned, depending on how it has been used by the Israeli and U.S. governments. Nonetheless, AIPAC and the Presidents Conference, driven by events in Washington, have largely taken over the "Israel" portfolio, even though the others still play an important part.

Given that an enormous part of American Jewish communal activity is devoted to Israel, American Jewish relations with others in the public square on domestic issues, which is the focus of the local community relations councils and their renamed national group, the Jewish Council on Public Affairs (JCPA), should be kept in perspective. As one veteran council professional put it, the give and take with other groups filled the bank of favors that could be drawn upon when Israel needed support, even if this involved Jews in issues not of direct concern to the community. Hence, every discussion of Jews in the public square has as its context the still overriding objective of protecting Jews abroad, especially the State of Israel.

Such discussions must also take into account that the American Jewish community has a numerous paid and trained cadre of professionals who run the organizations, in effect, the bureaucracy. The voluntary nature of the rest of the community means that the paid professionals are also more than that; they are leaders, too.

The Legacy

The traditional American Jewish organizations and their approach to the public square can claim many achievements. They removed obstacles to Jews throughout American society, many of them social rather than legal. They rallied massive support for Israel and for the rescue of Russian Jews, an effort that was especially important to the post-Holocaust generation who were far readier than their fathers or grandfathers to put public pressure on Washington to act. American Jewry's public life concentrated on the themes of Israel and the Holocaust, the "we are one" slogan. Its social dimensions or "civil religion of sacred survival," to use Jonathan Woocher's phrase, was connected to Judaism through the Hebrew concept of *tikkun olam*, "repair of the world." The Talmud uses this phrase to justify decisions made to keep social peace, and in this sense, much Jewish activity in behalf of other minorities and the poor would be justified as a way to avoid the European dilemma: the Jew caught in the middle between the poor masses and the rich few. A less stratified U.S. society was, therefore, arguably in the Jewish interest.[15]

Tikkun olam also has an esoteric kabbalistic meaning: a way to bring in the messianic age through repair of the human defects brought into the world when the earthly vessels could not accommodate the Divine Emanations. While one can doubt whether many American Jews advocating civil rights for American blacks or separation of church and state had the *Zohar* in mind, there was a sort of secular search for a utopia.[16] This was the American equivalent of a well-known pattern in modern Jewish life: the transfer of the religious longing for the messiah into a secular quest for a better society, with Marx or Herzl or the Bill of Rights replacing Moses and the Torah.

"Identity" Politics

The well-organized tradition of American Jewish activity in the public square has been challenged by several developments. The first and by far the most important for the longer term is what has been called the "disappearing American Jew."[17] This issue first surfaced almost forty years ago when *Look* magazine published sensationally, "The Vanishing American Jew," in May 1964. American Jewish leaders were already aware of the problem. Two years earlier, Rabbi Joachim Prinz, president of the American Jewish Congress, had proclaimed that assimilation more than anti-Semitism would be the great challenge of the future[18] and that the solution would be found in Jewish education, not exactly the focus of the AJC itself. Prinz defended the "Jewish" part of the AJC in the identification of Jewish values with liberal universalism, a position that held only so long as the liberal politics did not impinge on strong Jewish interests such as Israel, or racial preferences masquerading as civil rights. While these debates continued, so did the social process that took acceptance into assimilation. A generation of warnings by the sociologists turned into frightening statistical evidence when the 1990 National Jewish Population Study set forth what had been suspected for sometime. American Jewry's future was imperiled not only because of a lower birth rate, typical of the middle class (compared to the large immigrant families) but also most alarmingly, half of American Jewish marriages (between 1985 and 1990) were to spouses of another faith. As a recent survey phrased it: "a majority of out-married Jewish parents preferred another religion or ethnic identity for their children, leading to major percentage losses of the potential size of the new generation."[19] While definitions of Jewishness are variable for these estimates, there can be no doubt that out-migration is giving American Jews a significantly smaller population prospect.

There is also a change in the respective strengths of the religious affiliations within the community. The Orthodox, now estimated at 7 to 10 percent, could be 20 percent in fifty years, approaching that of the Conservatives (estimated to drop from 32 percent to 26 percent), with Reform holding steady at 34 percent. The last stream, "no affiliation," would hold at 22 percent.[20] Orthodoxy's increase, moreover, may be all the more impressive if the older pattern of interdenominational passage, whereby a considerable percentage of Orthodox children become Conservative adults, is reduced. By the early 1990s, the community found itself challenged at its most religious and least religious margins.[21] The latter set off the greatest alarm. The spiritual side of American Judaism—a secondary consideration of the primarily secular defense agencies, the social services, and the fund distributors, the Federations—had been left to the rabbinate and the synagogues. Observers had long remarked on the weak commitment of three-day-a-year Jews, three days (or less) a week, after-hours schools, and the virtual end of Jewish education following bar or bat mitzvah. (The late Yitzhak Rabin, himself not religious, remarked to this author in 1972, after two years as Israel's ambassador to the United States, that, in his view, support for Israel had become a kind of substitute for Judaism.) The dispersal of Jewish neighborhoods, Israel's increasing strength, and the waning of "lox and bagel" ethnicity had dissolved the old bonds. Now the failings of the educational system appeared to be a danger to the survival of the community itself.

The Continuity Decade

A decade of "continuity" experiments began, some initiated by the religious movements themselves, but by far the most interesting by the Federations. One approach might be described, to use Daniel Patrick Moniyhan's provocative phrase, as "defining deviancy down." Intermarriage was historically a very deviant Jewish behavior; but it had become a very large fact of American Jewish life. The Reform rabbinate, amidst enormous controversy, had in 1983, changed the millennia-old criteria of Jewish birth from matrilineal to patrilineal descent, a move not only hotly denounced by the Orthodox and Conservative movements, but also repudiated by the Reform movement in Israel. Equally difficult debates have broken out over rabbinical officiation at mixed marriages.

This change of the rules was accompanied by a new emphasis on the upbringing of the children of such marriages, including a prohibition in Reform schools against children also enrolled in Christian schools, synagogue programs for intermarrieds, and the like. These programs, and more aggressive conversionary efforts, became a regular part of many, if not most, American synagogues. But the notion that one can change the rules, reach out beyond historic boundaries, yet retain essential distinctions has not been very effective in practice. A recent American Jewish Committee survey showed a "thrust for accommodation and acceptance of intermarriage" and, worst of all, a belief by half the respondents that it was "racist" to oppose such unions.[22]

Jewish "identity" politics, however, were not restricted to the religious bodies. The Federations, heretofore primarily fund distributors, became highly active proponents of "continuity." Initially, this meant much more attention—and resources—for Jewish schools. Only 60 percent of Jewish children ever attend them and of those, some 40 percent now attend Jewish day schools.[23]

The day schools were, and still are, largely Orthodox. They had a good record of producing graduates who remained Jewish and both the Conservative and Reform movements have decided to enlarge their own systems. Meanwhile, day schools present two challenges to the traditional Jewish attitude toward the public square.

The Schools, Their Philosophy and Cost

The first challenge is to the public school's role as the integrating mechanism of Jews into a pluralistic society. When students equipped only with an adolescent's idea of Judaism are exposed to a sophisticated secular culture, Judaism is usually the loser, but this has mattered less to most Jewish parents than the quality of the public school itself. The decline of public school systems in the United

States has certainly encouraged Jewish migration from the big cities to suburban locations and to some extent from public schools to Jewish day schools. But the rise of the day school movement has presented to Jews the same issues presented to the failing schools of the inner city. If private schools can do it better, even if they are under religious auspices, is public financing not somehow justifiable? Are vouchers, for example, not only in the broader public interest but also in the parochial Jewish interest?

The fact is that even with Federation support and private philanthropy, the cost of Jewish day schools is outstripping middle-class family resources.[24] Those who argue for the strictest separation of church and state have to confront not only the Jewish need but also the historic American pattern of erecting a wall of separation and then making a series of small (or large) openings in it for pragmatic reasons. The greatest voucher program in history—the G.I. Bill after World War II—was applicable to all colleges regardless of religion. Every day public school buses transport parochial school children; public funds support lunch programs, science labs, and the like, depending on state law and local arrangements. Moreover, even the most avid Jewish proponents of separation have not sought to remove the tax exemptions of synagogues and schools.

Thus far, the Jewish school movement for more government assistance has made little headway and the most recent JCPA Statement seems to backtrack to the old position of separation. Only the Orthodox lobby in Washington has favored vouchers, joining with Catholics and Evangelical Protestants in the cause.[25] Jewish education, more specifically the Jewish day school, is one answer to the crisis of continuity, but it is an answer that faces its own financial crisis, apparently beyond the ability of the Jewish community to solve on its own. Moreover, the overall communal commitment to those schools is simply not yet great enough to overcome the twin historic American Jewish inhibitions against separate schools and public funding of religious schools.[26]

One interesting effect, however, has been to strengthen further the hold of the Federation and the Federation professionals on Jewish life. Renewed emphasis on American Jewish survival has certainly shifted the attention and resources of the Federations from Israel and rescue work abroad to what has become in effect a "self-rescue" at home. This, too, follows an American Jewish tradition: the volunteer community leadership, not the rabbis, are in charge.

The Federations Act

An active corps of professionals, much better educated and more religiously active than the typical American Jew, are now designing continuity programs.[27] Officials of the New York Federation, the largest and wealthiest in the country, see, for example, the answer not only in education but also in the larger Jewish experience—or the lack of it. The 1990 NJPS revealed that "Jewish homes do not include Jewish experiences." In the New York view the solution is not to burden the schools with more than they can manage, nor the community with a sense of guilt in the face of a society-wide assimilation affecting all religious and social groups. Instead, the community must strengthen what Daniel Elazar called the "marginal or intermittent" Jews by subjecting them to Jewish experiences: exposure to Israel for the youth, expanded Hillel programs on campus, adult education everywhere, moving toward personal commitment to mitzvot in small settings. "If a Jew has not experienced the power and beauty of Shabbat . . . why should he or she learn how to recite kiddush—or study about the origins of Shabbat in Genesis?" asked John Ruskay, executive vice-president and CEO of the New York UJA Federation.[28] The problem, he argued, is less one of skill to be learned in school than the absence of a "compelling Jewish community" where those skills find a home. In short, nothing less than a renewal of the Jewish community from the inside out is needed.[29]

There are, of course, serious questions about whether this strategy can succeed. Some have argued that the very individualism that is so marked a feature of American society and its religious counterpart—a kind of spiritualism—are not really compatible with the Jewish ethic of commandment and obligation, and that this is precisely what moves Jews to the margins.[30] The "first language" of American Jews having become individual, the "second language" of community, memory, and responsibility, to borrow Robert Bellah's terms, will be a vast jump indeed.[31]

Challenging the Consensus

Thus far, then, identity politics inspired by fear of assimilation do not seem to have substantially modified the Jewish position in the public square. But in the summer of 1999, the New York Federation complained that the JCPA was "out of touch" on key issues, singling out school vouchers and affirmative action. The New Yorkers depicted the Jewish community as more diverse than the JCPA position would suggest. More specifically, the New York Federation advised the JCPA to pay more attention to "Jewish issues," such as the Jewish elderly and how various social security reform programs would affect the Jewish community.[32] While key officials in both the Federations' newly organized umbrella group, the United Jewish Communities, and JCPA have stressed that JCPA's public policy agenda remains intact, these are warning shots clearly heard in the communal establishment.[33]

It may be premature to declare the end of the liberal consensus on the basis of such bureaucratic tidings, yet the episode suggests the question pungently put by Dennis Prager: "How do liberalism and Judaism differ? . . . [I]f liberalism and Judaism are essentially identical, why be Jewish?"[34] Defenders of the traditional JCPA approach have claimed that, far from following the liberals, the Jewish agenda has led politicians of both parties—although primarily Democrats—in the best direction for Jewish and general American social interests. Albert Chernin, a veteran leader of the JCPA, writing in the Philadelphia *Jewish Exponent* (February 10, 2000), anchored Jewish views on church-state separation and minority rights in the fight to overcome bigotry at its roots. The answer, in his view, was not to change positions on public funding for religious schools, for example, but rather to "give strong support" to day schools and Jewish education while also remaining committed to public schools, which most American and most American Jewish children still attend.

These views reflect accurately the surveyed opinions of Jewish professionals. While much more highly "Jewish" in education and religious practice than the general Jewish public, they are, on the whole, much more insistent on such matters as separation of church and state.[35]

Judaism and Public Policy

Jewish identity policies may indeed begin to restrict the scope and the resources applied by the Jewish community to broader issues, thereby turning the community inward and reassessing the American Jewish tradition that associates Judaism and liberalism. But it would be prudent not to exaggerate the extent to which Judaism itself will affect such positions. As one veteran JCPA leader put it, "we talk the talk [more religious input] but we don't walk the walk." The explanation here seems to be that American Jews are a community divided by a common religion. On top of that, most American Jews do not take too much direction from the rabbis, whomever they may be. Two social issues illustrate the disconnect between Judaism as defined by the rabbis and the stance taken by Jewish organizations. One is abortion. "Choice" as advocated by the feminist movement and endorsed by the major Jewish women's groups usually means the woman's right to an abortion by her own decision. This is completely contrary to the Jewish religious tradition, which allows for abortion only under very limited conditions.

Another is homosexuality. While homosexual and lesbian congregations have sprung up around the country, only the Reconstructionists have endorsed same sex marriages. Most recently, the Reform movement, while insisting on full rights for homosexuals and lesbians, still refused to grant same sex partnership the religious status of man and wife. Most other Jewish organizations, however, support by and large full rights for gays. As for the apparently explicit scriptural condemnation of homosexuality as an "abomination," one Federation leader, himself observant, explained that "you can torture the tradition until it gives up what you want of it." Both the Reform and Conservative rabbinical leadership have been put on the defensive by this issue.[36]

Arguably, both abortion and homosexual behavior are activities that diminish the Jewish future by reducing the potential birth rate and as such should be discouraged by the Jewish community simply for pragmatic reasons. Yet survey after survey has shown that American Jews are at the most liberal edge in sexual mores, including premarital sex.[37] Such positions on these so-called cultural issues place American Jews not only on the liberal side of the divide but contrary to Jewish religious tradition. Judaism is certainly absent from the public square on these matters.

To sum up: the American Jewish approach to religion in the public square shows some movement in the direction of a more identity-based politics. This is a crucial development for, in the end, such a community approach will overshadow the individualistic ethos that has dominated the Jewish public square. It will concentrate more on Jewish issues than general ones and define a Jewish approach that may or may not coincide with liberalism (or conservatism). Indeed, the communal "renaissance" that is now the focus of even the secular-minded Federations, by putting the American Jew more in touch with Judaism, is bound to influence positions on public issues. The key step will be more government funding of Jewish day schools.[38] Here, then, is the paradox: the American Jewish tradition has pushed religion out of the public square, the better to allow Jews to participate easily in it; now the very fruit of that success in the form

of dangerous assimilation is pushing Judaism (or the shadow of it)
back into the square in the guise of identity politics.

The Coalition That Was

American Jews, as noted earlier, are the second most loyal Democrats, just behind American blacks. Indeed, the coalition between
these two minorities is the stuff of legend for many American Jews,
who see in the substantial assistance given the black quest for equality the finest Jewish tradition of justice.[39] The breakdown of this
alliance over a whole gamut of issues provoked a domestic crisis
among Jewish liberals similar to the shock of the Yom Kippur War
in 1973 that gave birth to the neo-conservatives in foreign policy.

Beginning with the bitter Brownsville, New York, school district
strike that pitted black power advocates against the largely Jewish
teacher's unions, relations worsened notably in the subsequent big
city riots of the late 1960s when blacks looted and burned many
Jewish-owned stores. Black intellectuals espoused a third worldism
that was blatantly anti-Israel; crude anti-Semitic stereotypes became
a stock in trade on college campuses and ghettos alike.[40] Then Jews
became wary of "affirmative action," a concept of redress for past
discrimination that began to look like a quota system working to
Jewish disadvantage, especially in university admissions. "For Jews,
quotas were a way of keeping people out; for African Americans,
quotas were a way of letting people in."[41] There were also public
quarrels with leading Afro-American figures. Blacks widely believed that American Jews forced Andrew Young, U.S. ambassador
to the United Nations, to resign after meeting a PLO representative
in 1980. (It was actually Secretary of State Vance who insisted that
President Carter dismiss him.) Jesse Jackson made notably anti-
Israel and anti-Jewish remarks during the 1980s. Louis Farrakhan
and his Nation of Islam put anti-Semitic diatribes at the heart of
their movement. More recently, the Rev. Al Sharpton has been im-
plicated in anti-Jewish riots, especially during the infamous pogrom
in 1991 against the Lubavitcher Hasidim in Crown Heights after an
automobile accident killed a young black.

Thus, where American Jews and Afro-Americans crossed paths,
they found themselves increasingly at odds over Israel, the schools,
affirmative action, and anti-Semitism. It was small wonder that
many students of the situation saw the black-Jewish alliance to be
over—except that they both continued to vote Democratic and their
leaders, at least, advocated similar liberal positions.[42]

By the end of the 1990s, however, there was a determined effort to salvage the alliance, including a joint effort by Howard University and the American Jewish Committee.[43] On January 18, 2000—Martin Luther King Day—the Rev. Jesse Jackson, addressing the Third Annual Conference of the Jewish-funded Foundation for Ethnic Understanding, declared relations to be "better than ever." The new emphasis is on economic development. Jackson, for his part, had been asked earlier by Ambassador Ronald Lauder, chairman of the Presidents Conference, for his help in freeing thirteen Iranian Jews accused of spying for Israel.[44]

This extraordinary turnabout seemed part of a three-pronged Jewish strategy for recovery of the relationship: (1) coupling new programs of economic empowerment with an effort to cultivate black leaders amenable to dialogue; (2) making black-Jewish relations a regular part of Jewish school curricula, and identifying public service with help for blacks; and (3) ostracizing those leaders who were considered beyond the pale. The latter policy, however, has suffered serious reverses. One example was the Million Man March, sponsored by Farrakhan and addressed by Jackson himself. Farrakhan, later to appear on CNN as an opponent of racism, has taken major strides toward respectability but without shedding his anti-Semitic utterances.

Another incident, also involving Farrakhan, illustrated the difficulties that the Jewish community faced in trying to isolate him. In early 1997, the white working-class neighborhood of Gray's Ferry in Philadelphia erupted in racial tension over complaints of harassment by the few black residents, and white charges of unruly behavior by blacks renting there under the Federal Section 8 housing program. After months of rising trouble, the Nation of Islam threatened to organize a mass march through the neighborhood. Then Mayor Ed Rendell, later head of the Democratic Party and himself Jewish, was persuaded to invite Farrakhan to a rally against racism, and the Nation withdrew from the march. The two appeared together at a mainstream black church (Tindley Temple United Methodist) on March 19, a nice example of the traditional willingness of Afro-Americans, if not Jews, to fuse religion and the public square.[45]

There were no Jews living in Gray's Ferry, but the Jewish community vigorously protested the legitimacy conferred on Farrakhan by the mayor's action.[46] Notably, the Catholic archdiocese also refused to join the rally and very few whites attended. Rendell was stung; he complained that the Jewish organizations had only their "narrow" interest at heart but that he, the mayor, bore a larger responsibility.

Thus, Jews found themselves uncomfortably characterized as less than fully responsible by a powerful politician, even as he joined publicly with an avowed anti-Semite in the name of maintaining public order. Jews had been isolated politically by their own coalition partners—a profoundly unsettling incident.[47]

The black-Jewish coalition, like all political bedfellowships, can still be run at some levels despite the absence of once broader common interests. But for an American Jewish community still anxious about anti-Semitism, the direction of the black leadership must give pause. Insofar as the Farrakhans and the Sharptons gain acceptance as leaders without disavowing their anti-Semitism, and are courted by the Democratic Party, in turn, the Jews must wonder just what their coalition is worth. Moreover, some of the issues are still potential bombshells. Court decisions and the readiness of President Clinton to "reform" affirmative action have taken that issue down a peg, but there is gathering movement to see racial preference as more than just a way to assure the "social good" of diversity but "remedying past and present wrongs."[48] When the bill comes due for these remedies either through such preferences or claims for reparations, the Jews will find themselves in an awkward position. As a white, successful minority, the American Jew will have no claim for redress for past discrimination but will surely be classed among those who should pay by those who demand compensation. The successful Jewish campaign on behalf of Holocaust survivors is sure to be invoked by the claimants, repugnant though this may be to Jewish sensibilities. A "victim focused ideology of preferential liberalism," to borrow Shelby Foote's phrase,[49] will challenge the essence of the old Jewish civil religion's emphasis on equality of opportunity and equal treatment.

The Coalition That Wasn't

A decade ago, Irving Kristol summed up a decade of Jewish anxiety over religion in the public square: "The key question inevitably is whether a less secular, more religious society, will mean an increase in anti-Semitism."[50] Indeed, the whole issue of religion in politics had been brought to its current intensity by the appearance of Christian Protestant Evangelical movements, united under charismatic leadership with the open purpose of changing American society. While Kristol (and other neo-conservatives) saw secular humanism gone awry as the real threat, most Jews viewed the Christian Right as a bigger danger.[51]

The fundamentalists, as they were sometimes called, owed their roots to a conservative-liberal theological split that followed the shock of Darwinism and modern biblical scholarship in the late nineteenth century. They also drew on the periodic "awakenings" in American history that sought social change to reflect religious principles, such as abolition of slavery or the sale of liquor. The idea of making America a Christian society, if not a Christian state, of course, was not one that Jews could embrace. Organized in such groups as the Christian Coalition and the Moral Majority, the religious Right represented a protest against the encroachment of a secularizing Supreme Court and federal government that outlawed school prayer, imposed standards on religious groups through the IRS, and threatened morality through *Roe v. Wade,* itself, in their view, the logical consequence of a decadent society.[52] The fundamentalists soon proved reasonably adept at coalition politics, becoming a major force in the Republican Party, sometimes to the consternation of both moderate Republicans and the few but faithful Jewish Republicans.[53]

American Jews, for the most part, strongly opposed the domestic program of this very energetic political force and were extremely disturbed over the implications of a "Christian America." (The Anti-Defamation League summarized these objections in the very title of their 1994 report, *The Religious Right; The Assault on Tolerance and Pluralism in America.*) But the Christian Right did advocate one position of supreme interest to Jews: unflinching support for the State of Israel. Coming when many of American Jewry's traditional church allies in the separationist wars were turning sharply anti-Israel (e.g., the National Council of Churches), this offered an opening to a coalition.

Ultimately, the Jews found that they could oppose the Christian Right and still count on their support for Israel. The reason was religious, not political. The Evangelicals believed that a secure Jewish state would set the stage for the return of Jesus, at which time the Jews would accept him as messiah. This conviction, however repugnant to Jews, made leaders such as Pat Robertson and Jerry Falwell staunch political advocates of the less compromising Israeli politicians. Some Christian millenarians have even joined with Jewish groups who wish to build the Third Temple.[54] This very solicitude for Israel's welfare has been accompanied, however, by a worldview that in many particulars reeks of old anti-Semitic conspiracy theories. At one time or another, prominent leaders such as Robertson and Falwell have fallen into this category; others have offended by their public calls for Jewish conversions; and those

Jews advocating a coalition with the Christian Right have been embarrassed and apologetic.[55] These stirrings reinforce what Alan Mittleman has called Judaism's "basic trope . . . that of an adversarial relationship with Christianity and with the gentile world in particular."[56]

Moreover, the very theological underpinning of the fundamentalist position on Israel makes it unnecessary for American Jewish groups to pay much of a price in politics. The Christian Right may oppose American Jews on American domestic policy, but they will favor Israel "come hell or high water" because the survival and flourishing of the Jewish state is, in their view, fundamental to the fulfillment of Christianity itself.

In recent years, the Christian Right has waned as a political force, the Moral Majority disbanding and the Christian Coalition a shadow of itself, to name just two. Still, they have had a dramatic impact on American politics, not only because of what Neuhaus called their "aggressive defense" of their way of life, but their insertion of moral issues into the public square. "[T]hey did not really want to bash in the door to the public square, but it was locked. . . . Anyway the hinges were rusty and it gave way under pressure that was only a little more than polite."[57] The idea of making America a more upstanding society, defined by reference to religious (Christian) belief, has thus remained as a residue of the latest awakening.

This idea has now been coupled with another one, that religious organizations can help to solve social ills even as defined by secular society. The movement to entrust more public welfare services to "faith-based" groups represents the general consensus that liberal, secular methods have failed, and that more than money must be thrown at the problem. Advocates clearly believe that religious teaching on character, personal responsibility and regard for others can be employed without "establishing" a particular faith in the process.

This is in some way the counterpart to the argument that school vouchers in inner-city neighborhoods will allow poor parents to escape failing public schools for the more effective, faith-based religious schools, notably the remnants of the once teeming Catholic systems now often serving largely non-Catholic populations. But the "faith-based" experiment for social services has already progressed beyond the voucher issue, which is apparently stalled by a combination of the courts and lack of national consensus. In the 2000 presidential election, both candidates endorsed faith-based services and legislation allowing payments is already on the books (1996), although not much used as yet. George W. Bush emphasized this approach in his first meeting on the subject soon after his election, a meeting largely attended by black Christian ministers.

Unlike many churches, American synagogues do little in the way of general social services. The Jewish groups that do, such as Jewish Family and Vocational Services and the hospitals, are descendants of the earlier, less integrated phase of American Jewish history. They are also professional and secular. A large flow of funds toward "faith-based" groups will require a new set of Jewish organizational relationships if the Jewish community as a whole wants to participate in this experiment. (The two Jews attending the Bush meeting, Murray Friedman of the AJCommittee and Rabbi Daniel Lapin of Toward Tradition, represent organizations that do not deliver inner-city social services.) Thus far, the Jewish reaction to Bush's new Office of Faith-Based Initiatives might be described as carefully skeptical, and sometimes openly opposed.[58]

To sum up: a strong whiff of anti-Semitism from the Christian Right, plus real objections to the social ideas of the Evangelicals, prevented any real coalition between American Jews and the most active American Christian proponents of a more religious public square. Jews were able to act tactically to encourage the already theologically mandated support by the Christian Right for Israel without having to make any quid pro quo on domestic issues. (A similar detachment took place on the left, where Jews retained coalitions with anti-Israel groups, such as the National Council of Churches, for purposes of sustaining separation of church and state.) Overall, however, the Jewish debate with the Christian Right has been overtaken by a residual consensus that, in the face of failed secular approaches, religious organizations do have something significant to contribute to the solution of public pathologies. The movement to entrust "faith-based" groups with federal funds and a significant role in dealing with the homeless, welfare, and the like enjoys public support.

If the Jewish community wishes to participate in this movement, then a coalition with such groups will indeed have to be formed, even though this is a repudiation of the traditional American Jewish approach to the problem.

Uncertain Steps: American Jews
in the New Public Square

At the conclusion of this chapter, let us return to its beginning, the singular phenomenon of an Orthodox Jew nominated to be vice president of the United States. This "moment" of arrival in the Jewish relationship with others in the public square was regarded quite rightly as the ultimate sign of Jewish acceptance in America. Yet it was accompanied by the candidate's own fervent references to religion in the public square, the antithesis of a decades-old effort by American Jews to reduce the role of religion altogether in public policy. Or, as one acute observer put it, American Jews wanted to see a Jew in the White House but not too Jewish a Jew. Is Lieberman himself an anomaly or the forerunner of the American Jewish approach to a more religious public square? Are Lieberman's long held (if temporarily modified) views on vouchers, welfare, and the role of faith in public life a forecast of new relationships that may yet leave Jews largely voting for Democrats but more conservative overall? If so, the Jews would be aligning themselves with their fellow Americans: "Although the country leaned Democratic in the 1990s, it also leaned in a conservative direction."[59] In this context, Jews would remain part of a stable Democratic political coalition consisting of ethnics, Jews, and "seculars"; the Republican counterparts are the traditional white Protestants and Evangelicals. Put another way, the basic relationships of Jews to others in the public square would remain roughly the same even as the entire political discourse moved rightward.

The cases examined here suggest that American Jewish steps in this new, more religious atmosphere are not so certain. Identity politics, stimulated by fears for the community's survival, are reviving interest in Judaism and with it, an "inward" turn that is edging the community ever closer to a more elastic interpretation of what constitutes an unacceptable breach of the wall between church and state. I suggest that additional public funding for Jewish day schools will be a key step that will not only change Jewish attitudes toward that wall but also possibly ease Jewish opposition to a broader role for religion in public education for all Americans. In this case the old fear that Jews will be suspect if they are only for themselves may be transmuted into a view that Jews should advocate the same opportunity for others that the Jews have for themselves: a quality education.

A second but far more problematic change is less likely to occur except on a longer-term basis. Jews place themselves in surveys overwhelmingly on the more socially permissive side of the so-called culture wars when it comes to abortion, homosexuality, and sexual attitudes. This hardly comports with the traditionally strong Jewish family structure or Judaism itself, but then the data suggest that the stable, two-parent family is much less common than it used to be, with a substantial part of the Jewish population divorced or single. The very divisions among religious and community leaders over how to deal with a phenomenon such as homosexuality make a consensus to replace the current liberal views much less likely.

A third important change in the new public square concerns traditional allies. We have not explored issues concerning relations with the union movement on school reform or mainline churches on an Israel that finds itself embattled once more. The coalition under the most strain is likely to continue to be the relationship with African Americans. Many leaders have taken the historic quest for equality, so strongly supported by American Jews, into a new realm of racial preferences. The self-esteem of American Jews is heavily invested in traditional notions of help for society's less fortunate. But Jews have begun to share the views of other Americans that disadvantaged groups should not be assisted with special preference. Despite attempts to patch over the breaks in black-Jewish relations, these are bound to remain troubled, given the drift leftward of many black politicians and a readiness to accept the Farrakhans, anti-Semitism and all. The looming issue of reparations, we suggest, will put a new strain on this once most cherished of Jewish political alliances.

A fourth and final change examined here concerns Jewish relationships with openly religious organizations in the business of the public square. If fear of left-wing anti-Semitism has made Jews wary of tendencies among African Americans, then fear of right-wing anti-Semitism has forestalled any coalition—beyond support for Israel—with Christian Evangelicals. But Evangelicals have left their mark in the readiness of national politicians to speak of religion. More important, the failure of liberal ideas in dealing with social pathologies has stimulated a national consensus of sorts that faith-based groups have a newly important role to play in this field and that public funding should be available for it. The old Jewish insistence that the problem is lack of money or that the approach is too risky because it breaks down the wall of separation offers scant comfort in the face of successful pragmatism such as that practiced by Mayor Steve Goldsmith of Indianapolis.

Despite all the arguments for political change in the Jewish voting pattern, it remains predictably Democratic except when a candidate gives the Jews a good reason to vote otherwise in both national
and local arenas. (Reagan nationally, Guliani in New York, Whit-
man in New Jersey, and Goldsmith in Indianapolis all succeeded in
drawing much larger numbers of Jewish voters than usual, especially younger ones, although not a majority.) Jews voted overwhelmingly for Sam Katz during the tight mayoral race in Philadelphia and they voted much less overwhelmingly for Hillary Clinton
in the New York senatorial race. An AJCommittee survey in 1999
found that barely a majority of American Jews still describe themselves as Democrats, "suggesting that even the seemingly unshak-
able Jewish vote may be up for grabs."[60] This is new but has not yet
translated into a dramatic change of allegiances. There are other important elements of Jewish relations with others in the public square
that have not been covered here but are of great significance. In an
electoral system fed by huge amounts of money under ambiguous
legal rules, Jewish contributions to both parties play a significant
role. This is not new, nor is the influence of what one wag called the
"macherdom" in Jewish communal affairs to be underestimated. (As
the donor base of Federations shrinks and new private foundations
multiply, the moneyed Jews may even increase their importance.)
Emphasis on campaign reform may have the paradoxical effect of
reducing the influence of large single donors, but, given American
history, this is unlikely.

Another important issue is the community's ability to forge productive relationships with two fast growing immigrant minorities,
Muslims and Hispanics. In recent years, the Muslims have organized in both the local and the national arenas. Relations with the
Jewish community have occasionally been excellent on domestic
issues, but they range from polite disagreement to open antagonism
when Israel is the subject. Over the past few years, Muslim pressures on the Disney Exhibit on Jerusalem in Orlando, Florida, and
the dispute over a Burger King franchise in a Jerusalem Jewish
neighborhood beyond the 1967 lines have troubled the Jewish community. This was strongly reinforced by ambivalent and antagonis-
tic Muslim reactions to the September 11th attacks on the World
Trade Center and the Pentagon, disrupting Jewish-Muslim "dia-
logues" in New York, Los Angeles, and Cleveland.[61] Relations with
Hispanics, on the other hand, seem more susceptible to local rather
than national efforts, given the diversity of the groups described
best as originally Spanish-speaking. Efforts at building such local
coalitions have just begun and face serious demographic, geo-

graphic, and socio-economic differences.[62] The voting and economic clout of both populations will increase and Jews may find their status and power reduced unless they can forge common interests.

In conclusion, the new public square with its religious component finds American Jews pressed back upon their internal resources in unexpected ways. A community that elevated the right of individual choice must now alter the balance toward group loyalty in order to survive. A group defined by others in the public square by its religious affiliation must now seek fresh meaning in that religion to retain its cohesion. As one analyst of Jewish communal affairs wrote, "It is to be hoped that American Jews find a compelling Jewish voice, nurtured by their own authentic sources, which they can add to the ecumenical, political, and moral conversation on which republican renewal depends."[63] These new, albeit uncertain, Jewish steps in the public square are thus of significance not only to Jews but also to the broader American community.

Notes

1. Notably, the Anti-Defamation League, in a letter to Lieberman after the candidate's appearance in a Detroit church, noted that "there is a point at which the emphasis on religion in a political campaign becomes inappropriate and even unsettling in a religiously diverse society such as ours." Abraham Foxman, the ADL national director, noted a "mixed response" with many Jews unhappy about the criticism of a fellow Jew. See *Jerusalem Post*, September 19, 2000, for an interview with Foxman.

2. Senator Joseph Lieberman, "Vision for America: A Place for Faith," remarks prepared for delivery, Notre Dame University, October 24, 2000.

3. Norman Podhoretz, Irving Kristol, and Eliot Abrams, to name a few, are often called "neo-conservatives." Their political migration began with their objections to liberal foreign policy and their fears for Israel, and then broadened into a domestic critique as well. Murray Friedman has argued for domestic change on pragmatic grounds, that is, the failure of liberal solutions for social problems. Much further afield is Rabbi Daniel Lapin, who associates Judaism with social positions taken by Evangelical Christians, among others.

4. Daniel J. Elazar, *Community and Polity,* 2nd ed. (Philadelphia: Jewish Publication Society, 1995), 8.

5. Arthur Hertzberg, *The Jews in America* (New York: Simon & Schuster, 1989), 13.

6. Hertzberg, *Jews in America.*

7. Irving Howe, *World of Our Fathers* (New York: Harcourt, Brace, 1976), esp. chaps. 6, 9, and 14.

8. Abraham Cahan, editor of the Yiddish *Forward* and an avowed socialist with a talmudic education, gives a poignant picture of Rabbi Joseph's bewilderment in Leon Stein, ed., *The Education of Abraham Cahan* (Philadelphia: Jewish Publication Society, 1969). See also Sara Bershtel and Allen Graubard, *Saving Remnants* (Berkeley: University of California Press, 1993).

9. Donovan Fitzpatrick and Saul Saphire, *Navy Maverick: Uriah Philips Levy* (New York: Doubleday, 1963). The transcript of the entire "Defense of Uriah Levy before the Court of Inquiry Hall at Washington City, November and December 1857" (New York: William C. Bryant, 1898), contains an extraordinarily frank discussion of relations between Jews and non-Jews in pre-Civil War times.

10. Marc Dollinger, *Quest for Inclusion: Jews and Liberalism in Modern American* (Princeton, N.J.: Princeton University Press, 2000), 5.

11. Dollinger, *Quest for Inclusion,* see esp. chaps. 5, 6, and 7.

12. See Elazar, *Community and Polity,* chaps. 8-9.

13. See Steven Windmueller, "The Defenders: The National Jewish Community Relations Agencies," in the companion volume to this book, Alan Mittleman, Robert Licht, and Jonathan Sarna, eds., *Jewish Polity and American Civil Society* (Lanham, Md.: Rowman & Littlefield, 2002). See also Stuart Svonkin, *Jews against Prejudice: American Jews and the Fight for Civil Liberties* (New York: Columbia University Press, 1997).

14. Svonkin, *Jews against Prejudice,* Introduction.

15. Herzberg, *Jews in America.*

16. See Murray Friedman, *The Utopian Dilemma: American Judaism and Public Policy* (Washington, D.C.: Ethics and Public Policy Center, 1985).

17. Alan Dershowitz, *The Disappearing American Jew* (New York: Little Brown, 1997). Dershowitz, a prominent Harvard law professor, earlier published a book entitled *Chutzpah!* (New York: Simon & Schuster, 1992). He argued that American Jews should be confident enough to "demand" more out of society without fear of upsetting the majority. This optimism has been replaced in his latest book by anxiety over the Jewish future; Dershowitz's own son married out. His solution, however, turns out to be a kind of secular Jewishness that resembles the fading civil Judaism of the past plus a lowering of barriers to include the intermarried. For a devastating critique of such ideas and an opposite approach, see Elliott Abrams, *Faith or Fear* (New York: Free Press, 1997).

18. Svonkin, 188-90.

19. Sergio Della Pergola, Uzi Rebhon, and Mark Tolts, "Prospecting the Jewish Future: Population Projections, 2000-2050," in David Singer and Lawrence Grossman, eds., *American Jewish Yearbook 2000* (New York: American Jewish Committee, 2000), 110.

20. Pergola et al., "Prospecting the Jewish Future," 113.

21. See Samuel G. Freedman, *Jew vs. Jew* (New York: Simon & Schuster, 2000), for a highly readable account of the tensions between even the modern Orthodox and the non-Orthodox, esp. chap. 5.

22. Quoted in *The Forward*, English edition, November 3, 2000. See also Jack Wertheimer, "Surrendering to Intermarriage," *Commentary*, March 2001, for a strong critique of how "outreach" and blurred boundaries lend legitimacy to intermarriage. It has been estimated that one-third to one-half of Reform and Reconstructionist congregations are non-Jews. See Sylvia Barack Fishman, Mordechai Rimor, Gary A. Tobin, and Peter Y. Medding, *Intermarriage and American Jews Today: New Findings and Policy Implications* (Cohn Center, Brandeis University, October 1990).

23. Wertheimer, "Who's Afraid of Jewish Day Schools?" *Commentary*, December 1999, 49.

24. Wertheimer, "Who's Afraid," 52. See also Wertheimer's calculations in the American Jewish Committee's *A Statement on Jewish Education, Text and Responses*, December 1999, 67. His general conclusion, if not his numbers, was supported by John Ruskay, CEO of the New York Federation, 46-47.

25. See Lawrence Grossman's article in the companion volume, *Jewish Polity and American Civil Society,* for the debates among the Orthodox on this issue.

26. See the Leadership Survey in Steven M. Cohen, *Jews and the American Public Square: Attitudes of American Jews in Comparative Perspective* (Jerusalem: Jerusalem Center for Public Affairs, 2000), 15-16.

27. Sylvia Barack Fishman, "Spirituality and the Civil Religion," in Elliott Abrams and Robert Dalin, eds., *Secularism, Spirituality and the Future of American Jewry* (Washington, D.C.: Ethics and Public Policy Center, 1999), 28.

28. See Winston Pickett, "From Continuity to Caring Community," an interview with John Ruskay, executive vice-president and CEO of the UJA Federation in New York, *Manhattan Jewish Sentinel*, November 24-30, 2000, 12-16.

29. Pickett, "From Continuity to Caring Community."

30. "Post-War American Jewry: From Ethnic to Privatized Judaism," in Abrams and Dalin, *Secularism, Spirituality.* See the comments by Charles Liebman.

31. Abrams and Dalin, *Secularism, Spirituality.* See comments by Jonathan Woocher.

32. See *The Forward*, English edition, April 7, 2000, "An Open Letter to Hadassah," for a similar view by a disgruntled life member who criticized the women's organization, among other things, for its positions on vouchers and affirmative action, neither of which the author thought should be the focus of Hadassah's social action.

33. See *The Forward*, English edition, September 22, 2000, for an account of these developments. Portions of the New York letter were excerpted in the October 29, 1999, issue of *The Forward*.

34. Abrams and Dalin, *Secularism, Spirituality,* 35.

35. Steven M. Cohen, *Jews and the American Public Square.* For a debate on this issue between AJCommittee's Murray Friedman, who disputes such strict separation, and Marc Stern, director of social action for the

American Jewish Congress, see *Journal of Jewish Communal Service*, Winter 2000.

36. Jack Wertheimer, "Family Values and the Jews," *Commentary*, January 1994.

37. Wertheimer, "Family Values."

38. See the *AJCommittee Statement on Education*, statement of John Ruskay. He offers a "personal thought" that the traditional Jewish opposition to more funding for religious schools should be reexamined, a statement he has repeated since in other public forums.

39. See, for example, Hasia Diner, *In the Almost Promised Land: American Jews and Blacks, 1915-1935* (Baltimore: Johns Hopkins University Press, 1995).

40. Arch Puddington, "Black Anti-Semitism and How It Grows," *Commentary*, April 1994, details some of the more notorious incidents at Kean College and elsewhere.

41. Jerome Chanes, quoted in Jack Salzman, "Introduction," in Jack Salzman and Cornel West, eds., *Struggles in the Promised Land: Toward a History of Black-Jewish Relations in the United States* (New York: Oxford University Press, 1997), 14.

42. See, for example, Murray Friedman, *What Went Wrong? The Creation and Collapse of the Black-Jewish Alliance* (New York: Free Press, 1995).

43. See David Brian Davis, "Jews and Blacks in America," *New York Review of Books*, December 2, 1999, for a discussion of black thinking about the role of Jews.

44. *American Jewish Yearbook 2000*, 169.

45. The *Philadelphia Inquirer*, March 15, 1997, contains an account of the rally and speech excerpts; Rendell and Farrakhan both avoided controversy in their remarks.

46. The *Philadelphia Inquirer*, April 12, 1997, contains a letter from various Jewish groups protesting Rendell's invitation. See also the *Philadelphia Inquirer* of April 9 and April 20 for Jewish reaction. Every issue of April's *Jewish Exponent* resounded to denunciations of the mayor's action and Farrakhan.

47. *Philadelphia Inquirer*, April 1997, and *Jewish Exponent,* April 1997. The legitimacy conferred on Farrahkhan and his local representative, Rodney Muhammad, is reflected in Annette John-Hall, "The Voice of Devotion," *Philadelphia Inquirer Magazine*, February 25, 2001. From this largely favorable piece, one would hardly know that the Nation of Islam was rabidly anti-white and anti-Jewish.

48. See, for example, the letter by two national staff attorneys of the American Civil Liberties Union to the *New Yorker*, January 8, 2001, 5.

49. Shelby Foote, "Ideology as Identity," *Wall Street Journal*, January 11, 2001.

50. Irving Kristol, "The Future of American Jewry," *Commentary*, August 1991.

51. Jonathan Sarna, "Church-State Dilemmas of American Jews," revised version prepared for the Pew project and based on an article in Richard J. Neuhaus, ed., *Jews in Unsecular America* (Grand Rapids, Mich.: Eerdmans, 1987).

52. Abortion later became a useful coalition builder but was not the early focus of the movement. See Richard John Neuhaus, "What the Fundamentalists Want," *Commentary*, May 1985.

53. A long-time major contributor to the Republican Party confided to the author that he regarded the Christian Right not only as the greatest threat to the party but also to American tolerance of Jews.

54. See Gershom Gorenberg, *The End of Days: Fundamentalism and the Struggle for the Temple Mount* (New York: Free Press, 2000), especially chap. 1 on the Red Cow project.

55. See Norman Podhoretz, "In the Matter of Pat Robertson," *Commentary*, August 1995.

56. Alan L. Mittleman, *The Scepter Shall Not Depart From Judah* (Lanham, Md.: Lexington Books, 2000), 177.

57. Neuhaus, "What the Fundamentalists Want."

58. A good sample can be found in the *Philadelphia Jewish Exponent*, February 15, 2001. The American Jewish Committee and the Feinstein Center for American Jewish History at Temple University attempted to find a consensus on these issues. See *In Good Faith: A Dialogue on Government Funding of Faith-Based Social Services*, February 27, 2001.

59. John C. Green, "Religion and Policy in the 1990s: Confrontations and Coalitions," in Mark Silk, ed., *Religion and American Politics: The 2000 Election in Context* (Hartford, Conn.: Center for the Study of Religion in American Life, 2000), 32.

60. See Murray Friedman, "Are American Jews Moving to the Right?" *Commentary*, April 2000, 51.

61. See David Firestone, "For Some Jewish Leaders Partnership with Muslims Is a Casualty of September 11 Attacks," *New York Times*, October 22, 2001, B10. For an interesting capsule account of American Muslim organizations, see the "Symposium: American Muslims and U.S. Foreign Policy," *Middle East Policy* VII, no. 1 (October 1999).

62. See, for example, Steven Windmueller, "Rethinking Latino-Jewish Relations in Los Angeles," *Jerusalem Letter*, Jerusalem Center for Public Affairs, no. 407, June 1, 1999.

63. Alan Mittleman, *The Scepter Shall Not Depart,* 177.

8

The Jewish Debate over State Aid to Religious Schools

Jack Wertheimer

It has been a truism for the past half century that American Jews and their organizations are almost unanimously in favor of an impermeable wall of separation between church and state.[1] Less well known, perhaps, are the periodic eruptions of Jewish communal disputation over state aid to parochial schools. Simply put, proposals to channel government funds to religious schools have prompted debates among American Jews over broad legal principles and also particularistic communal interests.

One reason why state aid to parochial schools has prompted more debate than most other church-state issues is that such aid does not infringe upon Jewish equality: proposals for government funding have provided for the same types of support to schools of all religious denominations. As the historians Jonathan Sarna and David Dalin have observed, this evenhanded approach has narrowed the possible objections to state aid:

> Where Sunday closing laws and prayer in the public schools clearly disadvantaged Jews and could be fought on the basis of Jewish group interests as well as minority rights, state aid to parochial schools was offered to Christian and Jewish schools alike. The issue, then, was not the "equal footing" demand insisted upon since

the days of Jonas Phillips, but rather the "wall of separation" axiom
upon which Jews had built so much of their twentieth-century
church-state philosophy.[2]

In the waning decades of the twentieth century, this axiom would
collide with pressing communal needs.

As long as no other Jewish interests were harmed by strict separationism, it was a relatively simple matter for Jewish organizations to take a reflexively oppositional stance against all breaches
in the wall of separation. But matters were vastly complicated
when the attenuation of commitments to Jewish religious practice
and communal participation, especially among younger Jews, was
placed on the communal agenda. The welfare of educational institutions, chief among them day schools, suddenly assumed higher
priority. Faced with the hard reality of finite Jewish material resources to aid day schools, the skyrocketing costs of running such
schools, and the inability of many interested Jewish families to afford the high tuition expenses, Jewish communal leaders have
come under pressure to address the issue of day school *affordability*. Government funding could certainly help alleviate the crushing financial burdens. As communal leaders have come to regard
day school education as vital for the American Jewish future, they
have been pressed to balance the needs of this enterprise against
the widespread conviction that the strictest forms of separationism
are always good and necessary for America's Jews.

The Mid-Century Consensus

Organized Jewish opposition to government aid for religious
schools began in earnest only in the middle of the twentieth century. Indeed, for much of their prior history in the United States,
Jews not only supported state aid to religious school but, in some
localities, Jewish schools were recipients of state funding. All this
began to change in the second half of the nineteenth century as
public schools under nonsectarian auspices came to be regarded as
the preferred vehicle for delivering an education, a development
that hastened the disappearance of all but a few Jewish day
schools. Yet even when they had formulated positions on public
policy matters, such as state aid to religious schools, Jewish organizations lacked a unified structure to speak in concert. That
would only come under the press of anti-Semitism at home and

abroad during the 1930s and 1940s when so-called intergroup relations agencies joined together to articulate where America's Jews stood on a range of public policy matters.[3]

In the post-World War II era, Jewish agencies increasingly took positions on church-state issues. In 1948, a wall-to-wall coalition of Jewish organizations supported a statement drafted by the Synagogue Council of America and the National Community Relations Advisory Council, the former representing all the religious streams of American Judaism and the latter serving as the coordinating arm for public policy of mainly secular Jewish organizations, opposing all forms of government aid to parochial schools.[4] That same year, the three national community relations organizations—the American Jewish Committee, the American Jewish Congress, and the Anti-Defamation League—successfully banded together to influence a Supreme Court decision in the area of church-state relations; the success of their amicus brief emboldened them to engage in further efforts to thwart potential breaches in the wall of separation.[5]

Thereafter, throughout the second half of the century, the dominant organizations of the Jewish community consistently went on record as staunch opponents of almost every form of government aid to religious schools, ranging from broadly ambitious proposals to channel money directly to such schools, to providing funding specifically for the teaching of general studies in parochial schools, to offering parents vouchers to purchase an education for their children at the school of their choice, to encouraging states or the federal government to provide a tuition tax credit that would help parents shoulder the doubly onerous costs of paying for public schools with their taxes and for private education with their tuition payments. Many Jewish organizations also opposed more narrowly conceived programs to earmark money for purposes such as the transport of children to religious schools, the purchase of general studies textbooks for use in religious schools, the provision of remedial education in parochial schools, or the acquisition of computer equipment and other necessary supplies.[6]

The reasoning behind organized Jewish opposition to all these forms of state aid has remained constant over the past half century. First, and most important, there is the overarching goal of brooking no compromises in church-state separation, lest that principle erode. As the major agencies of the Jewish community candidly noted in a statement to a Senate subcommittee on constitutional rights in 1955,[7] they did not fear a "frontal attack" upon separationism since that "principle is so deeply ingrained in our tradition and so universally recognized."[8] Instead, they testified, "the danger to separation of church and state . . . lies in watering down, evasion, circumvention and compromise, while lip service is paid to the principle itself."

Once this broad approach was embraced, some Jewish organizations regarded any effort to channel government funds to aid religious schools as a potential "opening wedge,"[9] and therefore not to be tolerated any more than other types of breaches in the impermeable wall. The entrenched and, for some organizations, unbending logic of this thinking was candidly confirmed by a prominent attorney engaged in church-state battles during the latter decades of the twentieth century. Describing the decision of Jewish groups to fight against the use of federal funds to help parochial schools supplement remedial education for poor children, the central issue in the 1985 Supreme Court case of *Aguilar v. Felton*, Marc Stern, the lead attorney for the American Jewish Congress, observed:

> *Aguilar* gave people fits. It was litigated by PEARL [Committee on Public Education and Religious Liberty] on the theory that any form of government aid to parochial schools is bad. But that's their [PEARL's] particular ideology. We [the AJCongress] agonized over it. . . . We ask[ed] ourselves, "Why are we doing this case? What valuable social purpose does it serve?" But the answer was that you couldn't draw a line between this and something that was really bad. There was no way of knowing that the aid program would have worked out benignly because there would have been a whole new series of programs that chipped away at the edge of church-state separation. It was a rare case where the slippery slope argument made sense because politically that's what would have happened. . . . But it didn't leave anybody with a great feeling afterwards.[10]

Once committed to the preservation of the *principle* of absolute separation, many Jewish organizations felt they had no choice but to challenge every breach in the wall of separation—even when they recognized the unhelpful social consequences of their position.[11]

Second, separationists have put forth a particular interpretation of the First Amendment. As Leo Pfeffer, the chief architect of the post-World War II campaign for strict separationism, put it in 1971:

> If the First Amendment means anything, it means that religious freedom can be insured only when religious operations remain free

of government influence and that government can function on behalf of all citizens only when it conscientiously refuses to become the instrument of any religious interest group or groups. Those of us who vigorously defend our constitutional freedom to worship as we please—and that includes virtually all Americans—must understand that religious liberty includes the precious freedom not to be taxed to pay for anyone's religious education. Imparting religious values is the task of the home, the church, the synagogue—and for those who so desire—the religious school. It is not the task of government.[12]

In Pfeffer's view, the government was to be completely neutral about religion, and it was not to "meddle in the affairs of God, to hurt Him or to help Him."[13]

Implicit in this set of formulations is an assumption about the place of religion: it properly belongs in the private sphere *only*. In the just-quoted statement by Leo Pfeffer, the teaching of religion is limited to the home and church or synagogue. In other pronouncements on pending cases, Jewish groups spearheaded by Pfeffer warned against government aid that would "advance religion and entangle government in religious matters."[14] It was this fear of entanglement that spurred Pfeffer and others to have scant patience for any efforts to accommodate the needs of individuals for the free exercise of religion. As one professional in the field candidly conceded: "We have never been an accommodationist community. We like the naked public square."[15] In the view of communal affairs professionals, Jews—and American society generally—were not only better off with a public life denuded of religious influence; even more important, the First Amendment *required* the public square to be stripped of religion.

A third contention of those supporting strict separationism has been that *any* government aid flowing to religious schools entangles the state in support of religion. For this reason, separationists have consistently opposed funding for religious schools even if such money never went directly for the support of religious instruction—for example, if it was earmarked for the teaching of general subjects, such as math and science, in religious schools, or to purchasing textbooks for such general studies courses. In extreme cases, some groups have even opposed funds to bus children to religious schools, aid in remedial courses, or supply meals for poor children. As Samuel Rabinove of the American Jewish Committee put it: "In many denominational schools, there is no bright line of separation between secular and religious studies. Rather, the two are interwoven in much of the curriculum."[16] The underlying assumption is that it is impossible to distinguish between general educational goals in religious schools and narrower denominational ones. Therefore, no state aid should enter the parochial schools.

Still a fourth argument addresses charges that by consistently siding against religious institutions seeking aid, Jewish organizations are implicitly "antireligious." In defense of their policy positions, these groups contended that separationism is *good for religion* because "all religions will flourish best if government keeps its hands off, neither to hinder or to help them."[17] The assumption here is that "any religion that cannot flourish without governmental assistance does not deserve to flourish"; by extension, this also means that if religious schools cannot find adequate private funding, they are also unworthy of surviving. Moreover, proponents of strict separation also argued that only their position *protects* religious institutions from government meddling. In their view, the role of religions is to serve as a prophetic voice frequently at odds with government policies. The independence of religious leaders is best preserved if religious institutions are not beholden to the state.

Opponents of state funding almost invariably have linked their rejection of aid to religious schools to their strong commitment to the public school as the preferred vehicle for educating the next generation of Americans. They fear that the more governments support private education, the more they erode the privileged position of the public school. As a leader of the American Jewish Committee put it: "The public schools are the foundation stone upon which our democratic institutions are based, and we ought to very carefully consider changes which may adversely affect this unique contribution of American life. Directly put, we are concerned that if massive public aid is given to non-public schools, they will not only solve their present financial problems, but they will expand and grow at the expense of the public schools."[18]

Sometimes the argument has been put in general terms, with vague hints about efforts to undermine respect for public school education in the minds of America's citizenry; in other cases, fears were expressed that stronger students will flee to private schools and the public schools will come to be dominated increasingly by the weakest of students. "Inevitably," a spokesman for a Jewish organization testified at a public hearing in New Jersey, "more of the white students, and more of the better than average students, both black and white, will be diverted from public schools to the private schools."[19] Moreover, the likely source of money to aid religious schools, opponents have feared, would derive from funds siphoned off from public schools budgets. It was unthinkable for "private schools, traditionally supported by private funds, and optionally attended, . . . [to be] competing for state funding with compulsory education provided by public schools."[20]

Finally, opponents of state aid have periodically articulated their understanding of how the needs of Jewish educational institutions should best be addressed. At its annual meeting in 1971, the National Jewish Community Relations Advisory Council approved a statement endorsing Jewish education as essential for the perpetuation of the Jewish community and urging its constituent agencies to "help to interpret to the Jewish community the seriousness of the financial problems facing the Jewish day schools and to encourage adequate financial support of such schools by the Jewish community." But the signers counseled Jewish educational institutions neither to seek nor accept government funding for their programs and affirmed their view that "the Jewish community has the resources to finance Jewish education adequately without the aid of the government funds."[21]

These arguments in opposition to state aid were broadcasted by the major community relations organizations to a number of audiences. Perhaps the primary one has been the Jewish community itself. While organizational spokesmen commonly presented themselves as representative of their membership, the rank-and-file were not actively canvassed, and certainly they did not have a say in the day-to-day decisions of legal departments formulating amicus briefs. Jewish organizations issued statements on a range of church-state matters in order to inform and *rally* their members.[22] The second audience consisted of legislators whose votes Jewish groups sought to influence. Jewish organizations lobbied for or against legislation, and in the process they developed position papers to clarify where the Jewish community stood on issues of aid to religious schools. Finally, Jewish organizations sharpened their positions in order to play a role in the legal arena: the so-called "big three" and some other Jewish community relations agencies frequently filed amicus briefs to influence pending court cases.[23]

The Critics

Only one organized sector of the American Jewish community broke with the wall-to-wall consensus opposed to state aid—the major institutions of religious Orthodoxy. The first organization to break ranks was Agudath Israel, the standard-bearer for Haredi Orthodoxy, followed by Torah Umesorah, the primary agency coordinating Orthodox day schools, and the Young Israel synagogue movement.[24] By the late 1960s, the congregational body of modern Orthodoxy, the Union of Orthodox Congregations of America, a member of NCRAC, challenged the official consensus by issuing regular dissents from the "Joint Program Plans." Typical of these dissents[25] was the demurral appended to the above-quoted statement on the Responsibility of Community Relations for Jewish Education issued in 1971-72: "The Union of Orthodox Jewish Congregations of America believes that religious schools are entitled to government reimbursement for the secular instruction they provide."[26] In time, a legal arm was established by the Orthodox community named the National Jewish Commission on Law and Public Affairs (COLPA) with the express goal of addressing pending court cases and proposed legislation.[27]

These Orthodox groups were hardly shy about their motivations. As the sponsors of virtually all Jewish day schools in mid-century America, they fought for government aid for their schools. By the early 1960s, they had forged alliances with Catholic groups favoring aid to church-sponsored parochial schools.[28] In time, they broadened their critique and questioned why the organized Jewish community consistently favored secular institutions at the expense of religious ones. But their primary concern was to find means of aiding Jewish day schools.

A number of prominent American Jews not associated with Orthodoxy joined the fray. While the fate of day schools certainly preoccupied many of these writers, they were equally motivated by a desire to rethink the proper place of religion in American public life. Accordingly, they helped articulate the case for Jewish acceptance of state aid to religious schools by framing a set of arguments in favor of a broader reconsideration of church-state arrangements. Although they were mavericks and their views reflected nothing more than their own personal opinions, they were nonetheless important voices in the debate by virtue of their stature and also their ability to challenge the principle of strict separationism. Among the most prominent dissenters from the communal consensus on church-state matters generally, and particularly state aid to religious schools were: Morris B. Abram, an activist who served as a volunteer leader of major Jewish organizations, including the American Jewish Committee and the Council of Jewish Federations;[29] Arthur Gilbert, a Reform rabbi who held high executive positions with the Anti-Defamation League and, later, the National Conference of Christians and Jews;[30] Will Herberg, a leading social and theological thinker;[31] Milton Himmelfarb, editor of the *American Jewish Year Book*;[32] Wolfe Kelman, the long-time executive of the Rabbinical Assembly, the organization of Con-servative rabbis;[33] Jakob Petuchowski, professor of liturgy at the Hebrew Union College in Cincinnati;[34] and Seymour Siegel, a professor of Jewish thought at the Jewish Theological Seminary.[35]

Their critique of existing communal policy began with a challenge to the view that only the strictest, most rigid enforcement of separationism was in the interests of Jews. Rabbi Arthur Gilbert challenged a convention of Reform rabbis to rethink their reflexive position. "Our record is stuck in its groove," he admonished, as he specifically called for the use of public funds to pay for transporting children to religious schools.[36] Several writers observed that Jewish organizations were inconsistent in accepting some forms of state benefits for religious institutions, while adamantly rejecting others. For example, why was it perfectly permissible for Jews to fight for the appointment of rabbis as chaplains in the American military, but not at all acceptable to seek aid for religious schools on the elementary or secondary levels—especially if such aid were made available to schools of all religious denominations?[37]

More broadly, some of these writers questioned the assumption that separationism was always good for the Jews. Distinguishing between separation and separationism, Milton Himmelfarb contended that the former preserves the integrity of religious beliefs and American democracy, while the latter undermines both because it drains the public square of religious content and influence. "It is not true," he wrote, "that freedom is most secure where church and state are separated; separation and separationism are not the same; separationism is potentially tyrannical; separationism needlessly repels some from the democratic consensus; it is harsh to those who prefer nonpublic schools for conscience sake; and it stands in the way of a more important good (and a more important safeguard of Jewish security), the best possible education for all."[38] Himmelfarb cited the examples of Britain and the Scandinavian nations as models of countries hospitable to Jews, even though they still maintained state churches. By contrast, he cited the case of the Soviet Union, where the public arena was devoid of religious content—and the state persecuted religion.[39] Separation in and of itself, he argued, does not guarantee tolerance, nor does its absence necessarily promote persecution.

The harmful impact upon American mores and morality of a public square stripped of religious influence also worried these dissenters. Will Herberg addressed this matter already in the early 1950s in reaction to the secular drift of American society. By fighting for a society that relegated religion to the "merely private," Herberg wrote, Jews were dooming religion to play a peripheral role "to the vital areas of social life and culture."[40] Himmelfarb elaborated on the same theme a decade later, focusing on the beneficial impact of mediating institutions, including religious ones, for the enrichment of societies.

[F]reedom depends on society's having loci of interest, affection, and influence besides the state. It depends on more or less autonomous institutions mediating between the naked, atomized individual and the state—or rather, keeping the individual from nakedness and atomization in the first place. In short, pluralism is necessary.

Given that a shriveling of the non-public must fatally enfeeble pluralism, especially in education; and given that the agent of that enfeeblement is the unchecked operation of the economic law, the remedy is simple: check it. Let the government see that money finds its way to the non-public schools, so that they may continue to exist side by side with the public schools. That will strengthen pluralism, and so, freedom.[41]

In contrast with the official strict separationism of the organized Jewish community, which had no patience for religious contributions to public life, writers such as Herberg and Himmelfarb sought to find a healthy role for religion within American society, even as they accepted the need to limit its influence.[42] Clearly, what these writers were asking Jews to consider was the potential benefit to society of some flexibility on church-state matters as weighed against any losses caused by breaches in the wall of separation.

Even if Jews viewed this question only through the prism of their self-interest, warned Jakob Petuchowski, they owed it to themselves to avoid fighting the wrong battle: "Life in the medieval Christian world—in which, by the way, we no longer happen to live—certainly was no bed of roses for the Jews. But Jews fared infinitely *worse* in those modern societies from which the God of Abraham and of Jesus had been banished. If Jews cannot forget the Middle Ages, they owe it to themselves to remember the most recent past, too. One could argue, therefore, that the very self-interest of the Jews is at stake in preventing the United States from becoming a totally godless society." He therefore counseled Jews

to bend and avoid "pressing for the full extent of what the law provides" when it comes to separationism.[43] Strict separationism, its
Jewish opponents contended, in the long run will make America
less, not more, hospitable to Jews.

Still another line of argument directly addressed the First
Amendment, with its twin guarantees of non-"establishment" and
also "free exercise." Morris B. Abram, himself an attorney, noted
the tendency of courts "throughout the last forty-five years . . . to
recognize that a pragmatic accommodation of religion is mandated
by both the free exercise clause and the need to ensure that separation of church and state does not result in discrimination against
religion." Abram counseled Jewish groups to reconsider their in-
flexible opposition to state aid on the grounds of the "free exercise" clause. "By continuing to sanction a situation in which the
religious school option is so prohibitively expensive that only the
children of the rich can afford a religious education, we create a
system where only the wealthy can effectively exercise their religious beliefs." Abram urged a means of accommodating parents
who were intent on exposing their children to a religious education. "If free exercise is to be meaningful," he argued, "then should
it not be extended to young children as well as college students? If
a GI can use a grant from the state to study for the priesthood at
Notre Dame, shouldn't parents be given the option of using tax
money which presently goes automatically to the public school system to choose a parochial school for their child instead?"[44]

In contrast to the separationists' faith in public school education, Jewish proponents of state aid to religious schools expressed
serious reservations about the adequacy of public education, a concern that gained momentum during the 1960s when public schools
were manifestly in a crisis induced by the spread of drugs, crime,
and falling standards. Few questioned the important role public
education had played in the past as a key social instrument for
Americanizing immigrants; and few doubted the ongoing constructive role played by public schools. Rather, they worried aloud
whether such schools could do the job of educating young Americans alone, and whether private education could not play an important supplementary role. Moreover, they challenged the hypocrisy
of Jewish leaders who educated their own children in private
schools or in public schools located in posh suburbs, but nonetheless preached to others of lesser means about the virtues of public
education in the inner cities.[45]

Finally, proponents of state aid argued for governments to recognize the needs of religiously oriented families. Especially in

light of the fact that religion has been banished from public schools, should not parents who believed in the vital necessity of exposing their children to a religious education be given some support if they lacked the means to afford tuition at religious schools? These concerns were of growing practical interest as the population of day school children grew progressively larger. Particularly as ever more Conservative and Reform families opted to send their children to day schools, the crushing financial burden associated with such schools ought to prompt Jewish organizations to reconsider their positions on aid to religious schools, argued these critics.[46]

Shifting Attitudes at the Close of the Twentieth Century

Although the lines of division in the organized Jewish community—and the underlying arguments bolstering the position of opponents and proponents of state aid—hardly changed, a series of developments during the last fifteen years of the twentieth century intensified the debate. Perhaps the most important new circumstance affecting this dispute has been the altered perspective of the Supreme Court, the very setting where strict separationists had scored their most resounding victories during the middle decades of the century. Indeed, the high watermark for separationists was reached with the Court ruling in *Lemon v. Kurtzman*, a decision rendered in 1971 that defined a strict three part test for determining violations of the Establishment Clause: "1. Whether the law or program has a secular purpose; 2. Whether the primary effect of the law or program is to advance or inhibit religion; 3. Whether the law or program promotes excessive entanglement between religion and government."[47] The short-term consequence of this decision was to thwart virtually every piece of legislation designed to allocate public funds to religious schools. In the words of one scholar, the *Lemon* ruling had placed a "noose . . . around the government's discretion to provide aid to elementary and parochial schools."[48]

By the middle of the 1980s, the Court began to change direction. Chief Justice Warren Burger, the author of the decisive *Lemon* opinion, signaled this change in his own shift in favor of assistance for parochial schools.[49] This is how Marc Stern, the lead attorney for the American Jewish Congress and a strict separationist, characterized the changed mood:

In the 1980s a different note begins to appear in the Court's work. It begins to ask not whether religion is helped, but whether religion is getting special benefits. In a series of cases involving non-governmental religious speech, the Court has held that where religion gets only what secular speech gets, there is no establishment in allowing identical benefits to religion.

The idea that equal treatment cannot be equated with an established church has begun to spread to the funding arena. The Court has taken some tentative steps toward holding that where religion is funded only as one among many beneficiaries, there is no establishment of religion. These cases have involved only small amounts of funds.

Whether the Court would extend this rationale to comprehensive funding, under which the practical result is that the government has substantial responsibility for funding religious institutions, is the great unanswered question. Whether vouchers for religious schools (which would provide a form of equality with government financed public education) are constitutional depends on the answer to this question.[50]

Clearly, this shift in the attitude of the highest court emboldened activists eager to channel state funds to religious schools.[51]

The second important development of the late twentieth century, as Stern notes, was the intensification of legislative efforts to grant school vouchers to needy parents. Voucher plans were not an invention of this era and, in fact, had already been proposed in the 1960s, as the following description from an article published in 1970 makes amply clear: "One tactic that answers most church-state objections (no tactic answers them all) is to give a voucher representing a governmental allotment for each child's education to the parent, who is then free to purchase instruction from any approved school, public or nonpublic. Controls may be introduced to ensure that the funds are used for secular subjects exclusively."[52] Like GI bill funds and some forms of welfare payments, vouchers were thought to be direct grants to individual American citizens and therefore were not construed as state funding of religious schools. They could be employed by parents to make their own choices. In the 1990s, a number of state legislatures experimented with voucher plans, and at least in one case, the Milwaukee plan, students attending a Jewish day school were beneficiaries of a voucher program.[53]

Support for vouchers, and more generally, "school choice" has steadily increased within American society.[54] Opinion polls indicate that in the general population over 40 percent of Americans

favor "providing government aid (vouchers) to families for tuition
in private schools, including religious schools."[55] What has further
complicated matters for Jewish organizations was the embrace of
school choice by many of their usual liberal allies. As one of those
allies, former congressman Floyd H. Flake, a black pastor, put it:
"Nothing in our Constitution says public funding for education requires that it be delivered by the current construct. All citizens,
including those in the inner-city, deserve a quality education and
vouchers offer the best hope for delivering it to every child."[56]
Leaders of inner-city minority groups—and parents of minority
children—were quickest to throw their support behind school
choice, having endured decades of failed promises by administrators of public schools and officials of teachers' unions. With the
defection of their usual allies, liberal Jewish organizations were
forced to "reappraise" their traditional opposition to state aid, even
if they ultimately held fast to strict separationism.[57]

Two new realities internal to the American Jewish community
also propelled some organizations to reconsider their positions on
state aid. The first was the continual growth of day school enroll-
ment in the non-Orthodox sectors of American Jewry. Whereas the
Orthodox world began in earnest to construct a national day school
network during the 1940s and 1950s, the Conservative and Reform
movements established their networks a few decades later. The
Conservative Solomon Schechter Day School movement primarily
grew in the 1960s and 1970s, expanding to some fifty schools by
1977, and then adding another twenty schools in the next two decades. In addition, by the late 1990s, PARDeS, the Progressive Association of Reform Day Schools, encompassed twenty schools;
another fifty nondenominational day schools belonged to
RAVSAK, the Jewish Community Day School network.[58] By the
end of the twentieth century, an estimated 50,000 non-Orthodox
children attended these schools as well as day schools under Orthodox auspices.[59] The parents, and perhaps other members of
these children's extended families, formed a potential lobby to
sway communal opinion on the matter of state aid. For even if they
themselves could afford to shoulder the burden of ever-rising tuition fees, these members of the Jewish community surely also
knew of other families that were deterred by the high costs from
sending their children to Jewish day schools. The spiraling affordability crisis in day school education spurred parents and Jewish communal leaders to seek new sources of funding, including
state aid.[60]

This preoccupation with day school finances was further driven by a second development of the 1990s—growing communal anxiety over the ability of the American Jewish community to transmit a strong sense of group identification among younger Jews. With the release of data collected by the 1990 National Jewish Population Study, concerns over the question of "Jewish continuity" intensified, prompting communal leaders to pay far more sustained attention to Jewish educational programs, and especially to more intensive forms of education that showed some evidence of "success" in nurturing young people who would as adults embrace Jewish life. All the data pointed to high rates of Jewish observance and communal commitment among products of Jewish day schools, and suggested that the most intensive form of Jewish education also produced highly dedicated Jews.[61] In a community preoccupied with Jewish "continuity," the promise of day school education could not be ignored. Jewish communal leaders, therefore, came under somewhat greater pressure to find ways to help day schools.

In a few noteworthy cases, these altered circumstances prompted a reconsideration of, or at least a desire to consider, state aid to religious schools. In early 2000, John Ruskay, the chief executive of the UJA-Federation of New York, the largest of the Federations, publicly called for such a reappraisal. Noting his strong credentials as a church-state separationist, he nonetheless expressed his view that "the justifiable fears and concerns that led the Jewish community to be adamant in opposing any form of government support for Jewish day school education need to be seriously revisited." Though he did not endorse vouchers ("a subject that polarizes discussion in our community"), he did ask the Jewish community to contemplate "public funding to food services, physical education, guidance, clerical support, maintenance of facilities, and even reading and math."[62] Ruskay publicly spelled out a message that powerful leaders of the New York and Chicago Federations delivered privately to the Jewish Council for Public Affairs, the public policy arm of the Federation movement, namely, that the JCPA was "out of touch" on the question of vouchers.[63] Certainly, one of the concerns motivating these leaders of major Jewish Federations to reconsider state aid was their awareness that the Jewish community could not generate the necessary multibillion dollar endowments to address the affordability crisis of day schools.[64]

While there is no denying that support for some form of state aid for religious schools expanded in the Jewish community beyond its usual Orthodox base, there was no evidence that organizations committed to strict separationism were displaying any greater flexibility. Indeed, the extreme separationists triumphed when they forced a confrontation within the Jewish Council for Public Affairs in March 2000. Spurred by the National Council of Jewish Women, the JCPA voted in favor of a resolution ending their support for approved government aid to private schools "in those instances where the public funds are used for designated, extant, court-approved non-sectarian benefits." In the view of JCPA's then executive, the resolution was necessary so that the Jewish community could go on record against "court approved" infringements on absolute separationism. "Simply because the courts judge something legally appropriate," he declared, "it doesn't mean the Jewish community agrees."[65]

Thus as a new century dawned, the major communal intergroup agencies of the Jewish community remained as implacably entrenched in their strict separationism as they had been fifty years before. On the matter of state aid to religious schools, the so-called "big three" worked in concert with other organizations such as the Jewish Council for Public Affairs, the National Council of Jewish Women, and the Reform movement's Religious Action Center in opposition to virtually every proposed use of public funding.[66] Each employed the same arguments in defense of what they asserted to be "Jewish values:" (1) "Vouchers threaten the First Amendment's guarantee of religious liberty;" (2) "Public schools are the heart of American identity;" (3) "Voucher funding is a small bandage over a large wound;" (4) Via state aid, "the government could exert more control over religious institutions," an unacceptable intrusion; (5) "Jewish education is important, but government funding is inappropriate and illegal."[67]

What had changed a bit was the constellation of forces within the organized American Jewish community and the larger American environment: Orthodox groups now were organized to lobby on their own and worked to forge alliances with non-Jewish groups. A larger percentage of the American Jewish populace was considering the feasibility of vouchers, as is evidenced from the finding that a bit over one-fifth favored some forms of state aid to religious schools, as compared to only half that number of Jewish leaders who adopted that position.[68] Over 200,000 Jewish children were now enrolled in Jewish day schools, including about 50,000 from non-Orthodox homes; the parents of this vast population struggled to make tuition payments even as the organized Jewish community paid lip service to the vital importance of intensive Jewish education. There was also a growing awareness that American Jewish organizations were out of step with the rest of the country in their implacable strict separationism. Still, the dominant organizations remained convinced in the early twenty-first century, no less than they had been fifty years earlier, that only the highest and least permeable wall of separation could best protect the interests of American Jews. On the issue of state aid to religious schools, the priorities were best summed up by the head of the Washington bureau of the National Council of Jewish Women after she successfully led the campaign to pass a resolution in the name of the entire organized American Jewish community to oppose even court-approved forms of state funding: "We can't put a chink in the wall [of separation]," she declared, "just because it will benefit Jewish children."[69]

Notes

1. The point is made in the opening sentence of a survey of Jewish attitudes to church-state matters by Noah Pickus, "'Before I Built a Wall'—Jews, Religions and American Public Life," *This World* (fall 1986): 8.

2. Jonathan D. Sarna and David G. Dalin, eds., *Religion and State in the American Jewish Experience* (Notre Dame, Ind.: University of Notre Dame Press, 1997), 23. For examples of unequal programs of state aid to religious schools, one need look no further than Canada where in some provinces the religious schools of Christian denominations receive special privileges not accorded to Jewish schools.

3. On the transformation of the so-called "big three" Jewish defense organizations into intergroup and community relations agencies, see Stuart Svonkin, *Jews against Prejudice: American Jews and the Fight for Civil Liberties* (New York: Columbia University Press, 1997); see esp. chap. I.

4. This history is surveyed by Sarna and Dalin, *Religion and State*, 23-27.

5. The case of *McCollum v. Board of Education* concerned the use of public school facilities for religious instruction. See Gregg Ivers, *To Build a Wall: American Jews and the Separation of Church and State* (Charlottesville: University Press of Virginia, 1995), 4.

6. The primary record of such opposition is the Joint Program Plan issued annually by NCRAC, the National Community Relations Advisory Council, whose name was subsequently amended when the word "Jewish" was added, and more recently when it was renamed the Jewish Council for Public Affairs. See also the comprehensive listing of "Parochaid in the States," compiled by Edd Doerr, *Liberty* (November/December 1975): 18-19.

7. Quoted by Naomi W. Cohen, *Jews in Christian America: The Pursuit of Religious Equality* (New York: Oxford University Press, 1992), 130.

8. This awareness of just how ingrained church-state separation is in the fabric of American society has not prevented Jewish organizations from raising the specter of an end to the doctrine. See, for example, an advertisement by the Anti-Defamation League placed in the *New York Times* under the banner headline, "The Day We Lose Separation of Church and State, Start Saying Your Prayers," October 13, 1996, A13. The ad does not identify any actual impending threat to separation.

9. A report by the Commission on Law and Social Action of the AJCongress employs the metaphor of an "opening wedge" to describe "even the slightest departure from the principle" of separation of church and state. The report, dated October 13, 1967, and signed by Joseph B. Robinson, is in the Blaustein Library of the American Jewish Committee in a file called "Education-State Aid/AJCongress."

10. Quoted by Ivers, *To Build a Wall*, 206.

11. It would require a separate article to analyze the extent to which the range of Jewish organizations modulated their positions in response to specific court cases. The ongoing tensions between the AJCongress, with its extreme separationist stance, and the more nuanced positions of the ADL and AJCommittee are explored in depth by Ivers, *To Build a Wall*. See, for example, 97-98 on the AJCongress's "absolutism" on separationism.

12. From a press release by the American Jewish Congress dated August 27, 1971, located in the Blaustein Library of the American Jewish Committee in a file entitled "Education-State Aid/AJCongress."

13. Ivers, *To Build a Wall*, 149.

14. Press release dated August 1971, AJCongress.

15. Quoted by Alan Mittleman, "Toward a Postseparationist Public Philosophy: A Jewish Contribution," *This World* (winter 1989): 87.

16. Samuel Rabinove, "Separationism for Religion's Sake," *First Things* (May 1990): 8.

17. Rabinove, "Separationism."

18. Testimony of the Baltimore chapter of the American Jewish Committee before the agency's Commission to Study Aid to Nonpublic Education, January 12, 1970, in a file of the Blaustein Library entitled "Education-State Aid, AJC."

19. Testimony of Benedict M. Kohl at a public hearing on Assembly Bill No. 1078, June 16, 1970. In a file labeled "Education-State Aid/AJC" in the Blaustein Library.

20. Testimony of the Baltimore chapter.

21. Responsibility of Community Relations for Jewish Education, excerpted in the 1983-84 Joint Program Plan for Jewish Community Relations, issued by the National Jewish Community Relations Advisory Council, 62.

22. See the illuminating discussion in Ivers, who draws the distinction between the role of these spokesmen as "trustees, rather than as delegates or politicos, on behalf of their constituents," 205.

23. Gregg Ivers, *To Build a Wall*, provides the most extensive overview and analysis of the participation of Jewish organizations—especially the "big three"—in church-state cases. For a helpful listing of the cases involving state aid to religious schools that came before the Supreme Court between 1947 and 1994, see Wendy Lecker and Galit Kierkut, *Religion and Government: Interpreting the Establishment Clause* (New York: American Jewish Committee, March 1995), 12-14.

24. See "Marvin Schick on the Creation of COLPA, 1967," in Sarna and Dalin, *Religion and State*, 263-64, on the emergence of Orthodox agencies.

25. In the 1990s, one other member of NJCRAC also dissented on church-state matters—the Jewish War Veterans of the U.S.A. Typical of its dissents was the following issued in 1997: "JWV rejects the proposition that public funding should be limited to public education only. JWV continues to support the expenditure of public funds for non-public schools programs which are deemed constitutionally viable for educational essentials, such as health care, lunch program, remedial services for the handicapped and the provision of necessary educational material such as textbooks, computer programs and other supplies." *The Jewish Public Affairs Agenda, 1997-98*, Jewish Council for Public Affairs, 31-32.

26. Excerpted in the Joint Program Plan for Jewish Community Relations, issued by the National Jewish Community Relations Advisory Council, 62.

27. "Marvin Schick," in Sarna and Dalin, *Religion and State*. COLPA also represented the interests of individual Jews who encountered discrimination due to their observance of Judaism.

28. On this alliance, see Arthur Hertzberg, "Church, State, and the Jews," *Commentary* (April 1963): 277-88.

29. Morris B. Abram, "Is 'Strict Separation' Too Strict?" *Public Interest* (winter 1986): 81-90.

30. Arthur Gilbert, "A Catalogue of Church-State Problems," *Religious Education* (November-December 1961), reprinted as a pamphlet by the National Conference of Christians and Jews.

31. Will Herberg, "The Sectarian Conflict over Church and State," *Commentary* (November 1952): 450-62.

32. Milton Himmelfarb, "Church and State: How High the Wall," *Commentary* (July 1966): 23-29.

33. Wolfe Kelman, "Church and State Reappraised," *Conservative Judaism* (fall 1969): 71-72.

34. Jakob Petuchowski, "A Rabbi's Christmas," *First Things* (December 1991): 810.

35. Seymour Siegel, "Church and State," *Conservative Judaism* (spring/summer 1963): 1-12.

36. Quoted by Sarna and Dalin, *Religion and State*, 26.

37. Gilbert, "A Catalogue," 2.

38. Himmelfarb, "Church and State," 27-28.

39. Himmelfarb, "Church and State," 23.

40. Herberg, "The Sectarian Conflict," as summarized by Sarna and Dalin, *Religion and State*, 24.

41. Himmelfarb, "Church and State," 29.

42. Pickus, "Before I Built a Wall," 41-42.

43. Petuchowski, "A Rabbi's Christmas," 10.

44. Abram, "Is 'Strict Separation' Too Strict?" 89

45. See, for example, Himmelfarb, "Church and State," 27.

46. Kelman, "Church and State Reappraised," 71-72.

47. Lecker and Kierkut, "Religion and Government," 12.

48. Ivers, *To Build a Wall*, 183.

49. Ivers, *To Build a Wall*, 183.

50. Marc Stern, "Weakening the Wall of Separation between Church and State," *NCJW Journal* (winter 1997/98): 28.

51. By March 2001, some forty states offered some kind of assistance to nonpublic schools, mainly in the form of free lunches to aid poor children, textbook loans, or other types of assistance with school equipment and supplies. See James D. Besser, "State House Nixes Funds for Private Schools," *Baltimore Jewish Times*, March 18, 2001, Internet edition.

52. Donald A. Erickson, "Private Schools and Educational Reform," *Compact* (February 1970): 4.

53. Under the Milwaukee plan, recipients of vouchers may not have family incomes over 175 percent of federal poverty standards. Nonetheless, Yeshiva Elementary School in Milwaukee expected to receive over $400,000 in 2000-2001, about one-third of its budget. Alan Borsuk, "Fact Sheet on the Voucher/School Choice Situation in Milwaukee and Beyond," PEJE, Jewish Donor Assembly, Briefing and Background Papers, September 2000.

54. By the early 1990s, nearly thirty-five states had begun to experiment with school choice. See Jacob Sullum, "Educational Choice for Parents. I. Vouchers Will Make More Jews," *Moment* (February 1994): 12-13.

55. Steven M. Cohen, *Jews and the American Public Square: Attitudes of American Jews in Comparative Perspective* (Philadelphia: Center for Jewish Community Studies, 2000), 20. According to a Zogby poll, the figure actually reached 52 percent. See Nathan Diament, "Want Social Justice? Try Vouchers," *Forward*, June 16, 2000, 9.

56. Floyd H. Flake, "No Excuses for Failing Our Children," *Policy Review* (January/February, 1999): 48. See this entire issue devoted to "Questions on School Choice."

57. For an example of such a reconsideration, see *Vouchers for School Choice: Challenge or Opportunity: An American Jewish Reappraisal*, ed. Marshall J. Breger and David M. Gordis (Brookline, Mass.: Wilstein Institute of Jewish Policy Studies, 1998).

58. For the sources of these data, see author's essay, "Jewish Education in the United States: Recent Trends and Issues," *American Jewish Year Book 1999* (New York: American Jewish Committee, 1999), 20-21, 54-55.

59. Marvin Schick, *A Census of Jewish Day Schools in the United States* (New York: Avi Chai Foundation, 2000). The overall figure is broken down as follows: an estimated 14,849 attended community schools, 17,563 attended Solomon Schechter schools, and 4,485 attended day schools under Reform auspices (16). In addition, an estimated 3,100 non-Orthodox students were enrolled in Orthodox day schools (11).

60. Some opponents of state aid dismissed "the drift in Jewish opinion on vouchers" as motivated exclusively by disappointment with the public schools, rather than with any change in posture on church-state questions. See the remarks of Cleveland civil rights attorney Kenneth Myers, quoted in Marilyn H. Karfeld, "Jewish Reaction to Voucher Case Shows Changing View of Education," *Cleveland Jewish News*, December 13, 2000, Internet edition.

61. For some of the evidence of the day school impact, see author's essay "Jewish Education in the United States," 49-51.

62. The address is reprinted in *A Statement on Jewish Education: Text and Responses* (New York: American Jewish Committee, 2000), 45-48.

63. Ira Stoll, "Umbrella Group Criticized for Stance against Vouchers," *Forward*, December 3, 1999, 1.

64. Ruskay spelled this out in his assessment of schemes to help underwrite the costs of so-called internal Jewish communal vouchers, 47.

65. "Big Step Back for Support of Day Schools," *Forward*, March 3, 2000, 1, 3.

66. For the blanket opposition of these organizations to voucher proposals, see "American Jewish Committee Applauds Court Decision Striking Down Ohio School Voucher Program," a press release dated December 11, 2000, available on the ajc.org website; "AJCongress calls federal appeals court decision to invalidate Cleveland voucher program a 'signal' to other localities not to implement similar programs," at ajcongress.org website, dated December 12, 2000; the adl.org website, under religious freedom/vouchers. See also the annual Joint Program Plans, later renamed "Agendas," of the Jewish Council on Public Affairs.

67. These "Jewish values" are itemized at the website of the Religious Action Center of Reform Judaism. *Issues in Focus: School Vouchers*, dated June 29, 2000.

68. Steven M. Cohen, *Jews and the American Public Square*, 20. According to Cohen, about 22 percent of the "Jewish public" favored vouchers, as compared to only 11 percent of "Jewish leaders."

69. Sharon Samber, "Jewish Group Stiffens Opposition to Public Funding for Private Schools," *Jewish Telegraphic Agency*, March 14, 2000, Internet edition.

Part IV

Sociological Dimensions

9

Jewish Involvement in the American Public Square: The Organizational Disconnect

Sherry Israel

Background: American Jewish Hyper-Organization

Jews in America have been known to be, in Earl Raab's felicitous phrase, "politically hyperactive." For most of the twentieth century, the greatest part of that activity reflected a set of liberal democratic assumptions and commitments, aspects of a Jewish civil religion which closely tracked American civil religion. Peruse the leadership and membership lists of any American political or social action group with a liberal or progressive agenda, and you will find a disproportionate representation of Jews. It was no accident, for example, that a Jew (need we add, white) was the last national president of the NAACP before African Americans moved to take control of their own organizations. To the extent that the kinds of Jews who were politically and publicly active shared common positions, one might plausibly assert that there has even been a contemporary (not just biblical or historic) Jewish influence on American conceptions of the public square and what is proper to it.

When we speak of Jewish public activism, however, it is essential to distinguish between the activity of Jews as individuals and that of Jewish organizations. The framework for this study of "Jews and the American Public Square" focuses not on the impact of individuals but on the greater and more amorphous American Jewish community. Here we will attempt to address not philosophical or moral questions of collective Jewish involvement in the American public square but an issue of practical concern: that of the continuing possibility and efficacy of such involvement at all, at least in its present forms. We will examine a complex of interacting trends relating to the structures of American Jewish institutional life, new trends in religious and ethnic identity in America, and contemporary American Jewish demography.

The genesis of this overall project, as noted in its statement of purpose, was a concern for "the role of religion in shaping the American public square," and "the theme of religion and the public square in the context of the American Jewish experience." The formulation seems to assert that the context of the Jewish role in shaping the American public square is religious, that Jews collectively are concerned with issues of the public square qua members of a religious group in American life. Yet Jewish influence and participation in these matters has not come primarily from within a religious framework. The organizations and institutions most involved in the American public square on behalf of the Jewish community have been those of the Federation and community relations systems, not those of the religious sphere.

It is instructive to briefly note the origins of this anomalous state of affairs. Until the recent advent of multiculturalism, American public discourse did not sanction the public and institutional perpetuation of subgroup differences except along religious lines. Jews adapted superbly to these norms and have presented themselves for public purposes as one of the Three Great Religions of American Life.[1] Yet, as most Jews know but most other Americans sometimes have not figured out, it is not so simple. Jews are both a religious and an ethnic community, with allegiance to the Jewish people as well as to Jewish religion. In some eras and for some purposes, this nonreligious (which for Jews is not quite the same as "secular") alternative has overshadowed the religious in American Jewish life. The public square is one such venue. Thus, as several other authors in this volume point out (or assume without even bothering to make it explicit), the organizational channels through which American Jews have expressed their collective public concerns since at least the earliest decades of the twentieth century have been almost exclusively those of the secular (or, better, the civil religion) side of the American Jewish polity—the Federations, the JCRCs, the "Big Three" defense/advocacy organizations and their more recent companions in promoting Holocaust awareness and combating anti-Semitism, and the various Israel-related lobbies. This is not to dismiss the contributions of groups like the Reform movement's Religious Action Center or Orthodoxy's COLPA, but simply to note that they have not been the major players.

American public and political life, rather remarkably in light of the historic thrust toward an ethnic melting pot, have accepted the participation in the American public square not just of individual Jews and of Jews as members of synagogues and denominations, but also of the Jewish community qua community—that is, within the framework of the voluntary American Jewish polity. It is primarily *this* organizational activity that brings Jews *as a group* into significant engagement with other religious and ethnic groups, with government, with the press, and in all other arenas of the public square. It is through the Jewish community's "civil" organizations that most Jewish positions about and in the public square have been represented in ongoing conversations about particular issues and about American civil religion more generally. It is these organizations on which we will primarily focus.

American Jews have also, correctly, been called "hyper-organized." It is not just that there are so many American Jewish organizations (students invariably express astonishment the first time they look at the "Institutions" section of any *American Jewish Yearbook*). These organizations have also, especially in the years since World War II, been highly effective at what they do. American Jews learned how to use the system, and the resulting organizational prowess has been the envy of many another American group. A crucial element of this effectiveness has been the capacity of the organizations to back their policy positions and practical demands with personal contacts, communication networks, funds, media exposure, and votes—all coins of the realm in the effective public use of power. For all the great historic differences within American Jewry, for a long time there was significant enough consensus on what the major Jewish-linked issues of American public policy were (support for Israel, overseas relief and rescue, combating anti-Semitism and other forms of bigotry, church-state separation, civil rights, civil liberties, intergroup relations, the government's role in social and economic justice) and on the "correct" positions on these issues, that the community's organizations could take positions and mobilize the necessary support for them. It is thus worth stating what may be obvious but can easily be overlooked: the credibility of these organizations in representing Jewish views in the public square and the continuing effectiveness of their participation in these conversations are deeply dependent on the continuation of a credible base of support for both the organizations themselves and what they stand for.

Changing Patterns of American Jewish Affiliation

On this front, the news is complex. First, there is less Jewish consensus than formerly on many of the current debates in the public square. In fact, on several of them, different organizations have begun to take divergent public stances. True, such public differences of opinion are a positive development, insofar as they are a sign of American Jewish self-confidence and feelings of security. Beleaguered minority groups do not usually even acknowledge differences among themselves, much less go public with them. This new Jewish multivocality may be seen as the organizational counterpart of the demographic and identity developments which we will turn to shortly. However we understand it, though, the lack of consensus probably diminishes the impact of the Jewish "voice," raising as it does the question, what *do* Jews stand for? Who speaks for the Jews now? And so it poses a challenge for effective Jewish participation in the public square.

Equally crucial is the matter of organizational support. Here, the Jewish community is on new ground, much of it shaky. The most fundamental indicators of support—membership, participation, and contributions—are on the wane for most of the organizations which have been in the forefront of Jewish activity in the public square. Measured from within the organizations themselves, the trend to diminished affiliation began to show up first in the mass-based organizations, notably B'nai Brith and the historic Zionist groups. These days, none of these organizations remain as major players in the public policy arena. More recently, the American Jewish Congress, which has been at the forefront of some of American Jewry's most significant involvement in the public square, has encountered difficulties in sustaining all its regional offices, which depend heavily on local membership dues and contributions. The Los Angeles Congress office has, in fact, separated from the national organization.

Confirmation comes from social research as well. Ever since they began studying these matters systematically, sociologists and demographers of the American Jewish community have used two measures as standard indices of Jewish attachment to the civil side of the Jewish polity—belonging to (non-synagogue) organizations and donating to Jewish philanthropy. Every local and national demographic study has included questions to measure these two variables, and a clear pattern has emerged over the past generation: overall Jewish organizational membership is down, as is philanthropic activity in the domains of Jewish civil religion (that is, UJA and the Federations and their agencies). The trend shows up both over time and at a given time in relation to generational and age cohorts. Over time, as one moves from the 1970s through to the 1990s, a smaller proportion of Jews in each decade are affiliated with or giving to these Jewish civil organizations and causes. Currently, if we compare the immigrant generation to subsequent generations of Jews or older to younger Jews, in any current cross-section of Jews, we see the same pattern of decreases in both participation and giving.

As a concrete example, the following data is from Boston's last two community demographic studies. Let us start with philanthropy.

Table 9.1
Donations to Boston Combined Jewish Philanthropies
By Age, 1985-1995
(in percent)

| | Proportion Who Donated to CJP in Listed Year | |
Age	1985	1995
18-29	16	14
30-39	34	25
40-49	52	38
50-64	64	52
65+	55	64
Overall	39	38
Number	1446	1200

Source: S. Israel, *Comprehensive Report on the 1995 CJP Demographic Study* (Boston: Combined Jewish Philanthropies, 1997), 60, Table 3.21.

What Table 9.1 demonstrates first is that in 1985, Boston's Jews showed a pattern of decreased giving by each younger age group. At that time, it was possible to interpret the findings to mean that this lower giving by younger Jews was a developmental phenomenon; that is, that as these Jews got older, they would become more Jewishly philanthropic. But the 1995 data undermined this interpretation. The newer data replicated the earlier finding of lower giving by younger Jews. In addition, the table shows that for every age group below age 65 in 1995, giving levels were lower than they had been a decade earlier. The giving patterns established ten years ago were holding; younger Jews were not "developing" into Federation donors as they grew older. The data on membership in Jewish organizations displayed the same pattern, and when the demographic variable was distance from the immigrant generation, the phenomenon appeared even more strongly.

Note that we are speaking of overall patterns. Many Jews continue to give to Jewish philanthropy, read the Jewish press, and join the mainstream organizations and support their agendas. Indeed, by all indicators, such involved Jews are becoming more engaged, more active, and "more Jewish" than ever before. There are enough activists to keep the organizations going and to provide plenty of compelling anecdotes about "Jewish revival" for the Jewish press. Yet most current estimates suggest that these individuals represent at most about 20 percent of American Jews. It is important to note that this percentage is not strikingly lower than in previous decades. What has changed is that the affiliative impulses of the great middle group of American Jews (we speak here of Jews under age 60)—those whom Cohen has dubbed "marginal Jews," those who in the past provided the large and supportive underpinning of the civil organizations—are no longer predictable and reliable.

From a consideration of the overall picture, one might conclude simply that distance from the immigrant experience and (relatively) younger Jews' fuller American acculturation have resulted in weakened loyalty to the Jewish community. Jewish life in America, in this view, is doomed to gradual attrition and its impact in the public sector to a predictable fading away. This is the classic "straight-line assimilation" interpretation of American Jewish life. In fact, a large measure of the organized (especially Federation) community's concern about "Jewish continuity" has been as much a response to these documented decreases in affiliation and giving as to the more widely known statistics on intermarriage rates. But this straight-line assimilation view is too simple and it overlooks other important factors.

It is true that most of those who identify themselves as Jews (a requirement for inclusion in the sampling frame for local Jewish community studies) no longer express that identification by almost automatic support for the civic institutions of the Jewish community. From a communal standpoint, this is reason for concern and response, but it is not necessarily the same as a weakening of Jewish loyalty. Rather, the context of American life at the end of the twentieth century allows—or even compels—a more complex interpretation of the current trends, one that may suggest different organizational conclusions. Let us turn to that context.

Religion and Ethnicity in America: New Trends

One way to begin is to look at changes in the nature and meaning of both ethnic and religious identity in America. Mary Waters published an excellent little book a decade ago entitled *Ethnic Options.*[2] This title would once have been read as ironic: how can ethnicity, one's ancestry, what has always been thought of as an ascribed characteristic, be "optional"? Yet such is now increasingly the case.

Waters and others have now convincingly demonstrated that ethnicity has not disappeared as a category of identification in American life. Rather, its meaning has changed. Increasingly, ethnicity now involves nonexclusive identification and fluidity over the life course. Three factors distinguish this new kind of ethnicity: people pick and choose (or ignore and discard) elements from their ethnic backgrounds to fit the rest of their lifestyle, and they have no apparent problem with combining aspects of different ancestral strands as they make these choices. In addition, while it persists as an identity category, this kind of ethnicity does not make strong or consistent behavioral demands. It was a Jew, Herbert Gans, who first coined the phrase "symbolic ethnicity" to describe the phenomenon.[3] What is most relevant for us in his formulation is that symbolic ethnicity does not require ongoing personal contact with other individuals *or institutions* of the ethnic group. Ethnicity is carried in the individual's head as an inner identity, and it is expressed sporadically, often in response to life cycle or other individually related stimuli. Charles Liebman, borrowing Alba's terminology, called what is happening "the decline of ethnicity,"[4] but he was writing from a "straight-line" position. Yet Waters's research can equally be interpreted to suggest not decline but redefinition. That is, there is a new American way of being a member of an ethnic group. For our inquiry, the operative question then can change from whether this new way is "good for the Jews" given current organizational structures and norms—which it probably is not—to whether it can become so.

These new American definitions of ethnicity allow individuals to claim identity without requiring regular public demonstrations of behavior to support the claim, but allowing them as matters of individual choice. From this perspective, Jewish acculturation may be seen not as abandoning Jewishness for an American identity (the usual assimilationist interpretation), but of internalizing the new cultural definitions of ethnicity, which permit and encourage the persistence of an ethnic subidentity and allow for its expression in both private and public ways. American patterns set the basic template, within which Jewishness functions as an enriching addition to be hauled out when occasion or feelings call for it. A young or fourth-generation Jew can therefore feel him or herself loyally Jewish, without feeling obligated to express being Jewish in any ongoing public ways, and sense no contradiction.

The implication for organizational attachment is obvious: it cannot be taken for granted that such a Jew—even one who "feels very Jewish"—will follow in the path of his or her predecessors in terms of formal connections with Jewish organizations and institutions (or, for that matter, in much else that Jews have "always done"). And indeed they are not, at least not with the old war-horse organizations. But it need not mean that there are no public paths onto which this Jew will choose to walk when pulling out his or her ethnicity. Given the element of fluidity, the fact that individuals do not currently express their ethnic self-definition in public ways at any given time does not imply that they never will. Both of these matters are questions open to study, not givens.

A parallel shift pervades religious identification in America as well. There is fluidity, to start. Large numbers of Americans of all religions switch their denominational affiliations each year. Jews are not exempt from this process, as the analysis of the 1990 NJPS data on denominations has demonstrated.[5] In fact, the driving force behind much of this switching is the same elevation of personal choice that we have already seen functioning with respect to ethnic identification. As many have noted, the standard of judgment for religious identity in America, increasingly, is not historic or family loyalty or group cohesion, but personal meaning. Bellah's "Sheilaism"[6] may be an extreme example, but the name caught on because it captured the phenomenon so well.[7] Because the focus of this kind of religion is more inward and personalistic, religious identification (at least for the non-Orthodox) no longer carries with it nearly automatic expression in communally-related behaviors. The operative framework is not community and tradition but individual autonomy and choice.

Privatization and Organizational Life: Two Views

In today's Jewish world, the new rhetoric of "we are all Jews by choice" sums up these developments. Contrary to the fears of the religious Right, the alternative to traditional religion in contemporary American life is neither secularism nor paganism, it is privatization. In that same essay, Liebman noted that "the rhetoric of ethnicity concentrates on themes such as peoplehood, community, solidarity . . . [while that of] privatized religion . . . speaks in softer terms of individual meaning, journeys of discovery, spirituality, and the search for fulfillment."[8] He sees the connection between the rise of a privatized Jewish religion and the decline of public sector Jewish life, and—writing from within a framework of traditional definitions of what constitutes normative and healthy Jewish communal life—sees in all of this "a recipe for disaster."

Yet this is the way most American Jews now think about and enact their Jewishness. For increasing numbers of Jews in America, the expression of Jewish identity—both ethnic and religious—no longer functions in a protected space. It must compete with many other possibilities in the marketplace, not of philosophic positions but of leisure and lifestyle activities. To declare, as Liebman does, that this is the end of Jewish communal life is to be a pessimist about the staying power of Jewishness in twenty-first-century America.

But another perspective calls our attention, rather, to the creative energy that this essentially entrepreneurial situation has engendered. It appears that American Jews are now "doing Jewish" in a new and staggeringly wide variety of ways, about which we are only beginning to have reliable information. In her pioneering research, Bethamie Horowitz has begun documenting the existence of Jews for whom Jewish identity remains of central importance but whose expressions of it vary along multiple axes not previously noted in Jewish research.[9]

Liebman is correct in identifying "the search for fulfillment" as a central aspect of the rhetoric of the new privatized ethnicity and religion. What he overlooks, however, is that personal fulfillment can be found by participating in meaningful collective and public activity. It was Wade Clark Roof, one of the earliest chroniclers of these new trends in the religious realm, who observed that individuals' personal choices can lead them to seek membership in communities.[10] Horowitz's work suggests that Jewish journeys of discovery, made for the most personal of reasons, are ending up in new forms of Jewish group activity, or can be led to do so. We need to learn more about the ways, if any, that "new identity Jews," these privatistic and differently attached ones, are connecting with the public square as Jews. We simply do not yet know enough about what touches them, and whether there are or can be things that touch them in the public, not just the personal, realms.[11] What we do know is that the new forms of identity present a challenge to old structures and approaches. As always in times of change, the future is not clear, but we can be sure that a stance of negation will be a self-fulfilling prophecy. If new paths are not opened, Jews of this new sort will certainly not be able to walk on them.

New Directions in Research

To its credit, the community has begun to look for additional information. In most demographic studies before the 1990s, there was a fairly standard set of questions used to measure Jewish behavior and affiliation. These included the previously noted items relating to Jewish organizational membership and philanthropy, plus questions about observing traditional Jewish rituals, Jewish education, support for Israel, and belonging to JCCs and synagogues. If these were to continue to be the only ways of measuring Jewish identity and Jewish attachments, we know what the data would show: the outcomes would support Liebman's diagnosis of "disaster." But sticking with the standard measures would leave us in the dark about possible new developments. Hence, in the development of the next national sociodemographic study of the American Jewish community, NJPS 2000, the sponsoring organization, UJC (United Jewish Communities, the organization formed by the merger of the Council of Jewish Federations and the United Jewish Appeal) decided to go into new territory. To try to capture a fuller picture of the lives of American Jews, the questionnaire will plumb new realms of behavior and feelings. Some of these involve intensely private matters, some more public (or with the potential to become so). Items considered included, for example, attending Jewish film festivals, visiting Jewish Internet sites, going to Jewish exhibits at museums, engaging in environmental activities or volunteering in inner-city schools "as a Jew," visiting Jewish sites when traveling, meditating, or having mostly Jewish work associates. Only the limitations of a telephone interview format have kept all of them, and others, from being included.

The decision to expand the scope of the survey is not just a matter for technical specialists of survey design. It reflects a commitment on the part of key organizations of the Jewish civil polity to investigate the community's fundamental assumptions about the nature of Jewish identity in America and its contemporary expressions. It will be of great interest to discover, when the results of NJPS 2000 are in, if there are new discernible patterns of outward engagement that are complementing or replacing the older forms; if the choices Jews make to meet personal and private needs might be leading them to new forms of Jewish expression which can be harnessed toward the concerns of the public square.

Some Countertrends

In fact, it is not the case that all the institutions of Jewish engagement in the public square are fading. Some are flourishing. The most conspicuous nondenominational examples are the Simon Wiesenthal Center, ADL, and American Jewry's newest significant voice in the public square, the Holocaust museums and memorial groups. It should be noted that all of these are issue, not membership, organizations.

A return to the Boston data can offer some help in understanding these countertrends. The data support the notion we are proposing that Jewish attachments have not disappeared among younger and more acculturated Jews. Rather, they are becoming more differentiated. The 1995 Boston study included for the first time a new set of questions related to Jewish attitudes and sentiments. One subset of five questions delved into "Jewish values." Respondents were asked how important to them personally are "the exis-

tence of the State of Israel," "keeping people aware that the Holocaust took place," "Jewish ideals of social justice," "opposing anti-
Semitism in the United States," and "protecting Jews in foreign
lands from persecution." Respondents could say they found a particular item to be "extremely," "very," "somewhat," or "not at all"
important. An analysis using a variety of demographic variables is
revealing. Two tables are reproduced here, showing the proportion
of each subgroup who answered "extremely" important.

The first thing to note about this data is methodological: it is
differentiated. Respondents did not give the same response to all
five items, that is, they were not just giving some kind of global or
knee-jerk Jewish-values response, either positive or negative. As to
substance, what stands out is that "defensive" values commanded
the highest and nearly unanimous assent. Jews of all ages, generations, length of residence, denomination, of both genders, and with
and without children—variables that differentiate responses to
most of the other Jewish categories encompassed by this study—
agreed in their assessment of the high importance of keeping people aware of the Holocaust, opposing anti-Semitism in the United
States, and, although at somewhat lower levels, of protecting Jews
in foreign lands from persecution.[12]

Assuming that Boston's Jews are reasonably representative of
American Jews generally in these matters, we can note that the current successful public-sector Jewish organizations are precisely
those whose missions resonate with the personal values of younger
as well as older Jews.[13] These successful organizations represent
the communal analogue of that new phenomenon in the world of
advertising and the media, "narrowcasting." They are identified
with one agenda, which they pursue with vigor and very good media exposure.

An Organizational Disconnect

What they also represent is the fact that if American Jewish institutions can demonstrate, in a world of competing marketplace
choice, that their purposes and activities are relevant to the private
concerns of the Jews whom they wish to claim as members and
supporters, they will find ready listeners. In fact, however, this
task is problematic for many of the historic organizations. The
dominant public organizations of American Jewish life were
shaped in earlier eras when Jewish belonging was a given, and they

Table 9.2

Jewish Values by Household Income, Residency, and Denomination, 1995

(in percent)

Proportion Who Say "Extremely Important"	Overall	Household Income					Years in Current Town			Denomination			
		<$15K	$15-35K	$35-50K	$50-100K	>$100K	<5	5-9	10+	Orth.	Cons.	Reform	None
Keeping people aware of Holocaust	74	80	75	70	78	69	76	72	74	74	75	75	64
Combating anti-Semitism in the United States	66	66	64	70	68	66	66	66	67	74	69	65	56
Protecting Jews in foreign lands	56	60	51	63	58	54	65	66	67	69	57	57	44
Existence of Israel	53	49	45	53	51	55	46	51	57	81	65	50	39
Jewish ideals of social justice	41	34	38	45	38	45	37	44	42	67	45	39	28
Number	1200	120	112	132	327	271	316	187	695	422	394	491	62

Source: S. Israel, Comprehensive Report on the 1995 CJP Demographic Study (Boston: Combined Jewish Philanthropies, 1997), 90, Table 4.4 A.

Table 9.3

Jewish Values by Age, Generation, Children, and Gender, 1995

(in percent)

Proportion Who Say "Extremely Important"	Overall	Age				Generation				Children in Household		Gender	
		18-34	35-50	51-64	65+	1st	2nd	3rd	4th	Yes	No	M	F
Keeping people aware of Holocaust	74	76	74	72	76	84	76	71	74	76	73	71	77
Combating anti-Semitism in the United States	66	63	69	65	66	60	67	66	67	67	66	64	68
Protecting Jews in foreign lands	56	53	57	56	51	61	57	57	52	62	53	51	60
Existence of Israel	53	48	51	57	61	66	64	50	45	51	54	53	52
Jewish ideals of social justice	41	32	42	43	49	40	49	40	37	41	41	41	42
Number	1200	297	485	245	158	104	303	361	416	433	767	527	673

Source: S. Israel, *Comprehensive Report on the 1995 CJP Demographic Study* (Boston: Combined Jewish Philanthropies, 1997), 91, Table 4.4 B.

were formed to deal with the issues of the day, which were not those of personal meaning and relevance but relief and rescue, social service, and "mediation between the Jewish minority subculture and the majority Christian American culture."[14] There is, therefore, a mismatch between the needs and perceptions of most Jews and the basic assumptions and programs of most of the communally based American Jewish organizations. It remains to be seen whether these existing organs of Jewish engagement in the public square can find ways to reconnect with more inwardly looking Jews or to bring those inner searches into contact with more external and public concerns.

There are some interesting beginnings. At the local level, some Jewish Community Relations Councils have begun responding in just these ways, appealing to the individual language of *mitzvah* to motivate public action, and connecting their activities explicitly with individual Torah study. It is an approach that shows much promise. Whether the larger institutional structures of American Jewish life are willing and able to acknowledge these new realities, and others to be noted below, and to reframe their fundamental self-definitions accordingly, is the question posed by this chapter.

The Synagogue and Jewish Public Life

Although the major arena of Jewish public participation in American life, as already noted, has been in the organizations of the civil religion, a full discussion of organized Jewish life must include the role of the synagogue. This institution is not experiencing the affiliation declines of most of the realm of the civil Jewish polity. The majority of American Jews continue to affiliate with synagogues, although most do not join until they are married and begin to have young children. This pattern is consonant with what we have noted about the changing definitions of Jewish identity in America, for, of all the institutions of American Jewish life, synagogues are those most charged with dealing with individual needs, most able to respond to individuals' search for personal meaning and even spirituality. To be sure, many synagogues, perhaps even a majority, are still focused on the more peoplehood-oriented functions they served a generation ago. This accounts for the development of several new initiatives in this sphere, such as the Experiment in Congregational Education and Synagogue 2000, designed to help synagogues change so they may become more effective in realizing these more personal aspects of their missions.

By the same token, however, synagogues are not well positioned to function as voices in the public square. With the disappearance of the *landsmanschaften*,[15] synagogues in America are the quintessentially local organizations of the Jewish polity. Their focus is inward, to the personal lives of their members and the symbols and substance of congregational governance, not outward to public affairs. Those congregations that mount social action programs tend to do so in their local communities, and on a small—that is, personal and interpersonal—scale. Even the major apparent exception, political efforts on behalf of freedom for Soviet Jews, mostly took the form of bar/bat mitzvah twinning or letter writing to refuseniks. Continuing Jewish affiliation with synagogues does not provide a likely new locus for a Jewish public voice, except perhaps on the most local of scales.

Listen to what a proponent of synagogue revisioning has to say. Rabbi Peter Knobel has described a four-part vision for the transformation he sees as necessary for synagogues.[16] The synagogue, he writes, must "resacralize the primary institution of Jewish life, which is the home . . . be the locus of returning Judaism to the home . . . be the vehicle for serious adult Jewish education . . . re-energiz[e] the notion of obligation, of *mitzvah*, especially in terms of the personal needs of individuals," and be made up of "persons who depend upon one another to be there and to celebrate Shabbat together." This is a worthy vision. A synagogue in this mold would surely inspire both individual souls and institutional loyalty. But note that these goals are wholly focused on the internal lives of synagogue members as individuals and on the contained community of fellow members. This is not inappropriate, not shortsighted; it is what synagogues do best. Whether the broader community can harness the capacity of synagogues to attract and retain Jewish loyalty in the service of larger public affairs matters has not been tested. Indeed, it is not even clear that it would be good for the mission of the synagogue were this to happen on any scale.

Jewish Mobility

Another set of "disconnects" which are relevant to understanding the decreases in Jewish affiliation and organizational support are demographic. The first of these is geographic mobility. It affects

American Jews of all ages, and especially those below age 60. The second, changes in life-cycle patterns, involves primarily younger Jews.

The tendency of today's Jews to relate to Jewish (and other) organizations with a marketplace mentality is compounded by geographic mobility. Residential stability is an important basis for Jewish organizational loyalty. People who reside as adults in the communities they grew up in are more likely to continue earlier generational patterns of affiliation and support. Belonging is more of a given, "what we do," and less a decision to be made based on personal choice and the capacity of the institution to meet current individual or family needs. Conversely, mobility disrupts affiliation. Newcomers to a Jewish community are less likely to contribute to a Federation or to belong to its communal institutions than are long-time residents. Estimates of how long it takes Jews to connect with the Jewish institutions of their new places of residence—how long "newcomer" status lasts—range from three to five years (as noted below, Orthodox Jews and families with pre-bar/bat mitzvah-age children are the major exceptions to this situation). Jewish community centers, which are highly dependent on member and user fees and thus became aware of these trends before most communal organizations, now routinely have marketing consultants or even in-house marketing professionals to help them figure out how to attract members. The same cannot be said of the advocacy organizations.

As the 1990 NJPS demonstrated, Jews are among the most mobile of Americans.[17] If Jewish affiliation were a very high priority, newly arrived Jews would seek out and join Jewish organizations when they entered new communities. In fact, this does happen with synagogues; for Orthodox Jews, very quickly, for others, when their children reach religious school age. But, as we have seen, most Jews do not need public demonstrations of Jewish connection in order to feel Jewish, and so Jewish mobility compounds the already existing fundamental changes in Jews' relations to organizational life.

The organized Jewish community has been slow to recognize the national (or, more accurately, continental) nature of contemporary Jewish life. In relation to synagogues, Federations may be the "cosmopolitan" organizations of their own metropolitan areas, but viewed from a wider perspective, Federations are intensely local. Although many of the issues assailing the American Jewish community can be dealt with successfully only nationally, it has been extremely difficult to mobilize Federation commitments to efforts that cross local boundaries. Only two nationally planned Federation programs have been completely successful: support for loan guarantees to Israel and funding for refugee resettlement. Two other trans-communal issues—equitable funding for Hillel foundations and scholarship aid for graduate training for Jewish communal professionals—have garnered only partial support. The very slow pace of the creation of the UJC as a fully functional organization, which has been a more publicly visible process, is also in large part a reflection of the tensions between local and national/international perspectives in the Federation world. As for the impact of mobility, it is not even on local Federations' agendas. A system to systematically pass along information about Jews as they move from one part of the country to another would be a way to keep Jews on the community's institutional rolls under conditions of high mobility. It is not hard to imagine how to do this in today's electronic environment, but suggestions in this direction have received no effective organizational responses within the Federation or advocacy worlds.

The Long Singles Gap

The second demographic factor connected in fundamental ways to decreases in Jewish affiliation is the change in the age of marriage, with a host of concomitant consequences. Here, too, the organized community's responses have been meager. American Jewish organizational structures reflect a different time, not just with respect to the content of Jewish concerns but also with respect to life cycle patterns, specifically, the duration of single status.

Until the 1960s, the vast majority of Jews married in their twenties. This reflected a general American pattern, although because Jews attended college at higher rates than most other American groups, the Jewish marriage age was slightly older than the national median. In any case, young Jews moved very quickly from their parental homes through college to their own homes. They would connect to the organized Jewish community first through their parents, then on the college campuses through Hillel, and then, soon enough, as young marrieds in a variety of available organizations, most notably the synagogues but also other community organizations. If there was a gap in appropriate institutional availability, it was at most, say, five years, usually not enough time to have gotten deeply engaged with other, competing enterprises. In addition, the non-Jewish world and its organizations were not very welcoming of Jews, again reinforcing Jewish engagement with Jewish institutions.

Americans in general have been postponing the age of marriage. Much of this change is connected to increases in higher education. Jews, and particularly Jewish women, now represent the most highly educated of all American subgroups. The average age of first marriage for non-Orthodox Jews is now closer to 35 than to 25. But few mainstream Jewish organizations have changed in ways that recognize this new set of circumstances. Programs and fee structures continue to be built around the interests, values, schedules, and financial situations of settled adults. Even if organizational goals might appeal to young single Jews, the social milieu in which they are cast is not appropriate to their life stage.

What this means is that there is now a gap of fifteen years or more in which there are almost no appropriate institutional venues for single young adult Jewish participation in most mainstream Jewish organizations. But there is lots else—not Jewish—out there for single young adults to do and to connect with, and all of it is now open to Jews in once unimaginable ways. By the time our young Jew has married and has children—that is, fits into the mold for which participation in most of our organizations is designed— he or she has found other things to do, and perhaps, increasingly, a non-Jewish partner to do them with. In addition, of course, the young Jew now lives at a distance from his or her family and community of origin. All of this adds up to a loss of the "plausibility structures," the life givens that create a sense of necessity that *Jewish* organizational participation is the way to satisfy any needs for affiliation and social contribution that he or she might feel later as a more settled family person. In fact, we would identify this lack of appropriate structures and venues for post-college under-40 singles as the most glaring organizational lack in American Jewish life today.

In the late 1920s there was a new development in American Jewish demography—the presence for the first time of numbers of Jewish college students on campuses away from their parental homes. The communal response was the founding of the Hillel Foundations—the creation of a new institutional setting appropriate to the age group. But for the now huge numbers of unmarried Jews in their late twenties and thirties, no one has appeared with the equivalent of the vision that founded Hillel; and if they did appear, it is not at all clear that there is an institution able to mobilize local affiliates under a national umbrella, as B'nai Brith could do at the time of Hillel's founding.

Some Local Responses

There are some local attempts to provide new avenues of Jewish participation suitable for young and not-so-young, but still single, Jews. A web search turns up listings of "young adult" or "young leadership" activities sponsored by almost every major Federation, the local affiliates of some national organizations in the larger urban areas, and some synagogues and other local groups. But a more careful analysis reveals a piecemeal approach. Most of these attempts involve only sporadic programs, often targeted across the full span of singles (despite ample evidence that younger singles will not come to programs that 40-year-olds attend), or, in a continuation of the old patterns, designed and advertised for both singles and the partnered. Furthermore, in spite of all we know about the lack of institutional loyalty among today's younger Jews, competition and attempts at exclusivity, not city- or area-wide coordination, are the norm. Equally seriously, there is no linking between programs across metropolitan boundaries, in spite of all we now know about the great mobility of Jews in this life cycle stage. To the best of our knowledge, no national organizations in the civil realm have devoted anything resembling serious resources to an attempt to respond to the combined effects of these new demographic realities.

As for individual synagogues, with the exception of a few congregations in the largest cities with easily identifiable heavily young adult areas, in this respect most are still living in the 1950s. Activities, structures, and even membership forms reflect an assumption that the target population is married. The Reform movement's national organization is the only one to pay heed to the facts of Jewish mobility. It created the "Privilege Card," designed to reach out to younger single Jews by allowing the transfer of membership to any participating congregation when a person moved, without paying extra dues. The program was targeted precisely to the demographic combination of long single status and high mobility. It has been renamed "New Jewish Connections," with the new title signifying an attempt to also offer program and marketing ideas to help participating congregations be more effective in reaching the target audience. Some 400 congregations are currently enrolled in the program. Is it working? Are younger, single, mobile Jews finding their way to Reform congregations? Here, too, research is waiting to happen. However, even if these programs work, the Jewish community would be left with the issue of connection to the public square.

A Misguided Analysis

While some institutions are experimenting with new organizational forms, most of the effort has been in another direction. The Jewish community's attempts to respond to the decreases in affiliation and Federation philanthropy (and, of course, to the rise in intermarriage) have been almost entirely under the rubric of what is called "Jewish continuity." The emphasis has been on "strengthening Jewish identity." Yet, if our analysis is correct, this response is at best partial and, at worst, misses the boat. It is partial in its lack of full understanding of the new ways in which Jewish identity is being expressed, and it is off the mark in overlooking the interaction of demographic factors with organizational structural realities.

The "continuity response" to developments in the relation of Jews as individuals to Jewish organizational life is characterized by what social psychologists call the "fundamental attribution error." In brief, this explanatory rubric notes the common tendency to attribute others' behavior mainly to their internal states, to the kinds of people they are, even if we would have a considerably more complex and nuanced view of our own behavior in similar circumstances. For example, if you are late to a meeting with me, it must be because you are inconsiderate, or our meeting does not really matter to you, or some similar explanation whose locus is internal to you. If I am late, however, it is not because there is something wrong with me. It is because the phone rang, or traffic was bad, or something else external to me came along to make me tardy.

In the same way, the organized American Jewish community has been approaching the increasing nonaffiliation of the newer cohorts of Jews as if the issue is only internal—if today's Jews are not attaching themselves to Jewish community and Jewish organizations, it is because they are not "Jewish enough." The result has been an emphasis on strengthening Jewish identity as essentially the sole approach to ensuring Jewish continuity. It is as if, having recognized one paradigm shift—the one having to do with indi-

vidualism and choice—most community decisionmakers cannot
think about the other things that are also going on, specifically,
increased mobility and the young adult institutional gap. While
fostering strong Jewish identity is surely useful in light of the increasingly optional nature of ethnic and religious identity in America (although our analysis suggests it could use many more path-
ways than are usually involved in Federation Jewish identity
efforts), it is not sufficient.

The problem lies at least as much in the organizational realm,
specifically in the possibilities available (or not) for Jewish communal expression. Behavior equals motivation *plus* opportunity.
The once nearly automatic link between Jewish identity and Jewish
participation has been broken not only because younger Jews do
not *want* to connect, but also because the right kinds of opportunities for connection simply are not there at the right times. "Right
kinds" will involve both content (a wide variety of paths to connection, targeted to the increasing variety of ways Jews integrate
their Jewishness as an aspect of their personal identity) and form
(designed for single, young, mobile Jews). If Jewish participation
in the public square is to remain vigorous, institutions must reshape themselves to recognize the new realities of identity and demography in America. Doing so is no guarantee of success, but not
doing so will be a self-fulfilling prophecy of the impossibility of
change.

Putting It All Together

If the possibility of coherent Jewish activity in the public square
remains a desideratum, the organized community must pay better
attention to the entirety of what is going on in the arenas of ethnic
and religious identity and its expression, and to the changed demographics of Jewish lives. Jewish identity, even if it can be
"strengthened," no longer automatically implies communal participation. If and when collective activity will be one of the forms in
which Jewish identity is expressed, it is as likely to happen in ways
not yet even imagined as on past generations' paths. And if it is to
happen, there must be venues that recognize new life cycle patterns
and that are committed to communicating and coordinating efforts
across organizational and community boundaries.

All of these are matters for institutional structural change, not
instead of, but alongside of, and as necessary as, any attempts to

have an impact on individuals' Jewish identities. The challenge to the organized Jewish community is to re-vision attachment and affiliation through a multiply-focused lens. If it does not, it may be left with *rebbes* without enough *hasidim,* a set of organizations that are much clearer about how they want to represent Jews and Jewish life in the American public square, but fewer and fewer Jews engaged in the enterprise with them.

Notes

1. Will Herberg, *Protestant, Catholic, Jew* (Garden City, N.Y.: Doubleday, 1955).

2. Mary C. Waters, *Ethnic Options* (Berkeley: University of California Press, 1990).

3. Herbert Gans, "Symbolic Ethnicity: the Future of Ethnic Groups in America," *Ethnic and Racial Studies* 2, no. 1 (1979).

4. Charles Liebman, "Post-war American Jewry: From Ethnic to Privatized Judaism," in Elliott Abrams and David G. Dalin, eds., *Secularism, Spirituality, and the Future of American Jewry* (Washington, D.C.: Ethics and Policy Center, 1999), 7-18.

5. Bernard Lazerwitz, J. Alan Winter, Arnold Dashevsky, and Ephraim Tabory, *Jewish Choices* (Albany: State University of New York Press, 1998).

6. Robert N. Bellah, Richard Madsen, William M. Sullivan, Ann Swidler, and Steven M. Tipton, *Habits of the Heart* (New York: Harper & Row, 1985).

7. The author recently found "Shelaism" included in a list of world religions on a website, without comment to distinguish it from Hinduism, Buddhism, Judaism, or any of the other more expected religious "isms."

8. Liebman, "Post-war American Jewry."

9. Bethamie Horowitz, "Connections and Journeys: Assessing Critical Opportunities for Enhancing Jewish Identity" (New York: UJA-Federation of Jewish Philanthropies of New York, June 2000); and "Indicators of Jewish Identity: Developing a Conceptual Framework for Understanding American Jewry" (New York: Mandel Foundation, November 1999).

10. Wade Clark Roof, *A Generation of Seekers* (San Francisco: Harper, 1993).

11. I am indebted to Alan Mittleman for pointing out that one example of current Jewish spirituality having a political turn is the high premium placed on environmental consciousness, with several resulting environmental actions being organized under Jewish Renewal auspices.

12. The importance of the existence of the State of Israel ranked overall somewhat lower and also showed significant subgroup differences.

The personal importance of Jewish ideals of social justice was affirmed by the lowest proportion of respondents and also with significant differences between subgroups (parenthetically, the lower affirmation by self-identified Reform Jews came as a surprise).

13. Why so many Jews feel most strongly about these defensive issues, when American Jewry is arguably more secure than any other diaspora Jewish community in history, is another matter; cf. Jerome Chanes, *Antisemitism in America Today* (New York: Birch Lane Press, 1995).

14. Roberta R. Farber, and Chaim I. Waxman, *Jews in America: A Contemporary Reader* (Hanover, N.H.: University Press of New England/ Brandeis University Press, 1999).

15. Country/city/village-of-origin social support associations.

16. Peter Knobel, "The Rabbi, the Synagogue and the Community," in Abrams and Dalin, *Secularism, Spirituality, and the Future of American Jewry,* 54-57.

17. Sidney Goldstein and Alice Goldstein, *Jews on the Move* (Albany: State University of New York Press, 1995).

10

Public Jews and Private Acts: Family and Personal Choices in the Public Square and in the Private Realm

Sylvia Barack Fishman

This chapter explores issues connected to the family and personal choices that have evoked strong public advocacy responses among Jews, within the context of American Jewish liberal social and political attitudes. We trace the ways in which Jews express their attitudes toward family and personal choice in the public square, both as individuals and within institutional frameworks. At the same time, we look at information on the private lives of American Jews. We compare public stance and private lifestyles, and analyze the relationship between the two. We discuss factors influencing American Jews to champion causes that do not seem to be overtly connected to their own domestic concerns, and show that in some areas there is a disjunction between passionate public expression and private goals. Finally, we suggest that American Jewish preoccupation with the public square vis-à-vis family issues has obfuscated internal Jewish interests with regard to family formation.

In terms of internal Jewish public advocacy, we urge consideration of an alternative American Jewish stance, a two-tiered approach to issues of family and personal choice similar to the newly important American Jewish approach to issues of religious education.

American Jewish public advocacy today continues to oppose prayer in the public schools, while urging increased Jewish education for children in other settings. We argue that American Jews can similarly maintain advocacy on behalf of reproductive choice and other personal freedoms in the public square, while responding to a little noted Jewish fertility crisis by creating pro-natalist and family-support initiatives within the Jewish community.

American Liberalism as Religious Credo

We turn first to a brief discussion of liberalism as an exemplar of coalesced American-Jewish ethnic/religious values. Jewish advocational stances toward family and personal choice, the primary focus of this chapter, are symbolic and reflective of an American Jewish adaptive strategy that may be called "coalescence." As this author has explained in *Jewish Life and American Culture*, a sociology of American Jews, during the process of coalescence, the texts of two cultures, American and Jewish, are merged. Many classic American values are incorporated into American Jewish conceptions of what is authentically "Jewish." Moreover American Jews have not only created a coalesced American Judaism, they have also created a distinctly Jewish definition of the true American ethos, often characterized by activities on behalf of social justice. These American hybrids preferred by Jews provide a comfortable fit for Jews and Judaism.[1]

American Jews have a long-standing, well-documented reputation for socially liberal attitudes. For decades, political surveys, exit polls, and studies of varying ethnic family groups have revealed a pronounced attitudinal profile among Jews across the United States. Public opinion polls, such as those conducted yearly by the American Jewish Committee, demonstrate that American Jews have maintained liberal attitudes despite their attainment of widespread socioeconomic upward mobility. The 1998 AJC Annual Survey of American Jewish Opinion, for example, showed that 39 percent of American Jews define themselves as liberal, another 36 percent call themselves moderate or middle of the road, and only 23 percent define themselves as conservative.

Significantly, despite growing numbers of younger Jews who identify as conservatives, levels of liberalism are not declining. Rather, the number of Jews defining themselves as "moderate" declines with age. The AJC study shows that 40 percent of Jews under age 40 define themselves as liberal, with another 32 percent calling themselves moderate and 27 percent calling themselves conservative. Although the number of conservative Jews is greater among Jews under age 40 than among those age 40-59 (22 percent) or those age 60 or over (19 percent), the number of liberal Jews is also greater among younger Jews than older Jews. Thus, although pockets of Jews in certain areas of the country vote conservatively, and despite the recent growth of the sociopolitically "neo-conservative" Jewish intelligentsia which has attracted attention, proportionate numbers of conservative Jews remain small, and liberalism continues to grow among the young.[2]

The sources of this trademark American Jewish liberalism flow partially from historical Jewish feelings of vulnerability during centuries of intolerance and overt persecution in diaspora Jewish communities. In the twentieth-century American Jewish experience, Jewish liberalism has no doubt been influenced by the involvement of Jews in socialist and union movements. However, neither psychosocial nor historical factors which have helped to produce coalesced American-Jewish liberalism obviate the very real Jewish attraction to activities which express altruistic social ideals. As historian Stephen Whitfield comments, "The historical record and the data of political science disclose that Jews are more susceptible than other voters to a vision of human brotherhood, to ideologies and programs that can be packaged in ethical terms, and to politicians who can present themselves as apostles of social justice. More so than other Americans, Jewish voters are inspired by ideals that can be conceived to echo the prophetic assault upon complacency and comfort."[3]

One useful introductory example of continuing altruism in American Jewish liberalism is found in attitudes toward immigration. In the early part of the twentieth century Jews were more liberal on immigration issues than others associated with the Socialist Party, and this stance was connected to Jewish feelings of vulnerability, as Karen Brodkin points out. The official Socialist Party line declared many ethnic groups to be "backward races" who would be "incapable of assimilation," and thus should be discouraged from emigrating to the United States. Jews were told not to worry about socialist opposition to open immigration; the claim was that opposition "was directed against Asians, and that Jews should have no concern. However, Jews had a great deal of concern and were strongly opposed to any restrictions on immigration. Much of their opposition was based on the assumption that any restriction would be extended to the Jews."[4]

One might assume that with the turn of the twenty-first century, and the fading of their immigrant memories, Jews would become significantly more conservative on issues of immigration. However, the 1998 American Jewish Committee Public Opinion Survey shows that the vast majority of American Jews continue to believe that immigrants "make America more open to new ideas and cultures." Conversely, only 28 percent of American Jews believe that immigrants take jobs away from people who were born in America.[5] Thus, while durable Jewish liberalism on immigration issues grows partially out of the historical Jewish experience, it is also partially an expression of Jewish altruism and empathy for other disadvantaged groups.

Jewish liberalism has also been influenced by the particular "spiritual marketplace" which American Jews have chosen for themselves. An anecdotal comment by a Jewish professional in Columbus, Georgia, might well be applied to many Jews who adapted to life in the gentrified urban areas, suburbs, and smaller towns in the United States: "Jews in Columbus basically had a choice of looking like Southern Baptists, or looking like Episcopalians," he said. "We quickly chose to look like the Episcopalians." The social and political profile which the majority of American Jews have chosen to emulate values a kind of subdued religiosity, communal good works, and political liberalism. Decades ago sociologist Marshall Sklare noted that liberal American Jews "locate the source of their ethic in Judaism," although the "motive power for making such an identification comes from the general culture."[6]

American Jews often view their political activism as an expression of their Jewishness; this partially reflects their adamant identification as Jews. It also reflects their participation in an American society which is more favorably inclined to citizens who are religiously affiliated than it is to those who publicly declare themselves to be totally atheistic or secular. As Wade Clark Roof points out, "almost ninety percent of Americans claim an institutionally based religious identity." The religious communities with which Americans identify "serve as an important basis of social belonging." Although America, with its lack of an official church, has proven fertile ground for religious pluralism and an almost unimaginable number of splinter groups, these diverse religious movements provide the broader American culture with "an ascetic moralism deeply rooted in biblical tradition and Reformation theology emphasizing duty to family, church, and work. Reaffirmed are the twin ordering principles so embedded with this legacy, love of God and love of neighbor, that have long shaped religious and even secular notions of purpose in life, goodness, responsibility, and justice."[7]

Recent Gallup polls on trends in United States beliefs show that Americans are more religious than the populations of many other Western countries. Ninety-six percent of Americans say they believe in God (1995), for example, compared to 61 percent in Britain and 70 percent in Canada. Even younger Americans express this national religiosity. Ninety-five percent of American teenagers say they believe in God, and teenagers in all American religious groups are more likely to attend church or synagogue than their parents.[8] The broader American civic culture, from this vantage point, is perceived as based on the belief in God ("In God We Trust"), and as incorporating an amalgam, or a coalescence, of altruistic virtues gleaned from many religious traditions. Jewish activists participating in this vision can readily see themselves as being both better Americans and better Jews.

A striking institutional example of these sacralized liberal American Jewish values is found in the document *In Pursuit of Justice: Resolutions and Policy Statements*, put out by the Women of Reform Judaism, the Federation of Temple Sisterhoods (New York, 1998). The overall introduction to this document sets the stage for understanding the coalesced interpretive framework. Their "viewpoint is infused by Women of Reform Judaism's commitment to and foundation in the Judaic values of Torah, worship and loving deeds. Women of Reform Judaism have taken seriously the mandate to help repair a broken world," states Ellen Y. Rosenberg, the executive director.

In the Introduction to the 1988 edition, the authors reiterate a mandate which seems to focus primarily on issues which directly affect the individuals and institutions of Reform Judaism: "To carry out its objectives, the National Federation of Temple Sisterhoods shall continue to develop special relationships, concerns and interests on behalf of the Reform Jewish movement as well as on national and international issues . . . as the Women's Agency of the Union of American Hebrew Congregations [it] shall cooperate with the Union's various programs and projects as well as with its own, to strengthen the synagogue, Jewish education, family life, social advocacy, interreligious activities and concern for Israel."[9]

"Social advocacy" expands to provide most of the subject areas actually dealt with in this document, despite the Jewishly defined mission statement, in a wide-ranging list of resolutions and policy statements on the following topics: A. Arms control, disarmament, war, peace, and international understanding; B. Children and Youth;

C. Civil Rights; D. Crime and Terrorism; E. Economic Justice; F. Education: Religious and Secular; G. The Environment; H. The Family; I. Genocide; J. Health Issues; K. Immigration; L. Interreligious and Multicultural Issues; M. Israel and the Middle East; N. Poverty and Hunger; O. Public and Civic Concerns; Religious Living; Q. The United Nations; R. Women's Rights; and S. World Jewry.

A Judaic text is quoted from at the beginning of each section, with the goal of demonstrating the ways in which the stated policy decisions are grounded in historical Judaism. For example, the following quote is included at the opening of a segment on Affirmative Action (C-23): "In a well-known Talmudic story about a dispute between brothers, the rules of evidence were changed to put an excessive burden on the rich and powerful brother when witnesses for the weaker brother were fearful of testifying. "Thus do we do for all who are not powerful," says the text (B. Talmud, Baba Metzia 9b). The promise of equality is not sufficient if there are obstacles that make the reality of equality impossible."[10]

After a brief but coherent discussion of the history and main points of the issue, the Women of Reform Judaism articulate their resolutions as follows:

> Believing that there ought to be equal opportunity for all, and cognizant that discrimination against women and members of minority groups in regard to education and jobs continues, the Women of Reform Judaism:
> 1. Reaffirms its commitment to affirmative action or equity programs without quotas.
> 2. Urges Sisterhoods to provide educational events and resources about affirmative action or equity programs and their ongoing needs.
> 3. Opposes legislation and other initiatives and action at every governmental level that would prevent or eliminate necessary affirmative action or equity programs (C-24).

Significantly, these firm resolutions on behalf of women receiving equal access to job opportunities could well be perceived as going against the best interests of the institutional needs of the Temple Sisterhoods. Like most Jewish women's organizations, the Temple Sisterhoods have experienced a striking decline in the numbers of women able to put in long volunteer hours during the daytime because of the rise in women working outside the home for pay. However, despite the fact that promoting labor force participation by women may contradict the institutional interests of the group, they formulate their policy decisions based on an altruistic concept of justice and fairness and, above all, individual rights.

Feminism and American Jewish Public Activism

Similarly, Jewish liberalism on women's issues and Jewish advocacy on behalf of feminist agendas has a complicated etiology. Jewish advocacy for women's issues is composed partially of altruism and empathy for potentially oppressed groups, and is also influenced by individualism and the history of Jews as primarily an urban rather than a farming population. Smaller families are perceived as more nurturing environments for the women who endure pregnancies and for individual children, in modern, Western educated, urban societies, in contrast to preferred large family sizes in traditional rural communities, in which large numbers of children are absorbed into the family labor pool.

Although Jews are often colloquially considered to be exceptionally oriented toward family and children, American Jewish familism is not characterized by a preference for large families (with the exception of very small segments of the ultra-Orthodox community). On the contrary, in the American context, consistent family planning has come to be considered an ethnic marker of the Jewish community. American Jews have been associated with liberal attitudes toward family planning and personal choice for much of the twentieth century. American Jewish couples have been regarded as unique by demographers because of the accuracy with which they plan their families and use contraceptive devices to implement their plans.[11] Family planning is probably one of the first and most profound aspects of coalescence. The tendency toward smaller families among Jewish women actually began at least as far back as the middle of the nineteenth century. According to early twentieth-century Prussian figures, modernity affected the fertility of Jews more than any other group.[12] Among the early activists on behalf of birth control in twentieth-century America were women who lectured in Yiddish and probably felt that they were rebelling against Jewish culture. However, birth control no longer is perceived as transgressive, but instead appears to be an axiom of American Jewish culture for their daughters and granddaughters. Studies indicate that female contraceptive usage is the norm even among the majority of ultra-Orthodox American Jewish women. (It should be noted that women in ultra-Orthodox environments often do not begin using birth control until after they have had five children, do not always tell their husbands they are using it, and typically describe their motivation as being medical, rather than personal.)[13]

Jewish liberalism on family issues became even more pronounced with the spread of second-wave feminism in the late 1960s and early 1970s. On a personal level, the vast majority of American Jews have incorporated many feminist principles into their values and behaviors. The feminism of American Jews is demonstrated by numerous demographic facts: Jewish women have unprecedentedly high levels of education and occupational achievement, tend to continue their careers even when they are mothers of children under six years old, and are active in a broad spectrum of public leadership roles. Moreover, American Jewish women have been very influenced by feminism on a personal level. Conducting research for B'nai B'rith Women, Sid Groeneman studied middle American families from various ethnic faith traditions in 1985; he found that Jews tended to be almost as liberal in the heartland as they were on either coast. One of the striking characteristics of Jewish beliefs was what Groeneman called a "liberal, feminist package," which emphasized female competence and independence rather than docility and family orientation. Only 22 percent of Jewish women reported primary goals for their daughters as wanting them to "have a good family, husband, marriage, children" or being "loving, caring, good parents." In contrast, non-Jewish women ranked personal qualities such as thoughtfulness, neighborliness, and devotion to family much higher on their wish list for daughters than did Jewish women.

Ironically, Jewish women, who have often been perceived as very family oriented, reported themselves more concerned that their daughters have the capacity to be self-sufficient than they were that their daughters create and serve families. Although many of these women did not see themselves as "feminist," they had clearly absorbed feminist goals, especially when they thought of their daughter's lives.[14] This concern about the welfare of their daughters as independent individuals illustrates the extent to which American Jewish mothers have integrated a Western emphasis on the individual, in a clear departure from the social and religious norms of traditional Jewish societies, which often placed great emphasis on the needs of the social grouping, such as family or community.

American Jews often coalesce their dedication to individualism into their conception of American Judaism, as part of their preference for believing that the things they care about derive from their religious affiliation. When coalescence does not work, that is, when Jewish and American values do not fit well together, American Jews tend to ignore the area of Jewish dissonance.

Alternatively, American Jews often rhetorically juxtapose Jewish and American viewpoints, articulating both traditional Jewish and American sentiments but acting only on the more liberal American value system. Typically, Jewish values appear as a passive verbal expression, followed by action-oriented liberal advocacy. This strategy is emblazoned on the masthead of the newsletter of the Commission for Women's Equality of the American Jewish Congress: "Proudly Jewish, Actively Feminist." It is certainly significant that many American Jews find it important to connect their good works on behalf of liberal social and political causes to Jewish contexts. However, the subtext of this masthead seems to be: however "proud" one may be of Jewishness, it is on behalf of the feminist agenda that the organization articulates its goals as "active," while Jewishness is a dormant state of being. Within the body of the newsletter as well, the six pages of articles in the February 1995 issue provide equally interesting overt and subtle evidence of the characteristic outer-directed American Jewish public advocacy stance: First, the articles convey a uniformly liberal feminist message. Second, most of the articles address a larger, American civic social action agenda, with limited numbers dealing with subjects that have direct applicability to American Jews.

Family Planning as the
Prevention of Conception

Many demographers of the American Jewish community have noted that American Jews, like their socioeconomic Protestant peer group, are characterized by strikingly low levels of fertility. Changes in marriage patterns have affected both the timing and the size of today's families. In 1990, 93 percent of Jewish women aged 18 to 24 had not yet had children. More than half (55 percent) of those aged 25 to 34 had not yet had children. Among Jewish women aged 35 to 44, one out of four had no children. While almost all American Jewish women aged 45 and over reported having children, either biological or adopted, it is not clear that all or even most of the 24 percent of childless women in the 35- to 44-year-old age group will in fact achieve the status of motherhood. In contrast, during the 1950s, American Jewish women, like non-Jewish women, married early and started their families early. Half of American Jewish women had a child by age 22, and three-quarters had a child by age 25. But today, as a result of delayed marriage and childbirth, the American societal preference for smaller families, and unwanted infertility, most demographers now estimate that the completed size of the contemporary American Jewish family averages well under two children per married household.

The vast majority of Jewish women still place enormous value on having children. Jewish women are less likely than any other religious or ethnic group to state that they wish to remain childless. Most American Jewish couples hope to have children "someday." Unlike women of other ethnic groups, in which higher education is associated with lower expectations of childbearing, the more highly educated a Jewish woman, the more children she expects to have. Calvin Goldscheider and Francis Kobrin Goldscheider, relying on data that deal with expected family size, point out that among Jewish populations, "educational attainment is directly rather than inversely related to fertility expectations." Thus, "Jews with doctorates expect 2.2 children and only 11 percent expect to be childless."[15] However, highly educated Jewish women do not actually have as many children as they once expected to. Although Jewish career women are more committed to having children than other groups of career women, they are at least as likely as other white middle-class women to postpone the onset of childbearing until they have reached what they consider to be an appropriate level of occupational or financial achievement. In this new demographic, expectations often do not give way to reality. Jewish women aged 16 to 26 interviewed in a national study in 1969-70 expected to have an average of 2.5 children. That same demographic cohort, twenty years later, has in fact borne an average of 1.5 children, with a projected average completed family size of 1.7 children.[16]

This combination of postponing childbirth, and yet hoping to have children someday, has increasingly become characteristic of white American women. According to U.S. Census figures, by the end of the 1980s, 54 percent of women aged 30-34 said they were planning to have a child, compared to only one-third of such women in 1976. Similarly, the actual proportion of children born to mothers over 30 had increased: "In the twelve months ending in June, 1988, 33 percent of children born in the United States were born to mothers in their thirties, as against 19 percent in 1976," according to a report in the *New York Times*.[17] The article also notes that women who wait until their thirties to have children are far more likely to fall into the demographic which returns to work soon after childbirth. This profile very much matches information gleaned about Jewish women from the 1990 National Jewish Population Survey. Moreover, the same work commitments which play a role in Jewish women's postponing childbirth also play a role in their having fewer children than they had originally planned to have.

The demographic reality is thus that the true fertility crisis facing the American Jewish community is a crisis of low fertility. The family planning failure of the Jewish community, if there is one, is not the failure to responsibly use contraception to prevent unwanted pregnancies. It is, instead, an unwillingness to discuss the biological implications of postponed childbirth. The biological realities of women's childbearing lives are neither "fair" nor "politically correct." Indeed, when medical researchers have attempted to publicize findings on the relationship between advancing age and fertility, they have been roundly shot down and ridiculed by writers such as Susan Faludi. In her popular book, *Backlash*, Faludi contrasts two medical reports on infertility. Citing the report she views as more woman-friendly, Faludi declares that of women between ages 30 to 34 attempting to become pregnant for the first time, "only 13.6 percent" would suffer from unwanted infertility—"a mere 3 percent higher than women in their early twenties."[18] However, a 13.6 percent rate of primary infertility is not an insignificant figure among a population of married women who are currently trying to have children. What it means is that one out of every seven childless women between the ages of 30 to 34 will encounter difficulty or be unable to conceive altogether. Moreover, this figure does not include women who postpone beginning their families until their late thirties or early forties, when conception rates drop even further. It also does not include women trying to have a second child. Data from the National Center for Health Statistics indicate that infertility is actually higher in women attempting a second pregnancy than those trying for a first child.[19]

Despite the fact that Jewish women are far more likely to suffer from an inability to conceive than an inability to effectively use contraception, Jewish women's organizations overwhelmingly focus their reports on preventing pregnancy. Jewish organizations report and urge activism on family planning and fertility issues in one direction only: promoting access to information and techniques for the prevention of conception. For example, a recent issue of the newsletter of the Commission for Women's Equality informed readers about new research on Norplant, a contraceptive device implanted under the skin, which is effective for several months, and has successfully been used among inner-city teens: "The *New England*

Journal of Medicine recently published a study by Dr. Margaret Po-
lanetczky. The results showed that Norplant was 19 times more effective in preventing pregnancy than the pill among 98 inner-city
teen mothers who had just given birth at the University of Pennsylvania Hospital. After their delivery, 48 chose Norplant and 50 chose
the pill; 18 months later, 19 of those on the pill had become pregnant, while only 1 on Norplant had."[20] However, no space in this
journal was devoted to a discussion of the depressed fertility situation of direct concern to American Jews.

In American Jewish organizational newsletters, "family planning" is characteristically used as a synonym for preventing conception for those women who wish to have children. Thus, while Jewish
organizations play a prominent role in the American public square
advocating on behalf of controlling unwanted fertility, they play
little or no role in the Jewish public arena addressing the problems
of unwanted infertility that are germane to numerous young American Jewish women today, with the exception of exploring possible
problems with technologically assisted conception.

Reproductive Technologies and
Jewish Public Advocacy

The growing field of reproductive technologies is a relatively new
focus for Jewish public advocacy. In April 1999 the major national
Jewish women's organizations, including the Commission for
Women's Equality of the American Jewish Congress, Emunah, Hadassah, Jewish Women International, Na'amat USA, UJA Federation Task Force on the Jewish Woman, Women of Reform Juda-
ism/Federation of Temple Sisterhoods, and Women's League for
Conservative Judaism came together for a public conference on
"New Birth Technologies and the Jewish Community." As the
Commission for Women's Equality proposal articulated the Jewish
connection to this issue:

> Because they are substantial consumers of assisted reproductive
> technologies services (ART), Jewish couples are uniquely vulner-
> able to the inadequacies of current law governing reproductive
> medicine and to the excesses attributed to the commodification and
> commercialization implicit in a market driven fertility industry.
> Jewish women tend to marry late and postpone having children
> longer. They tend to go to college, be attracted to the professions,

and spend several years in graduate school. More and more Jewish women are remaining in the workforce and delaying the decision to have children to the point where age decreases their ability to become pregnant. Technological intervention then offers their only hope of becoming biological mothers. . . .

Jewish women and the Jewish community as a whole thus have a substantial stake in learning about the medical, bio-ethical and public policy issues involved in reproductive medicine.[21]

An in-depth look at the last three lines in this excerpt is instructive. The assumption here is that postponed childbirth is a given, and is not worthy of further discussion. One might suppose that any one of the diverse participating organizations in this conference might want to initiate a public information campaign within the Jewish community, providing information on the incremental biological implications of postponed childbirth. Contrary to popular impressions, this information is not widely available. Although delayed childbirth has a profound and sometimes heartbreaking effect on the lives of women and their partners, Jewish communal organizations seldom venture into the enterprise of publicizing known medical information about the relationship between age and fertility.

The subjects of the conference focused only on technological issues: What does Jewish tradition say about the new birth technologies? Should insurance coverage of fertility services be mandated? What should we do about the excessively high number of multiple births resulting from the new technologies? Should the ban on embryo research be lifted? Are additional measures regulating ART needed?[22]

This suspicion of technological aids to conception is encouraged by liberal and feminist ideologies. Feminist nurse Margaret Sandelowski charges that some feminist theorists take a harsh view of infertile women because the research and medicine in these areas is dominated by men. Such feminists concentrate on male technicians rather than on the infertility experiences of women. As Sandelowski summarizes: "Recent feminist writing has emphasized the continuing medicalization of childbearing and motherhood and the male expropriation of reproductive power from women, furthering female subordination. Reproductive technologies are tied to patriarchal concepts of womanhood, parenthood, and family, making their further development and use unjustifiable in terms of the potential consequences for women as a social group, despite the promise they might hold for some individual women."[23]

Ironically, the very organizations which wring their hands over Jewish women's increasing dependence on technological answers ignore any discussion of one overriding nontechnological answer: Jewish women, as they list their priorities and plan their life strategies, might wish to move their attempts at conception earlier rather than later. Naturally many factors enter into this decision, not least the critical factor of whether a woman has found a partner with whom she wishes to create a family with children. In addition, some women and some men will suffer from infertility-related problems at any age. However, all other things being equal, among the broad population the timing of conception has an enormous impact on the chances for success. Jewish women who have struggled with infertility, and their numbers are legion, already know this. Yet few young women who are "prioritizing" have access to this information.

In contrast with the American Jewish suspicion of a male-dominated assisted reproductive technology industry, Israeli Jewish society is markedly pro-natalist, and pursues assisted reproductive technology enthusiastically. As anthropologist Susan Kahn shows in her Hadassah International Research Institute on Jewish Women Working Paper, "Rabbis and Reproduction: The Uses of New Reproductive Technologies among Ultraorthodox Jews in Israel," and in her book, *Reproducing Jews: A Cultural Account of Assisted Conception in Israel*:

> It is important to understand that all Israelis, both ultra-Orthodox and non-ultraorthodox, have been enthusiastic consumers of the new reproductive technologies. Indeed, there are more fertility clinics per capita in Israel than in any other country of the world, and Israeli fertility specialists are global leaders in the research and development of these technologies. In addition, Israeli lawmakers have created legislation that guarantees insurance coverage for these treatments at unprecedented rates: not only are less invasive technologies and their associated treatments heavily subsidized, so are IVF and other advanced treatments. Every Israeli citizen, Jewish and non-Jewish, may receive up to seven rounds of in-vitro fertilization treatment, up to the birth of two live children, as part of their basic basket of health services. Moreover, these subsidies are available to Israelis regardless of marital status, which means that even unmarried women may receive the equivalent of thousands of dollars of fertility treatments at the state's expense. In March 1996, Israel became the first country in the world to legalize surrogacy agreements that are regulated by a publicly appointed government commission; since that time, numerous surrogacy contracts have been successfully negotiated and carried out.[24]

As surprising as these data may be, they illustrate the fact that Jews in Israel are much more influenced than Jews in the United States by the social and religious norms of traditional Jewish societies, which emphasized social groupings such as family or community. Not only historical Jewish values, but also the socialist philosophy which was influential in the founding and early years of the state, and the rigorous demands of Israel's early years upon its populace are each partially responsible for Israeli Jewish culture's characteristic focus, at least until recently, on the needs of the family, the community, and the state. This group orientation contributes to the fact that Israeli culture tends to be far more family-oriented and pro-natalist, even among secular Israelis. Thus, Israeli Jews marry earlier than American Jews, despite the required service in the Israel Defense Forces, and they have larger families than Americans, despite a more complicated economic situation.

Abortion as a Symbol of Individual Freedom

Abortion is an American right which Jews champion but use less often than others. The vast majority of American Jews articulate strong political support for the right of women to determine if and when they choose to become mothers. Included in this formulation of reproductive choice is the right of women to decide that they wish to abort any particular pregnancy. Given the nearly uniform, articulate support for abortion rights among American Jews, an observer might imagine that Jewish women are particularly prone to use of abortion. In fact, however, just the opposite is true. Jewish women and men have long been characterized by their determined, responsible use of birth control, minimizing situations that would call for abortion. As a cohort, Jewish women are actually less likely to make use of their legal right to abortion than women of other religious and ethnic groups because of their ubiquitous use of birth control.

So the direct need of Jewish women as a group is not the main reason that discussion of abortion rights is ever-present in Jewish public pronouncements. Jewish public advocacy on behalf of abortion rights is more accurately seen as yet another expression of Jewish altruism and sensitivity toward the needs of potentially vulnerable groups. Simply put, Jews advocate on behalf of reproductive choice because were the government to have control over women's biological fates, women could be perceived as an oppressed and profoundly unfree group of Americans.

American Jews are deeply, one may say religiously, committed to individual freedom. As individuals and in their communities, Jews suffered for centuries from an often dramatic absence of freedom, under the thumb of imperious, anti-Semitic governments that could revoke basic rights with whimsical malevolence. Jews as individuals had no say over their own destiny when intolerant rulers or neighbors saw them only as Jews, members of a pariah group. Emerging from the strictures of official bigotry, emancipated Jews cherished their privileges and responsibilities as citizens of democratic societies. The overwhelming majority of Jews who emigrated to America learned to embrace their adopted land and all its individual rights with patriotic passion. Disproportionately, during the course of the twentieth century Jews have labored in the public square to ensure that individuals have the freedom to follow their own visions of life, liberty, and the pursuit of happiness. Jews have overwhelmingly defended the right of each individual to make choices as an individual, rather than as an exemplar of any particular racial, religious, or gender-based group. In addition, Jews have been exquisitely sensitive to the encroachments of any state-based religion into realms that more correctly belong to the public square. Having experienced how onerous a state religion can be toward those not of that religious persuasion, many contemporary American Jews have worked hard to maintain the American separation of church and state.

Placed in this context, Jewish abortion advocacy is highly symbolic. It partially reflects the American Jewish repugnance against legislation which has the effect of restricting individual freedom, in this case the freedom of women to determine the fate of their own bodies: it is hard to imagine a servitude more violating than being forced to gestate a child against one's will. Jewish women are, of course, vulnerable to unwanted pregnancies. Women can find unwanted pregnancies devastating. Such pregnancies can threaten a woman's education, communal standing, and/or health. Letty Cottin Pogrebin's powerful "Hers" column in the *New York Times*, "Consequences," later published in her popular memoir, *Deborah, Golda and Me*, vividly recalls her anguish during an unwanted pregnancy at age nineteen, and her gratitude then and now that she was able to obtain an abortion.[25] The vast majority of American Jewish women sympathize with Pogrebin's experiences and emotions under these circumstances.

In addition, even for formally religious Jews, governmental control over abortion could cause severe problems because the rabbinic attitude toward abortion is far from identical to that of Christian teachings. According to rabbinic law, the potential mother is viewed as a human life receiving the utmost protection, while the fetus is viewed as a living thing, and deserving of respect, but not yet a human life; some rabbinic sources refer to the fetus as tantamount to a limb of the mother, rather than a separate being. As a result, when the mother's well-being is threatened by the fetus, such as in cases where the mother's physical or mental health is jeopardized by a pregnancy, rabbinic law can decide in favor of abortion to protect the mother. Not until the very moment when the fetus emerges from the birth canal, or the head emerges and the fetus starts to breathe air, is the child considered a human life on a par with that of the mother.[26]

Even in a case of what we might call "partial birth abortion," so abhorred by the contemporary pro-life political faction, the welfare of the mother is championed in Jewish law, as Robert Gordis elaborates: "The mishnah reads: 'If a woman is having difficulty in childbirth (so that her life is endangered), one cuts off the embryo, limb by limb, because her life takes precedence over its life. If most of the fetus (or the head) has emerged, it may not be hurt, for we do not set one life aside for the sake of another.' This classical passage embodies the principle that the fetus is a limb of its mother. In Rashi's words, 'The life of the mother in childbirth takes precedence over that of the embryo to the very last moment of pregnancy.'"[27]

Thus, it is difficult for knowledgeable Jews to have a political pact with the fundamentalist Christian anti-abortion movement because the two religious groups have deeply differing approaches to the appropriateness of abortion. On the other hand, the rabbinic attitude toward abortion is far from cavalier. Abortion is viewed by Jewish law as a sad necessity in cases where the mother's well-being is seriously compromised by a pregnancy. It certainly is not viewed as an acceptable mode of birth control, or a procedure to be undertaken for issues of "personal choice" or convenience. As a result, those Jews who view rabbinic *halakhah* as a binding mandate fit in with neither the so-called pro-choice nor pro-life movements. The great majority of American Jews, even Orthodox Jews, find themselves in the pro-choice camp at least by default. Having the government control the availability of abortion is unacceptable for American Jews, either because of religious ideology or the necessity for religious freedom.

Documentary evidence on the unmediated positive Jewish advocacy on behalf of abortion rights is ubiquitous. Good examples can be found in some publications of the Religious Action Center of Reform Judaism. According to its masthead, the Center is the Washington office of the Union of American Hebrew Congregations and the Central Conference of American Rabbis, "representing 1.5 million Reform Jews . . . in 875 congregations throughout North America." A Center press release of June 15, 1999, begins with the following bold-italicized statement: *"Rabbi Lynne Landsberg: 'The issue of abortion is profoundly religious and profoundly religious people are overwhelmingly pro-choice.'"*

The press release also quotes Rabbi Donald Weber, who declares, "those who oppose us are not against freedom of choice, they are against freedom of religion. They demand that we live our lives in accordance with their view of morality, with their view of life, and with their view of God."[28] Once again, the unnuanced, uniformly positive attitude toward abortion is striking. One would never guess from these declarations that historical Judaism had any negative or even conflicting feelings toward abortion, or that any thoughtful person today might have such feelings.

A more ambivalent approach is taken by the United Synagogue of Conservative Judaism Department of Social Action. An article dated June 15, 1999, first makes it clear that the organization unequivocally supports women's reproductive rights, including abortion rights. It quickly goes on, however, to define the difference between legal rights and religious and moral guidelines. Asserting that each religious tradition has its own set of guidelines on the issue, and that followers of each religion should have the right to turn to these guidelines, the statement turns to Judaism per se:

> Judaism has a great deal to say about the issue of abortion, and Jewish law provides both legal guidelines and ethical insights. Affirming the religious nature of this issue, much of the mainstream Jewish community, including the United Synagogue of Conservative Judaism, has supported laws to maintain the legality and accessibility of abortion. However, while it is imperative that our voices be heard on this issue to protect our own religious liberties, this position takes the risk of obscuring an important principle held by Conservative Judaism—abortion is not an appropriate form of birth control. In general, we believe that a woman's choice must be guided by principles of Jewish tradition and law, as interpreted by our rabbinic authorities.[29]

Despite this male, rabbinically authored statement expressing the Conservative movement's more traditionally Jewish and nuanced approach to the abortion issue, the Women's League of Conservative Judaism has taken an activist approach which is more in line with other Jewish women's advocacy groups than it is with that of the Conservative rabbinic leadership. In a Women's League Outlook newsletter, for example, the "Tikkun Olam" column written by League president Audrey Citak discourses with passion on the amended mandate of the organization. The revised document begins with an attempt to acknowledge that historical Judaism viewed abortion as a sad necessity in some cases, but clearly rejected the idea of abortion as a casual form of birth control: "Reverence for life is the cornerstone of our Jewish heritage. Since abortion in Jewish law is primarily for the mother's physical or mental welfare, we deplore the burgeoning casual use of abortion. Abortion should be legally available, but ethically restricted. Though abortion of a fetus is not equivalent to taking an actual life, it does represent the destruction of potential life and must not be undertaken lightly."[30]

Having articulated the concepts of deploring and ethically restricting abortion—an idea with no action component attached—the resolution Citak quotes with pride goes on to state its premise for action: "Women's League for Conservative Judaism urges its Sisterhoods to oppose any legislative attempts through constitutional amendments, the deprivation of Medicaid, family services and/or other current welfare services, to weaken the force for the Supreme Court's decision permitting abortion."

Citak immediately after this "mandate of Women's League" gives her own call to arms to other Conservative women: "We must take action now. March. Write letters to your elected officials and to the press. Speak out at public forums and join coalitions on state and local levels. Seek out the Religious Coalition for Abortion Rights or the National Abortion Rights Action League. Make your position known, and offer to help."

Citak's charge that Women's Leaguers "make our voices count" thrusts in only one direction: protecting abortion legislation. Nowhere in the article is the slightest indication that the first passage in the mandate, concerning spreading the Jewish teaching of reverence for life, can also be a basis for action. The article does not encourage Conservative women to educate themselves on Jewish law and attitudes toward abortion, or on the historical relationship of American Jews to the practice of family planning, or on fertility concerns in the American Jewish community today.

Individualism, Altruism, and the
Public Jewish Passion for Freedom

Differing psychic compartments are occupied by American Jewish reluctance to disseminate pro-natalist information within their own Jewish communities, and continued Jewish enthusiasm in advocating for abortion rights and other aspects of reproductive choice in the wider American community. Most American Jews, as individuals, and when they compose institutional statements, do not think about the ironies of a shrinking ethnic/religious group being associated primarily with limiting population growth. It is clear from Jewish public pronouncements that few Jews directly confront the curiousness of a family-oriented culture finding religious expression in this type of advocacy.

However, the ubiquitousness of Jewish pro-choice advocacy in the American public square and the near-absence of pro-natalist advocacy within the Jewish community are linked in important ways. American Jewish liberal leanings are for many not only a political preference but a moral and spiritual statement. For many American Jews, it would not be far-fetched to call these commitments religious in nature.

Nevertheless, in addition to the spiritualism Jews find in public advocacy, there are other factors at work as well in American Jewish reluctance to promote the family within Jewish public circles. When Jewish public advocacy on behalf of personal choice is placed in the context of broader American societal attitudes toward reproductive and abortion rights, it becomes vividly clear that American Jewish advocacy in this regard does not depart from the broader American public. Jews are not marching to their own drummer; they are simply carrying the batons at the front of a very large, well-populated parade.

Writing about a phenomenon she calls "the abortion myth," Leslie Cannold notes: "The 1995 Women's Equality Poll found that 74 percent of those polled support women's abortion rights, with only 18 percent opposing women's right to choose."[31] Similarly, a 1996 Gallup Poll found that 88 percent of Americans felt abortion should be legal when a woman's life is endangered, 77 percent in cases of rape or incest, 82 percent when a woman's physical health is endangered, 66 percent when her mental health is endangered, 54 percent when the baby might be mentally impaired, and 53 percent when it might be physically impaired. Only in the case of a woman wishing an abortion because she "cannot afford a child" did 62 percent of those polled say that abortion should be illegal.[32]

Interestingly, many thoughtful observers complain about the lack of nuance in the abortion debate. In her study of women facing abortion decisions because of information supplied by amniocentesis procedures, Rayna Rapp argues that the very availability of abortion has forced pregnant women to become "moral pioneers": "Situated on a research frontier of expanding capacity for prenatal genetic diagnosis, they are forced to judge the quality of their own fetuses, making concrete and embodied decisions about the standards for entry into the human community." Michael Berube comments on Rapp's book: "our national debates about abortion are just not complex enough to do justice to the extraordinary difficulty of the questions and decisions."[33]

It is not difficult to speculate on the reason for the silence which Jewish leaders and organizational publications maintain on the reality of unwanted infertility in the Jewish community. Living in the social and intellectual contexts in which they do, American Jews find it difficult to take a position which they fear may be perceived as being out of step. Roof comments on the frameworks which are most important to the now-aging baby boomers and to middle- and upper-middle-class Americans in general: "Concern about personal space and privacy . . . individual freedom and choice . . . gender roles, marriage, whether to have children, parenting . . . greatly concerned to preserve privacy over against the invasions of their space by government, corporations, and any other large-scale organizations. Privacy is a widely shared value, and one that blurs ideological differences except at the extremes."[34]

Fear that they may be perceived as encroaching on the privacy of others and perceived liberal social pressure makes Jews embarrassed to advocate internally for earlier childbirth and communal family-friendly policies. Writing and talking even within the Jewish community on behalf of earlier childbearing for those women who wish to have children exposes the advocate to disapproval as a perceived nonliberal. Discussing the negative fertility implications of postponing childbirth does not fit the liberal profile established within the American Jewish public advocacy community. When Jewish academics or communal leaders speak publicly or put into print the simple facts about delayed childbirth, they are quickly accused of pressuring women into pregnancies, or privileging families with children.[35] Indeed, even when they make it quite clear that their goals are providing information to those women who wish to enhance their chances for giving birth without having to turn to ART, their motives are publicly questioned. In a clear case of "shooting the messenger" which recalls the Faludi response to medical statements over a decade ago, those who have discussed age and fertility have quickly been silenced by charges that their concerns represent a conservative political stance—anathema to the majority of American Jews.

Notes

1. Sylvia Barack Fishman, *Jewish Life and American Culture* (Albany: State University of New York Press, 2000).

2. *1998 Annual Survey of American Jewish Opinion*, conducted for the American Jewish Committee by Market Facts, Inc. (New York: American Jewish Committee, 1998), 77.

3. Stephen Whitfield, *American Space: Jewish Time* (Hamden, Conn.: Archon Books, 1988), 87.

4. Karen Brodkin, *How Jews Became White Folks and What That Says about Race in America* (New Brunswick, N.J.: Rutgers University Press, 1994), 112.

5. *American Jewish Committee*, 1998, 74-75.

6. Marshall Sklare, "The Image of the Good Jew in Lakeville" (1967), in *Observing America's Jews*, ed. Jonathan Sarna (Hanover, N.H.: Brandeis University Press, 1993), 208-9.

7. Wade Clark Roof, *Spiritual Marketplace: Baby Boomers and the Remaking of American Religion* (Princeton, N.J.: Princeton University Press, 1999), 36.

8. George Gallup, Jr., and D. Michael Lindsay, *Surveying the Religious Landscape: Trends in U.S. Beliefs* (Harrisburg, Pa.: Morehouse Publishing, 1999), 122, 147, 159.

9. "Proudly Jewish, Actively Feminist," *The Newsletter of the Commission for Women's Equality of the American Jewish Congress*, III, no. 1 (February 1995): 3.

10. "Proudly Jewish," quoting from A. Vorspan and D. Saperstein, *Tough Choices* (New York: UAHC Press, 1992), 11-12.

11. Calvin Goldscheider, *Jewish Continuity and Change: Emerging Patterns in America* (Bloomington: Indiana University Press, 1986), 92-98.

12. Steven Martin Cohen and Paul Ritterband, "Why Contemporary Jews Want Small Families," in *Modern Jewish Fertility*, ed. Paul Ritterband (Leiden: E. J. Brill, 1981), 231.

13. Sarah Silver Bunim, "Religious and Secular Factors of Role Strain in Orthodox Jewish Mothers," unpublished doctoral dissertation, Wurzweiler School of Social Work, Yeshiva University, New York, 1986.

14. Sid Groeneman, "Beliefs and Values of American Jewish Women," report by Market Facts, Inc., presented to the International Organization of B'nai B'rith Women, 1985, 30-31. The data were drawn from 956 questionnaires divided between Jewish and non-Jewish informants.

15. Calvin Goldscheider and Francis Kobrin Goldscheider, "The Transition to Jewish Adulthood: Education, Marriage and Fertility," paper presented at the Tenth World Congress of Jewish Studies, Jerusalem, August 1989, 17-20.

16. Frank Mott and Joyce C. Abma, "Contemporary Jewish Fertility: Does Religion Make a Difference?" *Contemporary Jewry*, 13 (1992): 74-94.

17. Richard L. Berke, "Late Childbirth on the Rise: Census Bureau Says Most Women Ages 30-34 Plan to Have a Baby," *New York Times*, June 22, 1989.

18. Susan Faludi, *Backlash: The Undeclared War against American Women* (New York: Crown Publishers, 1991), 27-29.

19. Melinda Beck with Vicki Quade, "Baby Blues, the Sequel," *Newsweek*, July 3, 1989, 62.

20. "Proudly Jewish, Actively Feminist," 3.

21. "A Proposal for Funding of a Conference on Assisted Reproductive Technologies and the Jewish Community: Science, Ethics and Public Policy Issues," submitted by the Commission for Women's Equality and the Bio Ethics Task Force of the American Jewish Congress, New York, 1998, 8.

22. AJCongress Conference on New Birth Technologies and the Jewish Community to Confront Problems Arising from Growing Success of Fertility Medicine, in "Proudly Jewish, Actively Feminist" (March 1999), 1.

23. Margaret Sandelowski, "Fault Lines: Infertility and Imperiled Sisterhood," *Feminist Studies* 16, 1 (spring 1990): 33-51.

24. Susan Martha Kahn, "Rabbis and Reproduction: The Uses of the New Reproductive Technologies among Ultraorthodox Jews in Israel," *Hadassah International Research Institute on Jewish Women, Working Paper Series*, no. 3, 1998, 4.

25. Letty Cottin Pogrebin, *Deborah, Golda and Me* (New York: Crown Publishers, 1991).

26. David M. Feldman, *Marital Relations, Birth Control, and Abortion in Jewish Law* (New York: Schocken Books, 1974).

27. Robert Gordis, *Love & Sex: A Modern Jewish Perspective* (New York: Farrar Straus & Giroux, 1978), 141.

28. See http://rj.org/rac/news/012798.html.

29. See http://www.uscj.org/scripts/uscj/paper/article.asp? ArticleID=396.

30. Audrey Citak, "Tikkun Olam: Women's League's Mandate for Action," *Women's League Outlook* (summer 1992): 5.

31. Leslie Cannold, *The Abortion Myth: Feminism, Morality, and the Hard Choices Women Make* (Hanover, N.H.: Wesleyan University Press, 1998), 19.

32. Gallup and Lindsay, *Surveying the Religious Landscape*, 104.

33. Rayna Rapp, *Testing Women, Testing the Fetus: The Social Impact of Amniocentesis in America* (New York: Routledge, 1999), discussed in a review essay by Michael Berube, "Biotech before Birth: Amnio, Abortion, and (dis)Ability," in *Tikkun*, 13, no. 3 (May/June 2000), 74.

34. Roof, *Spiritual Marketplace*, 262.

35. One can think here about the silence which met Anne Roiphe's heartfelt book about Jewish fertility issues, *Fruitful: A Real Mother in the Modern World* (Boston: Houghton Mifflin, 1996).

Part V

Philosophical Dimensions

11

Jewish Critics of Strict Separationism

David G. Dalin

Since the 1940s, at least, most American Jews have conceived of religion and public life as being rigidly separate arenas. They have been, for the most part, strict separationists, committed to the proposition that the First Amendment was intended to erect a high and impregnable—an absolute—wall of separation between church and state. According to the prevailing liberal Jewish consensus, it is often assumed that Jewish survival and religious freedom are most secure where the wall separating church and state is strongest, and least secure where government and religion are intertwined.

For several decades, Leo Pfeffer, one of America's foremost scholars of church-state relations, was the preeminent Jewish spokesman for this strict separationist position. Pfeffer, for many years staff attorney and director of the American Jewish Congress's Commission on Law and Social Action, argued more church-state cases before the United States Supreme Court than any other person in American history, and did more than anyone else to shape and further the legal doctrine of church-state separationism.[1] Indeed, it has been widely recognized that Pfeffer's major books, such as *Church, State and Freedom* and *God, Caesar and the Constitution*, as well as his numerous articles and legal briefs, constitute the most "polished expression" of the strict separationist constitutional position. Moreover, during his forty-year association with the Commission on Social Action, Pfeffer was instrumental in formulating and planning Jewish communal policy on issues of religion and state, and was the "guiding spirit" of Jewish litigation in this area.

Instead of embracing the "narrow" interpretation of the Establishment Clause, Pfeffer and those who share his views consistently invoke the "broad interpretation" espoused by the Supreme Court in its famous *Everson v. Board of Education of Ewing Township* decision of 1947, wherein it claimed, quoting the words of Thomas Jefferson, that the Establishment Clause "was intended to erect 'a wall of separation between church and state.'" Speaking for the majority in the *Everson* case, Justice Hugo Black stated the "broad interpretation" of the Establishment Clause, in a famous—indeed, now classic—statement that is frequently cited by Jewish proponents of the strict separationist position, and that reads (in part) as follows:

> The "establishment of religion" clause of the First Amendment (said Black) means at least this: Neither a state nor the Federal Government can set up a church. Neither can pass laws which aid one religion, aid all religions, or prefer one religion over another. Neither can force or influence a person to . . . profess a belief or disbelief in any religion. . . . No tax in any amount, large or small, can be levied to support any religious activities or institutions, whatever they may be called, or whatever form they may adopt to teach or practice religion. Neither a state nor the Federal Government can, openly or secretly, participate in the affairs of any religious organizations or groups and vice versa. In the words of Thomas Jefferson (concluded Justice Black) the clause against the Establishment of Religion . . . was intended to erect a "wall of separation" between Church and State.[2]

Pfeffer and his fellow strict separationists within the Jewish community, who embrace this "broad interpretation," believe (with Justice Black) that the "intent" of the First Amendment is not merely to prohibit the establishment of a state church but to preclude any government aid to any and all religious groups or dogmas. In addition, as Pfeffer argued in *Church, State and Freedom*, any and all government support for, or involvement with, religion, "even on a nonpreferential basis," violates the Establishment Clause and is unconstitutional.[3] Reasoning that the Establishment Clause, broadly interpreted, was the best guarantor of both religious freedom and religious equality, they shared Pfeffer's oft-quoted assumption that the Establishment and Free Exercise Clauses of the First Amendment were "two sides of the same," or (as it were) two separate clauses, expressing the principle "that (religious) freedom requires separation," and that the nonestablishment of religion is an end unto itself, guaranteed by the First Amendment.

Beginning in 1948 with the landmark Supreme Court case of *McCollum v. Board of Education*,[4] which ruled that released time programs that used public school classrooms for religious instruction during regular school hours were unconstitutional, Pfeffer led an unrelenting fight against prayer and religious instruction in the public schools, state aid to parochial schools, tax exemptions for churches and synagogues, and the presence of any and all religious symbols in American public life. In the 1948 case, the McCollums challenged the constitutionality of a released-time program that used public school classrooms for religious instruction during regular school hours. Pfeffer supported their challenge in a "friend-of-the-court" brief on behalf of the Synagogue Council of America (an umbrella organization representing Orthodox, Conservative, and Reform rabbinic and congregational groups) and the National Jewish Community Relations Advisory Council (NJCRAC), which represents a wide spectrum of Jewish community relations agencies, including the American Jewish Congress, the American Jewish Committee, and the Anti-Defamation League of B'nai B'rith.

Like other immigrant Jews of his generation, Pfeffer had been taught by both Jewish history and his own experience to embrace strict separationism as the only defense against what they perceived to be a Christian-dominated state. For these strict separationists— and the vast majority of American Jews until the 1980s were strict separationists—it became axiomatic that any religious influence in the public institutions of Christian America impinged upon the full citizenship of Jews. Only strict separation, they believed, could ensure the kind of free society and political climate wherein Jews, and Judaism, could flourish.

Pfeffer's view that "complete separation of church and state is best for the church and best for the state, and secures freedoms for both" seemed to most American Jews to be logically consistent and historically convincing. When the Supreme Court in *Engel v. Vitale* (1962) and *Abington Township School District v. Schempp* (1963) outlawed state-composed prayers and state-sponsored Bible reading in the public schools, the overwhelming majority of American Jews applauded these decisions. Pfeffer proudly asserted in a 1966 address, "our absolutist policy has now become the law of the land through a series of decisions to which our test cases, briefs and other writing contributed substantially."

Will Herberg and Other Early Jewish Critics of Strict Separationism

Yet, it is important to remember that the separationist position did not go unchallenged in the Jewish community, even in its heyday. In articles published during the 1950s and 1960s, the Jewish theologian and religious thinker Will Herberg—the author of *Protestant, Catholic, Jew* and other important books—began to call for a reassessment of the prevailing Jewish consensus that religion should play no role in American public life. The authors of the Constitution never intended to erect a "wall of separation," said Herberg. The Establishment Clause of the First Amendment had been profoundly misunderstood: although the Founding Fathers did not want to favor any single religion, they were not against helping all religions, or all religion, equally. In drafting the Establishment Clause, they merely intended to prohibit the designation or establishment of any church or official state or "national" one, and to prevent "a preference of any one religious sect or denomination" over others. "Neither in the minds of the Founding Fathers nor in the thinking of the American people through the nineteenth and twentieth century," wrote Herberg, "did the doctrine of the First Amendment ever imply an iron-clad ban forbidding the government to take account of religion or to support its various activities."[5]

Herberg was especially vocal in his criticism of liberal American Jews and their insistence that religion be rigidly distinct from public life. In several articles published during the 1950s and 1960s, Herberg urged the liberal Jewish "establishment" to reassess its position. "The American Jew must have sufficient confidence in the capacity of democracy to preserve its pluralistic . . . character without any "absolute" wall of separation between religion and public life," he wrote in 1952.[6] Eleven years later, frustrated by liberal Jewish support for the 1963 Supreme Court decision banning Bible reading and recitation of the Lord's Prayer in the public schools, Herberg entered a plea for the restoration of religion to a place of honor in American public life. Writing in *National Review*, he said: "Within the meaning of our political tradition and political practice, the promotion [of religion] has been, and continues to be, a part of the very legitimate 'secular' purpose of the state. Whatever the 'neutrality' of the state in matters of religion may be, it cannot be a neutrality between morality and no-morality, . . . [both religion and morality being] as necessary to 'good government' as 'national prosperity.'"[7]

The traditional symbols of the divine presence in our public life," Herberg warned, "ought not to be tampered with."[8]

In 1958, Rabbi Arthur Gilbert also emerged as an early and trenchant critic of the strict separationist position, voicing and reiterating some of Herberg's earlier concerns in a major address to the annual convention of the Central Conference of American Rabbis. As Jonathan D. Sarna has pointed out, Gilbert, who was then the Director of Interreligious Affairs for the Anti-Defamation League of B'nai B'rith, challenged his rabbinic colleagues "to rethink their knee-jerk commitment to strict separationism," and the secular bias upon which it was predicated.[9] "Our record is stuck in its groove," he warned. Attacking the Reform Movement's unwavering opposition to religion in the schools generally, and to the use of public money to pay for the transportation of parochial-school children in particular, Gilbert called for Jewish policy positions that are formulated on religious grounds, and "that appear to be more realistic and respond in a more sophisticated fashion to the temper and needs of today's society."[10] In so doing, Gilbert, who was then one of the preeminent figures in the American rabbinate and who would later become the founding dean of the Reconstructionist Rabbinical College, emerged as the first prominent American rabbi to become an outspoken critic of strict separationism and to voice his critique at a national rabbinic gathering.

During the 1960s and 1970s, other prominent Jewish thinkers, such as Professors Jakob J. Petuchowski of Hebrew Union College and Seymour Siegel of the Jewish Theological Seminary, and Milton Himmelfarb, editor of the *American Jewish Year Book*, began to eschew their earlier liberal faith in separationism, and to develop a strong Jewish conservative argument for the desirability of greater religious involvement in American public life. Supporting state aid to parochial schools and questioning Jewish opposition to some forms of public school prayer, they (like Herberg) called for an abandonment of the Jewish separationist agenda in favor of a more pro-religion stance. Thus, writing in *Commentary* in 1966 on the subject of public aid to parochial schools, Himmelfarb argued:

It is not true that freedom is most secure where church and state are separated. . . . Separationism is potentially tyrannical. . . . It is harsh to those who prefer non-public schools for conscience's sake; and it stands in the way of a more important good (and more important safeguard of Jewish security), the best possible education for all. . . . It is time that we [American Jews] actually weighed the utility and cost of education against the utility and cost of separationism. All the evidence points to education, more than anything else, influencing adherence to democracy and equalitarianism. All the evidence points to Catholic parochial education having the same influence. . . . Something that nurtures a humane, liberal democracy is rather more important to Jews than twenty-four carat separationism.[11]

During the 1970s and 1980s, a Jewish neoconservative consensus began to emerge concerning the proper relationship between religion and politics, and the role of religious and moral values in shaping American public life. Himmelfarb, Siegel, Irving Kristol, and Murray Friedman, among others, all persuasively warned that an American moral and political culture uninformed by religious beliefs and institutions undermined the position of Jews and Judaism, and the health of a democratic society.

Their concern was also shared by Rabbi Abraham Joshua Heschel who, although "a man of the left," emerged late in life as a critic of the liberal strict separationist position. In his later years, as this author has noted elsewhere, he had increasing misgivings about the efforts of liberal Jewish leaders, such as Leo Pfeffer, to challenge the constitutionality of tax exemptions for churches and synagogues. The growth of Jewish day school education, to which Heschel was deeply committed, prompted him to rethink his own earlier opposition to state support for parochial schools.[12] His views on such church-state policy questions—as on other political and social issues that he addressed as a public theologian—were predicated on the assumption that his religious values and beliefs shaped his political commitments. Dissenting from the liberal Jewish consensus, Heschel thus did not subscribe to the view that religious values and theological insight should be expunged from American public life. His general view of the relation of religion to politics and public life was, in fact, a considerable departure from the prevailing Jewish consensus—and remains today much closer to the Jewish critique of strict separationism that most liberal Jews oppose.[13]

Government Support for Day Schools and the Jewish Critique of Strict Separationism

One issue that forced a reexamination and emerging critique of the strict separationist position for many Jews was whether the government should give aid to parochial schools. Prior to the 1950s, the issue of government aid to parochial schools, even when addressed by the Supreme Court, generated little interest or debate within the Jewish community. Thus, for example, the landmark case of *Pierce v. Society of the Sisters of the Holy Names of Jesus and Mary* (1925), in which the Supreme Court ruled unconstitutional a Ku Klux Klan-sponsored anti-Catholic Oregon law requiring all parents to send their children to public schools, did not seem to affect the majority of American Jews directly. Nonetheless, Louis Marshall, a renowned constitutional lawyer and one of the leading Jewish communal leaders of the era, representing the American Jewish Committee, filed an amicus curiae brief challenging the constitutionality of Oregon's public school law and attacking as "an invasion of liberty" any effort to make the public schools "the only medium of education in the country." Marshall asked the Court to affirm the basic right of parents to send their children to parochial schools and thus provide for their "religious instruction, the importance of which cannot be minimized."[14] In what has been described as the "Magna Carta of American parochial schools," the Court overthrew the Oregon statute and established this basic right of parents to educate their children in parochial schools that Marshall had sought.[15]

Yet, since there were very few Jewish day schools throughout the United States during the 1920s and 1930s, American Jewish parents did not advocate government aid for the parochial school education of their children. On the contrary, as late as 1948, in the aftermath of the Supreme Court's historic 1947 *Everson v. Board of Education of Ewing Township* ruling, which permitted states to fund the cost of transporting students to parochial schools, leading Jewish organizations and religious denominations, including the Orthodox, united behind the Synagogue Council of America-NCJRAC policy statement broadly opposing all government aid to parochial schools.[16]

Beginning in the 1950s, however, demands for a critical reassessment of this Jewish communal opposition to government support for parochial schools were increasingly heard within the American Jewish community. In 1962, as Jonathan D. Sarna has noted, the *American Jewish Year Book*, reviewing Jewish communal developments of the previous year, pointed out that "unexpectedly strong support for the Catholic position [favoring state aid to parochial schools] appeared within the Jewish community, especially among the Orthodox."[17] As the number of Jewish parochial schools began to proliferate during the 1950s and 1960s, Orthodox Jews abandoned their earlier opposition to state aid for parochial schools in the hope of obtaining funds for their own Jewish religious schools. They began to argue, as Catholics had before them, that education in a religious setting benefited not only members of their own faith, but also the nation as a whole, and that money used to support secular studies at these schools, should not be denied because the schools happened to teach religious subjects on the side.

As more and more private Jewish day schools were established during the 1970s and 1980s, and as the costs of parochial school education continued to escalate, a growing number of Jewish religious leaders and intellectuals began to recognize the "justice" of the Catholic claim to public support of parochial schools, whether in the form of textbooks, bus transportation and school lunches, or proposals for tax credits and vouchers. "In principle," as Herberg put it, "there is no reason why the religious school should be barred from governmental support because of what is said or implied in the First Amendment."[18] In 1965, when Congress debated the Elementary and Secondary Education Act, which proposed to extend $2.3 billion in federal aid to the nation's elementary and secondary schools, Rabbi Moshe Sherer testified before Congress in support of financial aid to private and parochial schools. Sherer, the executive vice-president of Agudath Israel of America, attacked Jewish separationists for their "rabid opposition" to state aid for parochial schools,[19] arguing that Jewish day schools faced "extremely difficult financial circumstances," and that denial of tax aid to these schools would constitute "a discrimination which is not in accordance with basic American ideals." He vigorously urged the extension of federal aid to the 251 Orthodox elementary and secondary religious schools he represented.[20] He was soon joined by representatives of other Orthodox religious groups, such as the National Council of Young Israel, the Jewish Day School Organization, Torah Umesorah, and the National Jewish Commission on Law and Public Affairs (COLPA), which was organized in 1965 to support aid to parochial schools and to defend the rights and interests of Orthodox Jews on other church-state matters. Dedicated to providing "legal and legislative services to Orthodox Jewish organizations and individuals, without charge, by submitting legal briefs to courts and preparing other legal materials," COLPA effectively served as a counterweight to the legal staffs of the American Jewish Congress and other separationist agencies in litigation concerning issues of religion and state.[21] In the ensuing years, COLPA has appeared as amicus curiae in numerous church-state cases before the courts, on issues ranging from the legal rights of Jewish Sabbath observers to the legal right of Jews to ask for religious symbols, such as the menorah, to be placed on public property.

Jewish critics of the strict separationist position on this issue began to emerge outside the Orthodox community as well. During the early 1960s, to the surprise of many Jewish communal leaders, aid to parochial schools had been endorsed by a leading Conservative Jewish leader, Charles H. Silver, who was also at the time president of the New York City Board of Education.[22] Throughout the 1970s and 1980s, the growth of Jewish day schools outside of the Orthodox community prompted some Conservative and Reform rabbis and educators also to rethink their earlier opposition to state aid. "The time has come," argued Rabbi Seymour Siegel of the Jewish Theological Seminary in 1970, in an argument that he (and others) would reiterate many times over the following two decades, "for the Jewish community to revise its stand . . . and to support the public officials who are in favor of state aid to all schools, including parochial schools, day schools and yeshivot":

> There is more and more realization in the Conservative movement that the strengthening of the Day School movement is essential for the maintenance of religious life. Even the Reform movement, once positively antagonistic, seems to be opening such schools, recognizing that they are vital to Jewish survival. So Jewish parents are now more sympathetic to the plight of Catholic parents. They have been complaining that without government aid for their parochial schools they are carrying a double load of taxation and that the special financial burden of supporting children in church-related institutions constitutes, in effect, a threat to their religious freedom.[23]

As Jewish parochial school tuition has increased enormously in recent years, government support for private religious schools, in the form of tax credits and vouchers, has emerged as a public policy alternative that more and more Jewish critics of strict separationism have begun to support.[24]

Jewish critics of the Jewish strict separationist position have frequently pointed out that the American Jewish community's commitment to separationism has never been absolute. On the contrary at the beginning of the Civil War, Jews in America, as a community, fought for the right of rabbis to serve with priests and ministers as chaplains in the armed forces.[25] Today, American Jews take it for granted that rabbis can and should serve as military chaplains, whose salaries are paid by the U.S. government. American Jews take it for granted that rabbis, together with priests and ministers, are invited to give prayers or benedictions at the opening of both houses of Congress and sessions of our state legislatures, and at our presidential inaugurations. They would protest vigorously if this tradition were ever abrogated. American Jews, like American Protestants and Catholics, never complained when the words "under God" were added to the Pledge of Allegiance during the 1950s, nor did they object to the fact that the words "In God We Trust" are on American currency.

Moreover, despite their commitment to separationism in other areas, American Jews (with few exceptions) have staunchly opposed legal efforts to challenge the constitutionality of tax exemptions for churches and synagogues. Most American Jewish leaders have, for several decades, consistently favored tax exemptions, some arguing, in fact, that to deny them would infringe upon the religious freedom of all religious groups. Such support for tax exemptions is, of course, not surprising. Synagogues and churches, and the religious schools they operate, are dependent upon the exemption of their property from taxes, and the deductibility of contributions made to them, for their very survival.[26] Most congregational rabbis of all denominations, even the more ardently separationist among them, agree that few synagogues could survive in today's economic climate without tax-exempt status. As one commentator has so aptly noted: "A court decision holding tax exemptions for religious institutions unconstitutional under the establishment clause" would do for the churches and synagogues of America "what Henry VIII did for the monasteries of England."[27]

School Prayer and the Jewish Critique
of Strict Separationism

The issues of government support for Jewish day schools and tax exemptions for synagogues and churches are only two of many issues that have forced many Jews to reassess and critique the strict separationist position. Also implicit in the doctrine of strict church-state separation, from which a growing number of Jewish critics have begun to dissent, is the assumption that any and all forms of school prayer, even the most innocuous and nonsectarian, are unconstitutional, an assumption shared by the vast majority of American Jews for many decades.

Indeed, since the mid-nineteenth century, Jews had been united in their opposition to prayer in the public schools. The development of the free public school system in antebellum America had coincided with the immigration to America of tens of thousands of German Jews, who had embraced the public school ideal, and whose children flocked to them in ever-increasing numbers. By the late nineteenth century, American Jews had become ardent supporters of public school education, enthusiastically embracing the opportunities and promise offered by a free, tax-supported school system open to all children, rich or poor, of all religious faiths.[28]

Jews who attended America's public schools in the late nineteenth and early twentieth centuries, however, were also uncomfortable with the "Christian ambiance" of the classroom, wherein the school day often began with the compulsory recitation of prayers, required Bible reading, the singing of hymns, and other Christian devotional exercises. Believing that prayer and religious instruction should remain a private matter, the province of church or synagogue, Jewish leaders opposed these practices, advocating the ideal of "unsectarian," religiously neutral public school education. "It is our settled opinion," said Rabbi Isaac Mayer Wise, the preeminent leader of Reform Judaism in America in the late nineteenth century, "that the education of the young is the business of the State, and that religious instruction . . . is the duty of religious bodies. Neither ought to interfere with the other."[29] Over the years, as Lloyd P. Gartner has noted, Wise's "settled opinion" became a principle of Jewish communal ideology[30] and, as a result, a Jewish consensus emerged in opposition to prayer and other manifestations of religion in the schools that would last for a century, until the 1980s.

Thus, when the U.S. Supreme Court, in its historic *Engel v. Vitale* decision,[31] outlawed state-composed school prayers in 1962, the vast majority of American Jewish leaders applauded the Court's decision as "an affirmation of the position that they had long espoused."[32] The prayer in question, however, a nondenominational one composed by the New York Board of Regents, was actually approved by several Orthodox rabbis and communal leaders, some of whom publicly dissented from the widespread Jewish community's support for Engel, and emerged as vocal critics of the Court's strict separationist position. In a letter to the *New York Times*, Immanuel Jakobovitz, then the rabbi of New York City's prestigious Fifth Avenue Synagogue and later the Chief Rabbi of the British Empire, strongly criticized the New York Board of Rabbis for its support of the Supreme Court's decision in *Engel*, expressing his "dismay at the alliance between teachers of Judaism and the spokesmen of secularism and atheism."[33]

Similarly, Michael Wyschogrod, a modern Orthodox professor of philosophy at the City University of New York, writing in the pages of the Orthodox religious journal *Tradition*, publicly criticized the

Court's decision in *Engel*, while urging the Jewish religious community to reconsider its opposition to prayer in the public schools.[34]
It was "in the interest of the American Jewish community," argued
Wyschogrod, "that America remain a God-fearing nation,"[35]
wherein Christians could recite their daily prayers and remain true
to their faith. Moreover, as Naomi W. Cohen has noted,[36] in making
his case in support of prayer in the schools, Wyschogrod dismissed
the arguments that such prayer caused emotional distress to Jewish
children. On the contrary, he argued, Jewish children secure in their
own religious identity and tradition would not be shocked or threatened by the religious prayers recited by their Christian classmates.

Rabbi Menachem Schneerson, the Lubavitcher Rebbe, also approved of the Regents' Prayer, and publicly challenged the Court's
ruling. The influential Hasidic leader, whose pronouncements carried considerable weight throughout the Orthodox Jewish world,
deplored the Court's ruling on the grounds of "Halakhah [Jewish
law] and common sense," stating that it was the duty of all Jews
committed to the Torah to work for the reversal of *Engel*. "It is necessary to engrave upon the child's mind the idea that any wrongdoing is an offense against the divine authority and order," argued
Rabbi Schneerson.[37] "The crux of the problem," Schneerson maintained, "lies in the success or failure of bringing up the children to
an awareness of a Supreme Authority, who is not only to be feared,
but also loved. Under existing conditions in this country, a daily
prayer in the public schools is for a vast number of boys and girls
the only opportunity of cultivating such an awareness."[38]

Menorahs and Yarmulkes: Religious
Symbols in the Public Square

Over the next three decades, Rabbi Schneerson, who died in 1994,
functioned as perhaps the most respected and authoritative Orthodox
Jewish critic of the strict separationist position. For close to two
decades, he voiced his opposition to the efforts of liberal Jewish organizations that, in the name of strict separationism, sought to keep
Jewish religious symbols, such as the menorah, outside of the public
square. The Lubavitch movement's vigorous campaign, beginning in
the 1970s, to construct privately funded Hanukkah menorahs on
public property in cities throughout the United States precipitated a
heated debate within the American Jewish community over whether
it was constitutionally permissible and proper to do so. The issue, as

popularly understood, involved a basic question: should the public square be devoid of any religious symbols, or should it be open to all religious symbols, including the creche and the menorah?[39] Liberal Jewish organizations, such as the American Jewish Congress and the Reform Movement's Central Conference of American Rabbis, have staunchly opposed the placing of menorahs (as well as creches) on public property, as an impermissible breach of the "wall of separation." Opponents of public menorah displays viewed them as a violation of the Establishment Clause, arguing that "the kindling of huge menorahs in public places across America opens a dangerous constitutional can of worms,"[40] and that "since there is no religious need to place sacred symbols of any faith on public property," there is no religious need to be accommodated by government.[41] Proponents of these displays, such as Rabbi Schneerson and the attorneys for COLPA, saw them as an expression of the very neutrality with regard to all religions that the First Amendment was enacted to guarantee. Orthodox Jewish groups, such as Chabad and COLPA, argued that Jews have a legal right to ask for menorahs to be placed on public property, especially alongside the permissible symbols of Christmas.

In a 1978 letter to Rabbi Schneerson, Rabbi Joseph Glazer, then the executive vice president of the Central Conference of American Rabbis, voiced his opposition to the Lubavitch campaign to erect menorahs on government property, calling it "as much a violation of the constitutional principle of separation of church and state as is the erection of Christmas trees and creches depicting the birth of Jesus. It weakens our hand when we protest this intrusion of Christian doctrine into the public life of American citizens."[42] In his reply, Rabbi Schneerson, the Lubavitcher Rebbe, tried to "allay" Glazer's "apprehensions." After presenting an alternative understanding of the First Amendment, and reminding Rabbi Glazer in effect that the American Jewish community's commitment to separationism has never been absolute, he emphasized that the Lubavitch organization placed menorahs on public property to encourage Jewish religious identity and observance ("Torah and Mitzvoth") as well as Jewish religious pride. Doing so increased the likelihood that the mitzvah of kindling Hanukkah menorahs would be fulfilled by all Jews. "Where Hanukkah lamps were kindled publicly," he wrote, "the results have been most gratifying in terms of spreading the light of Torah and Mitzvoth, and reaching out to Jews who could not otherwise have been reached."[43]

More recently, as part of the changing debate generated by the Supreme Court case *Allegheny County, City of Pittsburgh, and Cha-*

bad v. ACLU, the traditional liberal Jewish opposition to the public display of religious symbols has been countered by a growing demand for "equal time" for the display of the specifically Jewish religious symbols in the public square that Orthodox Jewish critics such as Rabbi Schneerson have long called for. This 1989 case, in which the Supreme Court ruled that a Chabad-sponsored menorah standing next to a Christmas tree in front of Pittsburgh's City Hall did not violate the First Amendment, forced many liberal Jews to reexamine their earlier opposition to the placing of Hanukkah menorahs in front of a public building or within a public park, and their earlier assumption that Jews have no legal right to ask for the public display of menorahs in the public square. In the decade since the Supreme Court's ruling in the *Allegheny* case, a growing number of Jews have been swayed by the arguments of Orthodox Jewish critics of separationism that such a legal right does indeed exist. Where religious symbols of differing faiths—for example, the Hanukkah menorah and the Christmas tree —are displayed side by side, say these critics, the government is not favoring one religion but rather is expressing equal respect for all religions. Promoting harmony among religious groups, they contend, is profoundly different from the "establishing" of one religion that the First Amendment seeks to protect us from. By giving a Jewish religious display "equal time" with a Christian one, Pittsburgh was showing the very neutrality with regard to all religions that the First Amendment was enacted to guarantee.[44] Moreover, as Nathan Lewin, a vice president of COLPA and the attorney for Chabad in the *Allegheny* case, has argued, public displays of a menorah symbolize to all the fact "that America is a country where Jews are welcome and are first class citizens," and "engender emotions of pride and confidence among Jews who see them." Banishing menorahs from public places, he and other proponents of public menorah displays contend, would mean "derogating religion and denying to Jews the equal access to public forums that are available to secular organizations."[45]

The issue of placing menorahs on public property has, for Jewish critics of strict separationism, been central to their critique of the strict separationist effort to keep religious symbols outside the public arena. Within the American Jewish community, in recent years, there has been a growing recognition that the triumph of strict separationism as a legal doctrine, with its promise to expunge any and all religious symbols from the public arena, may—and often does— infringe upon the free exercise of religion cherished by American Jews. For Jewish critics of strict separationism, and for many other Jews who have begun to rethink and reassess their traditionally liberal views on some issues of religion and state, the celebrated 1986 U. S. Supreme Court decision in *Goldman v. Weinberger* was illustrative of this tendency.

In *Goldman v. Weinberger*,[46] an Orthodox Jewish Air Force officer named Simcha Goldman challenged the military's uniform dress requirement that prohibited him from wearing a yarmulke while serving on duty. Goldman, an Orthodox Jew and an ordained rabbi serving as a clinical psychologist in an Air Force hospital, normally kept his head covered at all times in accordance with Orthodox Jewish practice. In May 1981, Goldman's superior officer notified him that wearing a yarmulke indoors while in uniform violated an Air Force dress code regulation, and he ordered him to remove it or face a court martial. Goldman, represented by attorneys from COLPA, filed suit, claiming that this regulation infringed upon his First Amendment right to the free exercise of his religion. The Supreme Court, however, upheld the Air Force regulation: The First Amendment's Free Exercise protection, it ruled, did not require the military to accommodate Captain Goldman's religious obligation. For many Jews, the Supreme Court's denial of Simcha Goldman's free exercise of his religious obligation to wear a yarmulke was a troubling example of what the Pfefferian ideal of strict separationism had wrought.

In his dissent, praised by all segments of the organized Jewish community, separationists and opponents of separationism alike, Justice William Brennan lamented the fact that "The Court and the military services have presented patriotic Orthodox Jews with a painful dilemma—the choice between fulfilling a religious obligation and serving their country." Orthodox Jewish servicemen, noted Brennan, would now be required to violate the tenets of their faith "virtually every minute of every working day."[47]

Congress subsequently enacted federal legislation to overturn *Goldman v. Weinberger*. Drafted by Nathan Lewin, the COLPA attorney who argued Simcha Goldman's case before the U.S. Supreme Court, and who would later be the attorney for Chabad in the *Allegheny* menorah case as well, and passed by both houses of Congress, this new law required the armed services to allow its members to wear a "neat and conservative" skull cap if it would not interfere with their duties. While the enactment of this legislation overturning *Goldman v. Weinberger* was a victory for COLPA and other Jewish critics of strict separationism, it was widely applauded throughout the organized Jewish community, and supported by individual Jews and Jewish organizations that, while traditionally part of the prevailing liberal Jewish consensus, were now dissenting from the strict separationist position.

Conclusion

No longer can it be said, as it could in the 1940s and 1950s, that American Jewry speaks with one "official" voice on issues of religion and state. To be sure, a number of American Jewish leaders remain wedded to a strict separationist position on many, if not most, church-state issues. But a growing and increasingly vocal minority of American Jewish leaders and intellectuals have emerged as outspoken critics of strict separationism, dissenting publicly from the liberal Jewish consensus that Jewish survival and religious freedom are most secure where the wall separating religion and state is strongest.

These Jewish critics of strict separationism have rejected the secular liberal view that the interests of American Jews, and American Judaism, are best served by what Richard John Neuhaus has called "the naked public square," one that is morally neutral and from which religious beliefs and values have been expunged. They think that religion has a legitimate place in American public life, that the Constitution does not embody what Supreme Court Justice Arthur Goldberg once described as "a brooding and pervasive devotion to the secular and passive, or even active hostility to the religious." The dissenting views of these Jewish critics of strict separationism, though they cannot be said to represent a mainstream Jewish consensus, command greater intellectual force and weight than ever before.

Notes

1. On Pfeffer's career, achievements, and legacy, see James E. Wood, Jr., ed., *Religion and the State: Essays in Honor of Leo Pfeffer* (Waco, Tex.: Baylor University Press, 1985); and David G. Dalin, "Leo Pfeffer and the Separationist Faith," *This World* 24 (winter 1989): 136-40.

2. *Everson v. Board of Education of Ewing Township*, 330 U.S. 1, 15 (1947).

3. David G. Dalin, "Leo Pfeffer and the Separationist Faith," 136-37.

4. *McCollum v. Board of Education*, 333 U.S. 203 (1948). On the Jewish communal involvement with, and response to, the McCollum case, see

Naomi W. Cohen, *Jews in Christian America: The Pursuit of Religious Equality* (New York: Oxford University Press, 1992), 140-47; and Gregg Ivers, *To Build a Wall: American Jews and the Separation of Church and State* (Charlottesville: University Press of Virginia, 1995).

5. David G. Dalin, "Will Herberg in Retrospect," *Commentary,* 86 (July 1988): 42.

6. Will Herberg, "The Sectarian Conflict over Church and State: A Divisive Threat to Our Democracy?" *Commentary* (November 1952), reprinted in David G. Dalin, ed., *From Marxism to Judaism: The Collected Essays of Will Herberg* (New York: Markus Wiener Publishing, 1989), 209.

7. Dalin, "Will Herberg in Retrospect," 42.

8. Dalin, "Will Herberg in Retrospect," 42.

9. Jonathan D. Sarna, "American Jews and Church-State Relations: The Search for Equal Footing," in Jonathan D. Sarna and David G. Dalin, *Religion and State in the American Jewish Experience* (Notre Dame, Ind.: University of Notre Dame Press, 1997), 25. Gilbert's address to the 1958 Convention of the Central Conference of American Rabbis is also discussed in Cohen, *Jews in Christian America,* 179-80.

10. *Central Conference of American Rabbis Yearbook* 68 (1958), 53 and 55.

11. Milton Himmelfarb, "Church and State: How High a Wall?" *Commentary,* 42 (July 1966), reprinted in Milton Himmelfarb, *The Jews of Modernity* (New York: Basic Books, 1973), 169-71. More recently, it is quoted in Sarna and Dalin, *Religion and State,* 264-65.

12. David G. Dalin, "The Jewish Theology of Abraham Joshua Heschel," *The Weekly Standard,* January 4/11, 1999, 38-39.

13. Dalin, "The Jewish Theology."

14. Marshall's brief is reprinted in Charles Reznikoff, ed., *Louis Marshall: Champion of Liberty: Selected Papers and Addresses* (Philadelphia: Jewish Publication Society of America, 1957), vol. 2, 957-67, and in Sarna and Dalin, *Religion and State,* 209-11. The historical context of Marshall's involvement in this historic Supreme Court case is discussed in Morton Rosenstock, *Louis Marshall: Defender of Jewish Rights* (Detroit: Wayne State University Press, 1965), 211-13.

15. Sarna and Dalin, *Religion and State,* 209.

16. Sarna, "American Jews and Church-State Relations," 25. On the Jewish organizational response to the *Everson* case, see also Cohen, *Jews in Christian America: The Pursuit of Religious Equality,* 139-40; and Ivers, *To Build a Wall,* 17-28.

17. Sarna, "American Jews and Church-State Relations," 26.

18. David G. Dalin, "How High the Wall? American Jews and the Church-State Debate," *Conservative Judaism* (spring 1997): 69.

19. Moshe Sherer, "The Great Society and Aid to Religious Schools," *Jewish Observer* 2 (January 1965): 3-5; and Sarna and Dalin, *Religion and State,* 256-58.

20. David G. Dalin, ed., *American Jews and the Separationist Faith:
The New Debate on Religion in Public Life* (Washington, D.C.: Ethics and
Public Policy Center, 1992), 5.

21. Sarna and Dalin, *Religion and State,* 261-64.

22. Sarna, "American Jews and Church State Relations," 26.

23. Seymour Siegel, "Church and State: A Reassessment," *Sh'ma* 1/3
(December 11, 1970).

24. On this point see, for example, Jacob Sullum, "Educational Choice
for Parents: Vouchers Will Make More Jews," *Moment* (February 1994):
38-41; and the comments by Murray Friedman, a senior official of the
American Jewish Committee, in his essay in Dalin, *American Jews and the
Separationist Faith,* 51.

25. Bertram W. Korn, *American Jewry and the Civil War* (Philadelphia:
Jewish Publication Society of America, 1951), 56-97; and Sarna and David
G. Dalin, *Religion and State,* 129-31.

26. These points are developed in greater detail in Dalin, "Leo Pfeffer
and the Separationist Faith," 136-40. On the issue of tax exemptions for
churches and synagogues, and their clergy, generally, see also: Leo Pfeffer, "Religious Exemptions," in Thomas Robbins and Roland Robenson,
ed., *Church-State Relations: Tensions and Transitions* (New Brunswick,
N.J.: Transaction Publishers, 1987), 103-8; Dean M. Kelly, *Why Churches
Should Not Pay Taxes* (New York: Harper & Row, 1977); and Ronald B.
Flowers, "Tax Exemptions and the Clergy: On Vows of Poverty and Par-
sonage Allowances," in Wood, *Religion and the State,* 359-76.

27. George Goldberg, *Church, State and the Constitution: The Religious Clauses Upside Down* (Washington, D.C.: Regnery Gateway, 1987),
79.

28. On this general topic, see Lloyd Gartner, "Temples of Liberty
Unpolluted: American Jews and the Public Schools, 1840-1875," in
Bertram W. Korn, ed., *A Bicentennial Festschrift for Jacob Rader Marcus*
(New York: Ktav Publishing House, 1976), 157-89.

29. Sarna and Dalin, *Religion and State,* 181-82.

30. Gartner, "Temples of Liberty," 177; also quoted in Sarna and
Dalin, *Religion and State,* 182.

31. *Engel v. Vitale,* 370 U.S. 421 (1962). Leo Pfeffer's detailed discussion of the case can be found in Leo Pfeffer, "The New York Regents'
Prayer Case," *Journal of Church and State* 4 (November 1962): 150-59; a
thorough discussion and analysis of the Jewish reaction to, and communal
debate over, the Supreme Court's decision in this case can be found in
Cohen, *Jews in Christian America,* 171-86.

32. Sarna, "American Jews and Church-State Relations," 23.

33. Cohen, *Jews in Christian America,* 177-78.

34. Michael Wyschogrod, "Second Thoughts on America," *Tradition* 5
(fall 1962): 29-36.

35. Wyschogrod, "Second Thoughts," 33.

36. Cohen, *Jews in Christian America, Religion and State,* 182.

37. Quoted in Sarna and Dalin, *Religion and State,* 212.

38. Sarna and Dalin, *Religion and State,* 216.

39. Sarna and Dalin, *Religion and State,* 288-89.

40. Alan Nadler, "Lubavitchers Setting Fire to Wall of Separation," in Sarna and Dalin, *Religion and State,* 290-300.

41. Dalin, "How High the Wall?" 76.

42. Letter from Rabbi Joseph Glazer to Rabbi Menachem Schneerson, April 25, 1978, reprinted in Sarna and Dalin, *Religion and State,* 290-91.

43. Letter from Rabbi Menachem Schneerson to Rabbi Joseph Glazer, 3 Sivan 5738, reprinted in Sarna and Dalin, *Religion and State,* 292-94.

44. Dalin, "How High the Wall?" 76.

45. Quoted in Sarna and Dalin, *Religion and State,* 290.

46. The *Goldman v. Weinberger* case is discussed in Sarna and Dalin, *Religion and State,* 278-80; and in Martin Edelman, "Goldman v. Weinberger: Yarmulkes, The Supreme Court and the Free Exercise of Religion," *Jewish Law Annual* 8 (1990): 210-20.

47. Sarna and Dalin, *Religion and State,* 279.

12

Under His Own Vine and Fig Tree: The Contemporary Jewish Approach to Religion in American Public Life and Its Problems

Hillel Fradkin

What should be the role of religion in American public life? What is its place in either the public square or our public institutions? Should it be broad and rich or narrow and austere? Like all other Americans, American Jews have tried to find proper answers to these questions for more than 200 years. They have had a special, though not unique,[1] incentive to do so as the victims of religious persecution and discrimination in other times and places.

By and large, American Jews have inclined to more rather than less austere prescriptions, inspired, first, by the desire to take adequate precautions against persecution and, second, by the hope that America would fulfill its promise of full equality as citizens. In very large part, indeed in amazingly large part, America has accepted the Jewish interpretation of the relationship of religion and public life, especially since World War II. In addition, America has delivered on its promise. Anti-Semitism is for almost all intents and purposes not a problem for American Jews. In addition, they occupy positions of respect, influence, and power and may aspire to any office in the land. This was made completely manifest through the nomination of Senator Joseph Lieberman for the office of vice-president, but it was already evident throughout the last decade.

On the other hand, America has never accepted a completely austere or simple view of the role of religion. Taken as a whole, America's answers to this momentous question have been complicated, reflecting the very rich and very complicated role of religion under our constitutional system and in our national life. To be sure, the American constitution proscribes the establishment of a national religion, creating a separation between any particular church and the state. But it also guarantees the free exercise of religion and Americans have been very energetic in that exercise. They have frequently brought their religious faith into the public square to bear on public matters. They have even enjoyed the direct and indirect support of government. This has frequently led to questions about the meaning of the separation of church and state. Should there be a so-called wall of separation and, if so, how high and thick ought it be? Even today, after 200 years, these questions remain unsettled and complicated.

The question for American Jews today is whether the views they now offer are able to stand up to these complications and provide proper guidance for themselves and their fellow citizens. There is, unfortunately, good reason to doubt that they are. Today in the absence of meaningful religious persecution, discrimination, and indignities, not to mention material privation, we generally seek a still more austere separation of religion and public life than any heretofore realized, through which religion might be almost altogether absent from public life. We go beyond asking for the separation of church and state to seek a wall of separation between religion and society. Indeed, any connection between religious belief and some aspect of public affairs—public policy and even public rhetoric—is sufficient for us to complain. We oppose school vouchers which might be used at religious schools by poor and illiterate students; moments of silent prayer; charitable choice, which entails government funds for religious groups in the struggle against addiction, crime, and poverty. We are indignant over the involvement of groups like the Christian Coalition and the Moral Majority in politics. We complain when our politicians invoke God or their faith in public discourse. In doing so, we sometimes invoke the specter of the religious discrimination, persecution, and even strife of the past. With survivors of the Holocaust still among us this is understandable. But in contemporary America, it is also implausible and fanciful. It is clear that this is not a truly credible concern and will become clearer in the future. In fact, we speak more and more in terms of comfort, both for ourselves and others. The discomfort we decry is not material or physical, the result of active persecution, but psychological and subjective. No one, including us, should be made to feel uncomfortable by the religious beliefs of others. Put positively, we seek the new goal of the so-called tolerant and inclusive society, a society which would in effect be utterly and completely purified of religious expression.

This proposal has the advantage of being simple and clear. But it has the disadvantage of being simplistic and crude, and it fails to do justice to the history and experience of this country and the religious rights and duties of Americans, including ourselves. It is a proposal that is unnatural, presupposing that human beings normally make an absolutely strict division between their private and public lives. As a result, it is also probably impractical without the application of force, especially given the fact that Americans, uniquely among modern peoples, are and are likely to remain religious. Many Americans think that no further austerity is required and not a few think it is already too severe.[2]

The austerity we propose is so unnatural and impracticable that we cannot or at least do not adhere to it ourselves, frequently invoking Jewish teachings, like *tikkun olam*—which means the repair of the world—in our own public discourse. Hence we are unlikely to persuade others of its virtue or necessity. Indeed we have opened ourselves to the charge of confusion and even hypocrisy. Worst of all, the new austerity may well undermine its apparent objective—that all Americans, including we American Jews, enjoy the twin blessings of self-respect and mutual respect. For it may be that the most solid source of respect or tolerance for our fellow Americans available in contemporary America are the teachings of its various religious groups. It may even be the case that our only serious prospect of having a meaningful understanding of the concept of "respect" now depends upon religious teachings. Of this possibility, we take almost no note.

Our behavior frequently implies that as Jews and Americans we have no other choice but to seek greater austerity. American principle requires it as well as American tradition. But this is far from obvious. Historically speaking, it is clear that this would entail new conditions of American life. Never in the past was religion really absent from American public and political life and it was frequently prominent, beginning with the American Revolution itself and continuing through various later political movements—abolition, temperance, civil rights, etc.[3] Hence, its justification requires the possibility and desirability of "progress," of rather sudden and dramatic progress, since it was but just yesterday that ministers, priests, and rabbis marched in America's streets for civil rights and against the war in Vietnam. That progress presupposes that we have also achieved an advance in our understanding of American principles since in the past those principles, including separation of church and state, never led to the austerity now proposed. But is this merely an advance in our understanding of old principles or the adoption of altogether new ones which lack the sanction of American tradition as well as American experience whose success, especially manifest now, tends to argue that no innovations are necessary? Since the answer is not obvious, it places upon us a very great burden of argument and proof for the merits of the society we seek. What is this glorious progress, why is it desirable, and how possible is it?

As indicated, the grounds of this austerity are the principles of toleration and inclusion. Today, many Jews and many other Americans uphold tolerance and inclusion as our highest virtues and aspirations; our greatest vices are to be judgmental and exclusive. As indicated below, these aspirations are not simply new, but they are newly defined and differently evaluated. Tolerance is today understood to require unqualified respect for any and all individuals and groups, no matter who they are, what they believe, and how they live their lives. It is only subject to the condition that such individuals and groups be themselves tolerant and accord similar respect to others. It is important that all groups and individuals be aware of such respect as a condition of their enjoying self-esteem, which is subjectively and objectively the highest human good. Hence, it is not sufficient that Americans avoid criticizing or blaming other Americans. They must be actively embraced so as to feel "included." Their subjective lack of such feeling is sufficient to call our tolerance into question. This is said to be implicit in the fundamental requirements of democracy and the equality of all its citizens.[4] Thus, in pursuing tolerance and inclusion we often claim to be doing no more than fulfilling the full democratic promise of the American foundings of 1776 and 1787.

Moreover, it has been argued by eminent authorities that the present state of American society indicates that the promised land of tolerance and inclusion, thus understood, is nearly within our reach. According to sociologist Alan Wolfe, we are "one nation, after all." The vast majority of Americans eschew "judgmentalism" and are emphatically tolerant, though not yet completely inclusive; for example, they are tolerant of homosexuality, but they do not embrace it with respect. Racism, sexism, and other forms of discrimination have declined to near vanishing points. If there is anything which still disturbs the unity and inclusion of all Americans it is religion, including the moralism associated with some religious groups. This is almost inevitable since the particular teachings of many religious groups typically conflict with one another. As they are made on behalf of divine authority, the highest possible authority, it is likely, if not simply inevitable, that they imply some disrespect for the beliefs and therewith the person of other Americans. Happily, according to Wolfe, the religious beliefs of Americans are increasingly easygoing and are defined less by ancient teachings than by modern views and life. Though some Americans may still take their religious differences seriously, they are increasingly confined to the margins of American society. Their impact on American life may be rendered still more marginal and less upsetting to the tolerant and inclusive society if they have few, if any, outlets in public life. This is in part the logic of pursuing greater and greater public austerity in matters of religion. Through it we will get closer and closer to the fulfillment of the fundamental principles of America, the tolerant and inclusive society. American Jews, including Mr. Wolfe, may help lead the way.[5]

There are a number of difficulties with this view of contemporary America and its requirements. Some of them emerged in the 2000 elections, in which religious rhetoric played a particularly prominent role as did groups which were alleged to lie at the margins of American society.[6] Moreover, an American Jew, Senator Lieberman, who is now also America's most prominent and distinguished Jew, was a leading exponent of such religious rhetoric. This does not look like an America which is ready to banish religion from public life.[7]

But this is not decisive. If American principle truly requires the tolerant and inclusive society as currently conceived, it would be necessary to pursue it in fair weather or foul. It would be our duty. But as already indicated, it is far from clear that we are simply expounding American democratic principles. To be certain that we are right, it is also our duty to study with great seriousness, worthy of the Jewish tradition of study, the facts of the matter. Do authoritative American accounts of the relationship of religion and public life describe a vision of society similar to our own, if not completely, at least in embryo? If not, what deficiency do they have and how compelling is our remedy?

For the purposes of the American Jewish community, if not Americans as a whole, it would be helpful if such an authoritative statement took cognizance of the American Jewish community and their particular concerns.

Remarkably enough, this is actually ready to hand through the primary and indeed chronologically first "official" view of the status of the Jews in the new United States. It was offered by the new and first president of the United States, George Washington, in a famous letter to the Hebrew Congregation in Newport, Rhode Island, which had congratulated him on his election with "expressions of affection and esteem." It deserves to be cited at length for its comprehensive and nuanced discussion, albeit in a short space, of the relevant issues. In fact, it offers a vision of a "tolerant and inclusive society," thus, in a way, confirming our claim. On the other hand, its vision is vastly different than that of contemporary Jews. It has the immediate advantage of conforming to America's historical experience; indeed, it is in no small part responsible for forming that history, at least its better angels. Above all, it offers a different account of the "tolerant and inclusive" American society which is more thoughtful, practical, and, above all, more admirable than our own.

In his letter, Washington asserted that the citizens of the new country had "a right to applaud themselves for having given to mankind examples of an enlarged and liberal policy: a policy worthy of imitation." The essence of that policy was that "all possess alike liberty of conscience and immunities of citizenship." Moreover, the grounds of the policy were emphatically new. "It is *now* no more that *toleration* is spoken of, as if it was by the *indulgence* of one class of people, that another enjoyed the exercise of their *inherent natural rights*. For happily the Government of the United States, which gives to bigotry no sanction, to persecution no assistance requires only that they who live under its protection should demean themselves as good citizens, in giving it on all occasions their effectual support."[8]

Washington closed his letter with a passage which expressed both a hope and a prayer, whose language was plainly drawn from the Hebrew Bible. "May the Children of the Stock of Abraham, who dwell in this land, continue to merit and enjoy the good will of the other Inhabitants; while every one shall sit in safety under his own vine and fig tree, and there shall be none to make him afraid. May the father of all mercies scatter light and not darkness in our paths, and make us all in our several vocations useful here, and in his own due time and way everlastingly happy."

The first part of Washington's message is emphatic in asserting that it is precisely not toleration or tolerance, as we would say today, which defines the legal status of Jews in the United States but right. Nor should toleration play that role. For tolerance is a species of indulgence by a superior to an inferior and depends upon the good will of the former for the latter. Indeed, it necessarily implies a critical or, as we would say, judgmental stance to others. Our current discourse is actually confused on this point. More important, from Washington's point of view our present stance toward tolerance would amount to a regress to an older and inadequate view of the situation of minorities rather than a progress as we would have it.

Washington asserts that the rights which are the foundation of the American polity are natural and inherent and thus shared equally by all. Thus it may always have been so, at least in principle. However, the innovation of the United States and its new constitution has been to give these natural rights the force of law, which makes it possible to use the machinery of law to oppose any actual or prospective state bigotry or persecution. Washington is confident that these innovative, indeed unprecedented, features of the American constitutional system make for a revolution in the legal status and political condition of Jews. All of American history since is a testament to the correctness of that conviction. For, in fact, the federal government of the United States has never in more than 200 years given "bigotry" its "sanction" nor "persecution" its "assistance" and on the amazingly few occasions when a threat arose it was swiftly eliminated. More positively, American Jews have always enjoyed "liberty of conscience."

Washington's repudiation of tolerance as the standard for political and legal rights, indeed his insistence that it is a defective and undesirable standard for such rights, precisely for Jews, who would thereby depend upon the indulgence of others, necessarily the majority of their fellow citizens, does not mean that he is entirely unappreciative of the virtues of tolerance or, as he puts it, "good will." The conditions of life are not entirely determined by law and, under the federal constitution, not entirely by federal law.[9] Hence, he expresses the hope and the prayer that American Jews would "merit and enjoy the good will" of their fellow citizens. But this precise hope and prayer is not something that can be guaranteed by the constitution and its workings. They may even merit the good will of their fellow citizens and not enjoy it. This is clearly not true of Washington himself and his letter to the Newport Jews is clearly designed to set the proper tone and example for other non-Jewish Americans, and in substantial, though not complete, measure it has.[10] But Washington had much too much experience of the weakness of human beings to place his confidence in their good will and indulgence of others, and, hence, he separates the issue of constitutional right to liberty of conscience from that of good will or toleration.

Today it is likely that American Jews would disagree with Washington's assessment. For unlike Washington who thought of good will or tolerance as something to be earned or gently encouraged by force of argument, Jews today now think of it as something to be prescribed. We would hold that Washington was insufficiently ambitious or at least that we are now in a position to make progress beyond what was possible in his time.

But is such a resolution really possible? Is such progress really desirable? A resolution might be possible but it would not be easy within the American constitutional framework which permits and encourages religious expression. Due to the fact that religious teachings are likely to be at some important level exclusive, the only way to achieve complete inclusion would be to alter all such teachings in such a way as to lead to a unitary and inclusive teaching. Historically speaking, this has been politically possible in one of two ways: the establishment of one national religion and church or the suppression of all religious teachings in the name of a completely unreligious or antireligious teaching. The former was, of course, the situation in many countries prior to the founding of America.[11] It was also sought in a different way after America's founding by fascist movements. The second method was that characteristic of communist regimes which imposed state atheism. Neither of these approaches had a happy outcome from the point of view of tolerance for Jews, not to mention other matters. It was precisely to avoid the consequences of these kinds of "inclusion," both after and before the fact, that the United States was founded as it was, without an established church but with full liberty of conscience. But according to some, today there is a third possibility—the transformation of religious belief such that there will be no differences which have meaningful societal impact.[12]

Washington effectively doubts that this is possible when he speaks of "our several vocations," meaning by that the separate religious groups into which Americans were then and would continue to be divided. But even more important and in contrast to current views, he suggests that this is not even desirable, as those separate vocations may be the source of our being "useful here." They may be the source of a great utility to the nation, a common utility. They may be the foundation, among other things, of tolerance and inclusion. In fact, American tolerance and inclusion may actually depend upon religion, properly understood and applied, rather than require its absence.

The prospect of tolerance and inclusion depends in the first instance on what Washington calls the comportment of religious Americans, Jewish or otherwise, as good citizens. This will certainly merit good will and may be hoped to earn it. All good citizens should and hopefully will be considered equal members of the American public.

Good conduct as citizens and the good will it generates may have a strong, if complicated, relationship to religion, at least the religions with which Washington was directly familiar. As Washington implied in his letter to the Newport Jews, good citizenship involves less the assertion of rights than the assumption of duties, large and small, toward one's fellow citizens. But a sense of duty rather than an assertion of rights may depend very heavily on the fact and efficacy of religious teaching. The duty of tolerance and inclusion may be especially dependent upon such teachings.

Washington developed this point on a different occasion, his famous Farewell Address.[13] There he asserted that "of all the dispositions and habits which lead to political prosperity, religion and morality are indispensable supports; . . . these firmest props of the duties of men and citizens." He added, "let us with caution indulge the supposition, that morality can be maintained without religion."

Today many do indulge that supposition. They believe that morality, including and especially the moral duty of tolerance and inclusion, can be maintained without religion. Indeed, they argue that the duties of tolerance and inclusion, our highest and almost only duties, can best be maintained through the dilution, if not the withering away, of religion. The question is whether in the long run they are right or whether Washington's understanding is deeper and more accurate.

A certain form of that question arose in the 2000 election, occasioned by some remarks of vice-presidential nominee Joseph Lieberman. As in times past, Lieberman, invoking, without citation, Washington's statement, asserted that the future moral condition of the country depended upon religion and its revival as a force in American public life.[14] He implied that our capacity for duty must be sought in religion.

For this Lieberman was criticized by some, though not many, of his fellow Jews. It was charged that he was claiming that only religious Americans could be moral and that this claim was intolerant and therefore itself immoral. Lieberman quickly denied both. But he might have added that neither was this Washington's position, and that the question is more complicated than his critics appreciate. For in his Farewell Address, Washington went on to say "that whatever may be conceded to the influence of refined education on minds of peculiar structure, reason and experience both forbid us to expect that National morality can prevail in exclusion of religious principle."

As is evident, Washington did not believe that morality and duty was impossible without religion. It could result from a refined or enlightened education in the case of some individuals. What he denied was that this was sufficient for society as a whole. For the majority of Americans, religion would remain important.

Today's invocation of tolerance and inclusion presupposes that such is no longer the case. In effect, it presupposes that today such a refined education is universally available and efficacious or might be with just a bit of effort. It believes that the morality of tolerance and in particular the duty of inclusion can be inculcated with such an education. Both this morality and this education are meant as improved substitutes for the morality and education of religion. For even if religion is a teacher of duty it must inevitably bear the liability of exclusivity. Tolerance and inclusion are the essence of citizenship and may teach it to us. It is only this which could make possible and justify the new and present vision of the tolerant and inclusive society.

How persuasive is this? There is certainly something to it. Tolerance and inclusion are on everybody's lips; it has become conventional wisdom and enlightenment. But it is not the only theme of conventional wisdom. Our general discourse is as dominated, if not more so, by the multiplication of rights and ever greater demands on their behalf. What is lacking is much talk of duty. Duty, except in the form of tolerance, is lacking as a subject of our education. Moreover, the duty of tolerance depends in no way on whether or not others perform their duties, great or small. It does not even attempt to encourage such duties. It offers esteem under any and all circumstances. It does not require that we merit that esteem or earn good will as citizens, as Washington proposed. It is a much diminished and therefore weaker form of respect and duty. It might suffice to provide for some general level of tolerance, but it is unlikely to lead to any serious and meaningful embrace of our fellow citizens. Nor can one be certain that it will triumph when and if it comes into conflict with the passions nurtured by our concern with our rights as individuals.

Worse still, the more "refined" forms of enlightened opinion are now postmodern, which is to say, among other things, that by their own admission they can no longer make any sense of morality or duty at all, in the proper sense of these words. All forms of morality are as such relative or merely values, which is to say preferences. The source of such preferences is the desire for power. Every formulation of a moral duty is nothing more than the attempt of some individual or group to impose itself on others. It is at bottom nothing but a form of oppression. There is in fact no reason to tolerate and include others or to champion these virtues except as a tactic. In terms of the "refined" and "enlightened" contemporary understanding of morality, tolerance and inclusion could be at best only the outcome of a shared desire for peace, including peace of mind. If we avoid blaming others, maybe they will avoid blaming us. We can avoid all feelings of shame and guilt. It is a desire for comfort, as much psychic as well as material, rather than any real sense of duties to others which is the content of the contemporary understanding of tolerance and inclusion.

To be sure, many Americans do feel a real duty to others. But due to our rights talk and postmodern enlightenment, that must be taken to be something of a "miracle." Like many "miracles," this probably has more to do with religion, even the most simple piety, than it does with "refined" opinion. It is most likely to be a function of religious teachings which espouse generosity of spirit to our fellow man on the grounds that we are all created equally in the image of God, the same grounds to which Washington appealed in his letter. For Americans who believe this, and there are many, there is an absolute duty of tolerance and inclusion of a certain kind. The survival of this sense of duty is at the same time a testament to the good sense in Washington's vision of what the tolerant and inclusive American society would look like and require.[15]

As already noted, at the end of his letter to the Newport Jews, Washington spoke of the "separate vocations" of Americans, meaning by that the separate religious communities and ways of life of Americans. He obviously expected that to continue but hoped that it would constitute the grounds of common good will. He knew, of course, that religion, like all other aspects of human life, had its darker as well as its brighter side. His whole Farewell Address, like that of another and biblical one—that of Moses to the People of Israel on the eve of his death[16]—is suffused with a certain pessimism. But precisely in that context, such optimism as he expressed was grounded in the future piety of Americans.

Despite many ups and downs which Washington anticipated, contemporary American society seems to have vindicated his optimism rather than his pessimism, at least with regard to the role religion might play. Today America embraces many religious groups, each pursuing its own vocation, sometimes in private, sometimes in public. Despite the intertwining of religion and public life, the conflict between religious groups is minimal. In addition, given the changes in "enlightened" and "refined" opinion between Washington's time and our own, our age may be in more need of religion than his. For as indicated before, today, religion is the only voice which speaks unequivocally on behalf of duty in general and in particular of the duty to respect others. If we want vigorous tolerance and inclusion as we claim that we do, rather than tepid civility mixed with indifference, religion may be our primary resource.

Many Americans today seem inclined to that view, concerned with what is perceived as a national moral decline, including a decline in significant respect for others. Americans may frequently invoke the language of tolerance and respect; after all, everyone now knows that this is expected. But their actions frequently belie these pious expressions.[17] The general public's sense that this is the true state of affairs has been recorded in many polls which also record an associated appreciation of the potentially beneficial influence of religion.[18] We American Jews to some degree share in this sense without directly expressing it or in fact frequently denying it. Nonetheless, it is shown by the fact that we are frequently impelled by its logic. When Joe Lieberman spoke, as he often did, of the Jewish roots of his public service, he engaged in a practice which has become ubiquitous among American Jews. It has become commonplace for Jews to appeal to an ancient Jewish concept, *tikkun olam*, to explain and defend their public doings, their justice and our duty. In light of our concerns about religion and public life, this is, to put it mildly, surprising. It is fair to say that we would not do it if we thought other moral resources would be adequate.

All this is to say that the character of our own behavior in the public square as well as the general weakness in American society of a deep understanding of duty and respect argue for a more benign view of the role of religion than is current in the American Jewish community. It argues for a thorough reconsideration along the lines laid out by Washington, to be sure updated in the light of 200 years of American history and experience. It would be best if the American Jewish community undertook this reconsideration at its own initiative; it would be best if it thoughtfully faced its current pieties and seriously examined them. It would be best because the objective of the tolerant and inclusive society requires it. It would also be best because sooner or later, and probably sooner, it may be forced to do so by other Americans. For the present position of the American

Jewish community is fraught with inconsistencies, both rhetorical and concrete. It is subject to the charge of confusion and worse—hypocrisy and even intolerance.

Rhetorically speaking, our problem is embodied in the practice, mentioned before, of appealing in support of our public activities to Jewish teachings; at the moment the most popular is *tikkun olam*. The most publicly active members of our community never tire of invoking this phrase. In fact, for many American Jews this has come to be the very definition of Judaism. Insofar as this is the case, there could not be a closer intermingling of religion and public life. Of course, we could decide to desist from this practice, but this is very unlikely. We continue to want an identification with the Jewish community and its traditions and this is often our only means.[19]

But unless we desist, there will be no reason to expect others to desist from their own forms of religious rhetoric. There will be no right either. If we continue to insist that others be silent, we will eventually be charged with being hypocrites, and we will be guilty.

American Jews have by and large seen no difficulty in this inconsistency, but other Americans have and in the future more will, as a result of Senator Lieberman's prominence. Moreover, many other Americans have and will welcome the fact that American Jews draw upon religious terminology to describe and defend their public activities. They have already welcomed Senator Lieberman's remarks both because they see something admirable in so doing and because they believe that it justifies their own inclination to bring religious beliefs and feelings to bear upon public life.

The difficulty of our present position is increased by the fact that it is our present practice rather than our current theory which is most consonant with American history, a history which is increasingly well known due in part to the energetic work of recent defenders of a religious role in public life. These authors, who include Senator Lieberman, have been vigorous in reminding the American public not only of the fact of public religious expression but also of the beneficial role it has played in American political history. They commonly cite the important and frequently decisive role religious groups played in important political movements of the past which aimed to remedy injustices and vices within American life. These include the abolitionist movement, the temperance movement, the woman's suffrage movement in the nineteenth century as well as movements which were important within living memory—the civil rights movement and the antiwar movement.

In fall 2000, Stephen Carter, a distinguished African-American author and professor at Yale Law School, published a book, *God's*

Name in Vain: How Religion Should and Should Not Be Involved in Politics, which once again rehearsed this history and defended the importance of its bearing on contemporary American politics. Carter, like others, has insisted that the role religious groups played in important political and social movements was not merely civic but depended upon and expressed itself through religious faith and sentiment. Though other not strictly religious grounds were available in each case, religious participation in these movements was expressly founded in religious faith and formulated in religious terms. Carter and others argue that the vitality of religious involvement and frequently the success of these efforts depended upon the sense of religious obligation.

These defenders of religion in public life might suggest that the efficacy of Jewish political action has some of the same religious quality. Why else invoke *tikkun olam* and other Jewish teachings on morality and politics? In any event, it is far too easy to point out that in the recent past American Jews did not complain of the undue influence of religion in public life when their clergy, volunteer leadership, and institutions were involved in political movements such as the civil rights and antiwar movements, precisely while flying a "Jewish" flag. It is also far too easy to suggest that present criticism of the political involvement of religious groups has less to do with the fact that they are religious than that the views they support are ones to which American Jews are opposed. Stung by such criticism, other relatively liberal religious groups have recently admitted as much. They responded by reinvigorating their own political activism with the founding of the Interfaith Alliance.

More broadly, the 2000 election campaign testified to the fact that it is still the case today that the most prominent American political figures feel free to invoke religion and that this is unobjectionable to the majority of American citizens. For it was not only Senator Lieberman who invoked religion. So, too, did Vice-President Gore and Governor Bush, and they did so well before Senator Lieberman was part of the race. Moreover and remarkably enough, despite many policy differences between Gore and Bush, they actually agreed on one thing: the propriety of legislation to assist so-called faith-based organizations as an instrument to deal with social problems.

This agreement presents an additional, more concrete, and immediate challenge to the merits of the views espoused by the American Jewish community. Such legislation is, in fact, already in place through the so-called charitable choice provision of the Welfare Reform Act. Its basic objective has recently been augmented by President Bush, who has already established a new Federal Office of Faith-Based and Community Initiatives. The purpose of this office is to make it easier for religious groups to participate in federal programs which address our gravest social problems.

This will occasion further scrutiny of the views of American Jews concerning religion and public life, in this case as regards legal rather than rhetorical matters. In fact, of course, we have already invited such scrutiny. Many American Jewish leaders have already announced their opposition, invoking as always the threat to separation of church and state and the specter of theological crusades, religious discrimination, etc.[20] Whether or not we realize it, it will be all too easy and correct to characterize this reaction as hysterical and even mean-spirited. After all, the purpose of such programs is manifestly not theological but social. They are directed at our most grievous and resistant social ills—drug and alcohol addiction, juvenile crime, family decay. In light of our well-publicized concern for a solution to these problems—our dedication to *tikkun olam*—it places upon us the burden of suggesting other means to the same ends. But this will not be easy to do and may be impossible. For the current proposals to engage religious groups in the fight against social ills are precisely not the result of a theological crusade but an expression of despair at the failure of thirty-five years of Great Society programs, which arguably made matters worse.

The American Jewish community, in its indignant reaction to these new initiatives, gives little sign of a generous appreciation of these basic motives. To the extent that it does, its position seems to be that despite these motives and even the help these programs might provide, the cost in terms of the violation of strict separation of church and state is too high. The importance of that principle trumps all other considerations.

This presents additional difficulties. It presupposes that the separation of church and state means that the government may not and has not provided support of various kinds to religious groups. It further presupposes that the Jewish community has in no way been the beneficiary of such support and has vigorously objected to and declined it. But neither of these propositions is true.

All religious groups in the United States are entitled to tax-exempt status, which applies both to their property and the contributions their members make to the support of their activities. As some have argued, this amounts to a state subsidy of religion and in fact a very large one, without which religious institutions would be unable to survive. (Moreover, it entails that the government engage in the definition of religion for the purpose of defining eligibility for this exemption.) The Jewish community has never opposed this status and is unlikely ever to do so since it would bankrupt its institutions.

More directly, the government has and continues to provide funds for religious groups in their capacity as providers of social services. The Jewish community has not opposed such funding. In fact, many Jewish social service agencies receive government funds, federal as well as state and local. Though this support goes for ostensibly neutral purposes, it also may be regarded as tantamount to a subsidy of religion. For example, in many Jewish communities, Jewish religious schools depend upon a subsidy from local Federations for their existence. Indeed, because of concern for assimilation, the American Jewish community has recently been energetic in encouraging the founding of such schools and they are growing in number. These schools and the subsidies they require would be difficult and probably impossible to maintain if Jewish communities could not count upon at least partial support of their social service agencies from local, state, and federal dollars. One might argue, then, that this support effectively supports religious instruction, which American Jews have claimed they regard as absolutely impermissible. It is on that basis that they have opposed school vouchers, even where their support of religious schools would be indirect.

To put the matter most simply, in the legal as in the rhetorical sphere, the American Jewish position on religion and public life is inconsistent and confused. A charitable explanation would be that we American Jews are or have grown obtuse and thoughtless, a testament to the actual ease of life we enjoy in America. But the most charitable explanation is that our confusion is consistent with the confusions and even the apparent contradictions of American experience, to the paradoxical character of America. For America is a paradox, combining as it does modern freedom and ancient faith. Whatever difficulties this entails, the fruitfulness of this combination has been extraordinary, both for us and our fellow Americans. Its dividends have been extraordinary freedom, security, and material prosperity, as well as tolerance and respect for our ancient ways. It has provided inclusion for us and all Americans.

However, to merit this charitable explanation we are obliged to appreciate this paradox, as George Washington asked us to do more than 200 years ago. Instead, we seem bound and determined to resolve it by our ever greater demands for religious austerity in public life. We claim to offer the prospect of greater tolerance, but the tolerance we offer is a pallid extension of a more or less thoroughly materialist view of human life, bound to champion comfort at all cost. Worse still, we denounce our pious fellow Americans in a most intolerant tone. We express little to no appreciation of their devoted service to other Americans and complain about their sense of moral duty. Allegedly preoccupied with the decline of our own families and the concomitant decline of our community, in both numbers and seriousness, we remarkably find time to complain about the efforts of others to preserve and protect their families and communities from moral decay through religious activity.[21] Instead of entertaining the modest thought that we might have something to learn from our fellow Americans and American experience, we are arrogantly certain that it is our right to lecture them, with insults and complaints.

If we fail to embrace the American paradox in a thoughtful and generous spirit, we may still escape a most uncharitable explanation of our behavior. We may owe that to the indifference of secular Americans or the appreciative, if sometimes critical, embrace of pious ones. Of the two, only the latter offers much prospect of genuine respect for us as Jews, of a truly dignified tolerance and inclusion worthy of the names.

Notes

1. American Jews today frequently overlook the need other religious groups, like Baptists and Catholics, had to protect themselves from the prospect of discrimination and even persecution in America and their actions to that end.

2. See, in general, "For Goodness' Sake, Why So Many Want Religion to Play a Greater Role in American Life," the report of Public Agenda and the Pew Charitable Trusts, 2001.

3. For the most recent account, see Stephen L. Carter, *God's Name in Vain* (New York: Basic Books, 2000), and my discussion below.

4. For a good discussion of the centrality of the issue of respect within liberal democracy, see Francis Fukuyama, *The End of History and the Last Man* (New York: Free Press, 1992). Fukuyama argues that mutual respect and individual self-esteem is the essential goal and driving force of modern liberal democracy, indeed of human history altogether, and that the recent triumph of liberal democracy through the Cold War is the essential fulfillment of human aspiration. However, in his account, democratic respect is still subject to one important condition, civic and moral self-governance.

5. Alan Wolfe, *One Nation, After All* (New York: Viking, 1998). Wolfe's subject is middle-class American attitudes. See also David Brooks, *Bobos in Paradise* (New York: Simon & Schuster, 2000), for an account of upper-class American views, especially chap. 6.

6. See the survey of voters in the 2000 presidential election by religious affiliation conducted by the University of Akron Survey Research Center under the direction of Prof. John Green. This survey reported increased polarization of voting along religious lines as well as the important impact of so-called marginal groups.

7. In general, the recent election called into question Wolfe's conclusions and supported an earlier critique offered by Gertrude Himmelfarb in *One Nation, Two Cultures* (New York: Knopf, 1999). Wolfe himself has bounced back and forth between insisting on the propriety of his conclusions and offering views which, in an important sense, amount to a retraction.

8. The text of Washington's letter used here is in *George Washington, Writings* (New York: Library of America, 1997). Emphasis is added.

9. At the time Washington wrote, several states had established churches and Jews were, in principle, liable to some disabilities as a result. The Constitution did not forbid such state arrangements and they continued for many years thereafter. They were altered by state action.

10. Washington wrote several similar letters to other religious communities. It would seem he had the intention to use his prestige and office to set a general tone of religious good will.

11. For two arguments on behalf of national unity in religion which come from the modern tradition of liberal political thought, see Thomas Hobbes, *Leviathan,* chap. 31, sec. 37 and elsewhere, as well as Benedict Spinoza, *The Theological-Political Treatise*, chap. 19. The purpose of both arguments is to prevent religious strife and persecution by outlawing sectarianism through an obligatory establishment of one national religion.

12. This is effectively the argument of Wolfe.

13. The text is available in *George Washington, Writings.*

14. For the fullest statement of his views, see Joseph Lieberman, *In Praise of Public Life* (New York: Simon & Schuster, 2000).

15. This view of the relationship of religious teaching or, more precisely, the teaching of the Hebrew Bible to American prospects for tolerance and inclusion is essentially the view of both Senator Lieberman and President George W. Bush. For the latter, see his Inaugural Address.

16. This farewell address comprises almost the whole of the Book of Deuteronomy.

17. An occasion which brought this out with particular force was the shooting at Columbine High School in Colorado. American newspapers were at that time full of accounts of the atmosphere at our nation's high schools. In general, they reported that the student body was divided into many and varied cliques, many of which were hostile and disrespectful of one another. At the time, this was attributed to high school "hormones." But it should have been noted that all contemporary American high school students have been, since kindergarten, instructed yearly in the virtues of tolerance and mutual respect.

18. See "For Goodness' Sake."

19. The practice of appealing to *tikkun olam* has been criticized by Marc Stern in *Tikkun Olam: Social Responsibility in Jewish Thought and Law*, David Schatz, ed. (Northvale, N.J.: Jason Aronson, 1997). So far, that appeal has gone unheeded.

20. For example, Rabbi David Saperstein, director of the Religious Action Center of Reform Judaism, declared that this office "takes us down a path that too often in our history has turned out to be disastrous for religious freedom and religious tolerance." *New York Times*, January 29, 2001.

21. In point of fact, a good deal of our objection to religion in public life has less to do with theology than family and sexual morality, in particular, abortion. See Steven Cohen, *Attitudes of American Jews in Comparative Perspective* (Philadelphia: Center for Jewish Community Studies, 2000). This presents curious questions: Why do most American Jews, known in the past for their attachment to tradition and family, today embrace most untraditional views of sexual morality and family? Why is this "Jewish"? In what way can struggles over these issues be understood, as we are inclined to do, as presenting a "religious" or "theological" problem? These questions are, however, beyond the scope of this article.

13

Toward a Jewish Public Philosophy in America

David Novak

American Jews or Jewish Americans

To ponder the question of how to formulate a Jewish public philosophy, it might be useful to locate the question itself in history, in my own case the history of a Jew in his late fifties, born and raised in the United States, and who has lived most of his life and done most of his work here. Let me begin with the following vividly remembered anecdote: In the early 1950s, when I was about twelve years old, I went with my parents to a barbecue at the newly built summer home of close family friends. During the course of the conversation among the ten or so people there, the following question arose: are we American Jews or Jewish Americans? That is, are we Jews who happen to be part of America, or are we Americans who happen to be of Jewish origin? The exact wording of the question was: "Are you a Jew first or an American first?"

The question was taken very seriously for a number of reasons. First, the adults present were mostly the children of immigrants, who themselves were sensitive about still being considered "foreigners" in America even though by then they all had become quite successful here. Second, it was the time when Senator Joseph R. McCarthy was questioning the American loyalty of a number of prominent persons, accusing them of being loyal to another country, the Soviet Union. Many of those so charged were Jews. This was the age of "loyalty oaths." Third, it was only a few years after the establishment of the State of Israel. To be sure, none of those present were anti-Zionists of the type who had survived in any numbers or influence until 1967. All of them were proud of the new Jewish state. Still, there was much nervousness about having to answer charges of "dual loyalty," or being dubbed what Senator Barry Goldwater, an American presidential candidate (and himself of partially Jewish origin), about a decade later sneeringly called "hyphenated Americans." Accordingly, the overwhelming consensus there was that we Jews here are, in effect, "Americans first" (ironically, words very close to the name of a notoriously anti-Semitic isolationist organization of the 1930s, "America First"). In effect, everyone there agreed we are essentially "Jewish Americans," with the adjective "Jewish" moderating and thus subordinate to the noun "American."

Remembering quite well all those adults present then, I am quite sure almost all of them had little or no Jewish education. So they were not in a position to figure out just how and why they were still Jews. But they were all quite sure what it meant to be an American which, for them, was the categorical imperative to make their American identity their primary identity. Anything less would be "un-American" (remember, this was during the heyday of the House of Representatives' Un-American Activities Committee), and, thus, dangerous to the newly won benefits of American life, especially for Jews.

Being a somewhat bold child who liked to insert himself into adult conversations, I announced: "As for me, I am a Jew first and an American second." Since I knew my own Jewish education was already better than that of the others present that summer evening, I gave the answer that just about any Jew would have given outside that time and place. After all, my reading of the Bible had taught me that what God has made takes precedence over what humans have made. Since God chose the Jewish people and by my birth chose me to be one with this people, and since the United States of America was clearly the creation of humans, it stands to reason that being a Jew is more important than being an American—however much a Jew might rightly enjoy being an American. Nevertheless, my parents became quite uncomfortable and quickly apologized for their impertinent child. On the way home they told me how wrong they felt I was and they asked that, if I persisted in this very wrong opinion, I at least not embarrass them in public by uttering it. Considering the time and place and their background, their reaction is quite understandable.

However, since the 1960s, when the explicit patriotism of the "my country right or wrong" variety has very much declined in the United States, and when ethnic particularism is very much accepted and even encouraged (thus, the name "African Americans" has now become de rigueur in polite conversation), most American Jews or Jewish Americans would probably not be so sure of the answer to that question about the priorities of one's loyalties. They would have much less certainty than my parents and their friends had almost half a century ago. Whether they would accept the answer I gave then and that I believe even more so is now at least arguable. In any event, my answer today would be far less embarrassing and the question itself much more likely to be critically engaged.

We Jews have to carefully rethink our relation to America—indeed, to any Western democracy in the diaspora (and perhaps even to the State of Israel)—precisely because we are more settled in these societies and more actively involved in their political and cultural life than ever before in history.[1] The most important indication of this fact are the increasing occasions for presenting "the Jewish point of view" on questions of public policy, which since the Vietnam War especially have become more explicit questions of public morality. Now just about everybody knows that the Jewish tradition is morally earnest; in fact, so much so that even many of those Jews who have noticeably departed from its specific norms have still retained the moral earnestness that characterizes our tradition in general, the tradition that has given even them whatever Jewish identity they have left. Furthermore, even though what is presented as *the* Jewish point of view is more accurately always *a* Jewish point of view, such points of view are quite frequently being taken seriously by many outside Jewry (especially by Christians). Thus, Jews are being asked to present a point of view not only on what directly affects us but also on what affects society in general. Moral earnestness is expected of us, both from ourselves and from others. In other words, how Jewish would we be if we did not have strong moral opinions?

Judaism Public and Private

The question of a Jewish public philosophy is very much connected to the question of the role of religion—or better, religions—in American life. Both the vast majority of Americans and the vast majority of American Jews see the Jews as a religious community just like they see the various Protestant denominations, the Roman Catholic Church, or the Mormons, for example, as religious communities within the United States. Even so-called secular Jews have to appeal to ultimately religious criteria such as religiously ascertainable direct descent from unmistakably Jewish ancestors, evidence of ritual circumcision, having been named in a synagogue, or conversion to some form of religious Judaism in order to be taken for Jews by anyone. In our society, communal claims seem to be limited to those that can be made in either religious or racial terms. (Even current claims made on the basis of "class" or "gender" turn out to be indistinguishable from basically racial claims.) Yet, very few Jews are willing to present themselves in racial terms. Therefore, what sort of Jewish claims can Jews as members of a religious community make on American society as a whole? That is, how can Jews ask society to recognize their religious uniqueness? (Even claims made by the Jewish community on behalf of the "secular" State of Israel are made in terms of the *religious* attachment of American Jews to the ancient Jewish homeland.) This is where the formulation of a Jewish public philosophy begins.

Until quite recently, the only voice of American Jews heard in public was the voice of those Jews who made their Jewish claims in terms of the classic liberal principle of the separation of church and state. Those who argue for this strict separation inevitably base it on the distinction between the public and private realms. That is, in order to protect minorities like the Jews, all religious claims are relegated to the realm of individual privacy, lest a majority religious community seize the public realm and either drive everyone else out or turn everyone else into a political outsider. For that reason, the public realm is not only to be protected from the claims of a majority religious community, it is to be emptied of the claims of any religious community at all.[2] In the words of one prominent American social theorist and critic, it is a "naked public square."[3] Religion is relegated to the realm of privacy, and it is argued that this is good for society and good for religion. It is good for society because it protects it from the imperialist claims of a majority religion upon the whole society. It is good for all the religions because it prevents state endorsement of any one religion at the expense of all the others, something that could both marginalize the minority religions into powerlessness and corrupt the majority religion with power.

In this view, everyone participates in public life as an anonymous individual or as an association of anonymous individuals. As public persons, these individuals are regarded as if they had no backgrounds in historical cultures that are themselves inevitably religious and which long predate the founding of the American polity. Thus, one's historical origins are consciously ignored, and one's goals are strictly mundane. One cannot base one's public philosophy, then, on anything that transcends the state and its interests. This type of public secularism has very much characterized the public philosophy of American Jewry both in their own eyes and in the eyes of the larger American public. It is evidenced by the fact that some of the most important Supreme Court cases on religion in recent years, cases whose legal rulings have sought to very much privatize religion, have been successfully argued by attorneys representing some major American Jewish organizations. In fact, only quite recently has this whole program been seriously challenged by other American Jews.[4] If so, what is wrong with it? Beginning to answer this question might lead us to an outline at least of a very different public philosophy of and for American Jews. Thus, it will be argued that this whole approach is bad for Jews. It is also bad for American society and, for that matter, bad for any democratic society in which Jews presently live, although this is not the place to discuss that more general issue.

It is bad for Jews because it makes the very justification of our distinctive life here our right to privacy. But that right is itself a public entitlement, that is, it is an area given to us by the state as, in effect, something beneath its concern. As such, what the state gives it can just as easily take away. We have no real arguments to use against the state if our own communal interests come into conflict with its interests. Furthermore, since morality is what governs relations *between* persons, it is by definition public. But if we have already ceded the governance of the public realm to the state and its law, then we become increasingly incapable of governing ourselves as Jews based on our own moral law. As Americans it is far better for us to argue that the First Amendment "religion clause" should be read as prohibiting the state from privileging one religion over all the others, not a relegation of religion away from civil society to, in effect, a private prison.[5]

As an example of this, I recall an occasion about ten years ago when I was a scholar-in-residence for a weekend at a Hillel Foundation on a campus in Washington, D.C. The director of the foundation, knowing that most of my work is in Jewish ethics, asked me to make my presentations on some ethical questions. Even though I told him I was already tired of talking about abortion in public, he insisted that I discuss that topic at the Sabbath dinner, which was the first event of the weekend.[6] Perhaps he thought controversy attracts and keeps the attention of an intellectual audience. Anyone reading the publicity for this event could not help but notice the topic of the first presentation. Being his guest, I somewhat reluctantly agreed to talk on that hotly debated moral and political question. (I really wanted to begin with a question in which I could rely on more agreement between myself and that audience and thus build on that agreement for the rest of the weekend.) Since my conservative political opinions on abortion are no secret, I was not too surprised, considering the time and the place, to learn that two lawyers who work for a prominent right-to-abortion organization were present in the audience. But in order to get away from abortion as an issue in American politics and concentrate on it as an issue in Jewish ethics, I said that I would concede—for the sake of confining the argument to an inter-Jewish context—that one could be opposed to the right of elective abortion on moral grounds (exclusive of abortion to save the life of the mother, which is not just the mother's right but her duty and the duty of everyone else capable of saving her life), yet not necessarily support the legal prohibition of abortion in a secular society. In the American context, the moral argument could be kept separate from the legal argument, even though in fact I am "pro-life" politically.

One could make that distinction based on theological or political grounds. Theologically, one could hold that the prohibition of elective abortion is based on a religiously based commandment that can only be cogently presented to the specific community that accepts the basis of that prohibition in divine revelation and the tradition of interpretation that follows from it. Politically, one could hold that there is not enough consensus in our society on the question of elective abortion to be able to enact its prohibition into law, let alone properly enforce it. I emphasized that on the Sabbath especially, when we Jews withdraw from civil society into sacred time and space, I only wanted to discuss the criteria for a faithful Jewish woman deciding whether to abort her unborn child or not.[7]

Is this type of discussion public or private? As a religious question it seemed to be private inasmuch as I purposefully confined discussion of it to the Jews celebrating the Jewish Sabbath that evening. I explicitly bracketed how the question could or should be answered by secularists, or by Christians, or by Muslims, or by anyone else who is not Jewish. Yet, as a moral question it is public inasmuch as it involves more persons than just the pregnant Jewish woman deliberating whether to have an abortion or not. It involves other persons with her: her husband or male partner, and medical personnel who might very well not be Jews themselves. Other persons are involved even if one does not consider the fetus whose abortion is being debated to be a person. (There can be other reasons than the "personhood" of the fetus for the general Jewish proscription of abortion, although I think ascribing personhood to the fetus is the most sufficient reason. Again, the point was made for the sake of argument.[8])

This leads us to the following dilemma: if we confine Jewish religion to the private realm, and if Jewish religion and Jewish morality are intricately intertwined, then we have one of two possibilities—either Jewish religion has to become a public matter, or Jewish morality has to be severed from Jewish religion and be subsumed under some other morality. In other words, before we can discuss a moral question like abortion before the general public, we have to discuss it within our own community. Thus, it is not that we move from the private realm to the public realm; instead, we move from one public realm to another.[9] As such, the question is only a matter of "private conscience" at the point when every individual person involved in this public question has to decide in her or his mind what she or he is to do here and now freely. The decision is private in that it begins with an individual person's thoughts; the criteria by which the decision is made are, however, public because they concern other people as well as oneself.

Because the two lawyers present that evening only wanted to talk about abortion as an issue of American law and politics, it seemed that they—and others who think like them—have, in effect, denied that Judaism has a viable morality even for Jews. But since morality and culture are so intricately intertwined, this approach, itself a practical application of the dogma of the absolute separation of civil society and religion, is a recipe for the cultural extinction of the Jews in American public life. How can any self-respecting Jew really buy it? Jews have to learn how to make public arguments that are authentically Jewish for public questions that involve the whole society in which we participate. Only this assertion will enable our unique voice to be heard in increasingly pluralistic public discourse. Surely, our claims *for* the public good are not like those of conscientious objectors, who claim exemption *from* public involvement. We want to be heard *in* the larger public realm, not just to be tolerated *by* it when we stay away from it, off among ourselves.

The old claim to the right of privacy, on the other hand, not only prevents our own voice from being heard but prevents anyone's unique voice from being heard. Only "the view from nowhere," to borrow the title of an important book by an American philosopher, can be heard following this logic.[10] But, since no one is really from nowhere, is this not a recipe for constructing a society in which being a liar is a prerequisite for having a significant opinion on anything? It is like those Jews of a generation or so ago who felt that they had to change their names to overtly Anglo-Saxon ones in order to "be accepted" where it really counts in American society. As nature abhors a vacuum, society eventually abhors such deceit.

The Social Contract

One of the most enduring ideas used to justify democracy in general and American democracy specifically is the idea that society is constituted by a hypothetical contract between all the members of that society to live together in peace.[11] This appeals to two of the most important aspects of our democratic experience—freedom and equality. In terms of freedom, it means that no one need be part of a society he or she does not want to be part of. Just as one can check in, so can one check out. Anyone can leave the society with impunity just as he or she can join it without any prior status in it. Therefore, even persons born in the society, by freely remaining in that society, choose retroactively to be part of it in the first place. By freely remaining in the society of their birth, they give their tacit consent to its political authority in their lives.[12] In terms of equality, it means that no one has any greater claim to citizenship and political office than anyone else. No one can make any primordial claim on the society or anyone in it, as is the case in those societies where one's status is determined by the location of his or her birth. Nothing appeals to Americans more than the notion that we are a nation of immigrants and that we have no official aristocracy. American Jews are no exception.

If the social contract is seen as being between lone individuals among themselves, thus creating the state, then Jews should be wary of embracing this idea. As we have seen above, that type of private individualism leads to a moral anonymity that is deadly for Jewish cultural survival (which for many Jews is inseparable from Jewish religious survival), for Jewish culture/religion involves a necessarily public morality, and that morality regularly involves non-Jewish members of the larger society. However, what if American Jews were to see their participation in American society more along Canadian lines, that is, taking American society to be a contract between various founding peoples? Even if the American legal system, unlike the Canadian legal system, cannot really recognize the cultural origins of its citizens, the American political system and the American social fabric certainly can and do recognize them. Thus, Jews can very well regard themselves first and foremost as members of the Jewish people, and American Jews can recognize themselves as members of the Jewish people who are citizens of the United States and participants in its political and social life in good faith.

Fortunately, American citizenship does not require that one's absolute, existential loyalty be to the state. Such a requirement would thereby divinize the state. American citizenship only requires that one not betray the United States on behalf of any other humanly constituted state in the world. Absolute, existential loyalty to the state, conversely, is the requirement of fascism.

There are very few American Jews, indeed, very few Jews anywhere, who would not agree that America has been a very good place for the Jews. But that judgment must be made on the basis of Jewish criteria, and by these same criteria it must be at least possible to speculate how it could be that America might become a bad place for Jews. Thus, the same criteria that have enabled us to come here and stay here could be the basis of our deliberate departure.[13] The task of a Jewish public philosophy, here or elsewhere, is to determine what is good for the Jews and how that can be consistent with the common good of a non-Jewish society, yet not simply be subsumed under that non-Jewish common good. Participation rather than subordination should be the preferred modus vivendi.

Any judgment of what Jewish public policy is to be, and the Jewish contract with the United States of America is no exception, should be determined by three basic criteria: (1) Torah, (2) Jewish self-interest, and (3) general morality. These three criteria are, therefore, indispensable for the formulation of a Jewish public philosophy. But let it be emphasized for the sake of discursive pluralism that there can be great differences of opinion on what specifically constitutes these three criteria, and these differences can very well lead to different conclusions on a variety of particular issues that call for a Jewish public philosophy to respond to them. Accordingly, this author readily admits that other American Jewish thinkers could accept these three criteria and, nonetheless, disagree with every political conclusion I happen to draw in my own schematic application of them. (I find it hard to believe, though, that any American Jewish thinker could formulate a Jewish public philosophy without positing similar criteria, albeit with a different enunciation and a different order of priority.) So, let us now examine each of these three criteria before we proceed to consider my applications of them, which I respectfully offer to a wider Jewish public for their consideration and for which I take full responsibility.

Torah

The ninth-century Jewish theologian Saadiah Gaon famously characterized the Jewish people as being a people "only because of her Torahs" (*ki im be-torateiha*).[14] By "Torah" in the plural he seems to mean both Scripture and the whole Jewish tradition, which continually attempts to either be derived from Scripture, the direct word of God, or to at least be authorized by Scripture.[15]

Now there are, of course, great debates among Jews as to what constitutes authoritative Torah and tradition and how they are to be applied to current situations where moral judgment on the part of Jews is called for. Unfortunately, for contemporary Jews, there is not the type of consensus that pertained when the Jews accepted the Torah at Sinai in Moses' specification of it, or when the Jews accepted Ezra's designation of the correct text of the Torah, or when the Jews accepted the Babylonian Talmud to be the authoritative legal interpretation of the Torah, or when Jews accepted the *Shulhan Arukh* of Joseph Karo as the authoritative code of Jewish law, or when Jews accepted the "Law of Return" (*hoq ha-shevut*, namely, that any Jew can become an Israeli citizen upon arrival in the State of Israel) as the right of every Jew. That failure of consensus became evident, for example, when the first chief rabbi of the State of Israel, Isaac Halevy Herzog, admitted that he could not get the new state to acknowledge the Torah as its constitution.[16] Indeed, that might well explain why the State of Israel still does not have a written constitution, and why all the more so there could hardly be any version of the Torah or any part thereof that a diaspora community like American Jewry could presently accept as the authorization of its public policies. Nevertheless, that does not mean that any segment of the Jewish community can offer a public policy recommendation for its own members, let alone for the whole community, that does not root itself in the Jewish tradition going all the way back to the Bible. This point can be illustrated by an example.

In the 1970s I served as rabbi to a congregation in a medium-sized southern city. Although in the past there had been a considerable amount of anti-Zionism within the moneyed leadership of the community, after the Israeli victory in the 1967 Six-Day War, all that leadership became forcefully pro-Israel. In the city at that time there was a small but vocal congregation of Jewish converts to Christianity who called themselves "Messianic Jews." In addition, this group had the active support of a famous local evangelist, who was also a fervent supporter of the State of Israel. In fact, from his television station one could hear both pro-Israel opinions as passionate as those of any Jewish Zionist *and* appeals to Jews to accept Christ. Since the leadership of the Jewish community felt that the evangelist's support of Israel was in the best interest of the Jews, and since they went out of their way to pay him honor, this led members of the "Messianic Synagogue" to claim that their total exclusion from the Jewish community was hypocritical and unjust. After all, they, too, supported the State of Israel and, unlike the evangelist, no one could deny that they were still Jews—at least individually.[17] (Everyone knows that once a Jew always a Jew, a point about which both the Jewish tradition and anti-Semites agree, ironically.)

Needless to say, the members of my congregation were confused, so I felt it my rabbinical duty to clarify the matter for them. Concerning the evangelist, I pointed out that his active proselytizing efforts among Jews constituted a direct danger to our community and they far outweighed his support of the State of Israel. While we could not very well tell him to stop this gross inconsistency on his part, we should refrain from seeking his support. Following this logic, I pointed out that, according to solid Jewish tradition, any Jew who becomes a member of a rival religious community loses all privileges in our community such as being called to the reading of the Torah or being buried in a Jewish cemetery.[18] That would extend to excluding the voice of any such person or group of persons from any communal deliberations about anything. Jewish tradition teaches that a Jew is to die as a martyr if conversion to another religion is the only way he or she could survive.[19] That means that although these Jewish Christians are still Jews in the eyes of God, they are for all intents and purposes no longer members of the Jewish community—even if they are pro-Israel in their politics.

At the level of the most basic requirement of Jewish public discourse, namely, who can be included in it, the Jewish tradition trumps any notion of Jewish self-interest that allows Jewish converts to another religion (and, all the more so, non-Jewish missionaries to the Jews) to be participants in the life of the community at any level— even if they seem to be politically useful in the short run. The task of the members of that Jewish community, I concluded, was to keep our distance from the evangelist and pray for the return to Judaism of the Jewish converts to Christianity, who had strayed so far from us into other pastures. Since the maintenance of Jewish identity is the most important matter of Jewish self-interest, and since that can only be determined by the Torah and its tradition, all other matters of Jewish self-interest must also follow this criterion or, minimally, not contradict it. Happily, many of my congregants, especially those who were regular worshipers in the synagogue, expressed their agreement with my presentation of traditional teaching on this subject.

Jewish Self-Interest

Although the Torah ultimately determines what Jewish self-interest is to be, there are matters of Jewish self-interest that cannot be derived directly from the Torah and its tradition. The most important (although not the only one) of these issues of current Jewish self-interest is support for the State of Israel. Now one can certainly derive from the Torah that the Land of Israel has a special sanctity for the Jewish people. This is demonstrated by the fact that there are certain commandments a Jew can only fulfill in the Land of Israel (*Eretz Yisrael*).[20] Nevertheless, it is very hard to directly derive support for the explicitly *secular* State of Israel from the Jewish tradition. Yet despite all that, the overwhelming number of Jews in the world (including America) regard the existence and endurance of the State of Israel as being indispensable for their well-being, perhaps their very survival, both of which are surely matters of self-interest. That is so for two reasons, it seems.

First of all, the State of Israel has proved on many occasions that it is ready and able to rescue Jews suffering from persecution anywhere. (Indeed, one can see this factor at work even before the establishment of the state in 1948, when the proto-Israeli group Breicha enabled Jewish survivors of the Nazi death camps to get away from their hopeless situation as displaced persons in Europe by escaping to Palestine, despite the severe restrictions imposed by the British authorities at that time.) After the Holocaust, especially, no Jew, no matter how rich or powerful, feels totally safe even when relying upon the most benevolent non-Jews. Second, the fact that Israel's founding law is the "Law of Return," which guarantees refuge in Israel to any Jew who seeks it, means that every Jew in the diaspora knows that he or she has an escape route, unlike the six million Jews who were trapped unto their deaths in Europe. (Should the Law of Return ever be repealed, as suggested by some contemporary Israeli thinkers who advocate "post-Zionism," which would mean that Israel is no longer "the Jewish state for the Jewish people," then support for the State of Israel would no longer necessarily be a matter of universal Jewish self-interest.)

American Jews should seek the self-interest of the Jewish people everywhere as a primary criterion of our public policy acts. This is like the American members of an extended family looking out for the welfare of other family members inside or outside America. American

Jewish attempts to rescue Soviet Jews from cultural extinction, or Ethiopian Jews from physical and cultural extinction, follow this same logic of Jewish self-interest. In addition, our notions of Jewish self-interest can differ from those of other Jewish communities, especially the Jewish community in Israel. This came out, for example, in the very successful attempts to resettle Jews who wanted to get out of the former Soviet Union.

The general Israeli position was that Israel is the only place to which Jews can legitimately aspire to immigrate. In this view, diaspora Jewish communities, whether in good places or bad places, are, in effect, Israeli colonies in which one does a limited amount of service until the time is ripe for return to the motherland. Nevertheless, most American Jews (and probably most other Jews in the diaspora) believe that the Jewish duty of "redemption of captives" (*pidyon shevuyyim*) means that one *rescues* Jews only *from* those places they themselves feel are intolerable for Jews, and only enable them to escape *to* whatever places they themselves want to go.[21] Moreover, this means that those Jews who are not "captives," in the sense of feeling that they are living in places (like America) where there is no great danger to Jews and no gross persecution of Jews, need not be "rescued" or rescue themselves therefrom. In this American Jewish view of Jewish self-interest, the immigration of American Jews to Israel (*aliyah*) is not, then, a matter of self-interest as much as it is the fulfillment of a Torah-related ideal of living in and building up the uniquely Jewish society and state of the Land of Israel (*yishuv Eretz Yisrael*). This itself is a matter of Jewish self-interest, since it would hardly be in the self-interest of American Jews, being the active citizens they are here, to present themselves to themselves and to others here as the "dispersed of Israel" (*nidhei yisrael*).[22]

General Morality

After the Holocaust, and after the 1967 Six-Day War, many Jews are now uncomfortable with talk of a general morality encompassing them along with all others. It is felt that affirming any universal moral criterion is a recipe for obsequiousness and assimilation. This is in large part a historical reading of two failed Jewish universalisms.

First, there is the universalism of pre-Hitler German Jewry (and of their American cousins of German-Jewish origin), which was convinced that it could justify the presence of Jews and Judaism in a larger society that seemed to claim to be constituted by universal criteria

of justice for all persons. Of course, we all know that Germany rejected any such universalism, adopting a racist, xenophobic ideology,
and that the Jews were its chief victims. In retrospect, then, these
German Jews (and similarly the French Jews whose devotion to France
and its ideals was betrayed by the Vichy government) are considered to
have been dangerous, self-deluded fools, who assumed a universalism
that was not there and had never been there. Perhaps, this type of
thinking concludes, Jews would have been better off if they had looked
out more for their own particular interests and those of the rest of the
Jews instead of looking out for the whole world, as it were.

Second, there is the failed universalism of the Jewish communists,
who were convinced that the "Jewish Question" would be solved by
the type of egalitarian society the Soviet Union claimed to be building
for itself and the entire world. The fact that this so-called egalitarian
project led to one of the worst forms of despotism the world has ever
known, and the fact that this communist despotism regarded Jewish
particularism to be an obstacle to be totally overcome by any means
whatsoever, has led most Jews to conclude that the universalism of the
Jewish communists (of whatever stripe) was a program for Jews to
willingly cooperate in their own cultural and political destruction and,
in many cases, their physical destruction as well. (What would Jews
like Julius and Ethel Rosenberg have said if Stalin had carried out the
mass pogrom against Russian Jews he was planning just before his
death in 1953? In their substitution of communism for Judaism, they
would have probably tried to rationalize Stalin's actions.)

Even if these two universalisms had not turned out to be so anti-
Jewish in both theory and practice, there is still the problem of submit-
ting Jewish public policy to criteria that are not Jewish and which are
taken to transcend Judaism. Is not any such acknowledgment a recipe
for the self-destruction of Jewish independence? But, on the other
hand, without the acknowledgment of some kind of general morality,
how can Jews possibly participate in a society with non-Jews, indeed,
in a society where the vast majority of the citizens are non-Jews? One
could say that this is only a problem for Jews in the diaspora, but, actually, it is also a problem for Jews in Israel, too. There it is the problem of how does Israel make a moral case in the increasingly international world society, and how does Israel make a moral case in its
treatment of non-Jews who live under its rule.[23] This is *the* Jewish
paradox that runs through all of modernity.

The solution to the above paradox is to see Jewish agreement to certain general standards of morality to be partial rather than all-
inclusive. Jews can agree to certain general moral standards when
these standards are not presented as being universal in the sense of be-

ing total, and when these standards are not presented as being ultimate in the sense of even being most important. To agree to employ certain general criteria in making a moral case in a multicultural, pluralistic context doe's not mean that these criteria are sufficient to govern all aspects of human life, nor does it mean that these criteria even govern the deepest aspects of human life. And, for Jews, the most important aspects of human life are those aspects of life which are specifically Jewish. Let me illustrate this by an example from recent history, both Jewish and general.

In the United States, one could well say that the most important moral debate our society engaged in during the last century was the debate over civil rights. After the defeat of Nazi racism in World War II, it became increasingly evident that the promise of the Declaration of Independence that "all men are created equal" was being seriously violated in the case of racial minorities, especially in the case of blacks or, as they are now called, African Americans. In fact, one could see *the* debate of twentieth-century America being a continuation of *the* debate of nineteenth-century America: the debate over slavery. In both cases the moral problem revolves around a group of Americans, unlike any other group of Americans (with the arguable exception of American Indians, who now seem to prefer the name Native Americans), who had not come here of their own free choice for the sake of freedom but who came here in chains. (One could say about Native Americans that they were put into chains here by their European conquerors.) Many Jews were in the forefront of the struggle for civil rights. But was their involvement because of specifically Jewish reasons or because of general moral reasons? The answer is that there were, no doubt, Jews whose motivation for involvement in the civil rights struggle was based on general moral criteria only. But there were other Jews whose involvement was based on specific Jewish criteria, one of which is that Judaism teaches certain elementary moral norms that apply to all persons, and which claim every human being by virtue of his or her basic humanity. This was the approach of my late, revered teacher, Rabbi Abraham Joshua Heschel, and this was the approach he urged his students to adopt and the example he urged his students to follow. Accordingly, I followed my teacher's precept and example and marched in Washington in 1964 on behalf of the Civil Rights Acts, with a *kippah* (skullcap) on my head, and I did so with many non-Jews (mostly Christians), whose presence in this moral struggle certainly did not require them to have *kippot* (skullcaps) on their heads, either literally or figuratively.

There was no conflict here between general morality and specific morality. There is only a conflict when Jews think that the general standard of *civil* equality is supreme, and civil equality turns into the ultimate and totalizing standard of doctrinaire egalitarianism. When this happens, as it has happened in some Jewish circles, then the separation necessary for the specific life of the Jews and Judaism in such areas as marriage and worship is deeply (and perhaps fatally) compromised. In other words, Jews can agree to general moral criteria only when these criteria are consistent with Jewish tradition and Jewish self-interest. In the case of the Jewish involvement in the civil rights struggles, though, that involvement was consistent with the Torah's teaching that there be one standard of interhuman justice (*mishpat ehad*) in civil society.[24] It was also consistent with Jewish self-interest in that Jews in America had suffered, although not nearly as much as African Americans, from American forms of racist discrimination and thus know that the elimination of such discrimination has been good for Jews to flourish in this democratic society. As such, in this case Jews could ascribe to a general morality not in spite of Judaism and the interests of the Jewish people but because of them.

Some Public Policy Implications for Jews Now

Heretofore I have employed certain examples from the immediate past to illustrate the points being made in this chapter in what might be termed Jewish political theory. However, in order to show some political relevance of what has been presented here to public policy questions facing the American Jewish community, let me offer brief opinions on three current questions of public morality, questions being debated right now, questions in which Jews are involved; indeed, questions we cannot very well avoid struggling with. Of course, this is the area where what I say is most subjective; nevertheless, without such particular focus, what I have said would be too abstract to tell whether it could be practically applied or not. The criteria I will employ here are those discussed above, namely, Torah, Jewish self-interest, and general morality. Also, the opinions I offer as applications of my method seem to go against the opinions of many prominent voices in the American Jewish community. But that is an advantage in offering one's opinions (hopefully, one's reasoned opinions) in a democratic context of opinion, and one that I think has characterized traditional Jewish discourse at its best.

Jonathan Pollard

The case of Jonathan Pollard, an American Jew who worked as a government defense analyst, and who in that capacity engaged in espionage for the Israeli government, has become a cause célèbre for many American Jews. Since his conviction for being a spy over a decade ago, Pollard has been held in a maximum security prison and his sentence seems to be interminable. Many Americans Jews, especially some prominent rabbis, have been involved in a struggle to free Jonathan Pollard and enable him to immigrate to Israel, where he desires to live. The U.S. government has argued against Pollard's release on the grounds that his espionage endangered the lives of many American agents working in hostile countries, and that he still possesses knowledge that could be detrimental to the interests of the United States if he were to be freed and thus able to share it with whomever.

It has been argued that Pollard ought to be released, and the three criteria presented above are invoked in that argument in one way or another. On Torah grounds it is argued that Pollard by now deserves to be freed and that seeking his release falls under the category of the "redemption of captives" (*pidyon shevuyyim*). Some have even compared his "captivity" to that of Alfred Dreyfus or Natan Sharansky, both of whom their fellow Jews (and many non-Jews as well) strove to free from imprisonment. On grounds of Jewish self-interest, it is argued that what Pollard did was in the vital interests of the State of Israel. On general moral grounds, it is argued that Pollard's sentence is far more severe than that of other American spies for foreign governments, hence the severity of his sentence strongly suggests an anti-Semitic bias on the part of those U.S. government officials who are determined to keep him in prison indefinitely.

In my opinion, all these arguments are wrong. By the three criteria of Jewish public policy, Pollard's imprisonment is just and, therefore, should not become a cause célèbre for Jews to challenge the justice of the U.S. court that sentenced Pollard.

On Torah grounds, Pollard is not a "captive" we are obligated to redeem. Unlike Dreyfus, who was convicted in a trial that was a mockery of justice and the French adjudication system, and unlike Sharansky, who was imprisoned because he asserted his right to live as a Jew in a totalitarian state, Pollard was convicted in a fair trial in a constitutional democracy; and Pollard was convicted for an act that was in violation of Jewish law. It was in violation of Jewish law because American Jews have a covenant with the United States to obey its laws in return for their equal protection by those laws. This is expressed in the classical Jewish legal principle of "the law of the state is the law [for Jews as well]" (*dina de-malkhuta dina*).[25] Traditional commentators were clear in pointing out that Jews have an obligation to obey the laws of a non-Jewish society in which they live when those laws are part of a system of law that employs due process of law for all those living under its rule.[26] The principle, though, does not apply in a society where laws are merely arbitrary decrees of tyrants, or where the law in both theory and regular application persecutes Jews or outlaws the practice of Judaism. Yet, most American Jews would consider the United States to be a country in which the rule of law largely prevails. It is, therefore, justified in making a moral claim on all its citizens—Jews included—not to violate those laws, and to be willing to accept appropriate punishment that is the result of the due process of that system of law. If Pollard was convinced that U.S. policy is intentionally harmful to Israel and the Jewish people, he should have defected to Israel, that is, if Israel would have taken him. The fact that he remained in the United States indicates his tacit acceptance of the authority of American law. Pollard is not a victim.

On grounds of Jewish self-interest, even Jewish self-interest on behalf of the State of Israel, Pollard's espionage was wrongheaded. First, he placed a strain upon U.S.-Israel relations that is hardly in the best interests of the Jewish people inasmuch as the United States is Israel's most important source of financial support, and its most powerful ally in international forums. Since U.S. government policy is heavily influenced by public opinion, as befits a democracy, Pollard's actions on behalf of Israel were interpreted by many Americans as Israeli/Jewish ingratitude for all that the United States has done for Israel.

On grounds of general morality, no one can justify espionage, which is a form of treason, against a nation of which one is a full citizen. That comes under the prohibition of robbery (*gezel*), which is where the Torah reconfirms what was available to human reason even before revelation. Pollard and his supporters have no cause to generally argue for his right to do what he did, nor against the right of the U.S. government to do what it did in legal reaction to Pollard. In this sense, American Jews can learn something from Israel's Law of Return, which grants the right of asylum to any Jew—except Jews fleeing just criminal prosecution in other countries.[27] In other words, we are to rescue Jews who are the victims of unjust persecution, not Jews whose actions have brought just retribution upon themselves, and who have brought shame upon the Jewish people (*hillul ha-shem*). Pollard's case has become a cause célèbre for some more conservative groups within the American Jewish community. By Jewish criteria, I think these conservatives are mistaken.

Same-Sex Marriage

One of the most keenly debated issues of public policy today has been the movement to recognize the right of same-sex couples to be fully married according to civil law as has been the case until now for heterosexual couples only. For many, this is the logical conclusion of the movement to recognize homosexuality as an acceptable way of life in our society. A number of Jews have been in the forefront of this movement and there are even some Jewish groups that have tried to argue for same-sex marriage as a matter of Jewish public policy. Of course, on grounds of Jewish tradition this has been virtually impossible inasmuch as the Jewish tradition seems to be unilaterally opposed to homosexual acts, whether between men or between women. All the more so is there no precedent in the tradition for the formal recognition of a homosexual union. Nevertheless, there have been some attempts to radically reinterpret the Jewish tradition to find some sort of opening for this new phenomenon of same-sex marriage, attempts that are admittedly tenuous.[28] Whether the tradition, though, can endure having been so radically reinterpreted is rather doubtful. On grounds of Jewish self-interest it is argued that the recognition of same-sex or gay marriages will include a segment of the Jewish community that has heretofore been alienated from the life of the community. On grounds of general morality it is argued that sexual orientation is a personal choice and that society should provide the benefits and obligations of marriage for any couple who wants it—straight or gay. No one sexual orientation should be in any way privileged.

In my opinion, the promotion of same-sex marriage should not be argued as a matter of public policy by the Jewish community, that is, any segment of the Jewish community seeking a wider Jewish consensus for its views. Since the Torah criterion is so unambiguously negative on this question, let us proceed to the questions of Jewish self-interest and general morality.[29]

On grounds of Jewish self-interest there is a very good reason to be opposed to same-sex marriage in the Jewish community. The reason is closely related to one of the gravest problems facing the continuity of the Jewish community—intermarriage between Jews and non-Jews. The argument for intermarriage is inevitably: Why can't I marry whomever I desire? Our opposition to intermarriage is only cogent if we argue that all forms of sexual desire cannot receive the communal endorsement of Jews because all forms of sexual desire are not in the best interests of the Jewish community. The only form of sexual desire that can be encouraged to the point of being institutionalized is the desire between a Jewish man and a Jewish woman to build a family whose primary (although not exclusive) purpose is the conception, birth, and rearing of children together. Yet we know that there are Jewish men who only desire non-Jewish women, and there are Jewish women who only desire, perhaps only can desire, non-Jewish men. What do we say to them? What can we say to them? We can only say: Either attempt to change your sexual desire—if they think that is possible or desirable—or be prepared not to have the union that is the result of your sexual desire have any official status in the community.[30] You are still a Jew, but your union is not Jewish. Without that admittedly harsh stance in general, we have no real argument against intermarriage or any other specifically prohibited unions.

Here is where considerations of Jewish self-interest and general morality overlap. That is, if Jews support same sex *civil* marriages, how can we cogently argue that somehow or other Jewish marriage is an exception to the policy of permitting anyone to marry who wants to marry? It is easy to argue for the further restrictions of Jewish marriage in a society that recognizes, more broadly to be sure, that marriage possibilities are limited. It is very much harder, if not most implausible, to argue for Jewish marital limitations in a society that recognizes no such limitations at all. Here is where general morality and Torah criteria overlap, since Judaism insists that every society is obligated to limit the range of acceptable sexual practices. Maximally, that means prohibiting certain sexual practices with punitive consequences; minimally, that means denying official endorsement to a number of sexual possibilities.

In a democracy there might be good reasons not to penalize persons for sexual acts committed in private by consenting adults. In a society that values privacy as much as our society does, it is hard to argue for criminal prosecution of any act that is not regarded by its human subjects as harmful to themselves and others. That seems to be the case when consenting adults have sex together. Yet that does not mean the state has any real interest leading to granting the status of marriage to anything but heterosexual unions, most of which produce children. How children are brought into the world and how they are raised is very much in the interest of the state to provide for the future of its society. But why should the state formalize same-sex unions, which themselves preclude producing children by design? There are numerous human relationships, friendship being the best example, in which the state has no direct interest and which it leaves, therefore, to the realm of privacy. Here, again, we have a case where liberal consensus ought not to be accepted as the basis of Jewish public policy opinions.

Public Prayer

As of the writing of this chapter (June 2000), the Supreme Court of the United States had ruled against the offering of officially approved prayers at public events such as school graduation ceremonies. This is consistent with most Supreme Court rulings in the area of religion for the last half century or so. In many of these rulings Jewish organizations took a leading role in arguing for what is perceived as the "high wall of separation" between church and state, either by supplying the plaintiffs themselves or providing the legal expertise to argue for the plaintiffs in such cases. In the public mind, both Jewish and general, there seems to be no issue on which the American Jewish community is so united as this one. Yet, here again, we need ask whether this public policy stance is justified by our three criteria: Torah, Jewish self-interest, and general morality.

The usual arguments against prayer on public occasions employ the three criteria in one way or another. Thus, by Torah criteria it is argued that since public prayers will inevitably reflect the theology of the Christian majority, Jews must be opposed to having Christian prayers, in effect, imposed upon them. By the criteria of Jewish self-interest it is argued that Jews are made to feel like second-class citizens at the vast majority of these public events where prayers are officially part of the program. By criteria of general morality it is argued that religion should not be endorsed in any way, even in a "nonsectarian" way by the secular state, and that only secular acts can receive official recognition. But, here again, I think this whole opposition is wrong-headed on the grounds of all three Jewish criteria.

On Torah grounds, Jews ought to encourage non-Jews to pray in public in order to show how much they believe the world, including the political order, is dependent upon God. Worship of God is not something Jews should ever claim is limited to ourselves alone. As long as Jews are not forced to utter prayers not authorized by our tradition, we should have no objection to being present at a public occasion where some citizen is asked to offer a prayer from his or her particular religious tradition. In fact, we should volunteer to offer a Jewish prayer on such occasions whenever possible. Even better, and this is becoming the case more and more in American public ceremonies, Jews should have no objection to the public recitation of any prayer that simply addresses God as creator of the universe and giver of natural law, and which does not explicitly mention the singular revelation of God to any particular faith community in history. We Jews should be opposed to the de facto public atheism that the elimination of religion from the public square strongly implies.

On grounds of Jewish self-interest, Jews ought to endorse public expressions of religion as the means for being able to express our own religion in public. Thus, for example, the Lubavitch community is in harmony with the spirit of American religious pluralism when it erects Hanukkah menorahs in public places all over North America. In fact, it is much more in harmony with American religious pluralism than are some of the secular Jewish organizations that spend untold sums of time and money fighting for no religion in public. Moreover, it is especially significant that this is done at Hanukkah time, for that is the time when American Christians most want to celebrate Christmas in public places, and that is the time when Jewish tradition requires Jews to "proclaim the miracle of the Hanukkah lights" (*pirsuma nissa*) to the entire world.[31] Whereas the militant secularism of some of the secular Jewish organizations creates animosity against Jews by Christians resentful of what they see as "Jewish atheism" at work, the pluralism practiced by Lubavitch, in this case especially, appeals to the widely held American belief that everyone has the right to practice his or her religion—in private and in public. I have never heard any objection from non-Jews that public Hanukkah displays are a way of forcing Judaism on the general society. In fact, the public display of Judaism is seen as giving something to society, whereas the militant secularist objection to any public display of religion is resented as taking something away from society. Religion in America does not belong in the closet.

On grounds of general morality, Jews should not be opposed to public displays of religion. Despite the fact that the separation of church and state is encoded in our Bill of Rights, all that this has meant for most of our history is that no one religion should have the official endorsement of the state, which would mean that all other religions are either outlawed and marginalized politically. It does not mean that our society must regard its moral foundations to be man-made. How could that be when our founding political document, the Declaration of Independence, explicitly invokes the creator God of nature as its moral warrant? Certainly, that does not force anyone in America to adhere to any one religion or any religion at all. But it does mean that the United States has always looked to a transcendent source of its foundational morality and law. Almost all our great moral struggles, from the movement to eliminate slavery to the movement for civil rights, have invoked God as the source of the justice we are to put into practice in our society. What would have been the moral attraction to leaders like Abraham Lincoln and Martin Luther King without their basic appeals to God's justice? Accordingly, it is hard to see how our national identity could continue if the official stance of our state becomes, in effect, antireligious. In fact, I am convinced that this aspect of American culture and society has made the United States such a hospitable place for Jews.

The enunciation of a public philosophy for American Jews is a desideratum. It cannot be done by any official body because no one body could possibly speak for all American Jews. Yet it is the responsibility of American Jewish scholars and thinkers to propose various versions of such a public philosophy and offer them for consideration when Jewish groups do have to make public policy decisions in American society. This is my own modest exercise of that responsibility for a community that has nurtured me and to whom I owe at least suggestions for its overall welfare in this country and for the overall welfare of this country.[32]

Notes

1. A number of the points made in this chapter are developments of thoughts expressed in the essay, "American Jews and the United States: The Mission of Israel Revisited" found in *Jewish Social Ethics* (New York: Oxford University Press, 1992), 225-43.

2. The doyen of all the American Jewish advocates of the strict separation of church and state was the late Leo Pfeffer, who for many years was legal counsel to the American Jewish Congress. Note how he begins his most important work, *Church, State, and Freedom*, rev. ed. (Boston: Beacon, 1967), 3: "Americans . . . today generally take it for granted that their religion is a private matter of no concern to the men elected or appointed to run their government." He then continues, "To the primitive savage, all of life may be said to be religious." Later, he notes that mention of God in official U.S. statements are "ceremonial verbalizations [that] could frequently not be avoided . . . [but] of themselves they are of no practical importance" (238).

3. In marked opposition to the whole approach of Pfeffer et al., see Richard John Neuhaus, *The Naked Public Square: Religion and Democracy in America* (Grand Rapids, Mich.: Eerdmans, 1984). As we shall see in this chapter, Jews can disagree with Pfeffer et al. and agree with Neuhaus on this question, even though Pfeffer was a Jew and Neuhaus is a Christian. That is because neither Pfeffer nor Neuhaus is making a primarily theological argument. Both are speaking primarily as social theorists.

4. For the beginnings of a changed perspective by a number of American Jewish public intellectuals, moving away from the Pfeffer position more to one like that of Neuhaus, see *American Jews and the Separationist Faith: The*

New Debate on Religion in Public Life, ed. David G. Dalin (Washington, D.C.: Ethics and Public Policy Center, 1993).

5. See David Novak, "The Idea of Covenant in Jewish and American Thought: A Suggestion for Creative Interchange," in *What Is American about the American Jewish Experience?*, ed. M. L. Raphael (Williamsburg, Va.: College of William and Mary, 1993), 41-53.

6. For my two basic statements on abortion, see *Law and Theology in Judaism*, 1 (New York: Ktav, 1974), 114-24; and *Covenantal Rights* (Princeton, N.J.: Princeton University Press, 2000), 128-31.

7. For what Jews should do on the Sabbath, note the first century CE Hellenistic Jewish sage, Philo of Alexandria: "Furthermore when He forbids bodily labour on the seventh day, He permits the exercise of the highest activities, namely, those employed in the study of virtue's lore . . . when the body takes its rest, the soul resumes its work." *De Specialus Legibus*, 2: 61-64, trans. F. H. Colson, *Philo* 7 (Cambridge, Mass.: Harvard University Press, 1937), 344-47. For similar rabbinic views, see Shabbat 150a-b based on Isaiah 58:13.

8. See David Novak, "Be Fruitful and Multiply: Issues Relating to Birth in Judaism," *Celebration and Renewal: Rites of Passage in Judaism*, ed. Rela M. Geffen (Philadelphia: Jewish Publication Society, 1993), 16-19.

9. If morality is a language, namely, what is spoken *between* persons, then just as there can be no private language, so there cannot be private morality but, perhaps, only private desires with which morality deals when they lead to public acts, and private thoughts that ultimately must be expressed in public language. See Ludwig Wittgenstein, *Philosophical Investigations*, 2nd ed., 1: 242-48, trans., G. E. M. Anscombe (New York: Macmillan, 1958), 88-90.

10. Thomas Nagel, *The View from Nowhere* (New York: Oxford University Press, 1986).

11. The idea of social contract, which goes back as far as Plato and which became central to the political philosophies of Hobbes, Locke, Rousseau, and others, has become the leitmotif of the most widely discussed political philosopher of the past fifty years, John Rawls, in his seminal work, *A Theory of Justice* (Cambridge, Mass.: Harvard University Press, 1971).

12. See Plato, *Crito*, 50A-54D.

13. Some American Jews are reluctant to express American patriotism because they fear they could become like those pre-Hitler German Jews, epitomized by the German-Jewish philosopher Hermann Cohen (d. 1918), who gave unconditional support to Germany, only to be betrayed by Germany posthumously (Cohen's widow died in the Theresienstadt concentration camp). See *Reason and Hope: Selections from the Jewish Writings of Hermann Cohen*, trans. E. Jospe (New York: W. W. Norton, 1971), 175-93. Cf. Novak, *Jewish Social Ethics*, 242, n. 42. Nevertheless, if a democracy is essentially based on a social contract, then no democracy can make an unconditional claim on its members. Only a covenant with God can do that.

14. *Emunot ve-Deot*, 3.7 (author's translation).

15. See Maimonides, *Mishneh Torah*, Introduction; "Rebels," chap. 1.

16. See M. Walzer, M. Lorberbaum, N. J. Zohar, and Y. Lorberbaum, eds., *The Jewish Political Tradition* 1 (New Haven, Conn.: Yale University Press, 2000), 471-76.

17. See David Novak, *The Election of Israel* (Cambridge: Cambridge University Press, 1995), 189-99.

18. See David Novak, "When Jews Are Christians," *First Things* 17 (1991): 42-46; "Edith Stein: Apostate Saint," *First Things* 96 (1999): 15-17.

19. Sanhedrin 74a.

20. See *Mishnah,* Kiddushin 1.9.

21. For the importance of this *mitzvah,* see Maimonides, *Mishneh Torah,* "Gifts to the Poor," 8.10.

22. There is a dispute between Maimonides and Nahmanides as to whether there is a scripturally based commandment (*mitzvah d'oraita*) for every Jew to live in the Land of Israel or not. Maimonides does not include any such commandment in the specification of the 613 commandments of the Written Torah in his *Sefer ha-Mitzvot,* but in his notes to this work (Addenda to positive commandments, no. 4; also his *Commentary on the Torah,* Numbers 33:53) Nahmanides insists there is such a positive commandment. Not to practice a positive commandment, when one is able to do so, is only permissible when it has been determined that a higher end takes precedence over this commandment (see Yevamot 90a-b). Otherwise, anyone not practicing any such commandment has sinned (see *Tosefta,* Kippurim 5.6). For Maimonides, it is clearly meritorious for a Jew to live in the Land of Israel and there are even legal rights such residence or intent of residence entails (see, e.g., *Mishneh Torah,* "Marriage," 13.19-20, based on *Mishnah,* Ketubot 13.11), but one has not explicitly sinned by not doing so (cf. Ketubot 110b and *Tosafot,* s.v. "hu"). So it would seem that those diaspora Jews, including of course American Jews who have chosen to remain in the diaspora, can only religiously justify that decision if they accept the approach of Maimonides and not that of Nahmanides.

23. See Novak, *Jewish Social Ethics,* 187-205.

24. See David Novak, *Natural Law in Judaism* (Cambridge: Cambridge University Press, 1998), 76-82.

25. See Baba Batra 54b and parallels; also, Menachem Elon, *Jewish Law,* 4 vols., trans. B. Auerbach and M. Sykes (Philadelphia: Jewish Publication Society, 1994), s.v. "law of the land is law."

26. See Maimonides, *Mishneh Torah,* "Entitlements and Gifts," 1.15.

27. See *Encyclopedia Judaica,* 10:1486, s.v. "Law of Return."

28. See Elliot N. Dorff, *Matters of Life and Death: A Jewish Approach to Modern Medical Ethics* (Philadelphia: Jewish Publication Society, 1998), 139-51.

29. See David Novak, "Religious Communities, Secular Society, and Sexuality: One Jewish Opinion," *Sexual Orientation and Human Rights in American Religious Discourse,* ed. Saul M. Olyan and Martha C. Nussbaum (New York: Oxford University Press, 1998), 11-28; also, *Jewish Social Ethics,* 84-103.

30. See Kiddushin 68b.
31. See Shabbat 21b.
32. See *Mishnah,* Avot 3.2 based on Jeremiah 29:7.

Index

Bible, 39, 91, 94-95, 316, 332, 340; reading(s), 24-25, 38, 56, 61, 293-94, 301
biblical scholarship, 205; teachings, 17
Big Three, 21, 40, 162, 167, 223, 232, 243
Bill of Rights, 49, 101, 106, 133, 135, 191, 195, 352
Bitburg crisis, 179
black-Jewish alliance, 175; coalition, 204; relations, 209
Black, Justice Hugo, 116-19
black power, 202
Blaustein, Jacob, 36
blood libel, 19
B'nai B'rith, 19, 31, 62, 154, 160, 244, 260, 272, 293, 295
Board of Delegates of American Israelites, 19
Board of Delegates on Civil and Religious Rights, 19
Bookbinder, Hyman, 159, 175
Bork, Robert, 88-89
Boston Combined Jewish Philanthropies, 245
Boy Scouts, 137-39, 143
Bradfield v. Roberts, 106
Brandeis, Justice Louis, 35, 105
Breicha, 342
Brennan, Justice William, 305
Brewer, Justice David, 49
British authorities, 342
Broder, David, 125
Brodkin, Karen, 267
Brookings Foundation, 164
Brown v. Board of Education, 123
Bunyan, John, 82
Burger, Chief Justice Warren, 228
Bush, George H. W., 164
Bush, George W., 188, 206, 324-25

Campaign Finance Bill, 177
Cannold, Leslie, 284
Cantwell v. Connecticut, 108, 110
Capitol Hill, 158
Carter, President Jimmy, 202

Carter, Stephen, 323-24
Catholic(s), 6, 24, 28, 49 52, 58, 81, 105, 115, 143, 198, 206, 297-300; Church, 141; communities, 143; education, 107; liberal, 17; Maryland, 73; schools, 6, 106, 116-18; tradition, 145
Catholic, Protestant, Jew, 294
catholicism, 3, 5
Center for Strategic and Institutional Studies, 164
Central Conference of American Rabbis (CCAR), 20, 44, 61, 282, 295, 303
Chabad, 58, 303-5
The Challenge of the Religious Right, 30
charitable choice, 4, 162, 312, 324
Chernin, Albert, 200
Chicago Federation, 167
Chosen People, 83
Christendom, 14
Christian(s), 14-15, 18, 20, 27, 29, 33, 41-42, 76-77, 123, 180, 191-92, 280, 333, 336, 345; America, 28, 49-50, 52-56, 59, 63, 205, 293; American culture, 255; Americans, 41, 49; animosity, 41; Bible, 192; churches, liberal, 37, 53, 56; commonwealth, 27; cultural establishment, 3; Evangelicals, 204, 209; law, 54; leaders, 21; majority, 41, 61; millenarians, 205; missionizing, 24, 30; morality, 53; nation, 48-49, 53; oath (Maryland), 21; political activism, 173; religion, 47-50, 53; Right, 26, 29-30, 37-38, 204-7; schools, 197; society, 48, 53, 205; state, 30, 40, 63-64, 205; zealots, 28
Christian Century, 37
Christian Coalition, 188-89, 205-6, 312
Christian Legal Society, 138-39
Christianity, 14, 24, 27-28, 39, 42, 44, 47, 49-50, 53-54, 56, 61-62,

About the Contributors

Marshall J. Breger, a fellow of the Jerusalem Center for Public Affairs, is a professor of law at Columbus School of Law, Catholic University of America. From 1983 to 1985 he was Special Assistant to the President and President Reagan's liaison to the American Jewish community.

Naomi W. Cohen, professor emeritus, taught American Jewish history at the City University of New York, Columbia University, and the Jewish Theological Seminary of America. She twice received the National Jewish Book Award for Jewish history as well as the Jewish Cultural Achievement Award in historical studies from the National Foundation for Jewish Culture. Her most recent book is *Jacob H. Schiff: A Study in American Jewish Leadership.*

David G. Dalin, a rabbi and American Jewish historian, is an adjunct scholar at the Ethics and Public Policy Center in Washington, D.C. He is the author or coauthor of six books, including *Religion and State in the American Jewish Experience* (with Jonathan D. Sarna) (University of Notre Dame Press, 1997).

Sylvia Barack Fishman heads the program in contemporary Jewish life/sociology of American Jews in the Near Eastern and Judaic Studies Department at Brandeis University, where she is an associate professor. She is also codirector of the International Research Institute in Jewish Women, established at Brandeis University by Hadassah. Dr. Fishman is the author of *A Breath of Life: Feminism in the Jewish Community, Follow My Footprints: Changing Images of Jewish Women*, and *Jewish Life and American Culture.*

Hillel Fradkin is president of the Ethics and Public Policy Center and an adjunct professor of government at Georgetown University. From 1986 to 1998 he was a member of the faculty of the Committee on Social Thought at the University of Chicago and vice-president of the Lynde and Harry Bradley Foundation of Milwaukee, Wisconsin. He has also served on the faculty of Columbia and Yale Universities. Dr. Fradkin has written on the history of Jewish and Islamic thought as well as the relationship between the Enlightenment and modern religious thought.

Sherry Israel is a fellow of the Jerusalem Center for Public Affairs and associate professor in the Hornstein Program in Jewish Communal Service at Brandeis University. She is the author of *Boston's Jewish Community: The 1985 CJP Demographic Study; The Comprehensive Report on the 1995 Demographic Study;* and co-author of the JCCA monograph, *Meaningful Jewish Community.*

Ralph Lerner is professor in the Committee on Social Thought and the Benjamin Franklin Professor in the College of the University of Chicago. He is the author of *Maimonides' Empire of Light: Popular Enlightenment in an Age of Belief* (2000), and *Revolutions Revisited: Two Faces of the Politics of Enlightenment* (1994). He also coedited with Philip B. Kurland the five-volume anthology, *The Founders' Constitution* (1987).

Alan Mittleman is professor of religion and head of the Department of Religion at Muhlenberg College. He is the author of three books on German-Jewish thought and political thought. He is the director of "Jews and the American Public Square" and co-editor of its publications.

David Novak is J. Richard and Dorothy Shiff Professor of Jewish studies at the University of Toronto. He is also vice-president of the Union for Traditional Judaism. He is the author of eleven books including *Covenantal Rights: A Study in Jewish Political Theory* (Princeton University Press, 2000).

Martin J. Plax is Cleveland area director for the American Jewish Committee and an adjunct associate professor of political science at Cleveland State University.

Jonathan D. Sarna is the Joseph H. and Belle R. Braun Professor of American Jewish history at Brandeis University and past chair of its Department of Near Eastern and Judaic Studies. He currently chairs the Academic Advisory and Editorial Board of the Jacob Rader Marcus Center of the American Jewish Archives, where he also serves as consulting scholar. He is author, editor, or coeditor of eighteen books, including *Religion and State in the American Jewish Experience* (with David Dalin) and *Women and American Judaism: Historical Perspectives* (with Pamela S. Nadell).

Harvey Sicherman is president of the Foreign Policy Research Institute in Philadelphia. He served as special assistant to Secretary of State Alexander M. Haig, Jr., 1981-82, consultant to Secretary of State George P. Shultz, 1988, and senior member of the policy planning staff under Secretary of State James A. Baker III, 1990-91. Among his recent works is "The Sacred and the Profane: Judaism and International Politics," *ORBIS* (spring 1998).

Marc D. Stern is codirector of the Commission on Law and Social Action of the American Jewish Congress. An expert on the law of church and state, he has been attorney with the Congress since 1977, conducting litigation, preparing amicus curiae briefs, drafting legislation, and giving public testimony on the full range of church-state issues.

Jack Wertheimer is provost and the Joseph and Martha Mendelson Professor of American Jewish History at the Jewish Theological Seminary. Among his most recent books are *A People Divided: Judaism in Contemporary America* and *Jews in the Center: Conservative Synagogues and Their Members*.